# CRITICAL READINGS: SPORT, CULTURE AND THE MEDIA

**ISSUES** in CULTURAL and MEDIA STUDIES

Series editor: Stuart Allan

# CRITICAL READINGS: SPORT, CULTURE AND THE MEDIA

Edited by
## David Rowe

OPEN UNIVERSITY PRESS

Open University Press
McGraw-Hill Education
McGraw-Hill House
Shoppenhangers Road
Maidenhead
Berkshire
England
SL6 2QL

email: enquiries@openup.co.uk
world wide web: www.openup.co.uk

First published 2004

A catalogue record of this book is available from the British Library

ISBN 0 335 21150 X (pb)    0 335 21151 8 (hb)

Library of Congress Cataloging-in-Publication Data
CIP data has been applied for

Typeset by RefineCatch Limited, Bungay, Suffolk
Printed in the UK by Bell & Bain Ltd, Glasgow

# CONTENTS

For all who toil in the CIPS salt mine

# PUBLISHER'S ACKNOWLEDGEMENTS

The authors and the publisher wish to thank the following for permission to use copyright material:

John Goldlust for: 'Sport as Entertainment: The Role of Mass Communications', in *Playing for Keeps: Sport, Media and Society*. © Longman Cheshire, 1987, Chapter 3, pp. 58–77. Reproduced by permission of Pearson Education.

Joan Chandler for: 'The TV and Sports Industries', in *Television and National Sport: The United States and Britain*. © 1988 by the Board of Trustees. Used with permission of the University of Illinois Press.

Lawrence A. Wener for: 'The Dream Team, Communicative Dirt, and Marketing Synergy: USA Basketball and Cross-merchandising in TV Commercials', in *Journal of Sport and Social Issues*, 18(1): pp. 27–47. Reprinted by permission of Sage Publications, Inc.

Toby Miller, Geoffrey Lawrence, Jim McKay and David Rowe for: 'Sports Media *sans frontières*', in *Globalisation and Sport: Playing the World*. © 2001, Sage Publications, Inc.

David Andrews for: 'Speaking the "Universal Language of Entertainment": News Corporation, Culture and the Global Sport Media Economy'. Reprinted with permission of the author.

Mark D. Lowes for: 'Sports Page: a Case Study in the Manufacture of Sports News for the Daily Press', in *Sociology of Sport Journal*, 14(2): pp. 143–59.

Michael Silk, Trevor Slack and John Amis for: 'Bread, Butter and Gravy: an Institutional Approach to Televised Sport Production', in *Culture, Sport and Society*, 2000, 3(1): pp. 1–21.

Maurice Roche for: *Mega-events and Media Culture: Sport and the Olympics* (2000), Chapter 6, pp. 159–93. Reproduced by permission of Routledge Ltd.

Miguel de Moragas Spà, Nancy K. Rivenburgh and James F. Larson for: 'Local Visions of the Global: Some Perspectives from Around the World', in *Television in the Olympics* (1995). Reprinted by permission of University of Luton Press.

Ketra L. Armstrong for: 'Nike's Communication with Black Audiences: a Sociological Analysis of Advertising Effectiveness via Symbolic Interactionism', in *Journal of Sport and Social Issues*, 23(3): pp. 266–86. Reprinted by permission of Sage Publications, Inc.

Michael A. Messner, Michele Dunbar and Darnell Hunt for: 'The Televised Sports Manhood Formula', in *Journal of Sport and Social Issues* 24(4): pp. 380–94. Reprinted by permission of Sage Publications, Inc.

Laurel A. Davis for: 'The Basic Content: "Ideally Beautiful and Sexy Women for Men"', in *The Swimsuit Issue and Sport: Hegemonic Masculinity in Sports Illustrated*. © 1997, State University of New York. Reprinted by permission from Michael Gelven, *Truth and the Comedic Art*, State University of New York Press. All rights reserved.

Kyle W. Kusz for: '"I Want to Be the Minority": the Politics of Youthful White Masculinities in Sport and Popular Culture in 1990s America', in *Journal of Sport and Social Issues*, 25(4): pp. 390–416. Reprinted by permission of Sage Publications, Inc.

Deborah Stevenson for: 'Women, Sport and Globalization: Competing Discourses of Sexuality and Nation', in *Journal of Sport and Social Issues*, 26(2): pp. 209–25. Reprinted by permission of Sage Publications, Inc.

David McGimpsey for: 'Representations of Football in Baseball Literature: the Lyric Fenway, the Prosody of the Dodgers, and Are You Ready for Some Football?' in *Imagining Baseball*. Reproduced by permission of Indiana University Press.

Robert E. Rinehart for: 'Sport as Constructed Audience: a Case Study of ESPN's – The eXtreme Games', in *Players All*, pp. 98–110. Reproduced by permission of Indiana University Press.

Brian Stoddart for: 'Convergence: Sport on the Information Super-highway', in *Journal of Sport and Social Issues*, 21(1): pp. 93–102. Reprinted by permission of Sage Publications, Inc.

Michael Sagas, George B. Cunningham, Brian J. Wigley and Frank B. Ashley for: 'Internet Coverage of University Softball and Baseball Web Sites: the Inequity Continues', in *Sociology of Sport Journal*, 17(2): pp. 198–205.

Every effort has been made to trace the copyright holders but if any have been inadvertently overlooked the publisher will be pleased to make the necessary arrangement at the first opportunity.

# SERIES EDITOR'S FOREWORD

This Reader has been devised as an accompaniment to David Rowe's highly praised and influential book *Sport, Culture and the Media: The Unruly Trinity*, which is being published simultaneously in its second edition. The Reader is a carefully selected anthology of 'classic' and contemporary work dedicated to understanding the relationships within what Rowe calls the 'media sports cultural complex'. Following a survey chapter by the editor that 'sets the scene' for the analysis of media sport, attention turns to how media sport is produced and the ways in which it can be interpreted (a two-part structure that mirrors Rowe's authored text). Part I, *Media sport construction: history, labour, culture and economics*, contains key chapters that address such timely topics as globalization, media convergence, the corporate contest for broadcast rights, the making of sports pages and broadcasts, and the staging of mega-media sports events like the Olympic Games. Part II, *Media sport deconstruction: readings, forms, ideologies and futures*, is concerned with issues including nationalism, gender, sexuality and ethnicity in sports television, the press, fiction and new media. Overall, then, the Reader promises to enhance our critical understanding of how the field of media sport studies has developed over the years. Apparent throughout the discussion is the cultural significance of media sport for everyday life, and the reasons why it continues to be such an important – and fascinating – area of study.

The *Issues in Cultural and Media Studies* series aims to facilitate a diverse range of critical investigations into pressing questions considered to be central to current thinking and research. In light of the remarkable speed at which the conceptual agendas of cultural and media studies are changing, the series is committed to contributing to what is an ongoing process of re-evaluation and critique. Each of the books is intended to provide a lively, innovative and comprehensive introduction to a specific topical issue from a fresh perspective. The reader is offered a thorough grounding in the most salient debates indicative of the book's subject, as well as important insights into how new modes of enquiry may be established for future explorations. Taken as a whole, then, the series is designed to cover the core components of cultural and media studies courses in an imaginatively distinctive and engaging manner.

*Stuart Allan*

# ACKNOWLEDGEMENTS

Compiling this Reader has been a real education in intellectual property rights, and I thank the authors and publishers who have agreed to the reproduction of various contributions to this collection. The authors, in particular, were unanimously enthusiastic about this book project, and I hope that they like this new setting for their work. I am also grateful to those who supplied new material or 'tweaked' earlier work for this collection, and who accepted with good grace my need to excise material in order to fit the book. Trying to reduce an entire interdisciplinary field of study to less than a score of chapters is obviously preposterous, and there are numerous worthy omissions that would have fitted perfectly into this book. It does not claim to be comprehensive or representative in any formal sense, or even the 'best' work in some academic version of 'Top of the Pops'. The book has a clear Anglo-American-Antipodean concentration that reflects the history of both editor and field, as well as the economics of English language publishing. Another collection, with a wider brief, greater word limit or different editor, can do fuller justice to the gathering force of work being produced beyond the old Empire. Nonetheless, all the selected work that appears here balances my editorial requirement of coherence, relevance and reasonable diversity, and has a significant bearing on the multitude of pressing questions raised when sport meets cultural and media studies.

Stuart Allan, again, was a kindly and calming series editor, while publisher Justin Vaughan supported the project at its inception before artfully passing on the baton. Miriam Selwyn, Cathy Thompson,

Chris Cudmore and Ellie Wood from Open University Press were unfailingly upbeat as many lonely, late night emails whizzed around the world looking for a friendly home. Paul Stolk and Erin Taylor from the Cultural Industries and Practices Research Centre (CIPS) also provided important strategic support at the right times. My CIPS colleagues, especially co-founders Deborah Stevenson and Kevin Markwell, continue to reinforce a sense of common purpose in the face of a seemingly endless series of scholarly commitments that, one way or another, inevitably bear down on the individual.

Finally, this was yet another academic activity that impinged on notional but perpetually receding 'quality time' with family and friends. My children, Daniel and Madeleine, have grown only too accustomed to the all-hours, staccato tap-tap sound of fingers on keyboard emanating from the cramped little study at the front of the house. I promise to stop when the siren song of media sport does the same.

*David Rowe*

# CONTRIBUTORS

John Amis is Associate Professor in Human Movement Sciences and Education, College of Education, University of Memphis, USA.

David L. Andrews is Associate Professor, Sport Commerce and Culture Program, Department of Kinesiology, University of Maryland, USA.

Ketra L. Armstrong is Assistant Professor, Sport Management, The Ohio State University, USA.

Frank B. Ashley is Associate Professor, Department of Health and Kinesiology, Texas A&M University, USA.

Joan Chandler is Professor Emeritus, Historical Studies, University of Texas, Dallas, USA.

George B. Cunningham is Assistant Professor, Department of Health and Kinesiology, Texas A&M University, USA.

Laurel Davis is Associate Professor of Sociology, Department of Social Science, Springfield College, Massachusetts, USA.

Michele Dunbar is Director of the Structured Curriculum Program in Disability Services, University of Southern California, USA.

John Goldlust is Convenor, Sociology and Anthropology, School of Social Sciences, La Trobe University, Australia.

Darnell Hunt is Professor of Sociology, Director of the Ralph J. Bunche Centre for African American Studies, and Interim Chair, Afro-American Studies, University of California, Los Angeles, USA.

Kyle W. Kusz is with the Northern Illinois University, Department of Kinesiology, University of Illinois, USA.

James F. Larson is with the Centre for Advanced Telecommunications and Training in Telecommunications, University of Colorado, Boulder, USA.

Geoffrey Lawrence is Professor of Sociology and Head, School of Social Science, University of Queensland, Australia.

Mark D. Lowes is Assistant Professor, Department of Communication, University of Ottawa, Canada.

David McGimpsey teaches Creative Writing in the Department of English, Concordia University, Montreal, Canada.

Jim McKay is Associate Professor of Sociology, School of Social Science, University of Queensland, Australia.

Michael A. Messner is Professor of Sociology and Gender Studies, University of Southern California, USA.

Toby Miller is Professor of Cultural Studies and Cultural Policy in the Centre for Latin American and Caribbean Studies, the Program in American Studies, and the Department of Cinema Studies, New York University, USA.

Miquel de Moragas Spà is Director, Olympics Studies Centre, Autonomous University of Barcelona, Spain.

Robert E. Rinehart is Lecturer in the Department of Kinesiology and Physical Education, California State University, San Bernadino, USA.

Nancy K. Rivenburgh is Associate Professor, Department of Communication, University of Washington, USA.

Maurice Roche is Reader in Sociology, Department of Sociological Studies, University of Sheffield, UK.

David Rowe is Director of the Cultural Industries and Practices Research Centre (CIPS), School of Social Sciences, University of Newcastle, Australia.

Michael Sagas is Assistant Professor, Department of Health and Kinesiology, Texas A&M University, USA.

Michael Silk is Assistant Professor in Human Movement Sciences and Education, College of Education, University of Memphis, USA.

Trevor Slack is the Canada Research Chair in Sport Management, University of Alberta, Canada.

Deborah Stevenson is Deputy Director of the Cultural Industries and Practices Research Centre (CIPS), School of Social Sciences, University of Newcastle, Australia.

Brian Stoddart is Pro Vice-Chancellor (Research and International), University of New England, Armidale, Australia.

Lawrence A. Wenner is Von der Ahe Professor of Communication and Ethics, Loyola Marymount University, California, USA.

Brian J. Wigley is Assistant Professor, Department of Kinesiology, Shenandoah University, USA.

# 1 | INTRODUCTION: MAPPING THE MEDIA SPORTS CULTURAL COMPLEX

## The functions of the Reader

This Reader has two main functions. First, it can operate as a 'stand-alone' introduction to the research and scholarship addressing the relationships between sport, culture and the media from the perspective of Cultural and Media Studies. This is a growing field of inquiry, and the Reader can operate as a useful point of entry into it through its selection of 'classic' and contemporary work in various countries. Once acquainted with the nature, scope and direction of work in the area, readers new to the field will be able to use the collection as a reference point for their own investigations and inquiries into what I believe, without a hint of editorial bias, to be a dynamic, fascinating subject of underestimated sociological significance.

The second intended function of this Reader is to operate as a companion volume to either or both editions of my book *Sport, Culture and the Media: The Unruly Trinity* (Rowe 1999, 2004). The necessary restrictions of length and scope for a monograph inevitably mean that many aspects of sport, culture and the media can often only be covered in a synoptic way. The publication of an accompanying Reader enables several topics to be treated more intensively and in greater detail. It should also be acknowledged, without disingenuous modesty, that any single author has their only-too-obvious limitations, and that it is sometimes better to allow the 'original' work to speak for itself than to gloss it. An edited companion collection can broaden understanding of the subject through exposure to different perspectives and styles of analysis. In addition, it enables students, teachers, scholars and researchers to become directly acquainted with a mixture of 'canonical' works and new insights that convey a strong sense of a field of study with its own history and intellectual trajectory.

Choosing a small selection of works from a large, growing and diverse body of literature is a humbling activity and, as noted in the *Acknowledgments*, I make no strict claim to formal comprehensiveness and representativeness. The primary aim of this book is to provide readers with a grasp of how the relationships between sport, culture and the media have been approached by former and current scholars broadly located within the interdisciplinary field of Cultural and Media Studies, and to give an indication of new research directions. Non- or limited availability of some works imposed unavoidable constraints on the shaping of the text, as did any *lacunae* in the editor's knowledge (a failing of which, *ipso facto*, he is blissfully unaware). But these limitations still leave a vast potential reservoir of fine work that could just as easily have occupied this restricted book space. I have also adopted a different approach to many other Readers by including mostly longer, substantial contributions rather than a large selection of brief 'tasters'. Only works that have not been previously anthologized have been included here. I believe that the result will be to satisfy scholarly appetites better (the difference between a snack and a full meal) so that these works, once digested, will stimulate new ventures in the kitchen of socio-cultural inquiry. Inevitably, given such intellectual riches, many editorial choices must be arbitrary in some respects.

Nonetheless, all the contributions to this volume are of obvious intellectual merit and reflect the editor's assessment of the quality and importance of the works reproduced here. Each illuminates a range of significant aspects of the production, circulation and consumption of media sport, and its immediate and enduring cultural ramifications. These are the concerns that have animated a field of study of considerable current vitality that, as is discussed below, took some time to emerge and prosper.

## Coming to terms with media sport

We are all, willingly or otherwise, daily confronted by the 'media sports cultural complex'. This concept 'embraces all the media and sports organizations, processes, personnel, services, products and texts which combine in the creation of the broad and dynamic field of contemporary sports culture' (Rowe 2004: xx). The sheer scope and scale of this complex and its culture means that, in advanced capitalist societies at least (and, increasingly, in many more besides), it can only be escaped with certainty in such sensorily deprived environments as hyperbaric chambers and deep space. Or by 'sleeping the big sleep', as crime writer Raymond Chandler (1939: 220) describes the state of death wherein 'you were not bothered by things like that'. Chandler may have been writing about the fictional gangster world, but the point can also be applied to media sport.

The popular 1989 film *Field of Dreams* proposes that even death may have no dominion over sport, as an Iowa corn field is mysteriously transformed into a nostalgic theme park where the paying public can watch reincarnated baseballers in action (Rowe 1998). A Marxist analysis would suggest that this is an ideal instance of the capitalist exploitation in perpetuity of the labour power of professional sports personnel and of its consumption by sport spectators. But this point need not be taken too literally – *Field of Dreams* is, of course, fiction, and Marxists don't believe that workers, even sportsmen, can return after compulsory retirement by death. What it reveals is the capacity of media sport to enable an endless trading of myths and images that doesn't have to rely on athlete reincarnation or cryogenic restoration. Through such media texts as sports books, statistical databases, television and radio documentaries, video and DVD sports highlight features, photo-essays, and films of both a fictional and non-fictional nature, sport can be kept alive across the generations, always offering new opportunities for representation and commercialization. The media, in other words, capture, record and 'memorialize' sport for everyone.

Media sport is closely interwoven into the everyday lives of sports fans and the uncommitted alike. It occupies vast tracts of electronic, print and cyber media space; directly and indirectly generates a diverse range of goods and services produced by large numbers of companies and workers; absorbs substantial public resources in the form of pro-grammes, subsidies and tax exemptions, and is strategically used by the political apparatus in the name of the people. The Olympic Games and the soccer World Cup are only two of the most spectacular examples where sport garners saturation media coverage, is respon-sible for the production and consumption of everything from soft drink to clothing, and is heavily subsidized by governments (Roche 2000). It is almost a civil duty, therefore, to try to come to terms with media sport by understanding, probing and criticizing it in order to be in a position to intervene in its operations, where necessary, in the name of cultural citizenship (Murdock and Golding 1989; Murdock 1992). This concept has developed to extend the traditional concern with the rights and duties of political citizenship to cultural entitlements and responsibilities under conditions where equitable access to cultural resources has become crucial to full participation in contemporary society (Stevenson 1995; Murdock 1997). Media sport is particularly important to contemporary cultural citizenship because there are no more culturally and economically prized texts, with correspondingly high rewards for controlling them, than 'live' televised media sports texts (Rowe 2003).

The collective public stake in media sport, then, is now of such significance that it demands a greater level of education about it and the recognition of substantial rights of public ownership over it and access to it. These principles apply to such obviously political issues as, for example, a commercial pay TV broadcaster attempting to 'siphon off' sports programming from free-to-air television or to buy a sports team like Manchester United (Rowe 2000), or a government underwriting a bid to host a mega-media sports event like the Olympics (Roche 2000), and allowing special legislative exemptions for tobacco advertising for televised sports like motor racing (Boyle and Haynes 2000). They are equally relevant to negotiating the politics of everyday life embedded in the task of being constantly presented with media sports texts such as live broadcasts and banner headlines, and simply trying to understand their origins and meanings. Citizens need, then, to be equipped with a working knowledge of the 'power lines' (Birrell and McDonald 2000) crisscrossing the media sports cultural complex.

This Introduction outlines the importance of studying sport for the field of Cultural and Media Studies. It provides a brief survey of the range of approaches and contributions to the understanding of media sports culture, laying the foundation for the following chapters selected for this Reader. The different theoretical currents and methodological techniques represent the overall framework for analysing the various dimensions of this conspicuous yet elusive analytical object. In addressing the *construction* of media sport (including its labour process, and the shaping of the relationship between culture and economics) and then *deconstructing* what has been produced by offering critical readings of media sports texts, Cultural and Media Studies is shown to be very well placed to provide a critically reflexive means of coming to terms with media sport.

## Sport in Cultural and Media Studies

Cultural and Media Studies is an interdisciplinary field that has developed since the early 1970s in response to major changes in society and culture. Among these trends, the twin processes of *culturalization* and *mediatization* are of particular importance. *Culturalization* can be described as the infiltration of culture, broadly conceived as the ensemble of institutions, practices and texts that turns simple existence into meaningful experience, into the heart of all dimensions of contemporary life, ranging from lifestyles and identities to political debates and economic decision-making. This is not to suggest, of course, that culture was unimportant in earlier epochs, but that there has been a vast expansion in the range of competing symbols, images, identities and values available to human subjects in most societies, and access to and command over them is crucial to human survival and prosperity in them. A key explanation for the daunting geographical and historical sweep of this change lies in a second and linked process – *mediatization*. This term is used to describe how developments in the channels and techniques of communication, including newspapers, radio, television, popular music and the internet, act as astonishingly efficient vectors of culture, conveying a dazzling array of symbols and their associated meanings to widely dispersed audiences.

Cultural and Media Studies (which for the sake of ease of argument I am conceptually combining) developed as an engaged intellectual response to this heightened importance of culture and media since the mid-twentieth century. What distinguishes this approach is its interdisciplinary nature – none of the established theories and paradigms in social sciences and the humanities seemed adequate to the task of comprehensively understanding and explaining the social world on their own (Barker 2000). The unconventional nature of this academic activity also reflects an urge to go beyond the 'canon' of key approaches and works that shaped the field of study into a hierarchy of 'good' and 'bad' culture (Appadurai 1996). Indeed, it sought to break down the boundaries between the detached world of academe and the world that it was trying to understand. This was because culture was viewed now as a key site of power relations in its own right, so demanding a politicized engagement with what was being studied in a critically self-reflexive manner (Rojek and Turner 2000). The increasing visibility of popular culture, and the appreciation of its 'politics of pleasure' (Rowe 1995) took scholars into areas that had been previously neglected. One of the most obvious and most academically marginalized of these was sport which, with its emphasis on the body, spectatorship and competitive performance, was for traditional scholars the antithesis of the approved, refined culture that they wished to cultivate in the wider population (Tomlinson 1999).

Sport came to be of greater interest to Cultural and Media Studies (and to allied fields like Sociology, Leisure and Communication Studies) because it is a socio-cultural institution that is deeply connected to the politics of everyday life. In barely a century, sport has made the transition from the regulated physical play of English villagers and schoolchildren to a global cultural phenomenon attracting massive investment, both material and symbolic, from business, government and the 'common people' (Sugden and Tomlinson 2002). The institution more responsible than any other for this spectacular rise of sport is the media, to the extent that these formerly separate institutions have interpenetrated to the point of merger (Rowe 2004). The symbiotic relationship of sport and media involves an exchange of visibility and capital for interest and audiences in a classic exemplification of the aforementioned processes of *culturalization* and *mediatization*.

Thus, there is unprecedented interest in the study of sport as the media have inexorably carried it into sundry cultural spaces, so prompting active debates concerning its socio-economic power and cultural influence. This realization has revivified the field of Sport Studies, which was formerly preoccupied, to summarize it rather crudely, with sports training techniques, athlete physiology, physical-moral education of the young, narrative sports history, and uncritical functionalist celebrations of the institution's contribution to social cohesion and consensus. These concerns and approaches have not gone away, and in the case of sport science are prospering as governments devote more public resources to high-performance international sport in search of national prestige. Sport Studies, nonetheless, has become a more diverse, critical and relevant field of study as the star of its object of analysis has risen.

Media sport is probably now the most vibrant area of study connecting orthodox academic concerns in social science and the humanities with the politics of everyday life. In the United Kingdom, for example, there has been a boom in association football since the early 1990s that can at least partially be explained by intensive media coverage, marketing and promotion. While this development is not without its disadvantages for other sports and for non-sports fans, it has helped create conditions where researchers and scholars can harness football's fashionability and popularity to academically productive effect (for example, King 1998; Giulianotti 1999). Sport's media visibility has also enabled scholars to tap into debates concerning important social, political and ethical issues. The perennial eruption of sport controversies over, for example, bribing International Olympic Committee delegates to host Olympic events; 'fixing' cricket, soccer and boxing matches; sexual, gender and racial discrimination; taking performance-enhancing drugs and secretly administering performance-damaging ones; and pressures to boycott international sports events like the 2003 cricket World Cup and the 2008 Beijing Olympics, are just some of the rich veins of analytical inquiry that take the researcher well beyond the sports arena itself. This research, if publicly communicated through the general media, draws on high levels of interest in such subjects and in the issues that they raise, and generates in turn more research material in what could be described as a virtuous intellectual circle created out of the more disreputable aspects of sport.

The development of the study of media sport echoes the expansion of the study of popular culture in universities across the world and the aforementioned unmistakeable growth and visibility of sport in the wider culture and society. But it was delayed by some resistance to the study of sport among intellectuals tending to construct their professional worlds around a hierarchy of mind over body, with sport's corporeality, and its association with aggressive masculinity, retarding its development as a field of research and scholarship (Rowe 1995; Tomlinson 1999; Miller 2001). Furthermore, sport's omnipresence, the sheer volume of sports texts, and the potential claim of any citizen to be an 'expert' on a form of popular culture that daily surrounds them, also made it paradoxically difficult to study. In this area of research, attempts to assert the 'authority' of the serious scholar were likely to be met with bemusement at best and derision at worst.

But there was a slowly progressing engagement from the 1970s onwards with the phenomenon that occupied so much media space and so much of the waking lives of vast sections of the population, among them academics who entertained the 'secret vice' of avid sports fandom (Sugden and Tomlinson 1998). The serious study of media sport from within the social sciences and humanities is, indeed, now flourishing, but it was only relatively recently that the importance of the subject was matched by academic attention to it. While there were pioneering works in the 1970s on sports television (such as Buscombe 1975) and in the early 1980s on the historical development of the commercial sports media (such as Cashman and McKernan 1981), it was not until the late 1980s that the momentum of media sport studies began to gather in book publishing. These first works were mostly concerned with television (for example, Goldlust 1987; Chandler 1988 [both represented in this collection]; Klatell and Marcus 1989; Real 1989; Wenner 1989), with these concerns mirrored in such key periodicals as the *Journal of Sport & Social Issues* and the *Sociology of Sport Journal*. In the wake of these influential works a steady stream of books on sport, culture and the media appeared in the first half of the 1990s, focusing on such issues as the changing public and private sports broadcasting environment and the gender politics of sports journalism (for example, Barnett 1990; Whannel 1992; Birrell and Cole 1994; Creedon 1994), with such work also finding outlets in a wider range of journals, such as *Media, Culture & Society*, *Cultural Studies* and the *International Review for the Sociology of Sport*. This corpus of works represents the solid foundation on which a somewhat belated boom in publishing on sport and media has occurred in books (for example, de Moragas Spà et al. 1995; Baker and Boyd 1997; Wenner 1998; Martin and Miller 1999; Birrell and McDonald 2000; Boyle and Haynes 2000; Andrews and Jackson 2001; Whannel 2001; Brookes 2002) and in journals (in both the growing roster of dedicated sport journals like *Culture, Sport, Society*, *International Sports Studies* and *Sport, Education and Society*, and in more generalist social science and communications journals such as *Sociology, Television & New Media*, and *Body & Society*. These works constitute more than just a numerical expansion in the field, with the scope of the subject matter continuing to widen as, for example, the sports media's involvement in racial ideologies and the media construction of sports stars and celebrities have been subjected to closer critical scrutiny. A notable characteristic of these works in Cultural and Media Studies has been their dedication to linking media sport to the wider social and cultural formation, with few that could be described as internalist or atomized analyses of the field. The explanation for this analytical expansiveness lies partly in the intellectual orientation of the scholars and researchers drawn to media sport. However, even were they not so inclined, the subject almost compels a widescreen approach, with each media sports text almost effortlessly harnessed to a rich range of significations and mythologies. This semiotic facility is responsible for both the excitement generated by researching media sport and a corresponding need to temper that intellectual exuberance in the interests of academic integrity. We turn next, therefore, to a consideration of how media sport has been approached within Cultural and Media Studies.

## Ways of analysing sport, culture and the media: theory and method

Media sport, as previously observed, comes in great profusion and variety. It ranges from live television broadcasts watched by billions of people and radio broadcasts heard by millions to specialist sports magazines read by a few thousand and personal websites accessed only by friends and family. It includes Hollywood feature films and paperback novels in which sport is a pretext for a story to daily newspapers in which sport is covered not just in the regular sports pages, but also in the general news, features, business and gossip pages. How can these diverse cultural phenomena be classified and understood? A good starting point is to consider the 'lifespan' of any media sports text. It has to be made by someone or something – be they multinational corporations or amateur fan groups. In being manufactured, the text acquires form and content that is now available for inspection. For it to exist in any significant social sense (like the proverbial tree falling in the forest) the text has to be 'read' by a sentient being, whether by billions of TV viewers or a solitary reader of a photocopied sports fanzine or webzine. In the activity of reading the media sports text, the reader will interpret it and derive direct (denotative) and indirect (connotative) meanings from it. In the hands of the reader, the text may change character from that originally intended by the producer, or it may be used for a different purpose. The television tribute to a sports star intended to be moving may to many be laughable, and the airbrushed, cheesecake image of an athlete intended to be alluring may find itself pinned to a dartboard. In other words, the reception and use of the produced text must also be taken into account. Acquiring greater knowledge of how media sport is made and its texts 'unmade' through theoretically, conceptually and empirically informed analysis enables a critical understanding of the institutional context within which media sport is produced that can, in turn, inform readings of media sports texts in their many forms and uses. By locating these texts within a wider cultural framework, the analyst can gain some understanding of media sport's contribution to the way of life of particular societies and to the relationships between societies, and can also use that insight as a way of understanding better whole societies and their cultures. This is an ambitious claim, but the best work on sport in Cultural and Media Studies, some of which is reproduced in this collection, performs this dual task with distinction.

The tripartite analytical structure of production, text and audience is at the heart of the study of media sport. In their historical survey of the field of 'MediaSport Studies', Kathleen Kinkema and Janet Harris note that:

> Work on sport and the mass media concerns three major topics: production of mediated sport texts, messages or content of mediated sport texts, and audience interaction with mediated sports texts . . . but at the outset it is important to acknowledge the lack of clear demarcation between them. Considerable overlap exists, and certainly it is difficult and somewhat artificial to discuss them separately, although efforts are made to explore linkages.
>
> (Kinkema and Harris 1998: 27)

Having noted these theoretically interconnected areas of focus, the authors go on to call for a 'more holistic research' that examines the detailed links between production, text, and reception in greater detail in order to articulate 'institutional, textual, and audience study' (p. 52). Raymond Boyle and Richard Haynes (2000: 14), in their book-length study *Power Play: Sport, Media and Popular Culture*, similarly map the field using the coordinates of political economy (products and institutions), representations of identity-formations (readings of media sports texts), and audience consumption (engagements by readers, listeners and viewers with media sports institutions and texts). These major features of the media sport landscape, Haynes and Boyle note, cannot be effectively isolated, requiring the placement of 'both sporting and media institutions within a larger frame of reference – a field of play which recognizes that sporting forms and mediated versions of these forms are continually being shaped by and in turn shaping culture as a whole' (p. 15).

The above-quoted authors, in surveying the subject from their vantage points in the key media sport sites of the USA and UK, also reveal its elusiveness and unruliness. In common with other areas of popular culture, such as rock and pop music (Rowe 1995), where media sport is broken down into defined analytical units in the interests of clarity and manageability, it is at some cost to the understanding of their inter-relatedness and complexity. For example, the mediation of the Olympic Games or the soccer World Cup can be analysed by concentrating on their production, a systematic knowledge of which is crucial to the understanding of any communicated text (Golding and Murdock 2000). This will demand a deep understanding of how sport is organized and governed, the relationship between peak sports bodies like the International Olympic Committee (IOC) or the Fédération Internationale de Football Association (FIFA) and corporate media organizations (like CBS, NBC and Fox), sponsors (McDonalds and Coca Cola), sports clothing companies (Nike and adidas), supra-state bodies (the United Nations and the European Union), national governments (China and Zimbabwe), non-government organizations (Amnesty International and the Global Anti-Golf Movement), and so on. Here the political and economic stakes are very high, and decisions taken at this level have very important ramifications, including economic collapse and political boycotts.

But there are many other levels of structure and process that have a bearing on media sport production, including the development of new audiovisual technologies and newspaper formats, the professional ideologies and practices of media sport personnel such as journalists and photographers, the emergence of new forms of sport and decline of older ones, and levels of support and subsidy from sub-national governments and businesses such as local councils and small traders. All these economic and institutional processes and exchanges are taking place in the context of much larger trends in which media sport is clearly implicated, such as the enhanced flows of people, capital, ideas, and technologies around the world that we commonly describe as *globalization*, as well as geo-political rivalries and conflicts, some of which are expressed, like the 'war on terrorism' in the wake of the 11 September 2001 destruction of the World Trade Centre, in various forms of diplomacy and military action. The complexity and, perhaps, unpredictability of these trends can be symbolized by the curious fact that, under the isolationist Taliban, Afghanistan joined the International Cricket Council (ICC) in 2001 shortly before the regime was toppled (Miller et al. 2003). As Alina Bernstein and Neil Blain (2003: 23–4) observe in surveying the research field of media and sport, this 'sense of complexity and ambiguity' is produced in a world where there are 'more and more connections across a variety of boundaries, accompanied by a growing sense of struggle between the local and the global'.

The myriad forces that combine in the production of media sport should not, however, deter those seeking to analyse it. Without a multi-layered knowledge of the political economic factors (large, medium-scale and small) that, first, make media sports texts possible, and then exert a profound influence on who is exposed to them and in which contexts, only a part of the picture has been completed. When trying to analyse live sports television broadcasts or sports reports or action photographs, it is essential to be equipped with a foundational understanding of their position in sport's cultural economy (Roche 2000). In the area of sports television, for example, it is important to understand how commercial development in the USA first transformed sport in that country, and subsequently influenced (without completely determining) the development of media sport in an international and, now, a global context (Guttmann 1994; Maguire 1999; Bairner 2001; Miller et al. 2001). To achieve this awareness it is necessary to undertake a deep examination of the ways in which media corporations struggle strenuously for the rights to broadcast sport, and sports compete to sell those rights to the highest bidder, while sponsors and advertisers seek the most visible and favourable brand association, and governments try to exert some influence to protect the rights of citizens. These exchanges are subject to constant change, with, for example, a sharp decline in the media sports market in the early twenty-first century, and a renewed interest by governments in its regulation (Rowe 2004). However, it is possible to become so preoccupied with economic issues of ownership, control and profit maximization that the specific characteristics of media sport disappear from view. Knowing how media sport is produced is not the same thing as understanding how it works *qua* popular culture.

Interrogating and interpreting media sports texts, and understanding both their formal properties and the ways in which they construct ideologies and mythologies of class (Hargreaves 1986), sexuality (Pronger 1990), race (Carrington and McDonald 2001), nation (Duke and Crolley 1996; Cronin and Mayall 1998), celebrity (Cashmore 2002) and so on, is also an important task. Much of this work in Media and Cultural Studies, Sociology and Sport Studies has involved the critique of the ways in which media sport has reproduced and promoted gender inequalities, with media sports texts consciously or unconsciously emphasizing male supremacy and reducing women to sexualized, subordinate and maternal roles in the language of sports commentators and journalists, the composition of sports photographs, public discussions of sport funding policies, and so on (for example, Creedon 1994; Hargreaves 1994; Thompson 1999; McKay et al. 2000; Hemphill and Symons 2002).

By such means media sport texts are read, inferences made and conclusions advanced about what they mean and how they will affect those exposed to them. These textual readings are often highly persuasive and acutely observed, and are sometimes supported with content analysis that provides quantitative evidence of, for example, the neglect of women's sport by the electronic and print media, or the differential ways of representing sportsmen and sportswomen to the detriment of the latter. They are also often informed by a knowledge and critique of the conditions of media sport production. But textual readings are vulnerable to the accusation that they reveal more about the reader than the texts themselves, with their decoding a product of the particular ideology or social positioning of the interpreter (Critcher 1993). Some 'decodings' of media sports texts might be described, following Stuart Hall (1980), as 'aberrant' because the meanings attributed to them might differ from the intentions of their producers, who do not in any case have 'divine rights' over the interpretation of culture. They might be read and used quite differently by other 'receivers', so vitiating claims of the meanings and effects of texts criticized on the grounds of being patriarchal, violent, sexist, and so on.

The point is not that these texts are inherently meaningless, and that they are not heavily scored with prevailing discourses and ideologies. Brief television exposure to the American patriotism of gridiron's Super Bowl or to the sexism of a male boxing bout (where lightly clothed female models parade around the ring informing innumerate patrons of the round number to a chorus of catcalls and whistles) would quickly disabuse viewers of that opinion. It is that there can be no final reading of any text, no singular, ultimate meaning that can be fixed forever for everybody without contestation. The same text is available to multiple readings across readers, time and space. Appreciating the theoretical impossibility of 'closing the book' of possible meanings is, then, as important for media sports texts as for any other type. Thus, in the introduction to Susan Birrell's and Mary McDonald's (2000: 6) collection *Reading Sport: Critical Essays on Power and Representation*, the editors adumbrate their commitment to 'critical cultural studies' and their concern with the intersecting 'power lines' of 'race, class, gender, and sexuality' that cross the field of sport. At the same time, they are aware that:

> An awareness that multiple readings of events and celebrities are always available precedes all critical analyses. We never want to become so confident that we cast our own particular readings

as the only authorized version and foreclose the possibility of other contradictory or complementary readings. All texts are polysemic, and the site of contested meanings, whether they are seen as dominant, subversive, resistant, transformative, or appropriative. Reading sport critically can be used as a methodology for uncovering, foregrounding, and producing counternarratives, that is, alternative accounts of particular events and celebrities that have been decentered, obscured, and dismissed by hegemonic forces.

(Birrell and McDonald 2000: 11)

This is a reasonable and increasingly orthodox theoretical stance within Cultural and Media Studies, but as a method it cannot satisfy all the requirements of media sport analysis. Not only does its emphasis on reading texts lead, inevitably, to a lesser concern with the context in which they are produced, but it leaves open the question of how to assess and adjudicate between competing readings of media sport texts. Rules of logic and evidence might be evoked, but these are in various ways as contestable as the texts they address are 'polysemic'.

In order to evade the implication that one reading of a media sports text is as good as any other, texts are usually embedded within coherent analytical narratives generated by the 'hegemonic forces' mentioned above that require to be countered. However, as Toby Miller (2001: 50) has argued with regard to the common claim (also made by Birrell and McDonald and, it should be acknowledged, on occasion by this author) that sport's gender order is characterized by 'hegemonic masculinity', there is a certain circularity in such arguments, and a tendency to explain away untidy phenomena 'inconsistent with standard political or textual moves' as 'symptoms of politics from elsewhere, and this "elsewhere" is the given of whoever currently rules'. Miller argues that readings of sports texts within a straightforward framework of hegemonic masculinity in sport have been 'destabilized' by political economic forces – namely the 'commodification of male beauty' (p. 52) that has made sportsmen much more objectified, subjected to surveillance, and vulnerable.

Yet, even if all textual readings were uniformly stable and fitted neatly within hegemonic narratives, their authority would still be in question where insufficient consideration has been given to how they are 'activated'. That is, media sports texts only come truly alive at the point where they encounter publics or audiences, at which point it is possible to assess how they are interpreted, used, accepted, challenged or adjusted. This is the third area of analysis previously identified by Kinkema and Harris, and by Boyle and Haynes. Close attention to audience reception and use helps overcome some of the speculative limitations of textual reading. Here, qualitative methods such as interviews, focus groups and observation involving sports fans, in some cases supplemented by quantitative surveys of attitudes, attendance and viewing, can compile a profile of the patterns of media sports text uses and of their users. As Gill Lines (2002: 198) argues, it is necessary to supplement 'textual analysis of media sport' with 'a more interpretative response incorporating audience voices in the research process'. Lines reports her methodological approach in a study of a group of young people's responses to the sports stars who were being intensively covered in the media during the 'Summer of Sport '96' (Euro '96 association football, Wimbledon tennis and the Atlanta Olympics). Her research 'combined quantitative and qualitative newspaper and television analysis' with a 'case study of twenty-five young people [aged fifteen who] completed daily diaries and group and individual interviews' (p. 198). Lines was especially interested in gender relations in this study, finding both anticipated and surprising readings of media sport texts involving stars by young people, and concluding that:

> Whilst there is evidence that gender relations are strategically mobilised and sustained through media representations and ongoing audience discourse, the precarious nature of the field of play remains as young people do negotiate the contradictions and acknowledge some elements of the power games being played.
>
> (Lines 2002: 212)

Lines's research links two of the elements – text and audience – that Kinkema and Harris believe constitute the main 'domains' of media sport research, but do not really incorporate the third – production. In fact, the only comprehensive study of this kind that they discovered in their survey of the field was reported in Laurel Davis's (1997) research, a section of which is reproduced in this collection, which 'Combined analysis of the *Sports Illustrated* swimsuit issue with interviews of both producers and consumers to show how ideas about hegemonic masculinity are generated and reinforced' (Kinkema and Harris 1998: 52). Nonetheless, Davis's use of the concept of hegemonic masculinity sets limits to the 'polysemy' noted by Birrell and McDonald (2000), and is open to the kind of criticism advanced above by Miller (2001) and others (*International Review for the Sociology of Sport* 1998). In methodological terms it also should be noted that there were only 39 subjects in the sample of consumers, that they were contacted on the basis of a combination of random and purposive sampling, and that as a result no statistical inferences could be drawn from the data.

The use of the case study method as represented in the above-cited work of Lines and Davis might meet the demands of audience researchers and reception theorists, but can still be criticized on the grounds that it cannot be generalized without further evidence. Of course, a case study of all media sport phenomena would be a practical impossibility, and there are constraints on how many comparative analyses can be performed between selected case studies (itself a process requiring a considerable degree of subjective decision-making). Large-scale studies of a 'multi-method and internationally collaborative nature' (de Moragas Spà et al. 1995: 6), like the one reported in *Television in the Olympics* (an excerpt from which is contained in this collection) involving 130 researchers in 25 countries, require the kind of long-term planning and resources that can rarely be achieved in the research field. Such studies would in any case be of limited value in the absence of a framework of theoretical explanation – the field of media sport research is rather more than the sum of 'joined up' analytical units. Research and scholarship on any subject involve elements of speculation, extrapolation, abstraction, selection and judgment, and media sport is no different in these regards. But there still remains a problem even if it were possible for production, text and audience and the relations between them in media sport to be fully accommodated in a wholly objective manner. This involves how the multifarious connections between media sport and the 'culture as a whole', as Boyle and Haynes (2000) described it above, can be tracked.

Social scientists and cultural analysts are expected to take cognisance of questions of causality, which can be briefly described as the separation of independent variables (causes) from dependent variables (effects) so that the former can be established as determining the latter. How can it be established where sport is shaping the wider culture, and where it is the other way round, especially when there are examples of mutual, simultaneous effects and influences? For example, there is keen debate about whether media sport is an agent of globalization or an outcome of it, with a variety of qualified positions in between (Maguire 1999; Bairner 2001; Miller et al. 2001). Answers to such questions must always be provisional, as those seeking to come to terms with the media sports cultural complex are required to chart and interpret the constant, multi-dimensional, multi-directional changes and continuities that they are not just looking at, but living in (Dandaneau 2001). This is a difficult balancing act, with various theoretical and methodological positions, including Marxism, feminism, Foucauldianism, and various 'posts' (including poststructuralism, postmodernism, postcolonialism), often in intricate blends, tracing explanatory patterns among sundry alternative explanations and counter-examples. Advancing macro-theoretical explanations of, for example, media sport and globalization while also documenting examples of nationally-based resistance to it, and also remaining sceptical about ideas of objectivity and value-free knowledge, can lead to accusations of wanting to 'have it both ways' (Hargreaves 2002: 37).

But this dynamic tension between grand theory and contingent explanation within Cultural and Media Studies is characteristic of a field that is self-reflexive. It fully appreciates the analysts' embeddedness in the culture and society that they are trying to analyse and, it is hoped, improve. Some recent writing in Sport Studies, for example, has displayed a self-reflexive, postmodern sensibility in attending to the 'craft' of writing by blurring the lines between 'realist' academic analysis and fictional narrative (Denison and Markula 2003). The intention of this approach is to generate new accounts and analyses of sport that resonate at different levels of experience and thought, thereby providing fresh insights and alternative 'truths' to those that dominate both the academic and media spheres. John Sugden and Alan Tomlinson (2002: 18) address this problem of 'truth' in the study of sport's 'power games' by recognizing that 'multiple vantage points' create 'multiple truths' with 'particular networks of power'. The critical sociologist of sport, they argue, must appreciate these different vantage points – including that their own is only one among many – in honest pursuit not of 'philosophical or absolute truth' but of a 'sociological truth' that can only be an 'impression' of reality. These authors are describing an investigative, ethnographic method that they apply to sports organizations like FIFA (Sugden and Tomlinson 1998) and to particular contexts like Cuba, which would not necessarily be suitable for all inquiry into sport, culture and the media. Nonetheless, its openness to different perspectives and attentiveness to power relations offers a workable basis for the interconnected study of media sport production, texts and audiences in their socio-cultural context.

## Conclusion: journeying with maps in media sport

In this chapter I have attempted a brief introduction to the study of media sport in Cultural and Media Studies that, it is hoped, will function as a useful springboard for the study of the subject and provide a context for the selected readings to follow. I have traced various approaches and debates, and attempted to show how a sceptical, reflexive and wide-ranging approach is required. It is important not to exaggerate the extent of some of the divisions and disputes in the field. As David Hesmondhalgh (2002: 42) has noted, there has been a rather debilitating and artificial split in the study of culture between a so-called 'political economy' approach primarily concerned with economic production and a so-called 'cultural studies' approach that is interested more in questions of textuality, identity, pleasure and so on. Hesmondhalgh (2002: 42) argues that, while there are genuine differences of emphasis, this division has exaggerated the cohesion of each side and the differences between them, and 'the key issue is how to synthesise the best aspects of the various approaches'. The fine work on media sport in this collection represents quite a diverse range of former and current work in the field. Those who become acquainted with this material here are invited to consider them and to 'synthesize' their 'best aspects' according to their own critical analytical orientation.

*Critical Readings: Sport, Culture and the Media* is divided, like the monograph on which it is based, into two parts. The first, *Media sport construction: history, labour, culture and economics*, establishes the institutional context within which media sport is produced, and then informs the second, *Media sport deconstruction: readings, forms, ideologies and futures*, which contains examples of critical readings of media sports texts in their many forms, so enabling a fuller exploration, interrogation and analysis of the media sports cultural complex. This is a division of convenience designed to illuminate different dimensions of media sport, but placing 'construction' before 'deconstruction' clearly indicates that, before media texts and their reception can be analysed, it is imperative to be knowledgeable about their provenance and current institutional position. Nonetheless, mechanically 'reading off' the meaning of media sports texts solely on the basis of their conditions of production will leave a clear analytical gap where the understanding of their cultural efficacy should have been. The 'trick' is to sweep back and forth ceaselessly between construction and deconstruction. In combining samples of key texts that have shaped the field of study with more recent works addressing media sport in Cultural and Media Studies, this Reader is intended to assist in the important task of making sense of a world that bears all the hallmarks of media sport saturation.

## References

Andrews, D.L. and Jackson, S.J. (eds) (2001) *Sport Stars: The Cultural Politics of Sporting Celebrity*. London and New York: Routledge.

Appadurai, A. (1996) Diversity and disciplinarity as cultural artefacts, in C. Nelson and D.P. Gaonkar (eds) *Disciplinarity and Dissent in Cultural Studies*. New York: Routledge.

Bairner, A. (2001) *Sport, Nationalism, and Globalization: European and North American Perspectives*. Albany: State University of New York Press.

Baker, A. and Boyd, T. (eds) (1997) *Sports, Media, and the Politics of Identity*. Bloomington: Indiana University Press.

Barker, C. (2000) *Cultural Studies: Theory and Practice*. London: Sage.

Barnett, S. (1990) *Games and Sets: The Changing Face of Sport on Television*. London: British Film Institute.

Bernstein, A. and Blain, N. (2003) Sport and the media: the emergence of a major research field, in A. Bernstein and N. Blain (eds) *Sport, Media, Culture: Global and Local Dimensions*. London: Frank Cass.

Birrell, S. and Cole, C.L. (eds) (1994) *Women, Sport and Culture*. Champaign, Illinois: Human Kinetics.

Birrell, S. and McDonald, M.G. (2000) Reading sport, articulating power lines: an introduction, in S. Birrell and M.G. McDonald (eds) *Reading Sport: Critical Essays on Power and Representation*. Boston: Northeastern University Press.

Boyle, R. and Haynes, R. (2000) *Power Play: Sport, the Media and Popular Culture*. Harlow: Pearson Education.

Brookes, R. (2002) *Representing Sport*. London: Arnold.

Buscombe, E. (ed.) (1975) *Football on Television*. London: British Film Institute.

Carrington, B. and McDonald, I. (eds) (2001) *'Race', Sport and British Society*. London and New York: Routledge.

Cashman, R. and McKernan, M. (eds) *Sport, Money, Morality and the Media*. Sydney: University of New South Wales Press.

Cashmore, E. (2002) *Beckham*. Cambridge: Polity.

Chandler, J.M. (1988) *Television and National Sport: The United States and Britain*. Urbana: University of Illinois Press.

Chandler, R. (1939) *The Big Sleep*. London: Hamish Hamilton.

Creedon, P.J. (ed.) (1994) *Women, Media and Sport: Challenging Gender Values*. Thousand Oaks, CA: Sage.

Critcher, C. (1993) In praise of self abuse, in C. Brackenridge (ed.) *Body Matters: Leisure Images and Lifestyles*. Eastbourne: Leisure Studies Association.

Cronin, M. and Mayall, D. (1998) *Sporting Nationalisms: Identity, Ethnicity, Immigration and Assimilation*. London: Frank Cass.

Dandaneau, S.P. (2001) *Taking it Big: Developing Sociological Consciousness in Postmodern Times*. Thousand Oaks, CA: Pine Forge Press.

Davis, L.A. (1997) *The Swimsuit Issue and Sport: Hegemonic Masculinity in Sports Illustrated*. Albany: State University of New York Press.

de Moragas Spà, M., Rivenburgh, N. and Larson, J. (1995) *Television in the Olympics*. Luton: John Libbey Media.

Denison, J. and Markula, P. (eds) (2003) *'Moving Writing': Crafting Movement in Sport Research*. New York: Peter Lang.

Duke, V. and Crolley, L. (1996) *Football, Nationality and the State*. Harlow: Longman.

Giulianotti, R. (1999) *Football: A Sociology of the Global Game*. Polity: Cambridge.

Golding, P. and Murdock, G. (2000) Culture, communications and political economy, in J. Curran and M. Gurevitch (eds) *Mass Media and Society*, 3rd edn. London: Arnold.

Goldlust, J. (1987) *Playing for Keeps: Sport, the Media and Society*. Melbourne: Longman Cheshire.

Guttmann, A. (1994) *Games and Empires: Modern Sports and Cultural Imperialism*. New York: Columbia University Press.

Hall, S. (1980) Encoding/Decoding, in S. Hall, D. Hobson, A. Lowe and P. Willis (eds) *Culture, Media, Language*. London: Hutchinson.

Hargreaves, Jennifer (1994) *Sporting Females: Critical Issues in the History and Sociology of Women's Sports*. London: Routledge.

Hargreaves, John (1986) *Sport, Power and Culture*. Cambridge: Polity.

Hargreaves, John (2002) Globalisation theory, global sport, and nations and nationalism, in J. Sugden and A. Tomlinson (eds) *Power Games: A Critical Sociology of Sport*. London: Routledge.

Hemphill, D. and Symons, C. (eds) (2002) *Gender, Sexuality and Sport: A Dangerous Mix*. Petersham, NSW: Walla Walla Press.

Hesmondhalgh, D. (2002) *The Cultural Industries*. London: Sage.

International Review for the Sociology of Sport (1998) The swimsuit issue and sport, Review symposium, *International Review for the Sociology of Sport*, 33(2): 189–203.

King, A. (1998) *The End of the Terraces: The Transformation of English Football in the 1990s*. London and New York: Leicester University Press.

Kinkema, K.M. and Harris, J.C. (1998) MediaSport studies: key research and emerging issues, in L.A. Wenner (ed.) *MediaSport*. London: Routledge.

Klatell, D. and Marcus, N. (1988) *Sports for Sale: Television, Money and the Fans*. New York: Oxford University Press.

Lines, G. (2002) The sports star in the media: the gendered construction and youthful consumption of sports personalities, in J. Sugden and A. Tomlinson (eds) *Power Games: A Critical Sociology of Sport*. London: Routledge.

McKay, J., Messner, M.A. and Sabo, D. (eds) (2000) *Masculinities, Gender Relations, and Sport*. Thousand Oaks, CA: Sage.

Maguire, J. (1999) *Global Sport: Identities, Societies, Civilizations*. Cambridge: Polity.

Martin, R. and Miller, T. (eds) (1999) *SportCult*. Minneapolis: University of Minnesota Press.

Miller, T. (2001) *Sportsex*. Philadelphia: Temple University Press.

Miller, T., Lawrence, G., McKay, J. and Rowe, D. (2001) *Globalization and Sport: Playing the World*. London: Sage.

Miller, T., Rowe, D., Lawrence, G. and McKay, J. (2003) Globalization, the over-production of US sports, and the new international division of cultural labour, *International Review for the Sociology of Sport* 38(4): 427–40.

Murdock, G. (1997) Base notes: the conditions of cultural practice, in M. Ferguson and P. Golding (eds) *Cultural Studies in Question*. London: Sage.

Murdock, G. (1992) Citizens, consumers, and public culture, in M. Skovmand and K.C. Schroder (eds) *Media Cultures: Reappraising Transnational Media*. London: Routledge.

Murdock, G. and Golding, P. (1989) Information poverty and political inequality: Citizenship in the age of privatized communications, *Journal of Communication*, 39 (3): 180–95.

Pronger, B. (1990) *The Arena of Masculinity: Sport, Homosexuality, and the Meaning of Sex*. New York: St Martin's Press.

Real, M. (1989) *Super Media: A Cultural Studies Approach*. Newbury Park, CA: Sage.

Roche, M. (2000) *Mega-Events and Modernity: Olympics and Expos in the Growth of Global Culture*. London and New York: Routledge.

Rojek, C. and Turner, B. (2000) Decorative sociology: towards a critique of the cultural turn, *Sociological Review*, 48(4): 629–48.

Rowe, D. (1995) *Popular Cultures: Rock Music, Sport and the Politics of Pleasure*. London: Sage.

Rowe, D. (1998) If you film it, will they come? Sports on film, *Journal of Sport and Social Issues*, 22(4): 350–9.

Rowe, D. (2000) No gain, no game? Media and sport, in J. Curran and M. Gurevitch (eds) *Mass Media and Society*, 3rd edn. London: Edward Arnold.

Rowe, D. (2003) Watching brief: cultural citizenship and viewing rights, *Culture, Sport, Society*, 6 (3).

Rowe, D. (2004) *Sport, Culture and the Media: The Unruly Trinity*, 2nd edn. Maidenhead: Open University Press.

Stevenson, N. (1995) *Understanding Media Cultures: Social Theory and Mass Communication*. London: Sage.

Sugden, J. and Tomlinson, A. (1998) *FIFA and the Contest for World Football: Who Rules the People's Game?* Cambridge: Polity.

Sugden, J. and Tomlinson, A. (eds) (2002) *Power Games: A Critical Sociology of Sport*. London: Routledge.

Thompson, S. (1999) *Mother's Taxi: Sport and Women's Labor*. Albany: State University of New York Press.

Tomlinson, A. (1999) *The Game's Up: Essays in the Cultural Analysis of Sport, Leisure and Popular Culture*. Aldershot: Ashgate.

Wenner, L.A. (ed.) (1989) *Media, Sports, and Society*. Newbury Park, CA: Sage.

Wenner, L.A. (ed.) (1998) *MediaSport*. London: Routledge.

Whannel, G. (1992) *Fields in Vision: Television Sport and Cultural Transformation*. London: Routledge.

Whannel, G. (2001) *Media Sport Stars: Masculinities and Moralities*. London: Routledge.

# Part I

# MEDIA SPORT CONSTRUCTION: HISTORY, LABOUR, CULTURE AND ECONOMICS

In trying to come to terms with lives of such rapid and far-reaching change, it is easy to forget (or never to have appreciated) that what seems to be a permanent feature of our existential landscape is often of much more recent tenure. Media sport is one such cultural feature, enveloping us every day in a familiar blanket of drama and cliché, and inducing collective memory loss about such matters as:

- television and sport were once uneasy bedfellows rather than red hot lovers;
- media sport is actually made by humans, not the product of spontaneous combustion or metal machine logic;
- media in different cultural contexts represent sport in significantly different ways;
- somebody, somewhere, is making cold-hearted economic decisions about other people's sporting passions.

This first part of the Reader, then, is something of a sobering reminder that media sport has various histories, that it is the product of work, is subject to considerable cultural variation, and is a massive economic enterprise. The first two chapters by John Goldlust and Joan Chandler are excerpts from 'classic', pioneering media sports books of the 1980s. They are reproduced here not just because of their importance to the field, but as historical documents in their own right. Both were written as the 'media sports cultural complex' was gathering force, but before its extraordinary growth (now slowing) in the last decade. Goldlust (Chapter 2) provides a useful discussion of the social-historical conditions that eventually gave rise to the inter-meshing of the institutions of media and sport. The sports press and radio are shown to emerge as part of a wider development of mass communication and commercialized leisure enabled by the growth of cultural capitalism and the success of organized labour in acquiring some of the surplus that they had generated. Goldlust takes us to the brink of sport's 'television age', while Chandler (Chapter 3) traces its flowering in Britain and the USA as the professionalization and televisualization of sport reinforced its industrialization. Chandler's chapter is extraordinary not only for showing how much has changed in broadcast sport since the 1920s, but the extent of change since her book was published in 1988. Her account, for example, of the non-competitive framework of British sports broadcasting and the 'curious gentility' of its football industry seems almost quaint in the light of developments documented elsewhere in this book. Nonetheless, some historical differences between the UK and USA television and sports industries have persisted, for example with regard to public broadcasting and to team franchising. These two chapters (historical in more than one sense) set up the later contributions by demonstrating continuities and discontinuities both in media sport and in its analysis within Cultural and Media Studies.

Lawrence Wenner (Chapter 4) neatly and incisively captures the dramatic outcome of this 'long revolution' of media sport as the new millennium approached. He uses a reader-oriented approach to analyse a range of television advertisements involving the USA's famous basketballing 'Dream Team' at the centre of a complex web of commercial arrangements with McDonald's, Visa, Pepsi and so on. Iconic figures like Michael Jordan, Magic Johnson, Charles Barkley and Larry Bird are shown to be potent vectors of consumer messages and wider ideologies in harnessing the power of the sport's 'dirt', liberally sprinkled through the apparatus of television. Toby Miller et al. (Chapter 5), on the other side of the epochal millennial moment, track some of the major developments in media sport and entertainment as part of a wider phenomenon that they call the New International Division of Cultural Labour (NICL) integral to the globalization of sport. They document some of the massive trans-actions that have seen an increasing convergence of sport and communications conglomerates, one of the best known and aggressive of the latter being the Rupert Murdoch-led News Corporation. David Andrews (Chapter 6) then examines News Corporation's strategies of using sports television to extend its overall activities across the globe, a 'vertical integration' that has seen massive investment in both broadcast rights and in the ownership and control of the sports properties appearing on screen. In this way, the position and influence of televised sport within the global media entertainment economy is reinforced.

While Miller et al. and Andrews focus on the global political economic forces framing the grand canvas upon which media sport is sketched, Mark Lowes (Chapter 7) and Michael Silk et al. (Chapter 8) reveal something of how these are translated into the 'nuts and bolts' constraints on the everyday working lives of professional media sport personnel. Lowes analyses the 'newswork routines' of the sports desk of a Canadian newspaper through an observational study. The routine work practices and news networks that combine to produce sports stories, coupled with the influence of commercial sports organizations and other economic forces on sports journalists, are revealed to produce the outcome common to many newspapers and magazines that 'some sports enjoy regular and voluminous press coverage and others virtually none'. Silk et al. move from print to the television production process in their case study of the coverage of the 1995 Canada Cup of Soccer. The authors researched the relationship between the conditions under which the broadcast was produced and the completed televisual texts that went to air. While the latter are not analysed in detail in the chapter, substantial understanding is gained concerning how they and comparable media sports texts are formed. This institutional approach is especially useful, as was argued in the Introduction, because it avoids the limiting disconnection of process and product in much media sport analysis. Silk et al. reveal a number of competing influences on broadcast sport, including prevailing 'industrial wisdom' and 'craft pride', the diffusion of international sports TV conventions, assumptions about the constitution and response of audiences, national cultural identity, and so on. This view of the 'labour process' in television production reveals a complex pattern of macro and micro influences that is, by various degrees, contested and accommodated.

The first part on *Media Sport Construction* concludes with a chapter that returns us from the coal face of media sport to its most glittering screen visage. Maurice Roche (Chapter 9) considers the Olympics as a 'mega-event' that becomes so by being a 'media-event'. He tracks the increasing infusion of broadcasting money into Olympic sport and deploys the neo-Durkheimian perspective of Dayan and Katz in analysing the construction of the Olympic media genre and narrative. The political economy of the 1988 Seoul Olympics is appraised, while Roche's use of the research of Miquel de Moragas

Spà et al. (1995) on media-stimulated nationalism and commercialism in the 1992 Barcelona Olympics provides a perfect bridge to the next section of this book, which opens with a chapter from these authors on the reception of the Games from different vantage points across the globe. The major phenomena and forces integral to the media sports cultural complex have, therefore, been analytically framed as a prelude to the analysis of the media texts seeking daily to imprint themselves on the collective consciousness.

# SPORT AS ENTERTAINMENT: THE ROLE OF MASS COMMUNICATIONS

## John Goldlust

Excerpt from *Playing for Keeps: Sport, the Media and Society.*
Melbourne: Longman Cheshire, 1987, Chapter 3: 58–77.

### The development of the commercial mass media

The emergence and spread of modern competitive sport can best be
understood in the broader context of the growth of urbanised,
industrialised society. Similarly, the structural and ideological characteristics associated with this process have been equally influential in
shaping the rise to prominence of another significant modern cultural
institution – the technologies and organizations of mass communications. The invention of the movable type printing press by Johann
Gutenberg in 1440 is conventionally considered to be the major technological breakthrough facilitating the possibility of mass production
of symbolic material, but, it was not until two centuries after this
that the first daily newspapers appeared in Western Europe and
North America. In Europe, from the time of their earliest appearance,
newspapers have been closely connected to political interest groups,
serving as a forum for the circulation and discussion of contemporary
issues, ideas and viewpoints. Consequently, from the outset, newspapers attracted considerable attention from authorities fearful of
their potential for disseminating troublesome and subversive material.
The battle over the 'freedom of the press' was an important element –
both practical and symbolic  –  in the ongoing struggle for
political control waged between the landed aristocracy and the urban
bourgeoisie in Britain and other parts of Europe from about the
seventeenth century onwards.

The newspaper quickly established itself as an important vehicle for articulating grievances, presenting arguments for social and political change and mobilising interest groups into action. Consequently, governments and powerful groups in society endeavoured, through licensing, censorship and the laws of libel and sedition, to exert some control over the contents of newspapers and thereby prevent the public dissemination of viewpoints they considered critical or in any way threatening – categories both extremely broad and often subject to the vagaries of arbitrary and authoritarian interpretation. However, in the United States, the positive involvement of the press in the colonial struggle for independence against Britain helped enshrine its absolute freedom from official authoritative interference. The United States became 'the first nation to detach its press from the official machinery of government' through the libertarian provisions of the first amendment to its constitution which stipulated that no law could be passed that might abrogate the absolute freedom of speech, of worship and of the press:

> The absence of political constraints and the nearly universal suffrage fuelled the growth of the press; the federal structure ensured its localism. Localism became an abiding characteristic of the US media; the detachment of the press from government and then from close party involvement led also to dependence on advertising. News and advertising grew together as two parts of a sandwich whose filling was entertainment.
>
> (Tunstall 1977: 3)

Thus, writing in 1835, Alexis de Tocqueville astutely noted:

> In France little space is given over to trade advertisements, and even news items are few; the vital part of the newspaper is that devoted to political discussion. In America three-quarters of the bulky newspaper put before you will be full of advertisements and the rest will usually contain political news or just anecdotes . . .
>
> In France the hallmark of the spirit of journalism is a violent but lofty and often eloquent way of arguing about great interests of state . . . the hallmark of the American journalist is a direct and coarse attack, without any subtleties, on the passions of his readers; he disregards principles to seize on people, following them into their private lives and laying bare their weaknesses and their vices.
>
> (Tocqueville quoted in Tunstall 1977: 24)

It was America, then, that was at the forefront of the development of an alternative to the partisan political newspaper. The commercial newspaper emerged as a business in its own right concerned with expanding its readership to the urban, working class among whom, understandably, the general level of literacy and formal education was not extensive. In order to attract such readers, vocabulary and sentence structure was simplified, items kept short and breezy, increasing emphasis placed on local personalities, issues, gossip and entertainment combined with a few brief descriptive articles on the broader political, economic and cultural affairs of the nation. More importantly, the sale of advertising space in a newspaper could become the primary source of financial return for the publishers, thereby subsidising the direct cost per copy charged to the reader. The greater the circulation of the paper the more advertisers were prepared to pay for space to reach potential customers, which in turn gave greater flexibility to newspaper publishers to reduce the purchase price. In large competitive markets such as New York, by 1833, the price of a daily newspaper was as low as one cent, yet the publishers could still operate profitably from advertising income, provided readership continued to expand.

A similar trend developed in Britain in the latter half of the nineteenth century. The last vestiges of governmental control over newspaper production were removed in the 1850s with the repeal of laws relating to advertising duties (1853) and stamp duty (1855) on each copy sold (Curran 1977: 212). This led to an intense competition between the more established, generally conservative newspapers and, somewhat ironically, to the virtual eradication of the radical, working-class press that had vehemently opposed and often evaded the taxes. Also, the repeal of the advertising duty tax increased the volume of advertising attracted by the more popular newspapers, which allowed them to reduce their price to as low as a penny per copy, thereby giving them an important competitive edge in the market place. Consequently, in the 25-year period from 1856, sales of daily newspapers in Britain increased by more than 600 per cent as compared with a 70 per cent increase over the previous twenty years (Williams 1965: 216).

Although several larger newspapers maintained strong partisan ties with various political factions and parties, the growing dominance of advertising as the basis of financially profitable newspaper publishing directed the British press into a broadly populist mode with a format, style and content not dissimilar from their American forerunners. To a large extent, and taking into account the segmenting of the market place through a broad division between 'quality' and 'populist' newspapers, the business rationales underlying the operation of the daily press that were first developed in America and Britain in the nineteenth century established both the principles of journalistic style and the range of content for the successful commercial newspaper. Both have changed very little to this day. As Jeremy Tunstall succinctly observes:

> The news-entertainment-advertising medium of the newspaper had a distinct technology and raw materials; it had a peculiar double system of finance – public sales and advertising; it evolved an elaborate division of labour-printers, journalists, commercial management. All of these were developed in ways which fitted with American (and British) circumstances, and were then copied, often in countries where quite different sets of circumstances obtained
>
> (Tunstall 1977: 23–4)

So, the technology of printing became a vehicle for the production of another form of consumer commodity – the daily newspaper – to be manufactured and marketed in accordance with those entrepreneurial principles of organization and distribution that worked most effectively in a capitalist economy. The direct link between the continued financial success of mass circulation newspapers and the consistent growth of advertising revenues tended to align the interests of the proprietors of commercial newspapers more closely to those of the owners of capital, rather than to the sellers of labour. This communality was further strengthened as newspaper publishing itself became 'big business'. In those societies in which industrialisation advanced most rapidly, and in which 'free enterprise' remained the dominant politico-economic orthodoxy, the structural trends that developed in the newspaper business paralleled closely those of many other industries. The process was typified by fierce competition for circulation, the swallowing-up of the smaller, less successful papers by the larger organizations and the establishment of chains or networks under the control of the most successful entrepreneurs within the industry. Following the economic 'laws' of capitalist mass production, the aim was to compete against other suppliers to produce a cost-efficient commodity attractive to a broad target market. In the newspaper business this translated into the development of a number of specialised sections and features of direct interest to particular sectors of the potential market, such as business, real estate, fashion (directed mainly towards women) and entertainment/leisure.

The period of the latter part of the nineteenth and the early decades of the twentieth century was one of significant growth and expansion for both the commercial daily newspaper and entrepreneurially-based forms of popular entertainment. The newspaper served as an extremely effective vehicle for the marketing of the latter. In addition to the direct purchase of advertising space by the producers and distributors of the various forms of popular entertainment, the more circulation oriented newspapers assessed the positive benefits of devoting increasing amounts of copy to 'news' items, critical appraisals, features, biographies and gossip that informed readers on almost every aspect of available commercial entertainment. Such welcome 'free' publicity greatly assisted the entrepreneurial develop-ment of first vaudeville, music hall and variety theatre, and later the Hollywood film, the popular music industry and spectator sports. The commercial newspaper thus operated as a promoter, an adjunct and itself a significant component of a modern social phenomenon broadly identified as 'mass culture'.

## Mass communication, leisure and commercialised culture

As evidenced by the history of the 'rational recreation' movement in nineteenth-century Britain, despite the respect accorded to the principles of liberalism and individualism, there were strong pressures from sections of the middle class to direct the populace as a whole – and, in particular, the working class – into gainfully filling their non-working hours with leisure pursuits that were 'uplifting', 'educational' and of 'cultural value'. For the more committed, this meant inculcating into the 'lower orders' a reverent appreciation of the carefully nurtured heritage of Western culture that had been preserved and patronised over the centuries by aristocratic and religious elites. But a position widely held within intellectual and political circles was that this rarified cultural world of theatre, art, literature and music would lose its integrity and its creative dynamism if it was to be made accessible to the 'rude mechanicals' who had neither the temperament nor the social background to appreciate its 'true worth'. Such views were particularly strongly felt by those who found many aspects of both political democracy and industrial capitalism a threat to 'civilised' values. Many still refused to accept the irreversibility of the recent political demise of the 'natural', aristocratic order, an example of the type of social structure they believed provided a necessary prerequisite for the operation and maintenance of any worthwhile expressive culture.

Such a position was further reinforced when the majority of the working class preferred to decline the entreaties of 'rational recreation' for the earthier pleasures of the communal ale house, brassy music hall, vaudeville theatre and the local sports field. Similarly, the general growth of literacy throughout the population did not translate into an immediate and insatiable rush to absorb the 'classics' of Western literature – although certainly some working people sought them out, read them and found them edifying – but rather stimulated an explosion in the publication of crudely written romance, adventure and fantasy. The working class in general stubbornly showed a marked preference for genres and styles that ranked fairly low on the institutionalised cultural scale of literary and creative merit. At the same time, the economic rationalisation of popular entertainment by leisure entrepreneurs and pioneers of the new media technologies was primarily directed towards maximisation of profit through the application of already established commodity production techniques of standardisation, centralisation of production, aggressive marketing, controlling costs of labour and equipment, increasing avenues for distribution, and the amalgamation of competitive enterprises in order to develop more effective economies of scale.

The economic success of the cheap commercial newspapers, 'pulp' literature and later other commercially-based entertainment forms amplified the already established tendency by intellectual observers to debate, from various theoretical and political perspectives, the supposed division between 'high' and 'mass' culture (or popular culture as it has more recently been relabelled). To many of the cultural critics, the rationalised materialism of industrial society was breaking down intermediary social groupings – regional, ethnic, religious, status and class – undermining particularistic group values and aesthetics with the resultant formation of a new entity identified as 'mass society' with its concomitant 'mass culture'. This 'mass culture' was continually portrayed as a corrupt and degraded derivative of the established 'high culture' forms of literature, art and theatre. Considered synthetic and exploitative, 'mass culture' was negatively contrasted with the 'authentic' alternatives of, on the one hand, 'high culture' as the refined expression of talented, independent creators, and, on the other, with 'folk culture', as the organically rooted examples of narrative, music, dance and ritual growing naturally out of the life and experience of pre-industrial rural communities.

While it has its origins as far back as the sixteenth century, the framework for the debate over the social, political and cultural effects of the rise of 'mass culture' intensified with the expansion of the newer communication technologies and remained the central paradigm for most critical discussions of modern culture until well into the 1960s (Rosenberg and White 1957; Lowenthal 1968; Gans 1974). Without entering into a detailed exposition of the various arguments in the debate, it does seem indisputable that with the general increase in material wealth and the consolidation of a new industrial order came a general reconstruction of the relationship between work and leisure. The 'folk culture' identified with rural society as an expression of religio-cultic communalism had little relevance to the everyday lives of the new generations of urbanised factory workers. The conditions of wage-labour provided a daily portion of discretionary time which, by the end of the nineteenth century, gradually increased as political pressures achieved a reduction in the hours that employers could reasonably expect employees to work each week in exchange for their 'living wage'.

Thus, what came to be perceived as 'mass culture' was constituted from the wide variety of commercialised performances, activities and artefacts increasingly presented to the public as attractive leisure or entertainment pursuits to be purchased from any money left available beyond obligatory survival needs. The most successful entrepreneurs of commercial entertainment quickly became attuned to 'public taste' and the marketplace of alternative pursuits, seeking to attract and nurture within their organizations those with the creative, administrative, technical and marketing skills most suited to the presentation of 'entertainment' that would return an attractive rate of profit. In style and content, the developing entertainment forms drew from the broader cultural experiences and recognisable performance styles most familiar to their potential audience. Many of the creative and performing talents who achieved the greatest commercial success came from the same working- and lower middle-class material and cultural environments as the people they entertained. For both performer and audience the 'great tradition' of the literary, artistic and performing arts was, in the main, alien and inaccessible; a culture expressed through forms and styles that were intellectually intimidating, nurtured by a numerically small community of creators and appreciators, and identified with the materially and educationally privileged classes in society. Within the range of commercial entertainments provided for them, the paying customers of popular culture clearly made discriminating choices. But the basis of such preferences did not often coincide with the aesthetic, moral and intellectual criteria of the institutionalised body of literary and cultural critics who authoritatively guarded a cultural hierarchy primarily concerned with 'high culture' or 'the arts'.

The new media technologies of the twentieth century proved eminently suited to the further expansion of popular entertainment. The novelty and creative potential of film introduced a medium that could draw upon and expand the narrative conventions of the novel and the theatre. But the organization of the American film industry as an entrepreneurial venture in cheap mass entertainment, the structure of which was definitively formed by a clique of predominantly immigrant sales and advertising men 'of a basically promotional disposition' (Tunstall 1977: 80), ensured that it set its course in the direction of primarily seeking to maximise the financial return on production costs. This could be most effectively accomplished through ensuring a steady output of material consciously tailored to attract the largest and broadest possible audience. The early establishment of the Hollywood studio system institutionalised the commercial basis of the film industry and its outstanding financial returns ensured the continued preference for 'entertainment value' (a convenient euphemism for the broadly popular) in production decisions over 'art' – meaning 'intellectual', 'high culture' or minority tastes. In this, the early Hollywood tycoons were merely extending the marketing principles previously established in the domains of the travelling circus, vaudeville and variety shows. They soon became aware that the new film technology might be applied to the creation of a standardised, easily distributable product that could be displayed concurrently in thousands of theatres to aggregate audiences numbering in the millions. Thus the mass communication technologies could be exploited to enormously expand the audiences for professionally produced entertainment and thereby create the conditions for universalised forms of cultural experience significantly different from either 'high culture' or the traditionally localised 'folk culture'.

The forms of presentation and distribution of the vast body of content making up 'mass' or 'popular' culture were further extended with the development of technologies for sound recording and reproduction, and for the transmission of sound and visual material directly into domestic receiving apparatus. The future characteristics of both radio and television were largely predetermined by the general assumption that the most rational and appropriate social application of their technological possibilities was as a means for the centralised distribution of professionally produced programme material to a mass of receivers. As some critical observers have pointed out, this is by no means the only arrangement by which the potentialities of these media technologies might be utilised. But the political decisions surrounding the introduction of radio and television transmission services were limited by the premise that these were essentially organs of 'mass communication'. Once this was accepted the question of what type of arrangement was most appropriate depended, in the main, on the particular society's broader political and economic structure. The decisions to be made concerned the nature and extent of centralised political control over the organization and/or content of radio and television transmission services; the economic basis upon which the cost of operating such services would be financed; the number of stations or channels that would be permitted to operate; the mechanisms for monitoring and regulating the content of the transmissions; and the broader responsibilities of television services to cater to certain social, political and cultural 'needs' of the 'communities' to which they transmitted.

Effectively, the resultant decisions on these questions produced three major models for the societal organization of radio and television services. In the United States the constitutional protection of the rights of the individual to freedom of speech and of the press which, as noted above, assisted the development of the commercial newspaper, also ensured minimal state interference in the process whereby privately owned organizations came to own and operate subsequent organs of mass communication. It was left to a Federal regulatory agency to administer the orderly allocation of transmission wavelengths. Licences were issued, first for radio and later television, to a number of individual or corporate applicants in each city, town and rural region. The licensee was legally entitled, within established guidelines, to beam a broadcast signal encoded with programme material into a specified area of the country. It was accepted that, as with newspapers, those granted radio and television licences could most effectively finance their operations through interspersing within their transmission commercial messages paid for by advertisers seeking to reach potential customers for their goods and services. Therefore, the costs of production and purchase of programme material and the other technical and organizational expenses incurred in the running of a broadcasting enterprise became directly linked to the sale of advertising time. In such a system, both the rates charged to the purchasers of advertising time and the level of profitability achieved by the broadcasting organization are broadly determined by total audience size as assessed in periodic 'ratings' surveys. Initially, the only major regulatory restrictions on the material broadcast required some sensitivity to established community norms with regard to language and sexual content, and specified a 'fairness' doctrine to be applied to material connected with candidates campaigning for electoral office. Other than these, the content broadcast was effectively constrained only by other relevant legal statutes relating to libel, sedition, incitement to riot, racial equality, and so on. Such a system was designed in principle to encourage a certain level of pluralism and community responsibility. However, it also institutionalized the commercial market principles in American broadcasting that led to the economic rationalisation of programme production – particularly with regard to television given its more potent marketing potential for advertisers and broader entertainment appeal to audiences. This resulted, at least for the first 30 years of operation, in the establishment of three major commercial networks that dominated American television broadcasting, each with hundreds of affiliated local stations throughout the country, transmitting, from centralised sources, a standardised range of programmes and competing for nationwide aggregate audiences to sell to large national advertisers.

As the United States has remained a major world economic and political power, it is not surprising that the basic elements of American commercial broadcasting have been widely reproduced in other societies, most notably in a number of Western industrialised countries, but also in many developing countries of Latin America, Asia and Africa. The latter has often been connected to a high level of economic dependence on the United States, as well as political control in these countries remaining in the hands of small 'client' elites sympathetic to America's international role in championing the principles of 'free enterprise' and supported by it against reformist or revolutionary movements (Schiller 1969). A second type of broadcasting model emanated from Britain. This evolved with the establishment of the BBC in 1926 as a government funded monopoly to control both the production and transmission of all radio broadcasting in Britain. The cost of such a service was to be financed through the sale of licences legally required by all households with a receiving device. The British conceived of broadcasting as a form of national 'public service'. Within certain guidelines laid down by the government, the BBC was to be a department of the civil service but nominally independent of political interference, with its own chairman and administrative structure and a budget allocation to employ the required personnel to produce and distribute programme material. As Raymond Williams comments in his analysis of this peculiarly British approach to the question surrounding the appropriate application of broadcasting technology:

> a dominant version of the national culture had already been established, in an unusually compact ruling-class, so that public service could be effectively understood and administered as service according to the values of an existing public definition, with an effective paternalist definition of both service and responsibility ... The flexibility which was latent in this kind of solution, though continually a matter of dispute, permitted the emergence of an independent corporate broadcasting policy, in which the independence was at once real, especially in relation to political parties and temporary administrations, and qualified, by its definition in terms of pre-existing cultural hegemony.
>
> (Williams 1974: 33–4)

The BBC's radio monopoly was extended to television when domestic services were introduced into Britain in 1946. The principle of direct state regulation and production of radio and television has been adopted by a number of Western European states. Such an arrangement can be expanded to allow for the establishment of alternative transmission channels catering to different cultural and regional interests, while all still remain under the umbrella of the government administered service. In countries where there exists a reasonably stable and securely legitimated liberal-democratic political culture, the American and British approaches to the organization of radio and television broadcasting have invariably served as influential working guides. In certain instances, notably Australia and Canada, broadcasting policy legislation was introduced to permit both privately owned commercial stations and publicly funded national corporations to operate side by side. In fact in Britain itself, in response to extensive public pressure on the government, the BBC's monopoly over broadcasting was broken in 1955 with the granting of the first commercial television licences. A third model of broadcasting tends to operate where effective political power is concentrated in a party or clique identifying itself with statist ideologies of Left or Right. In such circumstances all forms of public communication, particularly the organs of the mass media, are placed strictly within control of such groups or nominally at the service of 'the state' – which in most cases amounts to the same thing. Notwithstanding the considerable variations in the extent to which political power is exercised to limit the overall autonomy in the operation of mass communications systems, there has been an almost universal tendency to employ these technologies for the provision of public entertainment, however this term may be defined within a particular culture. Mass communication systems also operate as a source of general information, a forum for discussion or debate of social and political issues, an avenue for the dissemination of political propaganda and as an adjunct to formal educational training. But, in the main, they are considered, both by those who produce the transmitted material, and by the majority of their audience, as a major source for diversion and relaxing entertainment with which to fill some portion of discretionary leisure time. As such they have operated as an important institutional focus for the extensive growth of a wide range of popular performance forms such as music, variety, dance, fictional narratives of all types, and, most pertinently, the sporting contest.

The interpenetration of sport and the mass media has been greatly facilitated by the modern construction of the high-level sporting contest as essentially an expressive performance form and, therefore, as an appropriate vehicle for popular entertainment. The conceptualisation of sport as performance links modern sport to the Games of the Ancient Greeks. For in the Classical Games, the arts of poetry and music were included alongside the athletic contests, and exceptional performances in each treated with equal respect:

> Pindar devoted Pythian Odes to the winners in chariot races, horse races, wrestling matches, foot races, but without any incongruity the XII Pythian lauds, as no less worthy of the gods and noble ancestors Midas of Acragas, winner in the flute playing match, 490 B.C.
>
> (Kuntz 1977: 164)

The connection was certainly familiar to Baron de Coubertin [founder of the Modern Olympics] whose vision of a regular international sporting festival also included a place for artists, musicians and poets. Arts festivals and competitions, for which medals were awarded to entrants in a variety of fields, including town planning, architectural designs, sculpture, painting, literature, drama and music, were included as adjuncts to the sporting contests at a number of the modern Olympiads, but the practice was discontinued after 1948 (Kamper 1972). However, for modern sport, the relationship to performance is significant not so much in the sense that it might best be considered one of 'the arts' (such as theatre – Kuntz 1977) but rather the extent to which its attractiveness to spectators has influenced the development of sport as an important sector of the modern culture industry. Over recent decades, the latter has, from an economic and organizational standpoint, come to incorporate the marketing of all aspects of what is conventionally designated as both popular and high culture. Indeed, as Langer (1985: 20–1) argues, 'the myth that "high culture" is not "commercial" must be abandoned'. Thus, both the line of development of sport in the twentieth century and its relationship to mass communications may best be understood in the broader context of the general industrialisation of culture, promoted and packaged by interested parties as a consumer commodity competing in a market against similar products.

## Sport and mass communications before television

The reporting of sports events in daily newspapers began to appear intermittently in the early part of the eighteenth century with a predilection towards the sporting interests of the leisured class, notably horse racing, prize fighting, boat racing, fishing, hunting, golf and cricket. The *Boston Gazette* of 5 May 1733 is credited with carrying the first sports story – on a prize fight – in an American newspaper, but this was copied directly from a London daily (Greendorfer 1981: 162). Consistent with the earlier growth of a general interest in sport in Britain, the appearance of books, magazines and newspaper reports on sporting topics antedated their American counterparts. By the early 1800s, London magazines such as *Bell's Life* and the *Weekly Despatch* had developed a solid readership both at home and abroad by concentrating heavily on articles and stories about the sports mainly associated with the leisure pursuits of the rural gentry:

> *Bell's Life*, often cited as the 'Bible', was the authority for devotees of the turf, the ring, the hunt and angling ... Pierce Egan's *Boxiana* and other works were popular reading for ring enthusiasts. The *London Sporting Magazine* and the *English Sporting Magazine* were drawn upon for material or served as a model for American publishers.
>
> (Betts 1953: 40)

But the Americans very quickly produced their own indigenous journals on sport, beginning with *The American Farmer* that first appeared in 1819 providing its readers with 'the results of hunting, fishing, shooting and bicycling matches as well as essays on the philosophy of sports' (Greendorfer 1981: 162). The keen interest in horse racing in the Atlantic states and the American south stimulated the publication in 1829 of the *American Turf Register* and *Sporting Magazine* and, two years later, of *The Spirit of the Times*, 'which was destined to become the leading sporting journal of the middle years of the nineteenth century' (Betts 1953: 40–1). The numerous sports journals and magazines that proliferated in the nineteenth century in both Europe and America helped to form the sporting subcultures that grew up around particular games and competitions. Apart from describing events and providing results, they created a sense of cultural continuity – keeping records, lionising outstanding performers, developing the mythologies of 'golden eras' and in general operating as publicists, literary chroniclers and philosophers for the new codified games. The inclusion of sports results into the routine format of daily news was greatly facilitated by the development of the wire telegraph in the middle of the nineteenth century. It made possible the establishment of centralised news agencies such as American Associated Press and Reuters that provided subscribing newspapers with a daily selection of reports gathered by journalists employed directly by the agencies. Their services increasingly incorporated sporting information beyond localised sports cultures by bringing to keen followers of any particular sport or contest, through their local newspaper, results and descriptions of what had taken place a considerable distance away within a few hours of its completion.

Both the sources and distribution of sporting news were further expanded in 1866 with the laying of a telegraph cable across the Atlantic. The importance of sports news to the competitive commercial considerations involved in attracting and expanding newspaper readership is evidenced by the considerable sums that papers were prepared to pay correspondents and the wire services for the rapid transmission of such information. Thus:

> by 1867 the *New York Herald* only twice paid eight hundred pounds for dispatches: the first, to record the King of Prussia's speech after war with Austria: the second, to provide readers with a blow-by-blow description of the boxing match between Mace and Goss. The *Herald's* priorities were generally accepted.

When in 1888, William I lay dead in Berlin, the *New York Sun's* principal European correspondent, Arthur Brisbane, was concerned not with the future of the continent but with the aftermath of the Sullivan/Mitchell fight in Chantilly.

(Shergold 1979: 30)

In the 1880s came the beginning of the regular sporting section within the daily newspaper and the emergence of specialist sport journalists. There can be no doubt that the regular and detailed coverage of sporting events in the daily newspaper amplified an already broadening public interest in the major sporting leagues and, consequently, contributed towards providing such competitions with the cultural legitimacy that further propelled sport into the mainstream of popular culture. Newspaper attention, much more than specialist sporting journals, broke down the localism and class exclusivity previously associated with certain sports, transforming games such as cricket, baseball and soccer into truly national (and even international) spectator pastimes. The established leagues and competitions benefited, as evidenced by the steady growth in spectator attendance that developed concurrently in a number of countries between the 1880s and the 1930s. This, in turn, justified more prominent newspaper coverage. It allowed the press a direct involvement in the promotion of sporting events by focusing attention on peak events in the sporting calendar which helped build up an atmosphere of excitement and societal significance for a 'cup final' or a 'world series'. Local newspaper coverage often fuelled an atmosphere of intense partisanship for the 'home team' in inter-city or inter-community competitions.

Sports journalists frequently wrote their stories from the point of view of unabashed 'sports fans' consciously seeking to boost the popularity of the sport, and in particular the fortunes of the local team or the status of certain 'star' performers. In this manner, the expansion of sports journalism invariably assisted the entrepreneurial promotion of top level spectator sport – both amateur and professional. Most astute team owners, managers, officials and athletes themselves nurtured close friendships with selected reporters, eager to cooperate in providing them with 'inside' stories, interviews, leads and angles, well aware of the generous benefits to gate receipts that accrued from the free publicity they received from the newspapers' decision to treat sport as 'news'. As with other more specialist fields of journalism, there emerged a number of writers of considerable literary skill who brought to the genre of sports reporting a thoughtful, articulate and broadly philosophical approach, rooted both in the classical tradition and the nineteenth century ideals that saw sport as potentially ennobling to the human spirit and an expression of 'civilised progress'. Certainly, much of this kind of writing was concentrated upon sports such as cricket, golf, athletics, the turf, hunting and fishing and, in America, baseball, many of which had long associations with the leisured lifestyles of the socially privileged. Such writings helped to develop a formal aesthetic of appreciation, articulating many of the idealist beliefs of the participatory amateur value system that associated sport with self cultivation, social harmony, human achievement and the significance of 'good sportsmanship' to any 'civilised' culture. However, only rarely has the writing about sport in the daily press reached these levels of literary or philosophical sophistication. In the main it has been fairly mundane and descriptive with a heavy emphasis on results, individual performances and records. More importantly, rarely have newspaper journalists been critical of sport as a social institution. There has been some newspaper discussion of the contemporary trends towards increasing professionalisation and commercialisation of certain sports such as tennis and, more recently in Australia, cricket, but overall, after some initial soul searching, these are invariably seen to be ultimately 'good for the game'. Excessive violence, both on the field and among spectators, and drug-taking by competitors, are fairly universally condemned by the press, but generally in terms that carefully avoid linking any of these to broader social issues nor to any critique of the dominant values and ethics institutionally entrenched within the sporting culture. An assessment of contemporary sports journalism in Australian newspapers might serve as a harsh, but not inaccurate, summary of the somewhat dismal general history of the genre, applicable almost anywhere in the world. 'The press engages in crude sensationalism, often the promotion of rabid partisanship, overemphasizes violence and exaggerates the qualities and talents of the players' (Tatz 1982: 9). Certainly, the attention paid by the daily press to the world of sport, and the extent to which it has emphasised those aspects described above, have served to assist the successful development of high-performance sport as a commercially saleable spectacle.

If there is a certain ambiguity in the extent to which the content of daily newspapers might be considered 'entertainment', then this has been far less problematic for film and radio, both of which emerged as popular communication forms in the first decades of the twentieth century. Film's intrinsic ability to represent action and movement proved enormously attractive, and apart from the telling of fictional, acted stories it developed a documentary side very early, manifested in its most commercial form by the newsreel. Cinema programmes began to include a weekly summary of filmed news together with their feature film. Newsreel segments covering recent sporting events proved to be extremely popular. The already fine line between documentation and entertainment was soon blurred as many of the first 'news' films of sporting contests, while presented to the public as a true record, were in actuality reconstructions of the events set up especially for the newsreel cameras, sometimes featuring the sportsmen involved, but on occasion using hired actors to play their parts. While over the years one could compile a substantial list of feature films that have used sport or particular sporting heroes as the central theme, in the main producers of commercial cinema discovered that such movies had somewhat limited audience appeal. Consequently, sport has not figured as prominently in cinematic features as one might have expected. The number produced has declined considerably since the 1940s, when the subject of sport began to develop a widespread reputation in Hollywood as 'box office poison' (Cantwell 1973: 440–54)

The electronic media of radio, and later television, proved to be far more suitable than film for the secondary transmission of sport to the mass public. The cinema lacked immediacy and authenticity of experience, both of which are distinctive characteristics of radio and television. The technology of distribution brought broadcast sport directly to the audience via a small, portable receiving device that could be located almost anywhere. For the sports fan, a radio transmission describing, as it was happening, an ongoing sports event taking place a considerable distance away, was a positive substitute for the experience of attending in person. Sport thus played a prominent part in radio programming from the beginning of regular domestic transmissions in the 1920s. In the early years, technical limitations sometimes inhibited direct live coverage, but the absence of visual clues for radio audiences suggested the possibility of presenting 'simulated' or 'synthetic' sports commentary. This technique was occasionally employed in the United States (Rader 1984), but also independently developed in a sophisticated and ingenious manner in Australia. In the early 1930s, ABC radio introduced 'synthetic' broadcasts to Australian listeners of test cricket matches being played in England. 'Commentators' in the Australian studios 'described' the game from a continuous stream of cablegrams that provided them with the bare essentials of what was happening on the field in England. Although listeners were informed that such broadcasts were simulations, the verbal commentary was augmented by appropriate sound effects of crowd noises and bat striking the ball to provide a more convincing sense of 'reality'. Like the 'reconstructed' prize fights of the early newsreels, the simulated radio broadcasts reflect the value priorities of the mass media with regard to resolving any intrinsic conflict between the principles of journalistic veracity and keeping the audience entertained. Thus as one writer has noted:

> Synthetic cricket distorted the game in a number of ways. Not only were fictitious happenings invented to cover a break in the cables, the commentary even falsified the game itself on some occasions ... Radio also made cricket appear to be a faster-moving, more exciting game than it actually was ...
>
> (Cashman 1984: 102–3)

But live radio broadcasts of sports events signified the beginnings of an important economic relationship that was to develop between the mass media and organised sporting bodies. Unlike the newspaper reporting of sport, live radio descriptions incorporated the legal issues of proprietorship and copyright. The successful growth of spectator sport was premised on a set of well established entrepreneurial principles that applied throughout the 'entertainment' industry. As determined by the organisers, a price, or a range of prices was fixed, the payment of which entitled any member of the public to be admitted to a venue in which the performance or event would take place. The venue, be it a circus, vaudeville house, concert hall, theatre, cinema or stadium, was physically constructed in a manner that limited the potential audience to a finite number of paying customers who, from variably privileged vantage points – depending on the price they were prepared to pay – could experience that performance or event. Through the construction of some form of physical barrier or boundary, those unwilling to pay the cost of admission or unable to gain entry to the venue, because all the legally sanctioned audience space was already committed, were excluded. Until well into the twentieth century sports venues differed significantly from other entertainment structures in that most sports required fairly large playing areas and took place in the open. This factor encouraged the establishment of enclosed arenas that prevented non-paying spectators from obtaining a free view of the contest. The bodies administering the various sports, whether amateur or professional, claimed legal ownership of the events under their jurisdiction and, as they charged admission to the public, the matter of licensing radio broadcasters to transmit live descriptions and the question of payments for such rights emerged as issues for consideration. In the early years of radio broadcasting, most sports bodies considered it advantageous to provide free access to the event to any broadcasting organization and often were even prepared to pay the broadcasters for providing live transmissions. Despite strongly voiced fears by some sports administrators that allowing radio broadcasts would lead to a catastrophic decline in spectator attendance, the early experiences did not convincingly validate such fears (Cashman 1979: 94). An established view began to emerge that the increased publicity and extended audience offered by radio exposure was of some benefit in broadening public interest and awareness of the sport, and would contribute to an increase in the sale of admission tickets for future events.

However, it became increasingly apparent that sport was a form of commercial performance that provided radio with considerable programming content. Thus, for example, in the early 1930s, a number of commercial radio stations in Australia went as far as to position commentators in vantage points outside but overlooking suburban racecourses and proceeded to broadcast descriptions of the events to their listeners without paying the organizations involved for the rights (Inglis 1983: 36). As sports broadcasts of major events proved attractive to large audiences, which ultimately benefited broadcasters both economically (for commercial stations), and in terms of their corporate image for providing service and entertainment to the public, the relationship turned more and more into a complementary business arrangement between competing branches of the popular culture industry. Again, it was in North America where both sports and broadcasting had a well developed and unambiguously commercial basis that the formal components of the financial accommodation between sport and the electronic media began to take shape. Thus, already by the 1930s:

> networks and stations were paying for sports broadcast rights. Large sums of money were involved; moreover, profits from radio rights were evident by 1938. This development marked a reversal of roles between the networks (from benefactors to client) and sport owners (from client to supplier or benefactor).
>
> (Greendorfer 1981: 167)

However, once the basis of the relationship between sport and the electronic media was forged it was subject to significant change with regard to the relative strengths and bargaining power of the two institutions, particularly upon the successful development of a far more potent and comprehensive form of electronic communication – television. The required technology for the simultaneous transmission of pictures and sound, without wires and cables between transmitter and receiver, was available from the mid-1920s. Experimental services applying this new form of communication were already in operation, both in Europe and the United States by the 1930s, but the introduction of television as a medium of mass entertainment was postponed until after the end of the Second World War. The pattern of development in television followed closely that of radio. Most of the leading manufacturing, distribution and transmission organizations that had emerged with the development of radio as a domestic medium saw television as a natural direction in which to extend their interests, financial investment and accumulated expertise. Similarly, as noted above, the general policies decided upon by state authorities to regu- late domestic radio services in the most part determined the manner in which they approached the critical questions surrounding the later introduction of television services. Invariably, the principles, guide- lines and even the regulatory bodies set up to administer the orderly functioning of radio services were extended and adapted to include television. Initially no one seemed very clear as to what exactly tele- vision was going to do. As Raymond Williams (1974: 25) has pointed out, like radio before it, television was a system *'primarily devised for transmission and reception as abstract process[es] with little or no definition of preceding content'*.

Within a few years television showed itself to be a medium capable of usurping and absorbing many of the informational, and entertain- ment functions previously the domain of the daily press and radio. In its role as a provider of cultural experience and entertain- ment, television quickly challenged the entrepreneurial and market structure of currently dominant commercial forms, notably cinema, dramatic and variety theatre, and a number of other spectator-based leisure pursuits. As another rising branch of the popular entertainment industry it was obvious by the late 1940s to the administrators and controllers of spectator sport – both amateur and professional – that it was necessary and desirable to come to a satisfactory accommodation with television.

# References

Betts, J.R. (1953) Sporting journalism in nineteenth-century America, *American Quarterly*, 5(1): 40.

Cashman, R. (1984) *'Ave a Go Yer Mug!* Sydney: Collins.

Cantwell, R. (1973) Sport was box-office poison, in J.T. Talamani and C.H. Page (eds) *Sport and Society: An Anthology*. Boston: Little Brown.

Curran, J. (1977) Capitalism and control of the press, 1800–1975, in J. Curran, M. Gurevitch and J. Woollacott (eds) *Mass Communication and Society*. London: Edward Arnold.

Gans, H.J. (1974) *Popular Culture and High Culture*. New York: Basic Books.

Greendorfer, S.L. (1981) Sport and mass media, in G.R.F Luschen and G.H. Sage (eds) *Handbook of Social Science of Sport*. Champaign, ILL: Stipes.

Inglis, K.S. (1983) *This is the ABC: The Australian Broadcasting Commission 1932–1983*. Melbourne: Melbourne University Press.

Kamper, E. (1972) *Encyclopedia of the Olympic Games*. New York: McGraw-Hill.

Kuntz, P.G. (1977) Paul Weiss on sports as performing arts, *International Philosophical Quarterly*, 17: 164.

Langer, B. (1985) The culture industry: high culture as mass culture. Paper presented to Sociological Association of Australia and New Zealand Conference, Brisbane.

Lowenthal, L. (1968) *Literature, Popular Culture and Society*. Palo Alto, CA: Pacific.

Rader, B. (1984) *In Its Own Image*. New York: Free Press.

Rosenberg, B. and White, D.M. (eds) (1957) *Mass Culture: The Popular Arts in America*. New York: Fress Press.

Schiller, H.I. (1969) *Mass Communications and American Empire*. New York: Augustus M. Kelley.

Shergold, P.R. (1979) The growth of American spectator sport: a technological perspective, in R. Cashman and M. McKernan (eds) *Sport in History*. St Lucia: University of Queensland Press.

Tatz, C. (1982) The corruption of sport, *Current Affairs Bulletin*, September: 9.

Tunstall, J. (1977) *The Media Are American*. London: Constable.

Williams, R. (1965) *The Long Revolution*. Harmondsworth: Penguin.

Williams, R. (1974) *Television: Technology and Cultural Form*. London: Fontana.

# THE TV AND SPORTS INDUSTRIES

## Joan Chandler

Excerpt from *Television and National Sport: The United States and Britain*. Urbana and Chicago: University of Illinois Press, 1988, Chapter 5: 94–111.

The conditions that govern the TV industry on both sides of the Atlantic did not arise from the industry itself, but came originally from radio. Significant differences still exist between the American and British television industries because their radio industries were set in entirely different societal contexts. In the United States, Westinghouse began the first daily scheduled broadcast on radio in 1920; it fell into what TV producers later labelled 'prime time' (Barnouw 1982: 33–4). By 1924, perhaps 2.5 million sets were in use (Page 1975: 469), and stations scrambled to meet programming demands. They used amateur and then professional performers, and whatever material they could lay hands on. In 1923, a court had supported the American Society of Composers, Authors and Publishers (ASCAP) in its contention that WOR, Newark, was using copyright music for profit because listeners heard that the broadcast was coming 'from L. Bamberger and Company, one of America's great stores' (Barnouw 1982: 41). Incensed, broadcasters paid for the use of material, even as they realized that what ASCAP had begun, other groups threatened to emulate. In that case, where was the money to finance broadcasting to come from?

Various ideas were put forward and experiments tried (Lichty and Topping 1975), but while public debate was concerned with the financing of broadcasting another question was being asked in private. Who was going to make a profit from the use of radio sets and other broadcasting equipment? The Radio Corporation of America, founded in 1919, which included Westinghouse, United Fruit,

American Telegraph and Telephone, and subsidiary companies, had worked out patent and other marketing agreements, but by 1924, it seemed to the others that AT&T was trying to hog the market. None of the companies, however, wanted to discuss their differences in public because of the antitrust act. So RCA, GE Westinghouse, and AT&T decided to submit their claims to an arbitrator, in secret. But they had reckoned without the Federal Trade Commission, who chose this moment to charge these and other companies with conspiracy to monopolize broadcasting. Amid frantic and secret negotiations, the companies sorted out their empire; as a result, the National Broadcasting Company (NBC) was formed (Barnouw 1982: 21, 49–54). In the advertisements announcing NBC in September 1926, Owen Young, the chairman of the RCA board, and James Harbord, its president, proclaimed that the new company's purpose was 'to provide the best programs available for broadcasting in the United States', and that it was 'not in any sense seeking a monopoly of the air'. They also announced that one of the 'major responsibilities' of NBC's new president 'will be to see that the operations of the National Broadcasting Company reflect enlightened public opinion' (Barnouw 1982: 55).

Marketing arrangements having been settled, the public question remained. Where was the money to come from to produce 'the best' (or indeed any) programs for broadcasting? By 1928, the question had been answered; advertisers supported the new broadcasting industry. In 1924, Herbert Hoover, then secretary of commerce, had declared, 'I believe that the quickest way to kill broadcasting would be to use it for direct advertising . . . if a speech by the President is to be used as the meat in a sandwich of two patent medicine advertisements there will be no radio left' (Lichty and Topping 1975: 203). Yet having analysed the radio fare offered by New York stations in February 1927, George Lundberg wrote, 'The radio is at present used almost entirely as an entertainment device for the advertising of radio itself, and of the businesses which provide the programs' (Lundberg 1975: 323).

Further, when a network sold a time period, the sponsor decided what program should go into it; as Roy Durstine put it succinctly in 1930, 'The public wants entertainment. The advertiser wants the public's attention and is willing to pay for it. Therefore, let the advertiser provide the entertainment' (Durstine cited in Spalding 1975: 219–28). NBC's 'enlightened public opinion' therefore boiled down to the degree of enlightenment advertisers believed their audiences could stand. Meanwhile, a US District Court decided in 1926 that the secretary of commerce had no legal right to make detailed regulations about radio station licences, as he had been doing since 1923 when the fantastic increase in broadcasting had begun to make the ether cacophonous. The court decision led to immediate chaos, as stations increased power, changed wavelengths, and extended their air time. Broadcasters turned to Congress to have order restored. In 1927, the Federal Radio Commission (FRC) was established by the Radio Act; the granting of station licences was to be in accordance with 'public interest, convenience or necessity' (Barnouw 1982: 57–9). Further, these licences were not permanent; in theory at least, a station that did not serve the 'public interest' could find itself without a wavelength. Certainly, the FRC strictly enforced regulations that specified station location, frequency, and power; but while it concentrated on 'public convenience' the FRC seemed much less sure what to do about 'public interest', which the act had in no way defined (Lichty 1975: 621–31). When the BBC's Director General John Reith visited the FRC in 1931, he specifically discussed the public interest. As he wrote in his diary, the commissioners 'were immensely tickled with the idea that they should exert their powers' (Briggs 1965: 48).

Not surprisingly, as radio audiences grew bigger, advertising became more crass. Those who assume that television is responsible for the debasement of public taste cannot be aware of the complaints about radio in the 1930s. Not that the furore did much good; the Communications Act of 1934 that replaced the Federal Radio Commission with the Federal Communications Commission (FCC) did not create the non-profit channels that critics of radio had demanded (Barnouw 1982: 76). On April 30, 1939, RCA formally opened its TV broadcasting service. CBS formed in 1927 and, bought by William Paley in 1929, had also been experimenting with TV, as had other groups. By 1940, 23 stations were televising broadcasts. The FCC, however, had forbidden TV stations to sell time directly to advertisers. The FCC also ordered RCA to get rid of one of its two TV networks; in 1943, NBC-blue became the American Broadcasting Company (ABC). Wartime restrictions, however, stopped the growth of TV broadcasting (Barnouw 1982: 63, 89–96).

After World War II, television broadcasting was again licensed; by 1946, RCA had black and white sets for sale nationwide. It rapidly became clear that TV was very expensive; NBC decided that radio should finance it. The 'public-service' programs, put on in response to the public debate about radio quality in 1936, quickly became casualties. The FCC, however, was in no position to insist on a quality

TV product. Tuchmann goes so far as to suggest that the FCC and the TV industry originally enjoyed a relationship like that of 'a business and its house-union' (Tuchmann 1974: 8). Whether or not that is now true, the radio industry had found little to fear from the FCC, so when the commission tried to insist on standards for television it found itself swimming completely against the tide. In 1946, the FCC forgot its customary role and issued a memorandum entitled 'Public Service Responsibilities of Broadcast Licensees', which set out recommendations for programming in the public interest. This 'Blue Book', as it came to be called, listed specific instances of programming it deplored, and advocated balanced programming that would provide for minority interests and non-profit organizations, as well as giving listeners a chance to hear programs that had no proven commercial track record (Meyer 1975: 589–602). The public paid remarkably little attention to the FCC's concern for its welfare; broadcasters were outraged. Although the Blue Book may have prompted the National Association of Broadcasters to adopt a revised code for self-regulation in 1948, it affected the actual conduct of stations very little. Nor did the FCC really attempt to refuse licences to offensive stations; by 1952, TV licences had even been given to 30 of the 80 radio stations specifically cited for poor programming in the Blue Book, a number that amounted to about 28 per cent of the total TV licences granted (Pepper 1975: 142). 'Free speech' on the airwaves continued to be the most persuasive speech that money could buy. The alternative system of broadcasting set up under the Public Broadcasting Act of 1967 was watched by so few people and had such slender financial resources, that it is true to say that American television is a commercial enterprise.

For various reasons, the FCC refused to issue TV licences between 1948 and 1952. But after 1952, when licensing was resumed, sales of TV sets rocketed; competition between networks for listeners meant that whatever was popular on one channel was quickly copied on the others. The phenomenally successful 'Milton Berle Show' ('Texaco Star Theater') of 1948 was overtaken by 'Arthur Godfrey's Talent Scouts' in 1951. 'I Love Lucy' was followed by a host of comedy series in the early 1950s; the success of 'Gunsmoke' led to a spate of westerns in the late 1950s, while quiz and 'giveaway' shows proliferated, until Charles Van Doren was forced to admit in 1959 that he had been coached throughout his famous appearances on the 'Twenty-One' quiz. The revelations that followed were a disaster; the networks were demonstrated to have wantonly manipulated the public for the sake of profit. In reaction, the networks turned to news and public affairs shows; and as ratings increased, no one was prepared for the remarks of FCC Chairman Newton Minow at the National Association of Broadcasters contention in 1961. Calling network television a 'vast wasteland', Minow cited the 'procession of game shows, violence, audience participation shows, formula comedies about totally unbelievable families, blood and thunder, mayhem, violence, sadism, murder, Western badmen, Western goodmen, private eyes, gangsters, more violence, and cartoons, and, endlessly, commercials, many screaming, cajoling and offending, and, most of all, boredom' (Castleman and Podrazik 1982: 146).

Scathing as Minow's denunciations were, they had little effect. For the next twenty years, critics continued to protest, and programming decisions continued to be made on the same grounds as they always had been. Some excellent programs were produced, but the fundamental problems remained. Producers had to search for programs that would have the greatest appeal. Indeed, there was no possible way in which they could do anything different, unless they were to pull up their roots and start all over again. For the truth is that American network television does very well what it was set up to do. It simply continued the tradition established by network radio, an industry that by 1928 existed for the purpose of profitably distributing advertising copy nationwide. Officially, broadcasting was supposed to have other purposes; but like so many other public institutions on both sides of the Atlantic, what the broadcasting industry actually did and what it was supposed to do were different things. No one has yet been able to demonstrate how to serve 'the public interest, convenience and necessity' and to make a profit at the same time.

This confusion between the 'ought' and the 'is' in the American radio and TV industries is not unique to them, but to function at all, they simply have to ignore the spirit of the law and decide how far they need obey its letter. *Variety* made the point in 1972: 'It could be no secret that the manager of a major New York TV station was speaking for a good part of the industry when he told an applicant for the post of program director: Your job here will be to protect this station's licence. You'll have to take care of all that public affairs . . . (four letter word omitted)' (Lichty and Topping 1975: 527).

Occasionally such a bluff is publicly called. US District Judge Miles Lord neatly punctured the NCAA balloon when he pointed out that Mark Hall, a student athlete, had been 'recruited to come to the University of Minnesota to be a basketball player and not a scholar.

His academic record reflects that he has lived up to those expectations, as do the academic records of many of the athletes presented to this Court' (*Chronicle of Higher Education* 1982: 5). But in an heterogeneous society whose members cannot agree about the extent to which consumers should be protected from themselves, rhetoric and performance cannot normally be expected to match, however often Americans beat their breasts about the gap.[1] In Britain, the societal context in which the broadcasting industry grew was quite different. Hence, the purpose of and constraints upon it differed. Regular public radio broadcasting was initiated, as it was in the United States, by manufacturers of radio sets. In Britain, however, there was no question of a lack of governmental authority; the Post Office assumed itself to be in charge of wireless telegraphy, because it already controlled line telegraphy. After a Post Office representative attended Hoover's first radio conference as an observer, the Post Office was convinced that it wanted no part of a cacophonous ether. In May 1922, the postmaster general told the House of Commons that he proposed to call the radio manufacturers together to work out a system. Far from attempting to break up a monopoly, Post Office representatives then persuaded these manufacturers to form the British Broadcasting Company (BBC), whose income was to derive from the original stock (on which dividends were limited), royalties on receiving sets sold by members, and a licence fee from all who bought sets. In 1924, the royalties were dropped (Briggs 1961; Paulu 1956). From the beginning British broadcasting was set outside the context of the marketplace.

John Reith was appointed the company's general manager; he had strong views on what broadcasting should do. As he wrote in 1924, 'I think it will be admitted by all that to have exploited so great a scientific invention for the purpose and pursuit of entertainment alone would have been a prostitution of its powers and an insult to the character and intelligence of the people' (Reith in Briggs 1961: 8). Reith, however, was not swimming upstream; British observers such as Percy Scholes, who toured the United States between September and December 1925, came back convinced that competitive radio programming supported by advertising could not be of the quality provided by the BBC's licensed [*de facto* if not *de jure*] monopoly (Briggs 1961: 347). After a government committee had enquired into the future of broadcasting in 1925, the British Broadcasting Company was replaced by the British Broadcasting Corporation, operating under a royal charter. It was to be financed wholly by licence fees, which were collected by a government department, the Treasury, which was then to decide what proportion of the actual fee paid should be allocated to the BBC for its operations. Once that sum was settled, the Treasury was to bow out; it became the BBC's job to use the money in any way it saw fit, within the terms of its charter. The corporation was created in 1927 for ten years; five governors were appointed for five-year terms and Reith was appointed director-general. He insisted that while major policy decisions on topics such as the BBC's constitution did fall within Parliament's purview, no political or civil servant was to interfere 'directly or indirectly in management' (Reith in Paulu 1956: 133). That policy remains to this day, although the degree to which the BBC is really independent of government control has sometimes been questioned.[2] Reith had equally clear ideas about the BBC's functions. It was to cater to what was best in British life and aspirations, and by so doing, help to form public taste; by no means was it to please the greatest possible number of listeners by pandering to their whims. When Lord Reith published his memoirs in 1949 he articulated what the British establishment believed about public life. He wrote, 'it was, in fact, the combination of public service motive, sense of moral obligation, assured finance, and the brute force of monopoly which enabled the BBC to make of broadcasting what no other country in the world has made of it' (Reith quoted in Paulau 1956: 17–18).

Reith could not, of course, have set the BBC on this path and stuck to it, had he not had public opinion behind him. American radio continued to be a whipping boy; as an 'average listener' wrote in 1928, 'American broadcasting is designed for people who cannot concentrate' (cited in Briggs 1965: 47). The press, popular and august, supported the policy of monopoly; as the *Times* put it in 1934, 'To the British way of thinking, a service privately conducted and indirectly financed offers no attractions' (cited in Briggs 1965: 57). While there were those, particularly in advertising, who found the BBC's monopoly irksome, the nation as a whole was content with the establishment position. For Reith conceived of his audience as a unified group, whose taste could be formed. As the *BBC Handbook* put it in 1928, the order of the day was to 'give the public something slightly better than it now thinks it likes' in order to make that public 'not less but more exacting' (*BBC Handbook* in Briggs 1965: 55). But when Radio Luxembourg pirated the air in the spring of 1933, supported by advertising and broadcasting chiefly light music on records, the British began eagerly to listen to it (Briggs 1965: 361). By 1935, the Radio Manufacturers Association was restive; it sent a memorandum to the

program board, pointing out that people wanted more light entertainment than they were getting (Briggs 1965: 44). There was some
truth in this contention; a survey in the same year showed that 50 per
cent of the British listeners heard Radio Luxembourg on Sunday, an
'uplifting' day for the BBC, and 11 per cent during the week, when
BBC fare was more entertaining (Briggs 1965: 363). Reith was
unmoved; no serious listener research was begun until 1936, and a
choice of programs for the BBC meant that one could tune to regional
or national stations, both of which offered much the same variety of
material. Although 'light' and 'heavy' entertainment was available,
there was no special, continuous service for either before World War II;
the BBC's policy was explicitly to provide programs that were 'educative', not formally but in the sense of making 'life so much more interesting and enjoyable than it otherwise would be' (Reith quoted in
Briggs 1965: 185).

In November 1936, the BBC put out its first television program.
Always strapped for money, the corporation found the cost of the
service alarming; just as the FCC did not know how to manage a
technological revolution, neither did the BBC. The outbreak of war in
1939 sent Britain back to radio for the duration. During the war, the
BBC's reputation grew; the 21st birthday celebration in 1943 sparked
a 'round of congratulations' (Briggs 1970: 719). Yet after the war, the
BBC found itself facing mounting criticism, for a number of reasons.
The then director general, William Haley, pragmatically rearranged
programming, starting the Light Programme in 1945, and then the
Third Programme, the latter deliberately heavyweight; middlebrow
music, talks, drama, and similar fare were left on the Home Service.
But Haley insisted that he did not wish to segregate the BBC's
audience; rather, by giving people a taste of something, rather than
flinging them into it, he hoped to make progress. It was, he felt, 'a
subtler but more indirect method of bringing listeners to move up the
cultural scale . . . Maybe in a few years time the Light Programme will
be where the Home Service is now and the Home will have passed on
to other standards' (Briggs 1979: 76–7). When Norman Collins
became head of the Television Service in 1947, Haley instructed him
to continue the BBC's radio mission, which was to 'educate and entertain' (Briggs 1979: 227). On the BBC's 25th anniversary, Haley made
remarks on a Home Service talk that were quite unsurprising to his
audience, but that could never have come from the American broadcasting industry. Haley said, 'Broadcasting will not be a social asset if
it produces only a nation of listeners . . . It is not an end in itself . . .

The wireless set or the television receiver are only signposts on the way to a full life' (Haley cited in Briggs 1979: 162)[3]. The American example was always before British eyes; as Haley asserted in 1949, Americans were concerned not with the quality of material but in performer popularity. He wanted British TV to be built 'around ideas', not 'around personalities' (quoted in Briggs 1979: 284). This tradition still, to some extent, holds. As Paulu (1981: 198) points out, the BBC newsreaders are not 'anchor persons', and do not command anything like the status or pay of their US counterparts.

But other voices besides Haley's were being heard in the land. While the war was still on, the *Economist* published a series of articles challenging the BBC's monopoly. In 1946, Sir Fredrick Ogilvie, who had succeeded Reith in 1938, wrote to the *Times* also questioning the BBC's monopoly (Briggs 1979: 31, 42–43). The BBC's charter was to expire in 1951, so in 1949 a government committee enquired into the future of broadcasting. The Listeners Association declared to it that commercial broadcasting should be set up, outside the BBC's control. The Institute of Incorporated Practitioners in Advertising wanted commercial radio and TV, but under BBC control (Briggs 1979: 344, 363). Viewers were becoming disenchanted; the BBC had decided to extend TV coverage before putting on a new channel; and, given the range of Light, Home, and Third available on radio, it was annoying to have no choice on TV. In 1950, a group of young Conservatives entered Parliament, anxious to do away with wartime restrictions; a broadcasting monopoly seemed an easy place to start (Lambert 1982: 8; Sendall 1982). Although the Beveridge committee as a whole recommended the continuation of a monopoly, one member, Selwyn Lloyd, made a minority report in which he argued for the introduction of commercial broadcasting.

The government considered the Beveridge report, but found Selwyn Lloyd's position more to its liking. In May 1952, it suggested that the BBC's monopoly should end. Public feeling ran high, and again the spectre of American experience was called up. Once more, an influential ex-BBC man supported commercial television. In 1950, the BBC had belatedly raised the status of television from that of a department under a controller to a service under a director. Norman Collins, then head of TV, was not appointed director. In 1952, he wrote to the *Times* to point out that commercial radio and television did not necessarily have to follow the American pattern, because American and British standards were different. He argued that no one talked about the 'commercial' press; instead, they called it the 'free' press. Why should broadcasting be different? (Briggs 1979: 132, 886). The proponents of competition won; the BBC's monopoly came to an end on July 30, 1954. Yet the new commercial enterprise set up alongside the BBC had to operate within the rules of a game that were very different from those in the United States, as the government had proposed 'a typically British approach to this new problem' (Lambert 1989: 9). An Independent Television Authority (ITA) was set up which consisted of from seven to ten people, corresponding to the BBC's board of governors and appointed by the postmaster general. The authority was to oversee commercial TV, but its members were to have no stake in it, personal or professional. Programs were to be provided by ITV companies, for whose conduct the ITA was responsible. It was these companies, not the ITA as such, that would make or lose money. Sponsorship of programs was forbidden; advertisers could not contribute or control programs. All advertisers could do was to buy some specific airtime and produce an advertisement for it; they had no control at all over the content of the program surrounding the ad. The TV advertiser in Britain was thus required to send the visual ad into the equivalent of a usual newspaper or magazine. The timing, number, and content of advertisements was also spelled out by law, and advertisements for children were particularly strictly controlled. In fact, the Independent Broadcasting Authority (IBA) went so far as to preview scripts of almost all commercials.

By law, programming on commercial stations was also controlled, with the emphasis on quality. Nothing was to be broadcast that 'offends against good taste'; programming was to be balanced, news was to be accurate, and political and industrial controversies were to be presented impartially. The ITA was to use British programs in 'proper proportions', and was required to comply with, not simply sit through, recommendations coming from special committees set up on children's and religious programs. To prevent unseemly competition in bidding for 'sporting or other events of national importance', a government minister was given power to regulate broadcasting rights to such events. There is no First Amendment in Britain. The same kind of people were appointed to the ITA as were BBC governors; they were determined to see that British commercial TV did not resemble its American counterpart, for obvious reasons. What, however, they did not anticipate, was that they would have only one network to play with. They had assumed that the government would allocate frequencies in such a way that several commercial services could compete with one another; but when in 1955 they requested extra channels, they were refused (Lambert 1982: 9–10). The postmaster general made it clear that there would be no channel expansion at least until 1958, so that performance could be assessed and room left for technical developments such as colour. Thus, although monopoly had been broken, it was succeeded not by plurality, as some supporters of commercial television had assumed, but duopoly.

The BBC took the threat of ITA competition seriously and even began circulating a house organ called 'the competitor' in February 1955 (Briggs 1979: 937). But in terms of what US networks meant by competition, the efforts of both sides were derisory. As late as 1979, the *BBC Handbook* recorded audiences in terms such as '17½ million'. It was reported after lengthy trials and negotiations that 'the hope is that television audience measurement for both the BBC and ITV will be carried out by a service of the electronic type at present used by ITA, amended to accommodate the needs of the BBC; and this will be the only source of television audience measurement data'. The BBC also reaffirmed its commitment to quality, pointing out that this agreed method of audience assessment 'will involve a shift of resources away from the headcounting towards qualitative and audience appreciation studies, while continuing to meet in full the audience measurement requirements of the advertisers' (BBC Handbook 1979: 34, 37).

What, in fact, happened was that ITV's activities had brought several issues into sharp focus. The most obvious was that, in spite of years of careful tutelage, British viewers lapped up such programs as 'Emergency Ward 10', 'Popeye', 'Robin Hood', and 'Saturday Night at the London Palladium' when ITV offered them. To justify receiving licence fees, the BBC countered by offering equally 'popular' programs. In 1956, the BBC complained in its *Annual Report* that competition did not lead to better programming, but simply the same sort of programming on different channels; what listeners really required was complementary, not competitive, offerings (Lambert 1982: 13, 15). By 1962, the BBC had proved it could match ITV programs; but did it want its reputation to rest on such gems as the 'Billy Cotton Bandshow' and the 'Black and White Minstrel Show' (Lambert 1982: 14)?[4] The Pilkington committee report on broadcasting, published in 1962, was extremely critical of the ITA, saying that it had failed properly to exercise its responsibilities. The report cited poor programming, poor control of advertising, and power wielded by the few large program companies, who simply sought profits (Lambert 1982: 82–3). A Conservative government, however, could scarcely admit to having made a mistake in promoting free enterprise, and ITV was much too popular to abolish. What the government could do was to institute still firmer legislation for the ITA and allocate a second channel to the BBC, which could be used for 'minority' programming. The prospect of another channel was also offered to ITV with the provision that the ITA was to ensure that similar programs would not be shown at the same time (Lambert 1982: 17). The Pilkington report also drew attention to the high profits being reaped by ITV. The government therefore introduced a levy on them, in addition to the ordinary income tax already paid. Now it was ITV's turn to consider the disadvantages of competition, particularly as franchises were reallocated in 1967. By 1970, far from welcoming a competitive commercial channel, companies already in existence wanted what the BBC had, a channel as a complement to what was already in place. As Lambert (1982: 18) states, 'They too wanted the advantages of "try-outs", "repeats", and "cost-rationalizations", that a complementary channel could provide. In spite of the vision that sustained ITV's founders, in less than twenty years long-standing British attitudes to competition had resurfaced.'

Debate over a possible second commercial channel continued through 1970; in 1977 the Annan committee recommended that a second commercial channel should be started, but should be altogether separate from the IBA. Neither the Labour nor Conservative governments found that idea acceptable; so in 1979 a new commercial channel was authorized under the IBA's control, and in 1980 its constitution became law. The home secretary, William Whitelaw, made a speech in 1979 in which the responsibilities of the IBA regarding Channel 4 were made clear. The views expressed, like Haley's in 1949, would have been confusing to an American audience, because the rules of the game were so deliberately ambiguous. Whitelaw said that the IBA would 'be expected not to allow rivalry for ratings between the two channels for which it has statutory responsibility, nor to allow scheduling designed to obtain for each of those services the largest possible audience over the week'. The numbers game, as such, was not to be played. What was the IBA, then, to do? It was 'to add different and greater satisfactions to those now available to the viewer' (Whitelaw in Lambert 1982: 93). Channel 4 was to get its programs as much as possible from companies not contracted to ITV, so as to provide opportunities for creative people now locked out of TV program production. It was to increase the number of regional programs and provide time for educational and Welsh programs. Nor was advertising to be competitive between the channels; instead, the ITV companies were to provide the budget for the new channel, and that budget was not to depend on the revenue generated by advertisements on Channel 4. Apparently, Channel 4 was to be commercial but not competitive.

Some of the ambiguities in Whitelaw's statements were cleared up in the Broadcasting Act itself; but as Lambert points out, a great deal of interpretation was left to the IBA. Whitelaw also stated in the debate on the bill that Channel 4 would be expected to become financially self-supporting 'as soon as possible'. Questions were raised in Parliament and outside it as to how programming was to be both innovative and financially healthy; they were not answered (Lambert 1982: 108–10). In 1983, then, British broadcasting stood in ambiguous relation to the marketplace. It still does, although a committee was set up in 1985 to examine the question of allowing advertisements on the BBC. This ambiguity was reflected in sports programming, in that the service as well as the ratings facet of the industry was given more than lip service. The existence of Channel 4, with its mandate to be different, also affected sport. Channel 4 initially planned for only two one-hour weekly sports programs (Lambert 1982: 149), partly because the BBC and ITV both already covered sport well. But in these programs, the commissioning editor decided to broadcast 'new' sports such as basketball, badminton, and American football (Chandler 1978), or 'old' sports played by younger or older competitors than those usually seen. No one assumed that these sorts of programs were necessarily going to set ratings records; they were broadcast specifically for minority interests.

The American and British TV industries do not have quite the same purposes; the audiences they have for sport make different demands. Obviously, the most popular televised sports in Britain and the United States are different. But the scanty available evidence suggests that differences go beyond that. I have found no precisely comparable figures between Britain and the United States, but in 1979 and 1980 the BBC asked 'a quota sample of approximately 1000 adults' what sports they were 'interested in'. What precisely respondents understood by the words 'interested in' is not clear, nor whether they thought the question referred to participation, watching live or televised events, or all three. The combined results of these surveys indicate that *none* of the ten top-ranked sports mentioned by men were mentioned by women, and vice versa (British Broadcasting Corporation 1981: 93–4). The *Miller Lite Report* gives the replies of 1,139 randomly sampled

Americans to the request, 'Please tell me how interested you are generally in *watching* each of the following: [sports listed]'. The results show that only three of the eleven top-ranked men's sports were not mentioned by women and vice versa. Further, football was ranked first by the men and tied for second place among women, and baseball second by men and tied for second place among women (Miller Brewing Company 1983: 19, 176).

Another striking difference between Britain and the United States is that the traditionally British national games are not those in which the highest percentages of people, men or women, report that they are interested. For men, cricket ranks fourth behind boxing, Rugby League, and Rugby Union football, while soccer is ninth, behind racing in cars, on motor bikes, and on bicycles. For women soccer ranks fifteenth, and cricket twentieth (British Broadcasting Corporation 1981: 93–4). In the United States, football and baseball emerge as the two sports most people like watching, however the question is phrased (Miller Brewing Company 1983: 24–5). The range of interest is also different. In Britain there is a difference of only 12 per cent between men interested in the top sport and in the tenth; in the United States, there is range of 48 per cent between men who like to watch football and those who like to watch skiing, swimming/diving, or weight lifting, the sports equally ranked eighth (Miller Brewing Company 1983: 176).

The sports surveys also reveal some similarities between Britain and the United States. Although a higher percentage of women in Britain say they are interested in watching sport, the range of women's interests is similar on both sides of the Atlantic: 67 per cent of British women declare themselves to be interested in skating, and 43 per cent in table tennis and golf, their tenth-ranked sports; 46 per cent of US women like to watch gymnastics and 22 per cent track and field and marathon, their tenth-ranked sports. Thus, 24 per cent fewer women declare themselves interested in their tenth-ranked than in their most watched sport, in Britain and America. Also, on both sides of the Atlantic more men than women claim to be interested in or to watch sport. Boxing ranks as the sport most men in the United Kingdom are interested in, and as the third sport American men like to watch, while it does not appear in the top ten or eleven sports that women are interested in or like to watch in either the United States or Britain. Further, skating ranks first among British women and second among American women, while swimming, track and field (called athletics in Britain), tennis, and horse racing are among the top ten sports in which British women are interested and that American women like to watch

(Miller Brewing Company 1983; British Broadcasting Corporation 1981: 93–4). The BBC also asked their respondents to say whether or not they usually watched on TV the sports they claimed to be interested in, and found that some sports were watched on TV by a greater proportion of those interested in them than others (these data were not reported by gender). If the two surveys are combined, the greatest number of people claim to watch televised snooker followed by soccer, tennis, athletics, show jumping, skating, darts, wrestling, and cricket. Not surprisingly, given these interests and the relative amount of TV coverage accorded certain sports, more than 20 per cent of respondents complained that snooker, darts, and wrestling were not televised often enough (British Broadcasting Corporation 1981: 96–7).

On this evidence, it appears that American TV producers can be sure that they will have an audience if they televise football and base-ball, and sure that their electronic seats will be empty if they show soccer. In Britain, the BBC has a more complicated task. Men and women do not necessarily want to watch the same sports; and they do not necessarily want to watch on TV the sports they claim to be most interested in. Without better comparative data it is impossible to decide why this should be so. It seems possible, however, that the community-bonding functions that baseball and football provided in the years before television, and the paucity of opportunities for the development of other sports on a national rather than a regional basis in a sprawling, heterogeneous country, may account for American choices. Darts, for instance, have been available in British pubs for generations. But what is clear, is that in 1980 sports preferences on each side of the Atlantic were different. In 1984 British professional sport, while obviously in the business of entertainment, is not simply one facet of the entertainment business, as it is in the United States. While professional players and teams in Britain benefit enormously from TV, British professional sport as such is not dependent on it to anything like the extent that US professional sport has become. This is not simply because American TV got into the market earlier and has had more time to buy its way in. Rather, it is because the economic and social structure of British and American sports is entirely different.

The sports franchise does not exist in Britain; cricket and soccer are not financed as they are in the United States. No one owns a cricket or soccer club, and while to be invited to serve on the board of directors of either is regarded as an honour, it has often been a tribute to the length of one's purse, as club directors are always expected to bail their clubs out of financial trouble. Yet there is no way in Britain for a smart businessman to use a sports franchise as a tax shelter. Losses cannot be written off against other corporate activities, because the team is not owned by its board of directors. Through the long history of cricket until 1962, professionals were carefully distinguished from amateurs and had no part in the running of the game. Cricket clubs were organized by gentlemen for gentlemen; as the national structure of cricket began to emerge, it was the county clubs that became the focus of the professional game. A club represented its county. In 1873 (characteristically, halfway through the season) the Marylebone Cricket Club (MCC), cricket's governing body, agreed on rules to decide who could play for a specific county (Bowen 1970: 114). The counties competed with each other, but were not at all interested in profit, partly because so many outstanding players were amateurs. Even in 1930, fewer than 60 per cent of cricketers playing in what the MCC classified as first-class matches were professional (Bale 1982: 78). Although counties had a home ground, they did not expect to play most of their matches there. Rather, they took themselves to grounds around the county, so that everyone had an opportunity to see them play. County teams still continue this traditional and hopelessly uneconomic practice, although politicians have redrawn county boundaries in recent years and professional teams themselves (except Yorkshire) no longer require birth or even residence within a specific county, rendering county affiliation more or less meaningless. Yet, as Bale points out, on average six different places were used in 1950 for important matches for each of the 17 county clubs; by 1980, the clubs were each using an average of 8.8 different grounds. This average is the more startling when one considers that two clubs, Nottingham and Middlesex, since before 1950 have played almost all their matches at a single site (Bale 1982: 81–2). This economic folly is not as crass as it appears, for professional cricket was never designed to make money. Club patrons cheerfully supplied the difference between club receipts and expenditures as a matter of course until after World War II, when taxation made such a use of money impossible. Boards of directors now have to take different steps to avoid a cricket team's falling into bankruptcy, but they are not disposed to think of cricket itself as a marketable commodity. There is, in any case, no way in which individuals could secure a return on investment; nor is it worth spending a great deal on cricket to try to enhance one's own prestige.

The American football industry is specifically organized to corner the market. The British Football Association contains 92 professional clubs divided on basis of skill into four divisions, and talks of expanding into a yet larger association with a fifth division. However, professional soccer is run and marketed in the First Division, the very existence of some professional soccer clubs is dependent on community effort. Many Third and Fourth Division soccer clubs are normally on the verge of bankruptcy. They are kept alive by subscriptions from their directors, and by supporters, who voluntarily organize raffles, dances, and other money-raising activities. As Malcolm Musgrove, the manager of Torquay United, a Fourth Division club, wrote in the program notes of the last game of 1974, 'All supporters and officials have been working hard to raise money to make sure that the club remains in being as a League side'. He went on to point out that Torquay's opponents, Swansea City, 'are, if anything, in an even more serious position than we are' (Musgrove n.d.: 3). Such clubs are not regarded as the property of an owner, but as in some sense part of the local community. It is true that professional soccer is much less expensive to run than professional football, and travelling is far less costly in a country that can be fitted comfortably six times into Texas. But no soccer club board of directors could conceivably threaten to move their franchise to another city because they did not like their present supporters or facilities. Soccer has always been more commercialized than cricket; the soccer clubs that formed the Football League in 1888 were organized by men who knew how to run soccer as a business. But these clubs were not owned by individuals, and all fell under the jurisdiction of the Football Association and Football League. As George Keeton (1972: 49) puts it, 'The articles and memoranda of association of football clubs must fill outside persons with a feeling of wonder, for they bear no relation to modern company practice, and may give the impression that they were drafted on an off day in a fit of absence of mind – as perhaps they were'. Some professional clubs are also private; transfer of shares is therefore restricted. Shares have often gone to people uninterested in the game, or may never have been formally transferred. This lack of interest is not surprising since many professional clubs either never pay dividends or defer dividends for years. Football club shares are not quoted on the Stock Exchange.

This cavalier attitude to finance arose because when the game was first professionalized, it was run by the upper class who wanted to preserve the local loyalties soccer had always inspired and to make sure that the game was not ruined by money-grubbing. All articles of association of a new club therefore had to be approved by the council, and without exception, clubs were required to limit dividends, which in practice have been kept to 7.5 per cent, or 5 per cent tax free. Although the upper class soon departed, vestiges of its outlook remained. Directors cannot be paid, either as directors or employees, so no active player or manager can serve on a board; for many years no one who had ever been a professional player was allowed to serve on a board. As Desmond Morris (1981: 219) puts it, 'The directors remain the last outpost of what might be called the amateur enthusiasm of the Victorian era. And so we have the strange contradiction of a vast, modern, sporting industry run by unpaid part-timers as a kind of hobby.' The northern and midland clubs that rapidly came to dominate the professional game were organized by middle-class businessmen who paid lip service to the ideals of sportsmanship, but whose main concern was their club's prestige. They wanted professional players because professionals normally played better than amateurs; they did not, however, want to be held to ransom by talented players. So they agreed on a *maximum* wage that any player could earn, a restriction on players' opportunities that remained in operation until 1961. As the popularity of soccer grew, more and more clubs sought to join the league; directors of aspiring clubs dipped into their own pockets to buy players from other clubs (the fees for such transactions going into the selling club's coffers, not to the player's pocket), to hire managers, and to pay whatever club expenses seemed necessary to get their club into the league, and then to move up the various divisions. Paradoxically, even by the 1920s, most directors knew what kind of club they served and to what level of play it could and should aspire. To move up a division was of much less importance than to avoid moving down.

Similarly, a curious gentility ran through all the clubs' affairs. To this day, rituals remain. The home team directors may entertain the visiting team's board to drinks in the boardroom before the match; the two sets of directors then watch the first half of the match from the same box, although they sit separately. At halftime, tea is served in the boardroom, and a meal with tea after the match (Morris 1981: 217). For a soccer club has never been the private plaything of owners, but a community heritage. To be invited to serve as a director, therefore, is to have been given an accolade by one's peers; one cannot simply decide, as Americans do, to go out and buy a football team. Symbolically, the League and Association Cups are presented on the field, not in the dressing room, and not to the directors or manager (coach), but to the captain in the midst of his winning team. The losers, far from slinking away, are given medals; the crowd applauds them heartily also. Few British fans could name their team's board of directors; few American fans would not know their team's owner.

The structure of the British sports industry means that television cannot be used simply as a marketing device. There is no bidding war in Britain between networks to secure exclusive rights to particular sporting events. By agreement, the six major national sporting events, 'Wimbledon, The Derby, the Grand National, the Cup Final, Test Cricket and the Boat Race' (British Broadcasting Corporation 1974: 8), can be covered by both BBC and ITV, although ITV does not necessarily choose to show them all. Soccer officials are worried about what television will do to the game; in a report on sports broadcasting published in 1974, the BBC noted that the Football League's restrictions 'include a ban on the "live" coverage of matches and on the showing of recorded coverage before 10:00 pm, on the day of the match' (British Broadcasting Corporation 1974: 6). The Football League's 92 clubs in 1986 still do not regard television as a boon, anxious as they are to keep the party going at the gate. This fear arises partly from the small sums, in American terms, that British television executives have to offer sports promoters. In 1974, the BBC's entire 'annual expenditure on sport, both internal and external, amounts to some six-and-a-half million pounds' – at that time, less than US$18 million dollars (British Broadcasting Corporation 1974: 5). There is no means by which the sums of money US networks raise can be generated in Britain. Even in 1974, BBC officials were worried by the spectre of US exclusive rights to international events and their concomitant fees jeopardizing all the BBC's other sports programming. Nor can the British TV industry afford to pay very much to major sporting bodies in Britain. As the BBC put it, 'If the less popular sports are to continue to get a proper look in, the major sports will have to show more realism and exercise some form of restraint in their financial demands' (British Broadcasting Corporation 1974: 10).

In using TV as their primary marketing device, American sports promoters are merely reflecting one facet of US public life, its domination by electronic media. Important as 'the telly' is in Britain, it does not yet stand in the same relationship to public life and institutions, and probably never will. Much more important, however, is the fact that cricket and soccer are still not regarded in Britain primarily as commercial products. Those responsible for promoting professional cricket and soccer have often been ready to dig into their own pockets to support their team, and continue to do so; they have also encouraged members' and supporters' clubs. It is easy to think of ways in which cricket and soccer could be made more profitable; but even if they were, there is at present no entertainment tradition in Britain into which sports telecasting could readily be tied. The televising of cricket and soccer in Britain is done technically in ways similar to that of sports telecasting in the United States, but its purposes, rationale, and therefore its end product, are different.

## Notes

1 Michael Novak has made the point that Americans expect America to be morally better than other nations of the world; *The Joy of Sports: End Zones, Bases, Baskets, Balls, and the Consecration of the American Spirit* (New York: Basic Books, 1976), p. 18. There is no tradition in Britain of published breast beating, while Americans cheerfully buy books such as David Riesman, *The Lonely Crowd: A Study of the Changing American Character* (New Haven: Yale University Press, 1950); Vance Packard, *The Waste Makers* (New York: D. McKay Co., 1960); Christopher Lasch, *The Culture of Narcissism: American Life in an Age of Diminishing Expectations* (New York: W. W. Norton, 1979); Allan Bloom, *The Closing of the American Mind* (New York: Simon and Schuster, 1987).

2 Although Churchill wanted to commandeer it, during the general strike of 1926, the BBC remained independent, as it did during World War II (Briggs 1970). During the Suez crisis, the BBC gave airtime to the Labour, as well as the Conservative, position (Paulu 1981). During the Falkland Islands war, the Conservative government denounced the BBC for being too fair-minded. In 1985, BBC journalists walked out for 24 hours because a documentary on Northern Ireland was cancelled as a result, they alleged, of government pressure.

3 American broadcasters know their work is not an end in itself, but to say so is to suggest lack of commitment. The point of view that has to be established by commercial networks is reflected in a May 1978 NBC memorandum discussing plans for saturation hype of the 1980 Olympic Games. The aim was to ensure that 'anyone missing even so much as a half-hour of coverage will feel deprived. We will have turned the American people into a nation of Olympics addicts' (*New York Times* quoted in Powers 1984: 20).

4 Paulu (1981) considers that competition from ITV was helpful to the BBC, because it finally freed young, creative people working in television from the domination of those who had worked in radio. ITV also forced the BBC to pay more attention to what the public really wanted to see, without necessarily abandoning its quest for quality productions.

## References

Bale, J. (1982) *Sport and Place: A Geography of Sport in England, Scotland and Wales.* London: C. Hurst.

Barnouw, E. (1982 rev. ed.) *Tube of Plenty: The Evolution of American Television.* New York: Oxford University Press.

Bedell, S. (1981) *Up the Tube: Prime-Time TV and the Silverman Years.* New York: Viking Press.

Bloom, A. (1987) *The Closing of the American Mind.* New York: Simon and Schuster.

Bowen, R. (1970) *Cricket: A History of Its Growth and Development Throughout the World.* London: Eyre and Spottiswoode.

Briggs, A. (1961) *The History of Broadcasting in the United Kingdom Vol. 1: The Birth of Broadcasting.* London: Oxford University Press.

Briggs, A. (1965) *The History of Broadcasting in the United Kingdom Vol. 2: The Golden Age of Wireless.* London: Oxford University Press.

Briggs, A. (1970) *The History of Broadcasting in the United Kingdom Vol. 3: The War of Words.* London: Oxford University Press.

Briggs, A. (1979) *The History of Broadcasting in the United Kingdom Vol. 4: Sound and Vision.* London: Oxford University Press.

British Broadcasting Corporation (1979) *BBC Handbook* pp. 34, 37. London: British Broadcasting Corporation.

British Broadcasting Corporation (1981) *Annual Review of BBC Broadcasting Research Findings.* London: British Broadcasting Corporation.

British Broadcasting Corporation (1974) *The Coverage of Sport on BBC Television: A Study for the BBC General Advisory Council.* London: British Broadcasting Corporation.

*Broadcasting: Memorandum on Television Policy* (1953) London: Her Majesty's Stationery Office.

Brown, L. (1981) *Television: The Business Behind the Box.* New York: Harcourt Brace Jovanovich.

Castleman, H. and Podrazik, W.J. (1982) *Watching TV: Four Decades of American Television.* New York: McGraw-Hill.

Chandler, J. (1978) American pro football in Britain, *Journal of Popular Culture*, 12(1): 146–55.

*Chronicle of Higher Education* (1982) Jan. 13: 5.

Durstine, R. (1930) Audible advertising, in M. Codel (ed.) *Radio and Its Future.* New York: Harper.

Haley, Sir W. (1947) The place of broadcasting, *Listener*, 20 November.

Keeton, G. (1972) *The Football Revolution: A Study of the Changing Pattern of Association Football.* Newton Abbot: David and Charles.

Lambert, S. (1982) *Channel Four: Television with a Difference?* London: British Film Institute.

Lasch, C. (1979) *The Culture of Narcissism: American Life in an Age of Diminishing Expectations*. New York: W.W. Norton.

Lichty, L.W. (1975) The impact of the FRC and FCC Commissioners' backgrounds on the regulation of broadcasting, in L.W. Lichty and M.C. Topping (eds) *American Broadcasting: A Source Book on the History of Radio and Television*. New York: Hastings House.

Lichty, L.W. and Topping, M.C. (1975) *American Broadcasting: A Source Book on the History of Radio and Television*. New York: Hastings House.

Lundberg, G.A. (1975) The content of radio programs, in L.W. Lichty and M.C. Topping (eds) *American Broadcasting: A Source Book on the History of Radio and Television*. New York: Hastings House.

Meyer, R.J. (1975) Reaction to the 'BlueBook', in L.W. Lichty and M.C. Topping (eds) *American Broadcasting: A Source Book on the History of History of Radio and Television*. New York: Hastings House.

Miller Brewing Company (1983) *The Miller Lite Report on American Attitudes toward Sports*. Milwaukee: Miller Brewing Company.

Morris, D. (1981) *The Soccer Tribe*. London: Jonathan Cape.

Musgrove, M. (n.d., n.p.) *Official Programme: Torquay United*, 74–75: 3.

Novak, M. (1976) *The Joy of Sports: End Zones, Bases, Baskets, Balls, and the Consecration of the American Spirit*. New York: Basic Books.

Packard, V. (1960) *The Waste Makers*. New York: D. McKay Co.

Page, L.J. Jr. (1975) The nature of the broadcast receiver and its market in the United States from 1922 to 1927, in L.W. Lichty and M.C. Topping (eds), *American Broadcasting: A Source Book on the History of Radio and Television*. New York: Hastings House.

Paulu, B. (1956) *British Broadcasting: Radio and Television in the United Kingdom*. Minneapolis: University of Minnesota Press.

Paulu, B. (1981) *Television and Radio in the United Kingdom*. Minneapolis: University of Minnesota Press.

Pepper, R. (1975) The pre-freeze television stations, in L.W. Lichty and M.C. Topping (eds) *American Broadcasting: A Source Book on the History of Radio and Television*. New York: Hasting House.

Powers, R. (1984) *Supertube: The Rise of Television Sports*. New York: Coward-McCann.

Riesman, D. (1950) *The Lonely Crowd: A Study of the Changing American Character*. New Haven: Yale University Press.

Sendall, B. (1982) *Independent Television in Britain Vol. 1: Origin and Foundation 1946–62*. London: Macmillan.

Spalding, J.W. (1975) 1928: Radio becomes a mass advertising medium, in L.W. Lichty and M.C. Topping (eds) *American Broadcasting: A Source Book on the History of Radio and Television*. New York: Hastings House.

Tuchmann, G. (ed.) (1974) *The TV Establishment: Programming for Power and Profit*. Englewood Cliffs, N.J.: Prentice Hall.

# THE DREAM TEAM, COMMUNICATIVE DIRT, AND MARKETING SYNERGY: USA BASKETBALL AND CROSS-MERCHANDISING IN TELEVISION COMMERCIALS

## Lawrence A. Wenner

Excerpt from the article of the same name published in *Journal of Sport & Social Issues*, 1994, 18(1): 27–47.

By the time all was said and done in the 1992 Olympic Games, USA basketball's bringing home the gold rang to many as tin. Novelist Stephen King called the Dream Team a horror show following a new Olympic motto: 'Make Sure You're Going to Win, Then Go Ahead and Do It'. What purity was left in the amateur ideals of the Olympics had been put to rest. USA basketball's team was populated by the superstars of NBA basketball. They were bigger than life. Bigger than the Olympics. They stayed in fancy hotels. They played golf as if they were on vacation. Magic was back for a victory lap, AIDS and all. Never was the outcome of the basketball competition in doubt.

It is not surprising what took centre stage under such conditions. Along the way to the medal stand, we found the Dream Team quibbling with the various Olympic committees over who has what rights in the pursuit of commercialism. The issues were seemingly trivial. Charles Barkley was to be paid to write a column for *USA Today*. The International Olympic Committee (IOC) said no. Athletes may write only for their hometown paper. Michael Jordan, claiming loyalty to his Nike® contract, refused to wear a Reeboks® outfit on the medal stand. The U.S. Olympic Committee said athletes not wearing Reebok would not be allowed on the medal stand. In the latter dispute, international diplomacy yielded to the commercial code. Olympism recognised a new world order where new loyalties – endorsement contracts – reign. Jordan and other Dream Teamers in the Nike stable hit the medal stand, their jacket flaps consciously covering anything Reebok. In what might be taken as a perversion of Barthes's (1973) 'ex-nomination' process, these athletes nominated Nike.

The struggle over commercialism, endorsement contracts, and consumer loyalties in the modern Olympic Games is a competition with stakes far greater than those between athletes. This is because Olympism is an idealised premium product. In that idealised form, the Games celebrate the virtues of amateurism, sportsmanship, international goodwill, and 'healthy' nationalism, all in the context of heroic athleticism. And because of its four-year cycle, the product's potency has built-in curbs against market fatigue. The commercial value of the Olympics is great to sponsors and advertisers attempting to get a 'cultural rub' from values associated with the Games. The growth of cross-merchandising and 'synergy' as a marketing strategy among products recognizes this fact (Hewitt 1992). The IOC allows only 12 worldwide Olympic sponsors. The tariff is high. It is estimated that Coca-Cola® spent US$33 million (all dollar values discussed are US) to become the 'official' soft drink of the 1992 Games. Visa® International spent $20 million to be the Olympic credit card (Beckett 1992). NBC spent $402 million for the television rights to the 1992 Summer Games, more than double what ABC paid in 1984 (Elliott 1992). With such large figures at stake, the purity of Olympic ideals is necessarily compromised. *New York Times* television critic John J. O'Connor (1992) noted that it was such a big business undertaking leading to possible future payoffs for the athletes that the word hype was utterly inadequate. With so many jumping on the Olympic marketing bandwagon, some advertising executives feared that this amount of hype would backfire into consumer backlash as the event became archetypal of overcommercialisation (Marinucci 1992). Yet for most advertisers there was not enough of a good thing to go around. If they could not get in the front door, they would get in another way. A growing group of 'ambush marketers' including Pepsi®, Fuji®, American Express®, and Converse® developed ads that suggested an 'Olympic rub' without actually mentioning the Games. 'Ambush' ads were placed in close proximity to those of official Olympic sponsors. John Krimsky, Deputy Secretary General of the U.S. Olympic Committee, angrily called the strategy 'parasitic marketing' (Beckett 1992: B1).

The rush to get a commercial 'rub' from the Olympic Games recognizes the strong communicative power of sports 'dirt' in an 'interpretive community' of sports fans (Wenner 1991). It is ironic to hear Olympic officials single out 'ambush' marketers as parasitic. Official Olympic sponsors are parasitic as well; they just pay for it. Perhaps that is the difference between a sponsor and a parasite. The sponsorship and advertising of the Olympic Games is by necessity a 'dirty' one, parasitic if you will. As it is used here, the term 'dirt' has no inherent negative connotation. Rather, the term refers 'to the cultural borrowing that allows one cultural entity to adopt the logic of another' (Wenner 1991: 392). Hartley (1984) suggests that television texts are necessarily contaminated by seepages from other parts of culture. For example, dominant ideologies expressed in sports values (nationalism, patriotism, authoritarianism) are couched in the celebration of heroism, equality, commitment, and pride in the television sports text (Wenner 1989). Beer commercials use sports dirt – the logic and values of sport – to infuse alcohol consumption with athleticism (Wenner 1991). Nike commercials use nostalgic dirt from the Beatles' song 'Revolution' to empower their shoes (Howell 1991). The power of dirt ascends with its cultural primacy. At the apex of Olympic commercialism, Dream Team dirt was powerful. Through a reader-oriented analysis of the workings of dirt in commercials featuring the Dream Team, this study examines how we are characterised and positioned as readers through the use of sports dirt. Eleven commercials appeared during NBC's broadcasts of two games (a USA versus Cuba game in the Tournament of the Americas and a USA versus Angola game of the 1992 Olympics), some of which are analysed here. These ads were the only ones in these games that relied on Dream Team dirt as a primary strategy.

A reader-oriented approach is central to understanding the advertiser's agenda in sports. Attempts to position the reader are made easier because fans have many of the characteristics of an interpretive community (Fish 1980). Such group membership often contributes to a shared sense of place and cultural identity (Wenner 1990). The resultant group cohesiveness allows sports fans exposed to commercials featuring Dream Team dirt to be more easily identified as 'characterized fictional readers' (Allen 1987, 1992). Advertisers characterise the interpretive community when fans are directly addressed. We often see on-screen characterised fans as 'textual surrogates who do what real viewers cannot: interact with other performers and respond (usually in an ideal fashion) to the appeals, demands, and urgings of the addresser' (Allen 1992: 121). The structuralist version of reader-oriented criticism focuses on how the text attempts to control the reading act (Suleiman 1980). Television ads, in particular, attempt to position the viewer ' "some place" relative to the action in every shot' (Allen 1987: 90). The positioning strategy attempts to blur distinctions between the characterised addressee on the screen, the implied addressee viewing at home, and the addresser. The overriding goal in this attempt is to elicit a positive answer to the addresser's question 'Will you buy?' (Allen 1987, 1992).

The reader-oriented analysis that follows focuses on the reader in the text; the Dream Team fan who is the characterised fictional reader of these commercials. It is assumed that the fan as implied reader and the advertiser as addresser both bring dirt from sport to their constructed meanings of these commercials. Because dirt from sport is highly valued by the sports fan, a position is taken that negotiated readings of these commercials will be far more dominant than oppositional (Hall 1980). Although the study focuses on how sports dirt encourages preferred readings through characterising the reader, it is recognised that texts are interpreted in the context of a range of 'activations' (Bennett 1982). Thus, given indications of consumer 'backlash' to the 'overhype' of the Olympics, likely oppositional readings from within the interpretive community can also be explored.

## The world of dream dirt

All of the commercials that build on connections to the Dream Team fall into the category of being explicitly contaminated by sports dirt . . .

The commercials featured in the two USA basketball games often blurred the genres of active, implied, and idealised sports dirt. Given the sophistication of modern merchandising, this structural 'polysemy' should not be surprising. Still, a telling categorical scheme can be devised by asking, where is the locus of the sports dirt's power in the commercial? What central logics about sports and culture empower the connection to the product? By answering these questions, the commercials can be organized into three types:

1.  *Nationalistic sports dirt* focuses on sport as a tool for promoting nationalism and the metaphor of the team as soldiers.
2.  *Youth sports dream dirt* focuses on the idealised notion in the sports world that if one works hard enough, one's sports dreams can be realised.
3.  *Sports hero dirt* focuses on the ideal of the sports hero as a role model and the power of the 'reflected glory' that comes from identifying with the hero.

The analysis that follows considers the workings of dirt and the characterizing of the reader in each of these categories.

## Nationalistic sports dirt

### *Support the troops (team) and salute the flag (uniform)*

Champion® athletic clothes chose to rely on the notion of teamwork in the context of nationalism to smear sports dirt on its product. The 30-second ad relied on a simple, unhurried, but patriotic narration:

> This summer in Barcelona, 12 of our best men will be bound by a common path, a common goal, and a common thread. Champion is proud to be chosen to make the uniform for America's team. Because we understand teams. It takes a little more to make a Champion.

The narration directly addresses the characterised reader as powerful by assuming the reader's participation in collective ownership of the team. The 'bound' men are positioned in our service. Derivative of this, the reader is characterised as agreeing to the commonalty of 'path, goal, and thread'. This positioning has entailments, used in service of characterising the reader. The reader is a patriot, supportive of America's dream, team, uniform, and flag. Implicit is the reader's support of commonalty among the variant threads of America's melting pot. Implicit is support for our team as if its members are troops, and the last logical leap makes the last and most important dirty connection. In our supporting our team, we take 'pride' in the uniform our troops wear, and, as we see time and time again in the visuals, the uniform in red, white, and blue is a flag made by Champion.

Complex video imagery uses 61 shots to amplify these connections and position the reader. There are many visual juxtapositions of the USA basketball team competing and the Champion uniform being sewn. The direct address of the narrator positions us to accept the logic of this juxtaposition. As we root for our team, we root for the uniform being sewn. As we root for our powerful USA team's ball to go through the basket (5 shots), we root for the Champion's powerful needle to penetrate red, white, and blue fabric (8 shots). When the narration positions us to take 'pride' in 'America's team', we must take in the red, white, and blue of the uniforms. When we are positioned as having the knowledge to 'understand teams', we are positioned visually to equate that understanding with a consumer sweatshirt made by Champion. In the end, the 'little more' that it takes 'to make a Champion' amplifies the reader's position that nationalism makes sports a little better. Supporting Champion means supporting that dirty but potent mix.

### Fairy tales of US domination

Converse athletic shoes chose to rely on a fairy tale about the power of the Dream Team as a parable for the power of its 'magical shoes'. In one of what is known as the 'Larry Johnson's grandmother' ads, we see a grandmother sitting in a rocking chair reading a fairytale to a multicultural group of young children. Quickly, we find sports dirt. The grandmother is a large Black moustachioed man with a gold tooth who is dressed in a prim flowered dress and high-top basketball shoes. The grandmother says:

> This is a story about two of the baddest men that ever put on little short pants. One day they were surrounded by the Russians and the dreaded Italians! Arghh! They quickly put on their magical shoes from Converse and ditched them all big time! And snatched up all the gold and brought it home to Grandmama.

As the story unfolds, we find out who the 'baddest men' are by seeing storybook pictures of Larry Bird and Magic Johnson. The grand-mother is animated, excitedly telling the story. We see that the children are nervous and scared as the story unfolds. When the story's problem is resolved by putting on 'magical shoes from Converse' we see storybook pictures of the Bird and Magic Converse shoes. We see the children pleased as the story is resolved as Bird and Magic 'snatched up all the gold'. In the end, a small Black boy is incredulous, asking, 'Is that true, Grandmama?' The grandmother provides reassurance: 'It will be, child, it will be' as we see a closing graphic of 'Converse –

Official Shoe of USA Basketball'. Closing the ad with the questioning of the veracity of the story formalizes dual reading positions for the characterized readers. For the adult reader, it is clear from the start that this ad is a put-on. The reader is positioned outside the scene to appreciate the pictured children being taken in. For the child, the reading position is perched delicately on the edge of plausibility. This could be a fairy tale, and this could be a grandmother. Their on-screen textual surrogates are shown to be largely suspending disbelief.

Nationalistic dirt works on both reading positions in concert with sports hero dirt. As our 'bad' men are surrounded by the Russians and the 'dreaded Italians', nationalism is invoked. To the child reader, 'foreigners' are scary. For the adult reader, the Dream Team is an invincible national force and a foreign challenge laughable. The child is positioned to interpret Bird and Magic as mythlike, something the adults are already positioned to bring to their interpretation. The child is positioned as well to interpret Bird's and Magic's shoes as mythlike. For the adult reader, such positioning is unlikely. More likely, the ad works to position the adult to accept and expect the child's interpretation of the shoe as inheriting mythlike qualities. Thus the reading position of the adult specifies two roles. First, the adult is positioned as parent or prospective parent, who feels good about the myth the child may value. Second, the adult is positioned as adult-child, who can play along with the fairy tale and its assumptions. In either case, dirt works in a fairly straightforward way. Bird and Magic are America's team, they will win, they will wear Converse, and you should wear Converse if you want to support America and win.

## Youth sports team dirt

### Lifelong friendship as an Olympic value

Archetypal of the youth sports dream dirt commercials was AT&T's 30-second spot that featured a narrator telling an idealised flashback story about young Scottie Pippen and his childhood friend Ronnie Martin. The narrator speaks to us as implied readers who embrace Olympic ideals and hard work leading to athletic success. The narrator tells us that 'long before Scottie Pippen was chosen for the USA Basketball team, he knew he could count on his friend Ronnie Martin'. Meanwhile, we see a romanticised scene set in a warmly lit gym in Hamsburg, Arkansas in 1976. Young Pippen and Martin take on the challenge from an older, bigger, threatening boy named Big Harold. We see young Pippen and Martin work a play together to beat Big Harold. Here, the narrator tells us 'AT&T salutes all of our Olympic hopefuls and everyone that helped them get this far'. We enter the present by panning up an 'official' team jacket arm with signage 'Pippen' and the USA basketball logo. We see Ronnie Martin asking Scottie Pippen whether 'those guys in the Olympics gonna be tough?' Pippen asks, 'Why? Did they sign Big Harold?' as the two laugh. Theme music comes up as we see the USA Olympic logo that transforms itself into the AT&T logo while a graphic proclaims AT&T as 'Proud Sponsor of the 1992 Olympic Team'.

This ad works to position the reader in three interrelated places. In direct address, the narrator positions the reader as a USA basketball fan who can be counted on in joining AT&T in 'saluting' (as one would the flag) our 'hopefuls'. Second, we are cast as *voyeurs* of nostalgia, appreciative of a Horatio Alger story with a little bit of Tom Sawyer and Huckleberry Finn thrown in for good measure. Third, we are cast as privileged spectators of a private friendship, about which we share their private history. Throughout, sports dirt helps position the reader. As sports fans we are receptive to rooting for the underdog, sympathetic to the idea that hard work leads to sport success, seeing teamwork as an ideal in life, and interpreting sports histories as the culmination of these ideals. In today's sports world, we are treated to many tales of athletic prima donnas; thus the painting of Pippen as one who remains an Everyman who is true to a lifelong friend rings the bell of sports fans who likely hope that they, too, would remain unchanged with sports success. In short, we feel good about sport dreams, about friendship, and about AT&T. As dirt, these sport myths merely add power to a pre-existing crafted connection between friendship and AT&T, amplifying both 'reach out' and institutional 'feel good' campaigns . . .

### If I could be like Mike

One of Gatorades®'s generic 'Be Like Mike' ads appeared during the Tournament of the Americas game. We hear singing:

Sometimes I dream. The key is me. You've got to see that's how I dream to be. I dream I move. I dream I grew. Like Mike. If I could be like Mike. I'm gonna be, gonna be like Mike. Like Mike. If I could be like Mike. Be like Mike. If I could be like Mike.

The visuals intercut Dream Teamer Michael Jordan playing NBA basketball, multicultural girls and boys playing playground ball, and Jordan playing with the kids. The lyrics pose youthful sports dream as the driving dirty force that is energised by association with Jordan as sports hero. A variety of basketball-playing textual surrogates are seen: a teenage Black boy (seen with Jordanesque tongue hanging), a teenage White girl, a five-year-old White boy, and a ten-year old Black girl. A multicultural group of textual surrogates drinking Gatorade join Jordan as he goes to the playground. Other shots place the reader in a familiar spectator role, joining a crowd cheering Jordan as he slays the NBA. From any angle, and any age, readers are shown to like Mike and like being his friend. Only a step away is dreaming his dream and to do so is to 'be like Mike'. In that dream, we are those good textual surrogates shown to drink Gatorade 'like Mike'.

### McDonald's® Olympic dream

McDonald's youth sports dream spot relies on heavy doses of nationalistic dirt and sports hero dirt to round out the dream. The narration draws a bridge between nationalism and youth sports dreams:

> The 1992 Olympic Summer Games. The year basketball trades NBA colours for red, white, and blue. For everyone who's longed to see America send nothing than their very best. For every family whose hearts still beat faster when they hear the national anthem. For the young who dream that someday they too may soar so high. For every one of us. McDonald's is proud to sponsor the 1992 USA basketball team. To help Olympic dreams come true.

Quite simply, the commercial is dedicated to the implied reader. We are patriotic citizens. We are traditional families. We hold great hopes for our children. We share sports dreams with our children.

The visuals position us as well in the role of spectator. At the start, we see the Olympic flame and a montage of Dream Teamers on the NBA court. Our first textual surrogate is a middle-aged middle-American White couple with hands over hearts as the national anthem plays to start a game. The dreams 'we' have for our young to 'soar so high' are characterised by our appreciative reactions to the Dream Teamers in action. Our children with youth sports dreams are charac-terized by a young Black boy seen first in a stadium crow watching action and later cheering as a championship is won. Interestingly, the sealing of the championship for 'every one of us' is accomplished by a Larry Bird shot. This ushers in McDonald's 'being proud' to 'sponsor the 1992 USA basketball team' as we see the McDonald's arches blend with Olympic rings encased in red, white, and blue ribbon. As spectators, McDonald's has taken the time to position us to appreciate White heroism as a Black boy looks on from the sidelines. Admittedly, this is fleeting, but from the reading position established, it is the Black boy who needs help in making 'Olympic Dreams Come True'. The net result is a very paternalistic, traditional reading position that embraces sport as an agency for social mobility.

## Sports hero dirt

Almost all of the commercials discussed previously placed benefit substantially from sports hero dirt. The five commercials discussed in the sports hero dirt category de-emphasize nationalism and youth dreams. Rather, these commercials rely more directly on the importance of the sports hero as a public figure, the ideal of the sports hero, and the power of the 'reflected glory' of identifying with the hero.

### Visa as player on the all-defensive team

The Visa credit card relies on the collective strength and power of the Dream Team to make its dirty link between the strong Dream Team defence and Visa as defence against merchants who 'don't take American Express'. The audio pulses as the narrator introduces individual members of the Dream Team, saying 'They've been called the greatest team in Olympic history'. Implied readers are positioned as spectators seeing on-court exploits of the Dream Teamers. In mid-commercial, with the lead 'Olympic basketball may never be the same', the narrator queries the reader, 'But if you think they're tough, wait until you see the guys at the ticket window, if you don't have your Visa card'. We see tough-guy shots of Dream Teamers followed by a shot of a surly ticket seller. A textual surrogate saves the day: placing a Visa card on an elegant table emblazoned with the familiar dirty Olympic rings and telling us Visa is 'worldwide sponsor, 1992 Olympic Games'. When we are told that 'the Olympics don't take American Express' a montage of Dream Teamers blocking shots is followed by another textual surrogate whipping out the Visa card and then a

Dream Teamer getting off a tough shot. The ball goes into the basket as the narrator closes 'Visa, it's everywhere you want to be'. Again, we have three main reading positions. First, we are spectators of the Dream Team. Second, we are tormented textual surrogates caught without our Visa. Third, we are elegant textual surrogates playing the Dream Team game with our forceful defence – our Visa card. We are shown to appreciate the attributes of the Dream Team, and we are characterised on-screen using the desired behavioural path to demonstrate those attributes in our consumer lives.

### The magical ambush of Pepsi

Pepsi drew much criticism from Olympic worldwide sponsor Coca-Cola for its 'ambush' ads featuring HIV-positive Dream Teamer Magic Johnson (Marinucci 1992). Placed in the first games of the Olympics, the ad does not mention the Games. The ad is simple. It opens with inspirational classical music over the graphic 'We Believe in Magic'. A soft-focus shot of Magic dribbling to the basket is faded in. Dreamlike shots of Magic are intercut with a montage of shots showing a multi-cultural world of individuals and groups supporting him. We see Little Leaguers, a teenaged girl, a father and son, an Asian restaurant chef, a young White woman at a picnic, a Black garbage man, commercial fishermen on a boat, Pepsi employees in front of a Pepsi truck, young children in a multicultural classroom, and parochial school girls in uniform. Groups and individuals are shouting variously 'Go for it, Magic! Go Magic! Go get 'em, Magic! Good luck, Magic! Magic!' And from the young woman at the picnic, 'We love you, Magic!' This out-burst of affection from our many textual surrogates is contextualised mid-spot by a narrator who provides a contextual 'from all of us at Pepsi' to allow the brand to join in our fanship group and, in a sense, take ownership of it and responsibility for it. Pepsi and Magic become rallying points for our fanship group in supporting an AIDS-infected athlete in the Olympic games, although neither AIDS nor the Olympic Games need be 'nominated' (Barthes 1973).

Herein lies the inherent 'ambush' problem in Olympic dirtied ads. The Olympics has reached such a point of collective excess that the need to 'nominate' it only presents risks in marginalising its marketing impact. To not mention the Olympics may be far more powerful dirt than 'announcing' that the dirt was purchased for the purposes of fulfilling marketing goals. If Barthes (1973) is right, 'ex-nomination' is far more powerful, and the IOC really has something to worry about with these ambushes. AIDS, on the other hand, remains ex-nominated for more complex reasons. To name it, Pepsi would be patting itself on the back for being politically correct. Without doing so, it may have made a stronger statement in that Pepsi signifies that they know we know the story of Magic, thereby legitimizing their role as organizers in the interpretive community . . .

### Be Like Mike, Part 2

The last commercial featuring sports hero dirt focused on a discussion between Michael Jordan and his father over the attributes of Hanes® underwear. An opening graphic reads 'Hanes. Fashion Underwear'. Uptempo music accompanies Michael Jordan's entrance, shooting a basketball into an empty chair next to a man reading a newspaper. Another graphic reads 'Michael Jordan & His Dad. After the Game'. Jordan sits down. We see his dad pick up a pair of red underwear sitting on the floor atop blue and white underwear. Dad asks, 'Michael, are these your Hanes?' Jordan smilingly nods. His dad continues, 'Son, is there a reason you wear 'em?' Jordan's wife comes into the scene, hugging, then kissing Jordan, and answering the question with a fond 'Definitely'. Holding the underwear up, Jordan's dad quizzes Mike, 'Think Mom would like me in these?' Jordan responds, 'Maybe'. A graphic responds, 'Definitely'. Music comes up as we see a montage of shots of red, white, and blue underwear. A chorus is heard singing 'Just wait'll we get our Hanes on you' while Jordan smiles and a graphic reinforces the chorus's line.

The implied reader is a privileged spectator of a drama about a superstar who can do it all. For the male spectator, the textual surrogate is likely embraced by Jordan's dad, who wonders how the Jordan-empowered underwear might work for him. For the female spectator, a textual surrogate is found in Jordan's wife. She testifies to the power of the red, white, and blue underwear. The focus of the dirtiness in this 'Be Like Mike' ad is very different from the Gatorade ad. However, the workings of the dirt are similar. The power of the sports hero is transferred to the product and to the use of the product by the textual surrogate and implied reader. Both the Gatorade and the Hanes underwear make a great Jordan better, just as they could for you. Only in the Gatorade case it is fairly clean dirt. With the Hanes underwear, there is a layer of dirty dirt that commodifies and potentially reinforces cultural myths of sport and the Black male's sexual prowess (Majors 1990). As in the case of the ex-nomination of the Olympics connection and AIDS, the nomination of the stereotype would have worked against the cultural power of the ad and made placement of the implied reader that much more difficult . . .

This analysis of commercials featuring the Dream Team points out that advertisers have a strong working knowledge of cultural anthropologist Edmund Leach's (1976: 62) observation 'that power is located in dirt'. The collection of Dream Team commercials is rich with the workings of sports dirt. A triad of nationalism, youth sports dreams, and sports heroism interact in most of the texts to characterise or position the reader . . .

## References

Allen, R.C. (1987) Reader-oriented criticism and television, in R.C. Allen (ed.) *Channels of Discourse: Television and Contemporary Criticism*. Chapel Hill: University of North Carolina Press.

Allen, R.C. (1992) Audience-oriented criticism and television, in R.C. Allen (ed.) *Channels of Discourse, Reassembled: Television and Contemporary Criticisms*, 2nd edn. Chapel Hill: University of North Carolina Press.

Barthes, R. (1973) *Mythologies*. London: Paladin.

Beckett, J. (1992) Struggle over Olympic ads heats up, *San Francisco Chronicle*, 15 July.

Bennett, T. (1982) Text and social process: The case of James Bond, *Screen Education*, 41: 3–15.

Elliott, S. (1992) A top event: NBC's dash for the ads, *The New York Times*, 6 August.

Fish, S. (1980) *Is There a Text in this Class? The Authority of Interpretive Communities*. Cambridge, MA: Harvard University Press.

Hall, S. (1980) Encoding/decoding, in S. Hall, D. Hobson, A. Lowe and P. Willis (eds) *Culture, Media, Language*. London: Hutchinson.

Hartley, J. (1984) Encouraging signs: TV and the power of dirt, speech, and scandalous categories, in Rowland, W. and Watkins, B. (eds) *Interpreting Television: Current Research Perspectives*. Beverly Hills, CA: Sage.

Hewitt, J. (1992) Building media empires, in A.A. Berger (ed.) *Media USA*, 2nd edn. New York: Longman.

Howell, J. (1991) 'A revolution in motion': Advertising and the politics of nostalgia, *Sociology of Sport Journal*, 8: 258–271.

King, S. (1992) Dream team: just another horror show, *The New York Times*, 9 August.

Leach, E. (1976) *Culture and Communication*. Cambridge, England: Cambridge University Press.

Majors, R. (1990) Cool pose: Black masculinity and sports, in M.A. Messner & D.F. Sabo (eds) *Sport, Men and the Gender Order: Critical Feminist Perspectives*. Champaign, IL: Human Kinetics.

Marinucci, C. (1992) Olympics: Pinnacle of hype, hard-sell, *San Francisco Examiner*, 26 July.

O'Connor, J.J. (1992) These Olympic Games are brought to you by . . . , *The New York Times*, 13 February.

Suleiman, S. (1980) Introduction: varieties of audience-oriented criticism, in S. Suleiman and I. Crosman (eds) *The Reader in the Text*. Princeton, NJ: Princeton University Press.

Wenner, L.A. (1989) The Super Bowl pregame show: cultural fantasies and political subtext, in L.A. Wenner (ed.) *Media, Sports, and Society*. Newbury Park, CA: Sage.

Wenner, L.A. (1990) Therapeutic engagement in mediated sports, in G. Gumpert and S.L. Fish (eds) *Talking to Strangers: Mediated Therapeutic Communication*. Norwood, NJ: Ablex.

Wenner, L.A. (1991) One part alcohol, one part sport, one part dirt, stir gently: Beer commercials and television sports, in L.R. Vande Berg & L.A. Wenner (eds) *Television Criticism: Approaches and Applications*. New York: Longman.

# 5 | SPORTS MEDIA SANS FRONTIÈRES

## Toby Miller, Geoffrey Lawrence, Jim McKay and David Rowe

Excerpt from *Globalization and Sport: Playing the World.* London: Sage, 2001, Chapter 3: 60–8.

God wore number 23 – *De Morgen* (Belgium)
The 'Michelangelo' of sport shoes will not return – *Faz* (Germany)
His royal Airness will never fly again – *Telegraaf* (The Netherlands)
God is going home – *Yedioth Ahrnonoth* (Israel)
[B]asketball is alone – *La Repubblica* (Italy)
The King is Leaving – *Sport* (Spain)
Earthquake – *El Mundo Deportivo* (Spain)
A myth that has gone beyond sports – *El Periodico* (Spain)
Tell us it is not true – *El Pais* (Spain)
[H]e's the greatest – *Herald Sun* (Australia)
King Mike Abdicates – *Age* (Australia)
God will never fly again – *Asahi Shimbun* (Japan)
God finally to retire – *Tochu Sports* (Jordan)
[His] name is engraved on the heart of everyone – *Beijing Morning Post* (PRC)
Año Uno D. De J. [Year One After Jordan] – *Ole* (Argentina) (quoted in 'The World Bids' 1999)

These responses to Michael Jordan's retirement testify to three things – his exceptional athletic ability, the success of Nike world-wide, and the spread of the NBA across TV screens: *Rafaga NBA* in

Mexico, *La Magia de la NBA* in Argentina, *Give Me Five* in Belgium, *NBA Mania* in Japan, *NBA Jam* in Taiwan, and *Zou Jin* in the PRC (Andrews 1999: 508). Just as Nike and the National Basketball Association (NBA) built their strategies for growth around Jordan, so his career can only be understood in terms of those institutions. While this is perhaps the most spectacular instance of the media-sports link, TV in particular is inseparable from global sport, as both a marker of globalization and one of its prime movers.

IOC official history marks the Olympics in terms of broadcast revenues – a total of US$1.25 billion for the 2000 and 2002 Games – and their status as 'a social, even sociological event, which more or less reflects the state of the world' (Macleod 1996: 23; Verdier 1996: 34). This sense of sport standing for more than itself, always both representing and being represented, has a pre-commercial heritage. In its nascent medieval form, and as it matured in the moment of early modernity, sport was above all a local cultural pursuit, linked first to the 'rough play' of mainly young men in the festival seasons and later through more formal, regular contests between settlements in particular regions (Elias 1986). While never disappearing entirely, local sport has progressively given way to regulated professional competitions organized on national and international lines. The forces that, above all others, have transported sport from local pitches to the global stage are the mass (and especially electronic) media (Cunningham and Miller 1994; Rowe 1996). If a professionally-based economy of sport was first established through the enclosure of sports grounds and the charging for attendance at demonstration matches performed by or against visiting teams, then the capacity to carry sports action, advertising, and promotional messages enabled that economy to take on first a national and then an inter- and transnational character, as the game was transformed from a practice to a spectacle (Bourdieu 1999: 16).

In this chapter we examine how contemporary sport articulates with advertising, promotion, and commodification as it connects, disconnects, and reconnects collective experiences of space and time within and between nation-states. We are concerned with how local, regional, and national cultures are projected by the sports media into the domain of the global. It is then possible to analyse how the reception of the images and meanings of globally mediated sport affect those levels of culture. Certain contemporary sports seek to accommodate, mediate, or resist globalizing pressures according to their specific histories and geographies, institutional frameworks, and structures of culture. British (especially English) soccer, Canadian ice hockey, Australian rugby league, and women's tennis are all sites where the influence of television and enduring and shifting patterns of identification can be discerned. First, though, it is necessary to understand something of the global development of sport television.

## Mediated sport cultures

Sports reporting in the print and electronic media is deeply reliant on imaging the body. Still photography provides a sense of 'having-been-there' (Barthes 1977), often through minute attention to the bodies of athletes. Photographic presentations of sporting bodies are largely limited to rigorous motion (during competition) and inertia (for example, at a medal ceremony). The latter image carries most efficiently the idea of the nation. For many spectators, the medal ceremony at major international events like the summer Olympic Games epitomizes national identification and affect. Such rituals are *tableaux* of bodily dispositions. The athletes, their bodies draped in the colours and insignia of nation and corporation, are led to the ceremony by a functionary. The different heights of the blocks on which they stand spatially signify hierarchy. They bend to receive their medals as in a military service, then turn their gaze to their national flags, also hierarchically arranged, while the national anthem of the winning athlete/team reinforces visual supremacy with aural presence. Apart from flags fluttering in the breeze, the moment is still. At this point, athletes usually cry – moved both by a sense of individual and, heavily imputed by television and radio commentary, national achievement and responsibility. The stately nature of the ceremony demands that spectators and viewers be serious. It is not unusual for patriotic viewers at home to stand for their national anthem, disciplined, as Foucault (1977) argues, most effectively not by external repression but through externally induced and internally accepted discourses of the social self. If tears well up in their eyes, this discourse of nation has become powerful enough to produce involuntary physiological responses in those subject to it.

National mythologies prosper when internal fissures – class, gender, race, ethnicity, locality, age, sexuality, and so on – are submerged. The risk of displaying differences and divisions to a global audience, rather than asserting the existence of a unified nation, makes the medal ceremony and other less formal aspects of major sporting events subject to strict official control over communication in all its forms – verbal and non-verbal, abstract, and corporeal. Athletes are pressured by national sports committees and media organizations (especially those who have paid for privileged access to them) not to be controversial about issues 'back home' – to preserve the illusion of the united nation for the duration of the event. The International Olympic Committee (IOC), state-licensed and -funded national sports bodies, and the sports market's lucrative sponsorship and endorsement contracts, are decisive in disciplining athletes. The sporting body's marketability is significantly, but not exclusively, influenced by its degree of political quiescence. Race, gender, and sexuality also have a substantial impact on its place in the international cultural economy of sport. We shall examine now the vast and complex infrastructure that is hidden behind these sports *tableaux* of winners and losers.

Modern sport and the media developed simultaneously and symbiotically, supplying each other with the necessary resources for development: capital, audiences, promotion, and content. The sports media emerged out of a need, first, for the reporting of sports information through the print media and, later, through presentation of sports events via electronic media (Rowe 1992a and 1992b; Rowe and Stevenson 1995). In Britain and Australia, print sports journalism developed from notices about the time and place of forthcoming local sports events, match descriptions, results, and, rather quaintly, the hospitality (usually by 'the ladies') afforded to visiting players (Brown 1996). As sport became increasingly professional and commodified, it did not disappear from the local print media, but became secondary – even in provincial newspapers – to national and international sport (Rowe 2004). This progressive detachment of sport and place was first supplemented and then accelerated by radio and television. National public broadcasting organizations like the British Broadcasting Corporation (BBC), the Australian Broadcasting Commission (later renamed a Corporation) and the Canadian Broadcasting Corporation (CBC) used major sporting occasions like the FA Cup Final, the Melbourne Cup horse race, and the Stanley Cup play-offs, to develop the techniques of outside broadcast and to engage in state-sanctioned processes of nation-building (Hargreaves 1986; Whannel 1992; Gruneau and Whitson 1993; Haynes 1999). Once the nation could be reached through the agency of the public and commercial sports media (Wilson 1998), its boundaries could be exceeded as those media carried the nation to distant and dispersed sports events, further building a sense of national identity by encouraging readers, listeners, and viewers to support their national representatives in international sporting competitions.

There has been a dramatic shift in the nature of world television over the past decades. It has been transformed from a comparatively scarce resource to a common one in most parts of the world, moving from a predominantly nation-based and state-run medium towards internationalism and privatisation. The global fashion for neo-liberalism has: (a) cut down cross-ownership regulations (encouraging capitalists to invest across the media); (b) reduced public-sector budgets (drawing labour, product development, and technological initiative to profit-centred services); (c) opened up terrestrial TV to international capital (undercutting local production); and (d) attacked the idea of public broadcasting as élitist (blurring distinctions between education and entertainment) and inefficient (crowding out investment in the private sector).

Sport has been crucial to these recent developments. As the idea of a universal service that provides broad coverage of news and drama is displaced by all-entertainment networks, sport turns into a cheap source of hours and hours of TV-time. At the truly expensive, top end of TV sport, it offers a method of enticing viewers to make the massive monetary and technological shift to digital television (thereby rendering consumers' personal archives obsolete and making themselves guinea-pigs in the search for economies of scale) by showing favoured sports only on digital systems. France's Canal+ estimates that 40 per cent of its subscribers pay their monthly fees purely to watch soccer (Williams 1998: M3; Williams 1999: 104). In 1999, the rights to cover European soccer on television cost over US$2 billion as part of this enticement (Croci and Ammirante 1999: 500).

The IOC (n.d.) proclaims television as 'the engine that has driven the growth of the Olympic movement'. Just as we might associate shifts in capitalism with new technology (early nineteenth-century national capitalism and steam, late nineteenth-century imperialism and electricity, twentieth-century multinational capital and electronics – Jameson 1996: 3) so we might write a history of sport connected to technology – wire reports and the radio describing play across the world from the mid-twentieth century and television spreading cricket, soccer, and the Olympics since the 1960s, communicating ideologies of nationalism and the commodity. At the Sydney 2000 Olympics, not only was the Internet popular, but TV placed moving images of Olympic winners into commercials only seconds after they had won their event. The satellite and digital era promises to erase and rewrite relations of time and space in sport once more. This latter-day profit-making targets audiences defined and developed as part of nation-building by public services.

From the BBC's beginnings in the 1920s, its distinctively public mission has sought to unite the nation through live coverage of sport. Quality control in early radio times even included a visually disabled person alongside the commentators who could vouch for the vividness of description (Crook 1998: 85–6). At the same time, the BBC's payment of £1,500 to telecast the 1948 London Olympics set in train an entirely new relationship between sport and the audiovisual media, a precedent that has grown to consume the resources of its originator ('Sport and Television' 1996). Half a century later, the BBC's 1998 decision to commit vast resources to digitalization saw it lose the rights to cover English international cricket, leading to Cabinet discussion and public protest. The choice between technological upgrading and a traditional part of the national service was painful. In earlier times, it would not have *been* a choice – both innovation and national service would have been funded from tax revenue.

Sport has long been at the leading edge of TV and technology. When the Communications Satellite Corporation broadcast the 1964 Olympics, a new era began (Kang 1988) – the very name embracing the technological and the commercial as inseparable forms of technical and social relations. Expansion has continued apace. The number of TV hours watched globally tripled between 1979 and 1991, while more than half the 30 billion people who watched the 1990 World Cup did so from Asia, never a football power. The 32 billion viewers of the 1994 event spanned 188 nations, and the 1996 Olympic Games drew 35 billion. The third most significant event is the Commonwealth Games, which draws 500 million viewers. US audiences for NBC's Atlanta Olympics coverage were offered more advertising time than game time, while Hollywood now factors in a quadrennial overseas box-office disaster during the weeks when people stay away from the cinema and watch the World Cup. And the move into TV time is massive. The NBA is now seen on television in 206 countries across 128 networks and 42 languages, and has its own cable and satellite network ready for digital interactivity – NBA.com TV. Its start-up operation, the Women's National Basketball Association (WNBA), was seen on 37 broadcasters in 17 languages across 125 nations in 1999, its third season of existence. Major League Baseball (MLB) is seen in 215 countries. The 1999–2000 National Football League (NFL) season was telecast in 24 languages to 182 countries. Fans in Austria, the Netherlands, and Singapore, where no US football games are broadcast on Sundays, were offered webcasts from that season via broadband. The National Hockey League (NHL) is also seen around the world, and has web sites in France, Finland, Norway, Sweden, Germany, Japan, Slovakia, Russia, the UK, the Czech Republic, and Poland (Herman and McChesney 1997: 39; McAllister, 1997; Pickard, 1997; Smith 1997: 114; Muda 1998: 223; Burton, 1999; 'Country-by-Country' 1999; Dempsey, 1999a and 1999b; 'International Broadcasters' 1999; 'New Television Deals' 1999; 'NFL Full' 1999; FIFA n. d.; Wise, 1999). By contrast, Australian Rules Football is principally restricted to highlights shows given away to networks ('TV Times' 1999).

No wonder that Rupert Murdoch refers to TV sport as News Corporation's 'battering ram' into new markets, while TCI calls it 'the universal glue for global content' (quoted in Herman and McChesney 1997: 75–6). At the same time, national and regional identifications bring into question the 'benefits' of new technology and global capital. Even neoclassical economists have argued against satellite exclusivity, on the ground that 'key sporting events, like the Olympics, the World Cup and the FA Cup . . . generate positive social network externalities' when they are universally available. Folks talk to one another about the shared experience of viewing, which in turn binds them socially, and this 'social capital' would be lost if only a privileged few could receive transmission of such events (Boardman and Hargreaves-Heap 1999: 168, 178).

The state has been bombarded by complaints about the takeover of sport by private networks. Citizens regard national sport as a public good (or at least one for which they only pay profit-making entities indirectly). In Germany, for example, it became likely that parts of the next two World Cups of soccer would only be available locally on pay TV after the European Broadcasting Union (EBU), a consortium of public networks, was outbid by Kirch and Sporis in 1996, despite offering US$1.8 billion ('Sport and Television' 1996; Hils 1997; Boehm 1998). When the plan materialized in Germany, there was immediate uproar, with politicians proclaiming free viewing of national-team games as 'a basic right of our citizens' (quoted in Hils, 1997). And when Vittorio Cecchi Gori outbid RAI for soccer rights in 1996, the Italian state moved in to declare the auction contrary to the public interest, legislating to preclude anyone holding more than 60 per cent of the nation's rights to televise soccer (Tagliabue 1997: D4; 'Flirtation and Frustration' 1999). Similar legislation was introduced in the UK and France, although cricket authorities persuaded the Blair Government that 'their' sport did not belong on the 'A' list in 1998 (Boehm 1998; Boyle and Haynes 2000: 216). But then Telepiu bought exclusive pay rights for the four leading clubs in Italy, forcing audiences to make the digital move, and making it harder for competitors to gain custom. When Murdoch announced a second digital platform in Italy for 1999 via partnerships with local football clubs Mediaset, and Telecom Italia, he was also preparing a US$2.5 billion offer for six years' exclusive coverage of *Serie A* and *B* football, countering pay-per-view arrangements between Canal+, its Italian subsidiary Telepiu, and top clubs. Then he purchased a quarter of Kirch, staking out its non-broadcast rights (Williams 1998: M3; Zecchinelli 1998; 'Flirtation and Frustration' 1999; Boehm 1999; Boyle and Haynes 2000: 210). The criterion of national interest was being circumvented.

The Olympic Charter, which guarantees 'maximum presentation of the Games to the widest possible global audience free-of-charge' (IOC n. d.) may eventually be interpreted to mean that the Third World will receive analogue signals and the First World digital. Watching the Olympics on television is meant to be a similar experience for all, as host broadcasters produce the visual text (except for the US, which has its own feed, camera angles, and commentary position, unlike anybody else). Countries then re-territorialize the text with their own verbal track (Pujik 1999: 117, 119). Exhaustive studies of the Games as 'a communication phenomenon . . . initially produced in a city, but then "reproduced" in multiple places', suggest that locally modulated coverage constructs very different texts and generates very different responses. Local cultural policy regulated by the state also plays a part, notably the insistence by Arabic countries that women's events not be broadcast and that they hence pay on a *pro rata* basis (de Moragas Spà, Rivenburgh, and Larsen 1995: xvi, 22).

Disney/ABC's subsidiary ESPN has been a trendsetter in the televisualisation of sport. ESPN International, which began in 1983, telecasts in 21 languages to 182 nations and 155 million households. It has 20 networks across Asia, Australia, and Latin America (the latter has four networks of its own) in addition to syndication deals. A single executive sent to Hong Kong to cover Asia in 1993 is now one of 300 employees based in Singapore at a major production facility (Fry 1998b: A4; Sandomir 1999). In 1998, ESPN struck a programming arrangement with the Argentinian military to broadcast in the Antarctic, which had long been a target to enable the company to claim a truly global reach (Fry 1998a: A1; Fry 1998b: A4). That reach permits

Disney to address a social sector that has conventionally eluded it – middle-class men – and even to penetrate public TV: the PRC's sports network draws half its content from ESPN. The company's slogan is 'Think globally, but customize locally'. That means a degree of local coverage, such as table tennis in East Asia and cricket in India, while Latin American services produce 20 per cent of their programs (Grove 1998: A6). But from 1996, ESPN offered 'global buys' to advertisers – the global commodity sign could be attached to the local sports referent (Herman and McChesney 1997: 83, 63). The network used Princeton Video Imaging to edit computer-generated visuals advertising goods and services onto real-life stadia, streets, and public space, making it appear as though purely televisual billboards are present at the site of live action (Williams 1998). As a wonderfully double-speaking ESPN executive puts it, 'When we say "local" we don't mean that it has to be from that locality, it can be programming from half-way around the world' (quoted in Grove 1998: A6). Canal+ describes ESPN as 'one of the leading entertainment companies and brands in the "global information society"' (Lescure 1998).

Given the crucial role that multinational media-entertainment companies now play in marketing all sports, it is not accidental that a recent NHL expansion franchise in Anaheim was awarded to the Disney Corporation, which also owns the ABC network, MLB's Anaheim Angels, and 80 per cent of ESPN, and has partial rights to telecast NFL games for eight years. It is not surprising, then, that the 'Official City of Anaheim Web Site' lists Disneyland alongside the Mighty Ducks in projecting its civic profile. Wayne Huizinga, the owner of Blockbuster Video (which subsequently merged with Viacom), bought another new franchise in Miami via the Florida Panthers Holdings company. The Atlanta Thrashers, the NHL's most recent expansion team, belong to the largest media corporation in the world, AOL Time Warner, which also owns NBA and MLB teams in Atlanta, TNT Sports, the Goodwill Games, World Championship Wrestling, the CNN/SI sports network, *Time*, and *Sports Illustrated*, and is the NBA's cable partner.

This trend toward the vertical and horizontal integration of hockey in the sports-entertainment sector is part of a general process by which a small group of sport-loving millionaire cronies who owned teams as a hobby are being supplanted by a conglomerate of global communications MNCs (Bellamy 1998). Besides Disney/ABC and AOL Time Warner, the other major players in this new oligopoly are: Cablevision, the majority owner of both the NHL and NBA franchises in New York and Madison Square Garden; Comcast, owner of NHL and NBA teams in Philadelphia; Adelphia Communications, with 34 per cent of the NHL's Buffalo Sabres; and Murdoch, who is never far from view in the sporting mediascape. In addition to his global media empire of newspapers (over 100 Australian newspapers; UK publications like the *Times, Sun,* and *News of World*; and the *New York Post* in his adopted country), books (HarperCollins), films (Fox), broadcast television (the Fox network), and satellite services (British Sky Broadcasting [BSkyB], Star), Murdoch has telecast rights to about two-thirds of the nearly 80 MLB, NBA, NFL, and NHL teams in North America via complex joint ventures between Cablevision and Liberty Media, and his Fox Sports Net, which consists of over 20 regional cable channels with access to about 62 million households. In April 1999, media moguls Murdoch and John Malone struck the richest ($US 2.1 billion) deal in the history of the media industry. It was expected to be a precursor to joint ventures on the Internet between them. Malone would become the second largest shareholder (8 per cent) in Murdoch's News Corporation via his Liberty Media's purchase of US$1.42 billion of preferred shares in the former company. In return, Murdoch would tighten his grip on televised sport in the USA by doubling his control of Liberty's sports programming net-work, Fox Liberty Media, from 50 to 100 per cent. Liberty Media is the programming arm of the giant cable operator Tele-Communications Inc, which Malone sold in 1998 for over US$45 billion to AT&T, America's largest telephone company. Malone, who is known as the 'King of Cable' (described less charitably by Al Gore as 'Darth Vader') due to his formidable influence over cable TV, also has interests in Time Warner, Discovery Communications, USA Networks, and General Instruments.

Murdoch purchased MLB's Los Angeles Dodgers and also has a 20 per cent share of the new Staples Centre in Los Angeles, 40 per cent of the New York Nicks (NBA), 40 per cent of the New York Rangers (NHL), and options on 40 per cent of the NHL's Los Angeles Kings and the NBA's LA Lakers. He has a 40 per cent stake in Canada's newest sports channel, CTV's Sportsnet, which began broadcasting NHL games in 1998, thus giving him regional telecast rights to the 1999 Stanley Cup finals. When the Dodgers operated at a loss in his first year of ownership, and played very poorly, it really didn't matter – amortization of costs lay in programming for Fox and future use in Murdoch's Asian territories (Dempsey 1999c; Harper 1999; Williams 1999). The rationale for this corporate strategy is

obvious: by controlling both the content and distribution of programming, a scheme that is increasingly popular with all major TV
networks, companies can slash costs by eliminating third parties
and cross-promoting their other commodities for free while securing
much tighter control over the entire circuit of sports production and
consumption.

The New International Division of Cultural Labour (NICL) that
governs such processes as the globalization, televisualisation and
commodification of sport is partly formed through the increased
significance of the media in funding and displaying sport. Whereas
soccer players and other athletes are currently sold as screen actors
by governing sports organizations to television broadcasters and
advertisers, they may soon be more directly employed as TV talent
by sports that will simultaneously run and control the electronic distribution and display of competitions and events. Sports are engaging
in the vertical integration pioneered by sports management companies
like the International Marketing Group (IMG), which has simultaneously represented players and staged, promoted, marketed,
televised, and secured advertising and sponsorship for designated
sports events (Barnett 1990: 188; Rowe 1995: 112). Given satellite TV's
cross-border capacity, we may see more sporting competitions and
events shaped by the reach of media technologies, rather than by the
boundaries of nation-states and their contained audiences. New media
technologies always provide a stronger and more immediate sense of
'having been there' – in the 1930s, by simulating actuality radio commentary on cricket matches in England for Australian audiences, and
in the 1970s through vivid satellite coverage of global mega sports
events (Real 1989, 1996). In the late 1990s, a CBS internet affiliate
was providing US cricket fans with a high-quality web site for play-by-
play information on matches around the world ('SportsLine USA'
1999) and one-day cricket internationals involving South Asian teams
were available on pay-per-view TV.

This does not mean an end to national identification. In Ireland, Sky
and CNN beam foreign sports in, but RTE and the BBC continue to
cover Gaelic games, while the global Setanta Sport and Tara TV provide worldwide coverage to the Irish diaspora, and there are additional
highlights on airplane video programming (Cronin 1999: 68).
Diasporic spectatorship sees fans double-declutching between their
nations of origin and domicile and between regions. Since 1994, 14
MLB teams have offered domestic Spanish-language broadcasts. New
York City-based Dominicans congregate at a sports bar through

summer that provides simultaneous coverage of all games involving the two most prominent Major League sluggers from the Republic, Sammy Sosa and Manny Ramirez. Their team affiliations are over-written by their homeland in the eyes of spectators. Bulgarian viewers of NTV tune in to the WNBA to watch the Houston Comets' number-one draft pick, expatriate Polina Tzekova. Dozens of reporters from Germany covered the 1999 NBA game between Seattle and Dallas, which featured their countrymen Detlef Schrempf and Dirk Nowitzki (Cooper 1999; Dempsey 1999a; Marcano and Fidder 1999; Whitnell 1999). This form of identification is also a site of resistance to *le défi américain*, the cultural imperialism of American sports TV exports.

## References

Andrews, D.L. (1999) Whither the NBA, whither America?, *Peace Review* 11(4): 505–10.

Barnett, S. (1990) *Games and Sets: The Changing Face of Sport on Television*. London: British Film Institute.

Barthes, R. (1977) *Image-Music-Text*. Trans. Stephen Heath. London: Fontana.

Bellamy, R. (1998) The evolving television sports marketplace, in L. A. Wenner (ed.) *MediaSport: Cultural Sensibilities and Sport in the Media Age*. New York: Routledge.

Boardman, A.E. and Hargreaves-Heap, S.P. (1999) Network externalities and government restrictions on satellite broadcasting of key sporting events, *Journal of Cultural Economics*, 23(3): 167–81.

Boehm, E. (1998) Jocks itchy over costly cup, *Variety*, 8–14 June.

Boehm, E. (1999) Mergers alter euro dynamics, *Variety*, 13–19 December.

Bourdieu, P. (1999) The state, economics and sport, in H. Dauncey and G. Hare (trans.; eds) *France and the 1998 World Cup: The National Impact of a World Sporting Event*. London: Frank Cass.

Boyle, R. and Haynes, R. (2000) *Power Play: Sport, the Media and Popular Culture*. London: Longman.

Brown, P. (1996) Gender, sport and the media: an investigation into coverage of women's sport in the Newcastle Herald and Sydney Morning Herald 1890–1990. Unpublished PhD Thesis, University of Newcastle, Australia.

Burton, R. (1999) From Hearst to Stern: the shaping of an industry over a century, *New York Times*, 19 December.

Cooper, M. (1999) 2-TV Béisbol: Ramirez and Sosa, *New York Times*, 18 September.

Country-by-country schedule: WORLD. (1999) <http://nhl.com/hockeyu/international>.

Croci, O. and Ammirante, J. (1999) Soccer in the age of globalization, *Peace Review*, 11(4): 499–504.

Cronin, M. (1999) *Sport and Nationalism in Ireland: Gaelic Games, Soccer and Irish Identity Since 1884*. Dublin: Four Courts Press.

Crook, T. (1998) *International Radio Journalism: History, Theory and Practice*. London: Routledge.

Cunningham, S. and Miller, T. (with Rowe, D.) (1994) *Contemporary Australian Television*. Sydney: University of New South Wales Press.

de Moragas Spà, M., Rivenburgh, N.K. and Larson, J.F. (1995) *Television in the Olympics*. London: John Libbey.

Dempsey, J. (1999a) WNBA Games going global, *Variety*, 14–20 June.

Dempsey, J. (1999b) NFL kicks off online in 3 overseas markets, *Variety* 27 September.

Dempsey, J. (1999c) Sports-crazy showbiz finds score still iffy, *Variety* 20–26 September.

Elias, N. (1986) The genesis of sport as a sociological problem, in N. Elias and E. Dunning *Quest for Excitement: Sport and Leisure in the Civilizing Process*. Oxford: Basil Blackwell.

FIFA (n.d.) <http://www.fifa.com>.

Flirtation and frustration (1999) *Economist*, 11 December.

Foucault, M. (1977) *Discipline and Punish: The Birth of the Prison*. Trans. Alan Sheridan. London: Penguin.

Fry, A. (1998a) On top of their game: sports cabler casts net on four corners of the globe and scores, *Variety*, 19–25 January.

Fry, A. (1998b) Savvy dealmaking woos worldly auds and coin, *Variety*, 19–25 January.

Grove, C. (1998) Tapping into culture to find the right program, *Variety*, 19–25 January.

Gruneau, R. and Whitson, D. (1993) *Hockey Night in Canada: Sport, Identities and Cultural Politics*. Toronto: Garamond Press.

Hargreaves, J. (1986) *Sport, Power and Culture*. Oxford: Polity Press.

Harper, P. (1999) Future of sports: big money, big media rob games of their innocence, <www.msnbc.com>.

Haynes, R. (1999) There's many a slip 'twixt the eye and the lip': an exploratory history of football broadcasts and running commentaries on BBC Radio, 1927–1939, *International Review for the Sociology of Sport*, 34(2): 143–56.

Herman, E.S. and McChesney, R.W. (1997) *The Global Media: The New Missionaries of Global Capitalism*. London: Cassell.

Hils, M. (1997) Kickup in Germany: plan to air some soccer games on ppv under fire, *Variety*, 3–9 November.

International Broadcasters (1999) <www.majorleaguebaseball.com/u/baseball/mlbcom/int>.

IOC. (n.d.) <http://www.olympic.org>.

Jameson, F. (1996) Five theses on actually existing Marxism, *Monthly Review*, 47(11): 1–10.

Kang, J. (1988) Sports, media and cultural dependency, *Journal of Contemporary Asia*, 18(4): 430–43.

Lescure, P. (1998) Letter, *Variety*, 19–25 January.

Macleod, I. (1996) World forces and the Olympic Games, in C. Searle and B. Vaile (eds) *The IOC Official Olympic Companion 1996*. London: Brassey's Sport.

Marcano, A.J. and Fidder, D.P. (1999) The globalization of baseball: major league baseball and the mistreatment of Latin American baseball talent, *Indiana Journal of Global Legal Studies*, 6: 511–77.

McAllister, M.P. (1997) Sponsorship, globalization, and the Summer Olympics, Paper Delivered to the International Communication Association, Montréal.

Muda, M. (1998) The significance of Commonwealth Games in Malaysia's foreign policy, *The Round Table*, 346: 211–26.

New television deals mean more NBA worldwide (1999) <www.nba.com/ONTHE AIR>.

NFL full of foreign-born players (1999) <www.nfl.com/international>.

Pickard, C. (1997) Cup runneth over summer's o'seas B. O, *Variety*, 15–21 December: 9–10.

Pujik, R. (1999) Producing Norwegian culture for domestic and foreign gazes: the Lillehammer Olympic opening ceremony, in A.M. Klausen (ed.) *Olympic Games as Performance and Public Event: The Case of the XVII Winter Olympic Games in Norway*. New York: Berghahn.

Real, M. (1989) *Super Media: A Cultural Studies Approach*. Newbury Park: Sage.

Real, M. (1996) *Exploring Media Culture: A Guide*. Thousand Oaks: Sage.

Rowe, D. and Stevenson, D. (1995) Negotiations and mediations: journalism, professional status and the making of the sports text, *Media Information Australia*, 75: 67–79.

Rowe, D. (1992a) Modes of sports writing, in P. Dahlgren and C. Sparks (eds) *Journalism and Popular Culture*, London: Sage.

Rowe, D. (1992b) 'That misery of stringer's cliches': sports writing, *Cultural Studies*, 5(1): 77–90.

Rowe, D. (1995) *Popular Cultures: Rock Music, Sport and the Politics of Pleasure*. London: Sage.

Rowe, D. (1996) The global love-match: sport and television, *Media, Culture & Society*, 18(4): 565–82.

Rowe, D. (2004) *Sport, Culture and the Media: The Unruly Trinity*, 2nd edn. Buckingham: Open University Press.

Sandomir, R. (1999) When a TV network is your chef, *New York Times*, 8 November.

Smith, P. (1997) *Millennial Dreams: Contemporary Culture and Capital in the North*. London: Verso.

Sport and television: swifter, higher, stronger, dearer (1996) *Economist*, 20 July.

SportsLine USA and CricInfo launch 1999 World Cup site (1999) *Business Wire*, 13 May.

Tagliabue, J. (1997) Europe enters the big leagues: playing catch-up to the U.S., commerce takes the field, *New York Times*, 10 September.

'The World Bids Farewell to Michael' (1999) <http://nba.com/mjretirement/world-farewell.html>.

'TV Times' (1999) <www.afl.com.au>.

Verdier, M. (1996) The Olympic Games and the media, in C. Searle and B. Vaile (eds) *The IOC Official Olympic Companion 1996*. London: Brassey's Sport.

Whannel, G. (1992) *Fields in Vision: Television Sport and Cultural Transformation*. London: Routledge.

Whitnell, I. (1999) International players impact the NBA, <www.nba.com>.

Whitson, D. (1998) Circuits of promotion: media, marketing and the globalization of sport, in L.A. Wenner (ed.) *MediaSport: Cultural Sensibilities and Sport in the Media Age*. New York: Routledge.

Williams, M.L. (1998) Ad deals strike a cultural match, *Variety*, 19–25 January.

Williams, M. (1999) Soccer kicky for congloms, *Variety*, 20–26 September.

Wilson, H. (1998) Television's *tour de force:* the nation watches the Olympic Games, in D. Rowe and G. Lawrence (eds) *Tourism, Leisure, Sport: Critical Perspectives*. Melbourne: Cambridge University Press.

Wise, M. (1999) Empty seats are a concern for the NBA, *New York Times*, 19 December.

Zecchinelli, C. (1998) Murdoch streams into Italy, *Variety*, 28 December.

# SPEAKING THE 'UNIVERSAL LANGUAGE OF ENTERTAINMENT': NEWS CORPORATION, CULTURE AND THE GLOBAL SPORT MEDIA ECONOMY

## David L. Andrews

Previously unpublished.

Given its propensity for inspiring the interest and adulation of the global masses, it is easy to see why sport has been anointed the 'new Hollywood' (Bell and Campbell 1999: 22). This analogy becomes even more appropriate when considering the role played by major telecommunications corporations in the financing, production, and distribution of 'mediasport' (Wenner 1998). The size of the global sport media industry is difficult to measure, but its magnitude can be gauged by the fact that, within the United States alone, current sport media related expenditure has been estimated at US$36.54 billion per annum (all the following figures are in US dollars unless otherwise stated). This figure is divided between media broadcast rights ($6.99 billion); advertising ($27.43 billion); and multimedia ($2.12 billion) purchases (Broughton 2002: 28–9). Given the emergence of what is a highly rationalized, 'high-flying entertainment-media-sports industry' (Marantz 1997: 14), one needs to acknowledge the mutually constitutive relations linking sporting and corporate media interests. Media giants such as Disney, General Electric, News Corporation, and Viacom insert sporting spectacles into their programme schedules in a manner designed to benefit from (and indeed cultivate) sport's established popularity, through enhanced audience viewership and advertising revenue generation.[1] Despite a general acknowledgement of contemporary sport's interdependent relationship with corporate media interests (Alt 1983; Barnett 1990; Real 1998; Rinehart 1998; Jary 1999; Rowe 1999), there is a dearth of in-depth examination of such relations, which prompted this exposition of News Corporation's sport oriented media initiatives.[2]

Perhaps more than any other media industry hierarch, Rupert Murdoch (News Corporation's longtime Chairman and CEO)[3] has both recognized, and productively mobilized, sport's utility within the media entertainment economy. For this, he has garnered a welter of criticism from individuals and institutions troubled by such explicit commercialization of the sport domain. Much to his detractors' ire, Murdoch (1998) has forged a brazenly dispassionate contract with sport, which he avariciously describes as the 'universal language of entertainment'. Not that criticism has done anything but motivate Murdoch's competitive instincts (Shawcross 1997), the result being News Corporation's truly boundless sporting reach and influence, which has radically altered the global sport landscape (Pierce 1995; Rofe 1999; Rowe and McKay 1999). To be sure, News Corporation's acquisitional and diversified sport strategizing has created sport-media interdependencies which are bewildering in their complexity and scope. However, it is not the intention of this chapter to provide a descriptive litany of such initiatives.[4] Rather, the aim of the discussion is threefold. First, to provide a genealogy of News Corporation's development into a global media giant. Second, to examine the intricacies underpinning the paradigmatic manner through which News Corporation immersed itself within professional sport culture as a means of advancing its global media entertainment aspirations. Third, to highlight the manner in which the acquisition of sport properties (leagues, teams, and stadia) has contributed to the vertical integration of News Corporation's corporate structure. In sum, this discussion focuses on sport's pivotal role in establishing News Corporation as, arguably, the 'first vertically integrated entertainment-and-communications company of truly global reach' (Shawcross 1997: 399).

## News Corporation: the company behind the sport

Sport has not always been a staple of News Corporation's media strategies, which originated in much more conventional fashion with Murdoch's inheritance of two regional Australian newspapers (the

*Adelaide News* and the *Brisbane Courier-Mail*) following his father's death in 1952.[5] Through a series of increasingly audacious acquisitions, beginning in Australia, then moving into New Zealand, the United Kingdom, and the United States, News Corporation fashioned a vast stable of print media holdings that presently numbers more than 130 separate properties.[6] However, News Corporation only became a 'main player in the global media system' (Herman and McChesney 1997) with its incursion into the American movie and television industry. Specifically, the purchase of a 50 per cent stake in the struggling Twentieth Century Fox film and television studio for $325 million in 1985 proved a key initiative (News Corporation later bought the remaining 50 per cent to gain complete control of the studio). The acquisition of Twentieth Century Fox provided News Corporation with an established brand identity within the American market, extensive production facilities, and a vast library of media content, all of which helped realize Murdoch's goal of creating a fourth national television network to challenge the ABC-CBS-NBC media oligopoly. To this end, Fox Television Incorporated was founded in May 1985 with the $2 billion purchase from Metromedia of television stations in the major US TV markets (New York, Los Angeles, Chicago, Washington, Houston, and Dallas).[7] Fox Television's subsequent purchases (including the acquisition of 10 television stations resulting from the Chris-Craft Industries takeover in 2001) brought the number of News Corporation's US television station holdings to 33, by some distance the greatest rate of ownership among the US television network organizations. In a remarkably short space of time, and primarily through a financially aggressive business plan, the upstart Fox network built a national organizational structure and market presence to rival its more established competitors.

As was no doubt the rationale behind the initial investment, Twentieth Century Fox provided the facilities required for the production of considerable amounts of original network programming (supplemented by content drawn from Twentieth Century Fox's film library) required by the fledgling national network to help consummate its schedule. Predictably, and to the chagrin of many, Murdoch introduced his unapologetically populist production values – honed as they were in the highly competitive tabloid newspaper business – to network audiences. With scant regard for television's educative and informative potential, Fox originated a repetitious menu of entertainment oriented programming targeted at the lowest common denominators of popular sensibilities, and aimed at generating sizeable advertising revenues through the maximization of audience share. So, Fox Television signalled its arrival with an unrelenting diet of bawdy situation comedies, titillating teen dramas, irreverent cartoons, and tabloidic telejournalism, as *In Living Color*, *Beverly Hills 90210*, and *The Simpsons et al.* initiating a lowbrow revolution which is still being played out within the national network environment.[8]

Having secured a foothold in the all important American network television market, Murdoch's ambitions expanded to the colonization of the new media (specifically cable and satellite platforms) that emerged from the global spread of both new telecommunications technologies, and the widespread instantiation of media deregulation and privatization policies during the 1980s and 1990s (Barker 1997; Fairchild 1999). Despite not owning a controlling interest in a cable or satellite delivery system within the American context,[9] News Corporation made a concerted effort to assert itself within the new media universe through the establishment of channels such as the Fox News Channel, FX, the Fox Movie Channel, the various regional Fox Sports Channels, Fox Sports World, and the recently sold Fox Family Channel. Such new media ventures were not limited to the U.S., however, as News Corporation embarked on a truly global satellite television expansion. This process included substantial investment in satellite delivery systems and channels in, amongst others, the United Kingdom (BSkyB), Australian (Foxtel), Japanese (JSkyB), Indian (Zee TV), New Zealand (Sky), German (Vox), and Asian (Star TV) media markets. All of these initiatives combined to create a whole greater than the sum of its parts. They created a truly global, pay television structure that helps substantiate News Corporation's self-aggrandizing claims of 'Producing and distributing the most compelling *news*, *information* and *entertainment* to the farthest reaches of the globe' (http://www.news corp.com/index2.html, *emphasis in original*).

Murdoch oversaw the transformation of News Corporation from being a regional Australian print media concern to an economically and culturally imposing global media leviathan (rivalling, and in some cases surpassing, the financial might, sectoral diversity, and geographical reach of AOL Time Warner, Disney, and Viacom). In purely financial terms, News Corporation is presently one of the most significant media companies in the world, with assets in 2001 of $47 billion and annual revenues of $14 billion. Of the company's 2001 earnings, 27 per cent were derived from the television sector, 26 per cent from filmed entertainment, 18 per cent from newspapers, 11 per cent from cable network programming, 7 per cent from magazines and inserts, 7 per cent from book publishing, and 4 per cent from other sources. Lastly, with regard to the geographical distribution of News Corporation's total revenue generation, 75 per cent derived from the US, 16 per cent from the United Kingdom and Europe, and 9 per cent from Australasia (News Corporation 2001). In November 1998, News Corporation set up a subsidiary company, Fox Entertainment Group Inc. This company, 85 per cent of which is owned by News Corporation, incorporates armatures devoted to the development, production, and worldwide distribution of feature film and television programming (including sport). The assets of the Fox Entertainment Group approximated US$18 billion in 2000–1, with annual revenues of US$9 billion (Fox Entertainment Group 2001). The corollary of News Corporation's expansionist, acquisitional, and innovative strategizing has thus been the establishment of a truly global multimedia empire, incorporating nine media formats, spanning six continents, and purportedly reaching two-thirds of the world's population (Barker 1997; Herman and McChesney 1997).

The subsequent discussion focuses on the not inconsiderable role played by sport in News Corporation's ascent to the exclusive brethren of the global media oligopoly. However, before delving into the intricacies of the News Corporation sport complex, it is worth considering the unique properties and opportunities that sport offers the mass communications industry in general. Sport, or what Rowe succinctly described as 'the regulated expression of physical culture' (1995: 104), can be considered a unique form of mass entertainment due to its:

- explicit physicality (conjoined as it is with an implicit eroticism)
- innate competitive structure (which almost demands empathy inducing personal narrativizing)
- potential for generating visceral excitement (created by the uncertainty, real or imagined, surrounding the outcomes of sporting contests)
- nurturing of deep-rooted personal identifications and loyalties (the strength of which corporate brand managers can only dream)
- relatively straightforward and inexpensive production demands (especially compared with equivalent programming lasting more than two hours)

• continued widespread popularity (arising from these aforementioned factors) and especially its rare ability to attract high
concentrations of the 18–34-year-old male consumers (the demographics traditionally most prized by corporate advertisers).

It is precisely these properties and opportunities (Sugden and
Tomlinson 1994; Bellamy 1998; Dunning 1999; Miller et al. 2001;
Giulianotti 2002) that News Corporation and other media concerns
have sought to capitalize upon, quite literally, within their sport
programming.

Since the financial capital derived from the sale of advertising slots
represents network television's principal revenue stream (augmented
by sponsorship income and syndication fees), the fiscal exigencies of
the commercial television industry mean that the size and composition
of programme audiences assume critical importance. Given such economic pressure, in purely pecuniary terms (there would appear to be
little else motivating network executives) the relative size and quality
of the television audiences generated by sport has made live televised
sport an extremely attractive economic proposition for the major
networks. The recent decline in network sport's rating share, no doubt
caused in part by the increased viewer choices offered within what is
an ever fragmenting media culture, has, however, somewhat reduced
TV's sport's economic appeal. Nevertheless, high profile sporting
'mega-events' (Roche 2000) such as the Super Bowl, the Olympic
Games, and the FIFA World Cup Final continue to draw huge audiences from a broad spectrum of the viewing population. Moreover,
regular major league sport programming, often with modest television
audiences in terms of overall audience share, as noted above routinely
attracts high percentages of the important young male demographic
category. In other words, especially in terms of audience quality,
televised sport continues to be an important element of network
programming.

The continued cost benefits derived from the broadcast of sporting
spectacles explains the accelerated conflation of media and sport
industries in the latter decades of the twentieth century. This blurring
of the boundaries between various realms of cultural production –
otherwise indicative of the de-differentiation of production associated
with the conditions of postmodernity (Harvey 1989; Bryman 1999) –
has produced a hybridized culture industry, variously characterized as
'mediasport' (Wenner 1998), the 'sports/media complex' (Jhally 1989;
Maguire 1993), the 'sport-business-TV nexus' or the 'media sports

cultural complex' (Rowe 1996; 1999). Despite the complexity of the social and cultural relations that surround televised sport, the truism that 'the media have no inherent interest in sport' retains its validity in that media corporation investment in sport is motivated by its capacity to turn audience interest into profit (Sage 1990: 123). As illustrated in the following section, News Corporation's multifaceted investment in sports rights and properties certainly exemplifies such an economically driven rational pragmatism, with little or no sentiment for the traditions or protocols of sport culture.

## The global media battering ram

Of all the major media companies, News Corporation has demonstrated the most concerted incorporation of sport into its business model. As Rowe (1999: 191) has noted, 'There is no one in the media world who has a greater commitment to the commercial exploitation of sport than Murdoch'. He has been unambiguous in his identification of sport's unique televisual qualities, and their role in constructing a global media entertainment empire. His most revealing pronouncement on sport came in his 1996 speech at News Corporation's annual meeting in Adelaide:

> Sport absolutely overpowers film and everything else in the entertainment genre . . . Football, of all sports, is number one . . . Sport will remain very important and we will be investing in and acquiring long-term rights . . . We have the long-term rights in most countries to major sporting events and we will be doing in Asia what we intend to do elsewhere in the world, that is, use sports as a 'battering ram' and a lead offering in all our pay television operations.
>
> (quoted in Milliken 1996: 28)

At the heart of Murdoch's corporate media philosophy is the steadfast belief that 'sports programming commands unparalleled viewer loyalty in all markets' (Murdoch 1996), and can therefore be used as a 'battering ram' to penetrate media markets more effectively, and indeed rapidly, than any other entertainment genre. This point has been corroborated by Peter Chernin, News Corporation President and Chief Operating Officer, when identifying movies and live sport programming as the pivotal elements in their 'worldwide TV ventures . . . And sports is the more important' (quoted in Bruck 1997: 826).

Interestingly, however, while News Corporation is liable to charges of advancing a globally uniform process regarding the use of sport to penetrate national television markets, any global homogenization concerns are tempered by the nation-specific sporting content used to actually engage the local audience. As Murdoch himself outlined:

> You would be very wrong to forget that what people want to watch in their own country is basically local programming, local language, local culture . . . I learned that many, many years ago in Australia, when I was loading up . . . with good American programs and we'd get beat with second-rate Australian ones.
>
> (Murdoch, quoted in Schmidt 2001: 79)

Thus, News Corporation can be considered an archetypal transnational media corporation by operating seamlessly within the language of the local, simultaneously, in multiple locations (Morley and Robins 1995; Dirlik 1996).

News Corporation's first, and arguably the most financially consequential, use of sport as a media 'battering ram' came with British Sky Broadcasting's (BSkyB) securing of the television broadcast rights for the English Premier League in 1992. In 1990, News Corporation obtained a 50 per cent stake in the newly formed BSkyB following the merger of Murdoch's Sky Television with its chief rival in the United Kingdom satellite broadcasting market, British Satellite Broadcasting. The financial struggle which led to the merger resulted in News Corporation incurring massive losses which threatened the parent company's very existence. As a pay television service, BSkyB's long-term profitability, indeed its immediate viability, were dependent upon the attraction of significant numbers of subscribers (from whom BSkyB would derive significant subscription revenues, and who they could also use as a justification for levying premium advertising rates). This conundrum was solved in 1992 with BSkyB's signing of a £304 million, five-year deal for exclusive broadcast rights to the newly established English Premier League (EPL).[10] BSkyB executives felt the EPL to be 'the only sport that was clearly capable of attracting significant numbers of new customers to satellite TV', and their assumption proved correct (Williams 1994: 387). Within a year of signing the EPL contract, BSkyB subscribers doubled to approximately 3 million, effectively guaranteeing its future and, to all intents and purposes, that of News Corporation as a whole (Lefton and Warner 2001).

Having identified the EPL as its 'jewel in the crown' (Arundel and Roche 1998: 73), BSkyB moved quickly to quash any competitors by agreeing to pay £670 million for a four-year deal when its original contract ended in 1997. Four years later, the television rights to the EPL became the focal point of a more competitive bidding process, the main antagonists being Murdoch's BSkyB and the American cable television giant, NTL, bankrolled by Bill Gates. Not surprisingly, the outcome of this was a marked increase in the money required for securing broadcasting rights: BSkyB's £1.1 billion proving to be the successful bid in June 2000.[11]

Over the past decade BSkyB's relationship with the EPL has resulted in these two commercial entities becoming synonymous: 'Sky without football would be like Unilever without Persil or Mars without chocolate bars' (Anon. 2000a: 28). Moreover, BSkyB recognized the audience potential of other sporting contests, and subsequently embarked on a relentless pursuit of Britain's most coveted sporting events (including most of the English national soccer team's games, England's cricket test matches played abroad, many major rugby union games, rugby league in its entirety, and the Ryder Cup[12]), which allowed Murdoch (1996) to boast, as early as 1996, that 'Sky Sports has a lock on many of the commanding heights of British sport'. As a consequence, by the dawn of the twenty-first century, BSkyB's 'sport-centric strategies' had come to play an important role in securing more than 20 per cent of homes in the UK as subscribers, and thereby establishing the satellite broadcaster as a fixture within the British broadcasting landscape (Lefton and Warner 2001).

In an effort to encourage sport's migration to pay television platforms on a truly global scale, the BSkyB/EPL scenario has been replicated across numerous national media and sporting contexts, with News Corporation's local satellite subsidiary securing the broadcast rights to the sporting entities which most resonate with local audiences. News Corporation also adopted a similar sport-centered approach when building the brand identity and presence of its Fox Television terrestrial network in the United States. At the vanguard of this network building process was the $1.58 billion, four-year contract signed with the National Football League in December 1993 for broadcasting rights to National Football Conference (NFC) games. Justifying what was a vastly inflated sum, proffered in an ultimately successful bid to deter his more established and fiscally conservative competitors, Murdoch later conceded:

We put that $380 million a year on the table to help build Fox. We didn't do it so some quarterback can make another half million a year . . . That's just a by-product. What we did, we did selfishly, to build the network. It was a selfish business decision.

(quoted in Pierce 1995: 182)

Selfish it may have been, effective it most definitely was. Through the regular Sunday NFC schedule (and the Thanksgiving Day game), as well as NFC play-off games, and the rotational broadcasting of the Super Bowl spectacle, Fox's investment provided significant opportunities for magnifying the network's national visibility, elevating direct advertising revenues, and enhancing opportunities for network programming promotions. Fox's relationship with the NFC thus proved hugely influential in establishing and defining its network identity within the American popular consciousness. It also alerted television executives to that which they had long suspected, the fact that the NFL represents 'the most reliable programming on television . . . Football on television is the closest thing to essential, network-defining programming' (Carter 1998: C1).

Having aligned with the NFL to such great effect, Fox was predictably at the forefront of negotiations for the renewal of the contract and, in early 1998 Fox ($4.4 billion) joined with ABC/ESPN ($9.2 billion) and CBS ($4.0 billion) in signing an eight-year $17.6 billion (or $2.2 billion annually) contract for NFL television rights. By this time, Fox, in conjunction with NBC and ESPN, was also in the midst of a $1.7 billion five-year contract (1996–2000) for the television broadcasting rights to Major League Baseball (MLB).[13] This experience proved successful enough for Fox to subsequently sign a $2.5 billion contract with MLB baseball to be the sole broadcaster of every All-Star, play-off, and World Series game for the period 2001–2006. According to David Hill, Fox Sports Group Chairman and CEO, the value of this latest MLB contract can be measured in a number of ways, one of which speaks as much to the season's continuation into one of the twice-yearly auditing periods for television ratings (commonly known as 'sweeps'), as it does to the game's residual popularity:

The playoffs are in a great time of the year, just prior to November sweeps, and they are really an ideal platform for the entertainment boys to launch their wares . . . Add in the fact that they rate and the country focuses on the sport alone during that time of year, and we think it's an incredible property.

(quoted in McAvoy 2001: 26)

As well as dominating the national network delivery of the game, the Fox Sports Net[14] network of regional cable channels broadcasts more than 2,000 regular season games per season as part of the benefits derived from purchasing the local cable rights to 26 of the League's 30 teams. Fox and its affiliates have also come to dominate the local free-to-air delivery of baseball games, now controlling the rights to 15 teams. More disturbingly, perhaps, Fox's increasing control of the platforms through which baseball television coverage is delivered to the American public has allowed it to facilitate the continuing migration of baseball from free-to-air to cable television (McAvoy 2001). This strategy effectively necessitates the inclusion of the regional Fox Sports Net channel in local cable programme packages, even those owned by News Corporation's media adversaries. Through its procurement of national, local, and cable rights, Fox effectively commandeered baseball coverage, to the same extent that NBC has come to dominate, and indeed define itself through, its Olympic scheduling (Andrews 1998). In effect, Fox has fabricated what is tantamount to a televisual 'baseball monopoly' (McAvoy 2001).

Having secured broadcasting rights to two of the more established American sport properties, Fox subsequently turned its attention to NASCAR, the sporting phenomenon of the last decade (Hamilton 1996; Hagstrom 1998). Hoping to benefit from the sport's growing popularity (NASCAR is presently the second-rated sport on U.S. television behind the NFL), Fox joined with NBC and TNT in signing a $2.4 billion[15] television rights contract for NASCAR's Winston Cup and Bush Series races for the period 2001–2008. As David Hill admitted:

> The key to our interest, was very simple . . . In a world of fragmented entertainment choices where everything is slipping, you look at NASCAR and the ratings for the sport over the last five years have remained pretty static. What that means in this day and age is you had an increasing and very loyal fan base . . . To us, life is a gamble and we took a bet, but we think it's a pretty safe bet. I think NASCAR can get much bigger than what it is now, if it's on every week and people get used to it. From a ratings standpoint, I don't think it's anywhere near maxed out.
>
> (quoted in Schlosser 2001: 18)

The NASCAR contract was prompted by the same network-building impulses which underpinned Fox's initial relationship with the NFL. However, now the network could benefit from its earlier investment by directing, through strategic promotions, its established NFL audience to its new NASCAR offering. Within contemporary commercial culture, television programming represents a site for numerous promotional opportunities which, if successfully presented, become linked in a 'chain of mutual reference and implication' (Wernick 1991: 187). For example, Fox used its broadcasting of the 2002 Super Bowl as a forum for promoting both its first half season of NASCAR coverage on Fox and cable channel FX, and to announce the debut of its new cable outlet, The Speed Channel (the relaunched version of Speedvision which Fox purchased in July 2001).

With the NFL, MLB, and NASCAR in the Fox Television portfolio, it is clear to see why Murdoch has become such an important figure within the American sport economy (and, as will be evidenced later, in the broader global sport economy). He successfully identified, cultivated, and capitalized upon televised sport content as the core product within the new information-based mode of production that is emblematic of late capitalist economies (Poster 1990; Jameson 1991). Moreover, as well as crafting the hegemonic blueprint for sport media strategies, Murdoch has also practised a financially aggressive *modus operandi* which 'inflates cost and undercuts competitive balance' (Miller 1999: 32). Thus, both substantively and economically, he has thrust News Corporation to the vanguard of the global sport media economy, whilst forever changing the global sport landscape. Murdoch's power and influence, therefore, cannot be underestimated: As NBC Sports chairman Dick Ebersol commented in response to Murdoch's repeated ranking at the top of *The Sporting News Power 100*, the annual list of the top 100 most powerful people in sports, 'It isn't even remotely a race. You could make him Nos. 1 through 5' (Knisley 1998: 16).

According to the then News Corporation Co-Chief Operating Officer Chase Carey, 'Our entry into sports [is] driven by a belief that sports and live events are going to play a more and more important role in television' (quoted in Rofe 1999: 24). Such an assertion explains why News Corporation has increasingly looked beyond the mere securing of television broadcasting rights in its desire to exert its influence over the sport media economy. In short, News Corporation's goal has been to centralize ownership, and therefore control, over the various revenue generating nodes of the sport entertainment commodity chain, with the ultimate aim of creating a vertically integrated and globally encompassing sport media network (Gereffi and Korzeniewicz 1994; Castells 1996). The process of vertical integration is prompted by the desire to manage the market uncertainties which accompany reliance upon external units for core products and services. Hence, vertically integrating a corporation represents a process of internalization, whereby, 'The planning unit takes over the source of supply or the outlet; a transaction that is subject to bargaining over prices and amounts is thus replaced with a transfer within the planning unit' (Galbraith 1985: 28). The market uncertainties implicit within the sport media economy, particularly the imponderables surrounding the periodic, and increasingly hyperinflationary bidding wars for broadcasting rights, no doubt galvanized News Corporation's vertical integration agenda:

> We are really content providers. We look upon ourselves as a creative company [that] owns newspapers, books, whatever . . . but to ensure their distribution and also to ensure that no one has a choke hold on us . . . we'd like to be vertically integrated from the moment of creation right through to the moment of delivery into the home.
>
> (Murdoch, quoted in Schmidt 2001: 78–9)

News Corporation is well advanced in this process, being, alongside Disney and AOL Time Warner, a primary 'player in the vertical integration game' (Stotlar 2000: 2).

Having invested in the ownership of numerous broadcast platforms and channels, News Corporation subsequently turned to the procurement of the actual sport entities (leagues, teams, and stadia) from which programming content is derived, and the controlled predictability of vertical integration realized, according to the rationale 'that buying sports properties is cheaper than renting – and it heads off the competition' (Rofe 1999: 24). In more specific terms, as well as providing a position of ascendancy within the television rights fees scramble (indeed, the purchasing or establishment of sport leagues relinquishes the need to bid for television rights, while the ownership of sport teams puts media corporations in the advantageous position of negotiating with themselves), the mammoth financial outlay required for the purchase of sporting properties provides numerous other opportunities for direct revenue generation. Sport programming is customarily attractive to advertisers; it offers significant opportunities for intra and cross network promotion, and its popularity allows networks to increase the rates paid by cable systems for carrying their channels. The control afforded by sport property ownership also provides networks with the ability to generate significant revenue from the 'migration' of game coverage to lucrative pay-per-view television platforms. Despite his purported indifference toward sport *per se* (Pierce 1995; Bruck 1997), it is thus clear to see why Murdoch would consider sport property ownership to be vital in his grand global design for News Corporation.

Murdoch's initial steps toward vertically integrating his sport media empire came within the parochial domain of Australian Rugby League (ARL). Despite the global reach of News Corporation's various armatures, within the Australian media landscape Murdoch has struggled for pre-eminence with his media mogul rival, Kerry Packer.[16] Nowhere was Packer's presence more apparent than within the Australian televised sport marketplace, where Packer's terrestrial Nine Network had successfully commercialized and spectacularized cricket and ARL coverage (Miller et al. 2001). In the mid-1990s Packer ventured into the pay television domain in a collaborative venture with the telecommunications company, Optus Vision, which secured the pay television broadcasting rights to both the Australian Rugby League (ARL) and the Australian Football League (AFL). This latter development proved particularly troubling to Murdoch, since he was acutely aware of the need for popular programming content for his new Foxtel pay television network.[17] Thus, Packer's commandeering of Australia's two most popular football codes, Australian Rules Football and Rugby League, compelled Murdoch to produce Foxtel's own sporting content. As a consequence, in April 1995 News Corporation embarked on an AUS$500 million undertaking aimed at establishing the Super League, a rival to the ARL made up of six teams comprised of elite players prized away (by large financial inducements) from the ARL. Super League's subsequent poaching of player and coaching talent did not go unchallenged, yet the ARL's counter offers (bankrolled by Packer and Optus Vision) were often declined, and legal action seeking to prohibit individuals breaking existing ARL contracts proved ultimately unsuccessful. So, in March 1997, the Super League commenced in direct competition to the ARL.

Due to the perceived dilution of both Rugby League products, and the groundswell of public criticism deriving from the public and legal wrangling between these adversarial sport media coalitions, both the ARL and Super League fared poorly in terms of game attendance and television viewership. Given the economic impracticability of rival leagues competing for a diminishing spectatorship, in December 1997 the inevitable ensued with an ARL-Super League merger to form the National Rugby League (NRL), owned in equal partnership between the Murdoch and Packer camps and the ARL (Rowe 1997; Rowe and McKay 1999).[18] The NRL debuted in 1998 as a twenty-team competition, a figure that was reduced to a mandated fourteen clubs by 2000 through the team closures and mergers demanded by the market rationalities of the corporate media concerns now running the league.[19] So, despite a huge financial outlay for a share in the merged league, and the public relations debacle resulting from the perceived hypercommercial corruption of the game in Australia, the NRL scenario once again evidenced Murdoch's conscienceless and ruthless 'determination to secure whatever corporate advantage he can, regardless of the cultural or commercial obstacles' (Hiltzik 1997). In this case, the prize was corporate advantage accruing from the ability to control, even if in partnership, a pivotal source of televised sport content.[20]

The Australian Super League initiative was but one (albeit keystone) element of News Corporation's broader goal of developing a globally integrated Rugby League competition incorporating contests within, and between, clubs in the northern and southern hemispheres (Falcous 1998; Denham 2000). In order to facilitate this ambition, in 1995 News Corporation gained control of the British Rugby Football League (RFL) with the signing of an £87 million five-year contract, the financial details of which bound Rugby League clubs' very survival to Murdoch's corporate plans.[21] Put crudely, News Corporation effectively purchased a controlling interest in a 100-year-old sport culture, ingrained in the working-class history and experience of northern England, and transformed it from a financially troubled and poorly administered sport into a financially stable media production unit. BSkyB, Rugby League's *de facto* owners and administrators, soon set about changing the culture of the game, through the execution of a divisional restructuring, the implementation of aggressive management and marketing initiatives, and even the institution of pseudo-American team nicknames like the Bradford Bulls, Wigan Warriors, and Halifax Blue Sox (Kelner 1996; Arundel and Roche 1998). Perhaps the most radical change to Rugby League culture came with the switching of the playing season from the winter to the summer as dictated by the corporate exigencies of both British and Australian media markets. In terms of the former, the British Super League's summer scheduling meant that it would not clash with English Premier League soccer, BSkyB's prize possession within a British broadcasting rights context. With regard to the latter, News Corporation hoped that close season contests between Australian and British teams (realized by the alignment of playing seasons in different hemispheres) would add an unmatched international dimension, and thereby enhanced brand equity, to Foxtel's Australian Super League coverage. In this way, and as Falcous (1998: 8) noted, 'British Rugby League had been used as a tool in a broader global struggle'.[22]

Not infrequently, News Corporation has been confronted with sports organizations and cultures wherein league ownership, or new league development, was neither feasible nor even admissible. Within such circumstances, Murdoch has turned his attention to the ownership of professional teams as a means of exercising control over the sport media economy. However, his ambition of owning a high profile NFL franchise within a major US television market was stifled by the league's prohibition of corporate ownership of league franchises. According to NFL Commissioner Paul Tagliabue, a media corporation's involvement in the league 'would present a conflict of interest in competitive situations' over rights fees negotiations. "We always want our interests to have but one interest. That might be compromised" (quoted in Heath and Farhi 1998: A1). With such restrictions in place, Murdoch turned to America's other major professional sports. Most notably, in March 1998, and after protracted negotiations with MLB, Fox purchased the entire Los Angeles Dodgers organization for $311 million. Thus, Murdoch commandeered 'one of the great brand names in America in a world where brand names are increasingly important' (Peter Chernin, News Corporation's president, quoted in Heath and Farhi 1998: A1).

Through the investment in the Dodgers, Fox Entertainment purchased a permanent and high profile presence in one of the U.S.'s largest television markets by being able to offer a marquee programming attraction to the local viewing audience. The fact that information on the Dodgers is located within the 'Cable' section of the News Corporation website is illustrative of the purely instrumental value Murdoch places on sport. It certainly vindicates Miller's observation that:

> 'software' is what media empires call the teams they own. Fans may see the Los Angeles Dodgers or the New York Knicks as home teams with illustrious histories, but the new breed of owners – Rupert Murdoch's News Corp., Time Warner, Disney, Cablevision, Comcast – view them as content, programming fodder for the insatiable beast called television.
>
> (Miller 1999: 23)

Fox's position in the Los Angeles market is likely to be strengthened by Murdoch's stated intention to exercise his option to purchase 40 per cent of the Los Angeles Kings and 10 per cent of the Los Angeles Lakers, both clauses associated with his 40 per cent investment in the team's new arena, the Staples Centre in April 1998. Also in 1998, Fox Entertainment gained another foothold in the American sports franchise market with the 40 per cent interest in both the New York Knicks and the New York Rangers (and, incidentally, the Madison Square Gardens arena), acquired as part of News Corporation's purchase of a 40 per cent share in Rainbow Media Holdings, a Cablevision subsidiary.[23] Interestingly, through these dealings, News Corporation added ownership and control of sports stadia to its vertically integrated media delivery system.

Although successful in acquiring the Dodgers, Murdoch's even more audacious £623 million bid for Manchester United was ultimately blocked by the British government's Mergers and Monopolies Commission (MMC) in April 1999 (Brown and Walsh 1999). The rationale for this denial centred on the deleterious effects on competition in the broadcast sport industry arising from the competitive advantage that BSkyB would command, as owners of the most popular and high profile English Premier League club, when negotiating for the league's television rights. Murdoch consequently changed tack and has, through stealth as opposed to brute force, sought to garner influence over the future destination of English Premier League television rights. To this end, BSkyB embarked on a 'buying spree' of up to 9.9 per cent (the maximum percentage allowed for ownership in multiple clubs) of shares in individual clubs, with Manchester United, Manchester City, Leeds, Chelsea and Sunderland all added to its football portfolio (Cassy and Finch 1999).[24]

Having outlined, in admittedly brief terms, the various levels of its engagement with sport as part of realizing its goal of vertical integration, it becomes evident that News Corporation is simultaneously part of a horizontal web of competing, yet collaborating, companies within the contemporary media industry (Auletta 1997). This new industrial order, referred to by the Japanese as a *keiretsu*, is based on intricate networks of cross-company alliances and investments. These protect and strengthen the position of the conjoined megacorporations while simultaneously restricting the ability of external competitors to challenge their ascendancy:

> Like spiders, these companies compete by devouring others of their kind, and by spinning ever bigger webs to cover all of communications, from owning ideas, through owning the factories that manufacture the ideas as products, to owning the means of distributing those products, and on to owning their afterlife.

While the companies continue to do battle with one another, however, they increasingly collaborate, and the result is a horizontal web of joint partnerships . . . These companies join forces for various reasons. They do so to avoid competition. They do so to save money and share risks. They do so, as Microsoft did with Comcast and Murdoch is doing with Primestar, to buy a seat at an adversary's table. They join forces to create a safety net of sorts, because technology is changing so rapidly that no one can be sure which technology or which business will be ascendant. And they join forces with foreign companies to avoid arousing the ire of local governments.

(Auletta 1997: 227)

News Corporation's various collaborative ventures within the sport media economy include associations with a number of its fiercest competitors. These include: the aforementioned alliance with Kerry Packer over the Foxtel and NRL ventures; collaborations with rival American networks for shares of the broadcasting rights of premium sports properties (such as with NBC in televising NASCAR, and with ABC and CBS in televising the NFL); the convoluted web of relations involved in News Corporation's interest in Rainbow Media Holdings, which is also part owned by General Electric; and perhaps the most unlikely collaboration of all, the ESPN Star Sports partnership in Asia, which brings together News Corporation and Disney, in what has proved to be a highly successful venture. Evidently, the vertical integration celebrated by Murdoch cannot be viewed in rigid monolithic terms, such as that which the Ford Corporation instituted during its pre-war heyday, for each unit within News Corporation's vertically integrated structure relies, to varying degrees, on horizontal relations developed with its market competitors. Hence, in Auletta's (1997) terms, News Corporation could be said to exemplify a new order within the media entertainment industry. This could be called a sport media *keiretsu* dependent upon horizontal peer networking to share the risks and responsibilities of, yet continue to derive the benefits from, a vertically integrated organizational structure.

## A cog in the global media machine

Although virtually impossible to assess with any degree of certitude, the commonly accepted estimate is that News Corporation's satellite television platforms reach 66 per cent of global households owning a television (Stotlar 2000). With such a multi-channelled global television footprint, the cross fertilization of sport programming has become yet another lucrative option for News Corporation. For instance, BSkyB feeds of English Premier League soccer represent a staple part of Fox Sports Worlds offerings in the US, with live games on Saturday and Sunday mornings also available to pay-per-view satellite systems. Similarly, Star Sports broadcasts Australia's National Rugby League Telstra Premiership games across the Asian continent from Hong Kong to India. An indication of this trend came with the global simulcast in 2002 of an English Premier League game between Manchester United and Liverpool, the opening sequence of which demonstrated News Corporation's global reach and, by inference, significance:

> *Richard Keys*: Whoever you are, wherever you are, you'll not want to miss this. *Voiceover [against the backdrop of Manchester United and Liverpool game action, interspersed with mesmerized and euphoric supporters, drawn from around the globe]*: When the two biggest football clubs meet, the world watches . . . Across the globe half a billion people in 152 countries will see the biggest club game on the planet.
> *Richard Keys*: This fixture was first played in 1894 in front of just 3,000 people. Tonight, one in twelve of the world's population will tune in, somewhere. This truly is the biggest club game in the world.
>
> (Sky Sports coverage, Manchester United v Liverpool,
> January 22, 2002)

Evidently, the once implausible suggestion that News Corporation may one day 'be able to offer any game, any where, any time of day' is no longer as far-fetched (Heath and Farhi 1998: A1). Moreover, this scenario illustrates the promotional potentialities offered by media corporations who interlace sport within a broader business network (Maguire 1999; Miller et al. 2001). A game involving Manchester United (of which News Corporation owns, as noted above, a 9.9 per cent share) is framed to the world by the hyperbolic rhetoric of the BSkyB commentary team, and no doubt favourably reported upon by News Corporation's various national newspaper properties. Thus the circuit of intra-organization marketing and promotion is completed.

Despite its burgeoning global media architecture, all is not rosy in the News Corporation garden. Most pertinently, there is a growing body of evidence to suggest that, within the ever fragmenting American media market in particular, live television coverage of major sporting events is failing to maintain its audience ratings. Hence, News Corporation's strategically inflated investments in television broadcasting rights, and of other sport properties, have little chance of making significant, if any, returns. News Corporation itself has recognized this state of affairs by restructuring its television contracts through a 'one-time abnormal charge' of $909 million in February 2002. This payment, divided between the NFL ($387 million), NASCAR ($297 million), and MLB ($225 million), allowed News Corporation to adjust (or 'write down' in industry parlance) its future television contract payments based on the anticipated advertising revenues derived from projected viewing figures:

> The severe downturn in sports related advertising during the second half of calendar 2001, the lack of any sustained advertising rebound subsequent to September 11th and the reduction of forecasted long-term advertising growth rates, all resulted in a reduction of our projections of direct revenues from these contracts.
>
> (News Corporation 2002: 6)

In other words, News Corporation was admitting its overpayment on these contracts, and sought redress with the $909 million 'abnormal charge' in order that future NFL, NASCAR, and MLB coverage would be in a position to contribute toward, rather than deplete, the quarterly and annual earning statements from which public companies derive their market share value. As indicated in the statement, News Corporation attributes some of the revenue decline to the post-September 11th economic downturn, but some analysts view it as the most vivid manifestation of a long-term trend, 'This time there appears to be an across-the-board write-down of major sports and a walk away from major sports' (Neal Pilson, sports television consultant and former president of CBS Sports, quoted in Mullen 2002: 33).

In certain quarters, the death knell is already being sounded for major professional sport, which has for so long been dependent on television revenues as a means of financing its own inflationary economy:

> Sports could well have a lot less income in the future. They're going to have to look for corporate support at a very basic level if

they're not getting it from media . . . The media companies are almost to blame for it. They put the money up, and because their business models haven't worked out the clubs, which are used to a certain level of income, are going to suffer.

(O'Riordan 2002: 3)

Whether or not such doom-laden forecasts are realized, News Corporation may well have discovered the future of televised sport through the resuscitation of the 'trash sports' genre of television entertainment prevalent within the 1970s (Rinehart 1998). This came to the fore with the 'Celebrity Boxing' special aired in March 2002 on the Fox network. Pitting B-list, faded celebrities against each other in crassly themed bouts (for example, *The Partridge Family*'s Danny Bonaduce against *The Brady Bunch*'s Barry Williams; troubled ice skater Tonia Harding against Clinton-era figure Paula Jones) easily outdrew Fox's regular sport and general entertainment programming. Equally as importantly, the broadcast attracted major sponsors such as Chevrolet, McDonald's, and VoiceStream Communications.[25] Not surprisingly, Fox promised more to follow.

Of course the popularity of such novelty programming will probably prove to be fleeting. Nevertheless, its ability to grab even momentary public attention offers network executives a vindication of recent initiatives designed to broaden sport's appeal through the advancement of what the noted *New York Times* columnist Robert Lipsyte (1996) described as 'sportainment', a commercial cultural form through which the narratives and aesthetics of mainstream entertainment genres have increasingly commandeered the production of televised sporting events. Doubtless, Murdoch and News Corporation will be at the vanguard of such initiatives, for their corporate investment in sport is such that they are compelled to cultivate its broad-based appeal.[26] As Tracy Dolgin, president of Fox Sports Net, revealed:

We have some tricks up our sleeve to try to Foxify it [NASCAR coverage] . . . We're not only going to appeal to the hard core NASCAR fans, but we're going to try and reach out to the moderate fans and bring them in, trying not to alienate the serious fans at the same time.

(quoted in Schlosser 2001: 18)

Whether the process of *Foxification* is a good thing for sport *per se* is largely immaterial since, as has been demonstrated throughout this discussion, News Corporation's rational pragmatism approaches sport as nothing more than a 'cog in the machine' of global media capitalism (Miller 1999: 32). Periodic component modification, and even replacement, is merely part of the process of ensuring that the machine runs as efficiently and productively as possible.

## Notes

1 Of course, increased advertising revenue is not the only perceived benefit of televising popular sport spectacles, they also represent a priceless opportunity for promoting the network's other programming (particularly new shows) to otherwise unimaginable percentages of the national populace. In the cut throat world of primetime television, this access to audience consciousness can have important effects on establishing the popularity (and hence longevity) of new programming, thereby affecting the profitability of entire networks.

2 News Corporation's sport media strategies are widely acknowledged, but are generally only discussed as part of broader projects (Herman and McChesney 1997; Shawcross 1997; Cashmore 2000; Harvey et al. 2001; Miller et al. 2001).

3 There is a tendency, adopted within this discussion, to refer to institutional figureheads such as Murdoch as synonyms for the institutions that they have come to symbolize. Hence, this descriptive practice should in no way be viewed as contributing to the reification of Murdoch as the sole author of News Corporation's business strategies and initiatives.

4 An incomplete list of News Corporation's sport related holdings at the time of writing, with percentage ownership in parenthesis of those properties not wholly owned, includes:

**Sport Leagues**: National Rugby League (Australia: 50 per cent); Super League (England); Super 12 (Australia, New Zealand, South Africa).

**Sport Teams**: Los Angeles Dodgers (Major League Baseball, US); New York Knicks (National Basketball Association, US: 40 per cent); New York Rangers (National Basketball Association, US: 40 per cent); Chelsea F.C. (Premier League, England: 9.9 per cent); Leeds United F.C. (Premier League, England: 9.9 per cent); Manchester City F.C. (Premier League, England: 9.9 per cent); Manchester United F.C. (Premier League, England: 9.9 per cent); Sunderland F.C. (Premier League, England: 9.9 per cent).

**Sport Venues**: Dodgers Stadium (Los Angeles); Madison Square Gardens (New York: 40 per cent); Staples Center (Los Angeles: 40 per cent).

**Television Outlets**: Fox Television Networks (US, 22 stations); Fox Sports Net (US, 25 regional cable sports channels: 40 per cent); Fox Sports World (US cable channel); CTV Sportsnet (US cable channel: 20 per cent); Home Team Sports (US cable channel: 34 per cent); Golf Channel (US cable channel: 30 per cent); Outdoor Life Network (US cable channel: 34 per cent); Fox Sports Australia (20 per cent); Fox Sports Latin America (50 per cent); Fox Sports World Espanol (50 per cent); ESPN Star Sports (Asia: 50 per cent); Sky Sports 1 (UK: 40 per cent); Sky Sports 2 (UK: 40 per cent); Sky Sports 3 (UK: 40 per cent); Sky; Sports Active (UK: 40 per cent); Sky Sports.com TV (UK: 40 per cent).

5 For a detailed discussion of Murdoch's life, and especially the circumstances surrounding his inheritance and the early years at the helm of News Corporation, see Shawcross (1997).

6 News Corporation's newspaper acquisitions have included: the Perth *Sunday Times* in 1956; the Sydney *Mirror* and *Sunday Mirror* in 1960; the *Australian* and Wellington *Dominion* in 1964; the London *Sun* and *News of the World* in 1969; the San Antonio *Express*, *News*, and *Sunday Express and News* in 1973; the *New York Post* in 1976; the London *Times* and *Sunday Times* in 1981; the *Boston Herald* in 1982; and, the *Chicago-Sun Times* in 1984). Also, News Corporation ventured into the purchasing of magazines (i.e. *TV Guide*, the *Weekly Standard*, and the *Times Literary Supplement*), and publishing houses (i.e. HarperCollins, Regan Books, Zondervan). For more comprehensive listings of News Corporation's labyrinthine media properties, see Barker 1997; Herman and McChesney 1997; Harvey et al. 2001; News Corporation 2001.

7 Interestingly with regard to these purchases, and compelled by Federal regulations that forbade an individual owning a newspaper and a television station in the same city, Murdoch was forced to sell the *New York Post* (he later bought it back). The rule against foreign ownership of broadcasting licenses also forced him to change his citizenship from Australian to American.

8 This is most graphically illustrated in the demise of network news and current affairs programming over the last decade, which has seen the heightened succumbing of serious news reportage to the populist sensibilities of 'infotainment' (Downie and Kaiser 2002). Of course, the ABC's recent courting of chat show host, David Letterman, as a personal and substantive replacement for Ted Koppel's *Nightline* slot, speaks to the same phenomenon.

9 News Corporation owns a 5 per cent share in the satellite television company Echostar Communications Corporation. Moreover, much of 2001 was spent in ultimately fruitless takeover negotiations with Hughes Electronics Corporation (itself a subsidiary of General Motors) for the leading satellite television company in the US, DIRECTV.

10 BSkyB's £304 million deal for the EPL represented a staggering 600 per cent increase over the previous contract.

11 This figure was for live coverage of 66 Sunday and Monday games per season, for the period 2001–2003. Initially, NTL was successful in securing the EPL pay-per-view rights, having their £328million bid accepted for

40 premier league games per season. However, this deal fell apart in October 2000 due to the costs involved and NTL's inability to have first choice of pay-per-view games due to BSkyB's having rights of first refusal for each weekend's games. This allowed BSkyB to get onto the pay-per-view platform through a four-broadcaster consortium (BSkyB, NTL, ITV Digital, and Telewest) which secured the rights for a reduced fee of £181 million. More than any of the other broadcasters, BSkyB has benefited from this unexpected access to the pay-per-view market, with more than 100,000, £50 'season tickets' to all 40 televised matches sold in a matter of weeks (the charge was £60 after the initial sign-up period), in addition to the £8 charged to consumers of individual games (Henderson 2001).

12  BSkyB's successful procurement of the broadcast rights to many of the key events within Britain's sporting calendar led to government legislation protecting eight events deemed of national importance (FIFA World Cup, the Olympic Games, Wimbledon, the English and Scottish F.A. Cup Finals, the Epsom Derby, the Aintree Grand National, and home test matches for the England cricket team) for 'free to view' TV services (Arundel and Roche 1998).

13  It should also be noted that Fox controlled the television broadcast rights to National Hockey League (NHL) from 1995 to 1999, but decided not to renew the contract due to continuing disappointing television ratings. Indeed, Fox's attempts to engage a more mainstream audience through the advancement of more entertainment-oriented production values and technological gadgetry (most notably the infamous FoxTrax puck) proved doubly unsuccessful, in that it failed to attract new viewership while alienating the traditional hockey audience (see Mason 2002).

14  News Corporation had developed a significant sporting presence within the US cable television market through its setting up of the Fox Sports channel in 1993. Nine regional cable sports networks were subsequently purchased in 1996, laying the groundwork for the innovative Fox Sports Net, a network of 22 regionally-based cable sports channels linked by the national nightly highlight show 'Fox Sports News' and other nationally aired programming, but also incorporating a large proportion of regionally-focused sports coverage. Fox Sports Net presently controls the local cable television rights to an overwhelming majority of US based MLB, NBA, and NHL teams, placing it in a significantly stronger position than ABC's more established, but less regionally flexible, ESPN and ESPN2 cable sports channels. Indeed, such is its vigorous good health, one commentator recently referred to the '8,000-pound gorilla that Fox Sports Net has become' (Rofe 1999: 24).

15  Fox was thought to be contributing $1.4 billion of the total $2.4 billion NASCAR contract, for which it gained broadcasting rights to the races in the first half of the NASCAR season, and the Daytona 500 on a rotational basis with NBC (Schlosser 2001).

16 Packer is a director, and *de facto* figurehead, of the publicly-quoted and Packer family dominated media giant, Publishing and Broadcasting Limited, which controls significant proportions of the Australasian magazine and television markets. Also, as evidenced by his World Series Cricket (WSC) initiative in 1977, Packer is arguably the originator of media companies' migration into sport content organization and production (as opposed to mere broadcasting). This revolutionary counterpoint to the cricket establishment was prompted by the Australian Cricket Board's (ACB) rebuffing of Packer's bid to televise Test Match cricket. Through previously unheard of financial inducements for professional cricketers, Packer secured the services of the world's top players and also developed a series of entertainment-inspired game and broadcasting innovations, all of which contributed to the undermining of the ACB's cricket monopoly and, ultimately, led to his acquisition of broadcast rights to Test Matches (Quick 1991).

17 Somewhat like BSkyB's private/public organizational and ownership structure, Foxtel is a partnership between News Corporation and Telstra, the majority state-owned telecommunications company.

18 Interestingly, the NRL settlement saw the development of close working ties between Australia's premier media moguls, with Packer agreeing to use Foxtel as the vehicle for developing his pay television initiatives, and Murdoch consenting to Packer's purchasing of 50 per cent of his share in Foxtel (Anon. 2000b).

19 The South Sydney Rabbitohs, Australia's oldest and most successful Rugby League team, was excluded from the competition in the 2000 round of NRL rationalization due primarily to a combination of mounting debts, organizational problems, and poor playing performance. South Sydney's debarring sparked a considerable public outcry, much of which was targeted at News Corporation's, and particularly Murdoch's, apparent disregard for sporting tradition and community experience. The outcome of the ensuing lengthy, bitter legal battle was a Federal Court ruling which made unlawful South Sydney's exclusion from the NRL. The Rabbitohs, therefore, made a rather improbable return to the NRL in March 2002, so demonstrating News Corporation's fallibility. In 2003 News Corporation won its own appeal, but the Rabbitohs stayed in the NRL competition.

20 Interestingly, although holding only a 50 per cent interest in the league, in recent years, News Corporation has sought to further conjoin its sub-brands to the NRL product. For instance, in late 2000, Telstra paid AUS$400 million for a four-year contract for naming rights to the NRL, meaning that within the cross-promotional climate of the contemporary media economy (Wernick 1991) Optus 'faces having to broadcast rugby league games plastered with the logos of its rivals' (Anon. 2000b 13).

21 According to Denham (2000), the terms of the News Corporation deal

meant that each Super League team received a basic payment of £1 million per season, plus additional revenue determined by their final league position and success in post-season contests. Such financial compensation brought a previously unimaginable degree of financial stability to Rugby League, but also tied the game's future to News Corporation's purse strings.

22  Space considerations preclude an extended discussion of this development, but it should be noted that News Corporation similarly invested in the Rugby Union code in Australasia, South Africa and Britain. Indeed, within the Australian context, Murdoch again struggled for supremacy with Kerry Packer over the previously under-exploited Rugby Union code, so sparking what Fitzsimons (1996) described as a 'rugby war'. This contest eventually led to the spectacular commercialization and professionalization of what had once been an amateur game, or at least one where player payment was covert. This change is epitomized by the AUS$750 million investment in establishing the Super 12 competition, which pitted the major players and provincial teams of Australia, New Zealand, and South Africa against each other (Fitzsimons 1996; Hutchins 1996, 1998; Anon. 2000b).

23  Murdoch also acquired Dodger Stadium as part of his sports franchise dealings.

24  News Corporation is not the only media company to invest in English Premier League clubs, with NTL (Newcastle, Middlesbrough, Aston Villa, and Leicester City) and Granada (Liverpool and Arsenal) following suit.

25  The show garnered a 9.1 rating, and 14.0 share, having been watched by 9,646,000 households owning a television. These figures are based on there being an estimated 105.5 million television households in the USA. A single ratings point represents 1 per cent, or 1,055,000 households for the 2001–02 season, while share is the percentage of television sets in use tuned to a specific programme (Anon. 2002: 16; Carter 2002).

26  Of course, Fox has been at the forefront of such initiatives in their NFL, MLB, and NHL coverage, which introduced numerous production value and technological initiatives, many of which have which subsequently became standard within the televised sport industry (Mason 2002; Pierce 1995).

## References

Alt, J. (1983) Sport and cultural reification: from ritual to mass consumption, *Theory, Culture & Society*, 1(3): 93–107.

Andrews, D.L. (1998) Feminizing Olympic reality: preliminary dispatches from Baudrillard's Atlanta, *International Review for the Sociology of Sport*, 33(1): 5–18.

Anon. (2000a) Held to ransom, *Marketing Week*, 9 March.

Anon. (2000b) Murdoch's end game, *Sydney Morning Herald*, 23 December.

Anon. (2002) The week that was, *Broadcasting and Cable*, 18 March.

Arundel, J. and Roche, M. (1998) Media Sport and local identity: British rugby league and Sky TV, in M. Roche (ed.) *Sport, Popular Culture and Identity*. Aachen: Meyer & Meyer Verlag.

Auletta, K. (1997) The next corporate order: American Keiretsu, *New Yorker*, 8 December.

Barker, C. (1997) *Global Television*. Oxford: Blackwell Publishers.

Barnett, S. (1990) *Games and Sets: The Changing Face of Sport on Television*. London: British Film Institute.

Bell, E. and Campbell, D. (1999) For the love of money, *The Observer*, 23 May.

Bellamy, R.V. (1998) The evolving television sports marketplace, in L.A. Wenner (ed.) *MediaSport*. London: Routledge.

Broughton, D. (2002) Behind the numbers: how US sports dollars are spent, *Street & Smith's Sports Business Journal*: 30–9.

Brown, A. and Walsh, A. (1999) *Not for Sale: Manchester United, Murdoch and the Defeat of BSkyB*. London: Mainstream.

Bruck, C. (1997) The big hitter, *The New Yorker*, 8 December.

Bryman, A. (1999) The Disneyization of society, *The Sociological Review*, 47(1): 25–47.

Carter, B. (1998) NFL is must-have TV: NBC is a have-not, *New York Times*, 14 January.

Carter, B. (2002). Fox puts gloves on faded fame and achieves ratings glory, *New York Times*, 14 January.

Cashmore, E. (ed.) (2000) *Sports Culture: An A-Z Guide*. London: Routledge.

Cassy, J. and Finch, J. (1999) BSkyB linked to new Premiership buying spree, *The Guardian*, 11 August.

Castells, M. (1996) *The Rise of the Network Society*. Oxford: Blackwell.

Denham, D. (2000) Modernism and postmodernism in the professional rugby league in England, *Sociology of Sport Journal*, 17(3): 275–94.

Dirlik, A. (1996) The global in the local, in R. Wilson and W. Dissanayake (eds) *Global Local: Cultural Production and the Transnational Imaginary*. Durham: Duke University Press.

Downie, L. and Kaiser, R.G. (2002) *The News About the News: American Journalism in Peril*. New York: Knopf.

Dunning, E. (1999) *Sport Matters: Sociological Studies of Sport, Violence and Civilization*. London: Routledge.

Fairchild, C. (1999) Deterritorializing radio: deregulation and the continuing triumph of the corporatist in the USA, *Media, Culture & Society*, 21(4): 549–61.

Falcous, M. (1998) TV made it all a new game: not again! Rugby league and the case of super league in England, *Occasional Papers in Football Studies*, 1(1): 4–21.

Fitzsimons, P. (1996) *The Rugby War*. Sydney: HarperCollins.

Fox Entertainment Group (2001) *Annual Report 2001*.

Galbraith, J. K. (1985) *The New Industrial State*. Boston, MA: Houghton Mifflin.

Gereffi, G. and Korzeniewicz, M. (eds) (1994) *Commodity Chains and Global Capitalism*. Westport: London.

Giulianotti, R. (2002) Supporters, followers, fans, and flaneurs: A taxonomy of spectator identities in football, *Journal of Sport & Social Issues*, 26(1): 25–46.

Hagstrom, R.G. (1998) *The NASCAR Way: The Business that Drives the Sport*. New York: John Wiley & Sons, Inc.

Hamilton, M.M. (1996) NASCAR's popularity fuels a powerful marketing engine. *The Washington Post*, 26 May.

Harvey, D. (1989) *The Condition of Postmodernity: An Enquiry into the Origins of Cultural Change*. Oxford: Blackwell.

Harvey, J., Law, A., and Cantelon, M. (2001) North American professional team sport franchise ownership patterns and global entertainment conglomerates, *Sociology of Sport Journal*, 18(4): 435–57.

Heath, T. and Farhi, P. (1998) Murdoch adds Dodgers to media empire, *The Washington Post*, 20 March.

Henderson, J. (2001) Thousands sign up to pay more, *The Observer*, 12 August.

Herman, E. and McChesney, R.W. (1997) *The Global Media: The New Missionaries of Corporate Capitalism*. London: Cassell.

Hiltzik, M.A. (1997) Playing by his own rules, *Los Angeles Times*, 25 August.

Hutchins, B. (1996) Rugby wars: The changing face of football, *Sporting Traditions*, 13(1): 151–62.

Hutchins, B. (1998) Global processes and the Rugby Union World Cup, *Occasional Papers in Football Studies*, 1(2): 34–54.

Jameson, F. (1991) *Postmodernism, or the Cultural Logic of Late Capitalism*. Durham: Duke University Press.

Jary, D. (1999) The McDonaldization of sport and leisure, in B. Smart (ed.) *Resisting McDonaldization*. London: Sage.

Jhally, S. (1989) Cultural studies and the sports/media complex, in L.A. Wenner (ed.) *Media, Sports, and Society*. Newbury Park, CA: Sage.

Kelner, S. (1996) *To Jerusalem and Back*. London: Macmillan.

Knisley, M. (1998) All Rupert, all the time, *The Sporting News*, 14 December.

Lefton, T. and Warner, B. (2001) He's got global game, *The Industry Standard*, 19 February.

Lipsyte, R. (1996) Little girls in a staged spectacle for big bucks? That's sportainment! *New York Times*, 4 August.

McAvoy, K. (2001) Baseball gets the bucks, *Broadcasting and Cable*, 2 April.

Maguire, J.A. (1993) Globalization, sport development, and the media/sport complex, *Sport Science Review*, 2(1): 29–47.

Maguire, J.A. (1999) *Global Sport: Identities, Societies, Civilizations*. Cambridge: Polity Press.

Marantz, S. (1997) The power of air, *The Sporting News*, 24 December.

Mason, D.S. (2002) 'Get the puck outta here!': Media transnationalism and Canadian identity, *Journal of Sport & Social Issues*, 26(1): 140–66.

Miller, S. (1999) Taking sports to the next level: Start with teams, add arenas, media and you've got a sports empire, *Street & Smith's Sports Business Journal*, 23, 32.

Miller, T., Lawrence, G., McKay, J., and Rowe, D. (2001) *Globalization and Sport: Playing the World*. London: Sage.

Milliken, R. (1996) Sports is Murdoch's 'battering ram' for pay TV, *The Independent*, 16 October.

Morley, D. and Robins, K. (1995) *Spaces of Identity: Global Media, Electronic Landscapes and Cultural Boundaries*. London: Routledge.

Mullen, L. (2002) Losses make Fox wary of sports deals, *Street & Smith's Sports Business Journal*, 1, 33.

Murdoch, R. (1996) *News Corporation Annual Report: Chief Executive's Review*. Adelaide, Australia.

Murdoch, R. (1998) *News Corporation Annual Report: Chief Executive's Review*. Adelaide, Australia.

News Corporation (2001) *News Corporation Annual Report*. Adelaide, Australia.

News Corporation (2002) *Earnings release for the quarter ended December 31, 2001*, Adelaide, Australia.

O'Riordan, B. (2002) Good times may be over for professional sports, *Australian Financial Review*, 16 February.

Pierce, C.P. (1995) Master of the universe, *GQ*, April.

Poster, M. (1990) *The Mode of Information: Poststructuralism and Social Context*. Chicago: University of Chicago Press.

Quick, S.P. (1991) What a catch! The establishment of cricket on Australian commercial television, *Media Information Australia*, 61(August): 81–5.

Real, M.R. (1998) MediaSport: technology and the commodification of postmodern sport, in L.A. Wenner (ed.) *MediaSport*. London: Routledge.

Rinehart, R.E. (1998) *Players All: Performances in Contemporary Sport*. Bloomington, IN: Indiana University Press.

Roche, M. (2000) *Mega Events and Modernity: Olympics, Expos and the Growth of Global Culture*. London: Routledge.

Rofe, J. (1999) The 800-pound gorilla keeps growing: Fox discovers that buying sports properties is cheaper than renting – and it heads off the competition, *Street & Smith's Sports Business Journal*, 24.

Rowe, D. (1995) *Popular Cultures: Rock Music, Sport and the Politics of Pleasure*. London: Sage.

Rowe, D. (1996) The global love-match: sport and television, *Media, Culture & Society*, 18(4): 565–82.

Rowe, D. (1997) Rugby league in Australia: the super league saga, *Journal of Sport and Social Issues*, 21(2): 221–6.

Rowe, D. (1999) *Sport, Culture and the Media: The Unruly Trinity*. Buckingham: Open University Press.

Rowe, D. and McKay, J. (1999) Field of soaps: Rupert v. Kerry as masculine melodrama, in R. Martin and T. Miller (eds) *SportCult*. Minneapolis: University of Minnesota Press.

Sage, G.H. (1990) *Power and Ideology in American Sport: A Critical Perspective*. Champaign: Human Kinetics.

Schlosser, J. (2001) Revved up for NASCA, *Broadcasting and Cable*, 12 February.

Schmidt, R. (2001) Murdoch reaches for the sky, *Brill's Content*, June.

Shawcross, W. (1997) *Murdoch: The Making of a Media Empire*. New York: Touchstone Books.

Stotlar, D.K. (2000) Vertical integration in sport, *Journal of Sport Management*, 14(1): 1–7.

Sugden, J. and Tomlinson, A. (1994) Soccer culture, national identity and the World Cup, in J. Sugden and A. Tomlinson (eds) *Hosts and Champions: Soccer Cultures, National Identities and the USA World Cup*. Aldershot: Arena.

Wenner, L.A. (ed.) (1998) *MediaSport*. London: Routledge.

Wernick, A. (1991) *Promotional Culture: Advertising, Ideology and Symbolic Expression*. London: Sage.

Williams, J. (1994) The local and the global in English soccer and the rise of satellite television, *Sociology of Sport Journal*, 11(4): 376–97.

# SPORTS PAGE: A CASE STUDY IN THE MANUFACTURE OF SPORTS NEWS FOR THE DAILY PRESS

## Mark Douglas Lowes

Excerpt from an article of the same name originally published in *Sociology of Sport Journal*, 1997, 14(2): 143–59.

This chapter presents a study of the work routines employed by news-workers in the manufacture of sports news for the metropolitan daily press. More generally, I offer an account of the lived work experience of newspaper sport reporters and editors at a large Canadian daily, in an effort to explain why the sports pages are so regularly saturated with news of major North American commercial spectator sports (including 'amateur' sports spectacles like the Olympic Games and high-profile university sports) while noncommercial sports receive only minimal coverage at best.

The sports newswork environment of a metropolitan daily is rife with pressures and constraints; and newsworkers have responded by institutionalising various work routines to cope with these demands. By 'institutionalised' work routines I mean a distinctive set of patterns and rules of conduct that (a) persist in recognizably similar form across long spans of time and space; and (b) represent well-recognized and widely accepted ways of doing things in society (Giddens 1982: 10; Gruneau and Whitson 1993: 34). In other words, today's patterns of action tend to reiterate past patterns. 'Repeated time after time, these actions become standard operating procedures', they 'take on a life of their own', simply becoming 'the way things are done' (Sigal 1973: 101). In this way, sports newswork becomes routinised, which has the effect of standardising sports news content – it is mostly about major commercial spectator sports. I argue that, to understand why it is that some sports enjoy regular and voluminous press coverage and others virtually none, we have to examine how and why newsworkers choose what will become sports news in the first place.

## Method

Data were gathered during four months of field research conducted primarily in the newsroom of an eastern Ontario metropolitan daily newspaper, the *Bytown Examiner*. To protect anonymity, 'Bytown' and all individuals and organizations in it have been given pseudonyms. The *Examiner* has a weekly (Monday to Friday) circulation of approximately 52,290 readers in a market area of approximately 710,000 adults older than the age of 18 years (*Canadian Advertising Rates and Data* 1994). This field research consisted of both non-participant observation of activities at the paper's sports desk and extensive interviews with the paper's sports editors and reporters. In addition, several hours were spent interviewing and observing five media relations staffers from two major commercial sports organizations: the Hornets of the National Hockey League and the Flames of the Canadian Football League.

The *Examiner* has a staff of 10 sports newsworkers. There is one editor and one assistant editor, three beat reporters, and two columnists. In addition, there are two 'deskers' who split their time between reporting and preparing the sports section for publication every day; this latter task involves such things as copy-editing, photo selection, and page layout. Finally, the *Examiner* has one freelance reporter generally responsible for covering Bytown's university and college sports scene; he also regularly writes on harness racing. Based on biographical data obtained during interviews, the typical *Examiner* sports newsworker is a 33 year-old White male with about 10 years experience doing sports journalism, and he holds a diploma in journalism from community college. There was one female working as a desker . . . Sports newswork at the *Examiner* is carried out at a very hectic pace. Indeed, at first glance to an outsider activity in the newsroom seems completely incoherent, a senseless ball of confusion akin to the organized chaos that marks activity on the floor of the Toronto or New York Stock Exchanges. Sports newsworkers typically work a 3 p.m. to 11 p.m. shift, and as the evening wears on and deadline approaches the pace picks up. As reporters scramble to finish their stories, and editors and deskers await these news items so they can layout the sports pages, a constant barrage of questions and orders pounds the ears – 'Who pitched for the Jays last night? What's his ERA?' 'Do you know if Barrett is starting tonight or is he still benched?' 'Hey Colvin! What's going on with Turlotte? Can you get confirmation from the Hornets that he's on the trading block or not?' 'Who's covering the diving competition?' This cacophony made it necessary to conduct most of my interviews 'on the fly', as the organized chaos of the newsroom generally did not allow for long protracted interviews . . .

## Sports newswork at the *Examiner*

Although the primary focus of this chapter is on newswork routines, the economics of the news business and its influence on the content of the sports section cannot be ignored. Indeed, as we shall see, market forces play a big part in shaping the framework within which sports newswork is carried out. Metropolitan daily newspapers, like any other free market enterprise, sell a product to buyers. Their market is advertisers; the 'product' is readers. In effect, readers are a commodity generated by the news industry – an 'audience commodity' – and access to them is sold as advertising space. Further, newspaper organizations are fully attuned to the crucial importance of audience 'quality'. Advertisers are interested in purchasing clearly defined and highly concentrated audiences comprised of people inclined to purchase whatever product the advertiser is selling. This is what Ben Bagdikian (1992) calls 'the iron rule' of advertising-supported media; it is less important that people buy your product than they be the right people. For a metropolitan daily selling its sports readers, the 'right people' are 18 to 49-year-old males with disposable income. This demographic is considered to have the most buying power and can be swayed by effective advertising (Parente 1977; Jhally 1984; Sparks 1992). What's more, several studies show that the levels of knowledge and interest in sport are greater among men than women (Gantz 1985; Gantz and Wenner 1991, 1995). Thus, the prevailing philosophy in the news industry is that the most effective way to attract male readers is to provide extensive coverage of commercial spectator sports; that is, cater to perceived male tastes. Accordingly, the sports pages of metropolitan dailies are saturated with commercial sports news, as revealed by content analyses of several North American dailies (Scanlon 1970; Lever and Wheeler 1984; Rintala and Birrell 1984; Gelinas and

Theberge 1986). Commercial sports are cash cows and metropolitan dailies depend on them to 'deliver the male' (Sparks 1992).

The *Examiner* is an advertising-supported daily, dependent on advertising sales to generate most of its revenue. As such, the paper must produce a 'quality' audience commodity to sell to advertisers – one which is highly concentrated and identifiable. Accordingly, the paper openly courts male readers with its sports coverage – it covers primarily commercial spectator sports, widely considered most appealing to male readers. Wenner (1989: 15) suggests that in many ways the sports pages function as socially sanctioned gossip sheets for men, a place where 'a great deal of conjecture is placed upon "heroes" and events of little worldly import'. The sports section is primarily the domain of men. The philosophy that the *Examiner* should cover the major sports events and issues that have the widest interest primarily to male readers rarely embraces noncommercial sports, which are generally considered an afterthought at best. The paper's approach to covering sports is neatly summed up by one of its sports reporters:

> People want to read about professional sports, the big leagues . . .
> A lot of people don't watch little Billy go play ball at Trillium
> Park on a Friday night. I mean, how much interest is there in
> amateur sports like that? Not enough to warrant a lot of
> coverage.

Commercial sports thus consumes the majority of available column space in the *Examiner's* sports section each day by default – it's what readers want.

Developing this last point further, the first concern at the *Examiner* when planning its sports section each day is with the commercial sports scene – reporting what's happening in 'the big leagues'. The standard fare of the paper's sports news is game results from the previous day, player movement through trades and outright releases, injury reports on athletes, and the current status of any labour unrest. Indeed, reporting this news seems to be the *raison d'être* of any metropolitan daily's sports section: 'This is the stuff people want to read about . . . big time sports gets you readers', remarked the *Examiner's* sports editor. The paper's sports section is thus saturated with commercial spectator sports news, as this is how a quality audience is attracted and subsequently sold to advertisers. A commercial spectator sports bias is simply a matter of financial survival for the *Examiner*.

As we've seen thus far, the present logic of news industry economics leads metropolitan dailies like the *Examiner* to emphasise commercial sports coverage. Given this, the problem facing these organizations is how to cover such a vast expanse? After all, metropolitan dailies, like any news organization, have finite resources; they are not able to post reporters everywhere there is a major sports event happening. So, newspapers employ a coverage strategy that is an industry standard – the 'beat' system of reporting. Beats are a way of 'providing predictably available information to reporters and, as such, are an important means of reducing the variability of the news and bringing some order to the news world' (Theberge and Cronk 1986: 199). Briefly, beat coverage entails assigning a reporter to a particular organization in order to provide regular coverage of a subject. In regard to sports, it is exclusively major sports organizations that are assigned beat reporters. For example, a reporter is assigned to cover the Toronto Blue Jays beat. Day in and day out, he or she reports on the team's activities; that is, anything that happens involving the team's ownership, its management, and its players and coaches. The reporter is expected to know the beat intimately and write regular news items about its activities. In this manner, the newspaper gets regular coverage not only of the Blue Jays, but of Major League Baseball itself, because when the reporter writes about the Blue Jays, invariably this means covering the activities of all the other teams in the major leagues. The Blue Jays beat, therefore, generates a regular flow of baseball news not only about the team, but Major League baseball as a whole.

The beat system is used extensively by the *Examiner* to cover major commercial spectator sports. The paper has reporters assigned to three beats; namely, the Hornets of the National Hockey League; the Flames of the Canadian Football League; and the Badgers, a Triple 'A' baseball club. Coverage of noncommercial sports is a patchwork at best, usually by a freelance reporter or one of the paper's two deskers. Beat reporters only cover sports of such marginal interest when they're not too busy with their regular duties (Theberge and Cronk 1986). Establishing and maintaining a series of sports beats constitutes a significant investment of organizational resources. As the Examiner's sports editor remarked, 'It costs us a hell of a lot of money' to establish and maintain these beats. For example, it costs the paper in excess of CAN$10,000 per year to provide beat coverage of the Flames, the local CFL franchise, and 'several times that' to cover the Hornets of the NHL. Over and above reporter salary, the paper has to pay for reporter transportation on road trips, hotels, and *per diem* money to cover meals and incidental expenses. Not only are there significant financial costs to consider, but human resources costs as well. When a reporter is assigned to cover a sports beat they are mostly unavailable to write other sports news items, so making a significant impact on sports news content. The beat system limits the number of sports reporters available to cover noncommercial sports events – they're committed to major commercial sports teams. So, if the *Examiner's* three beat reporters are all occupied with their regular responsibilities (covering their respective teams), then that leaves only two deskers and one part-timer to cover Bytown's noncommercial sports scene. Obviously, under these conditions the opportunity for noncommercial sports to wrestle some news space from commercial spectator sports is minimal. Moreover, because only the paper's best reporters are assigned to these beats, it is arguable that the quality of noncommercial sports coverage is significantly less than that afforded to commercial sports. After all, it is unlikely that the paper will assign a cub or part-time reporter, or one with marginal or average skills to cover a major sports beat; the newspaper has far too much invested in these beats to assign anyone but its best reporters to them.

Beat subjects receive regular and extensive coverage in the most prominent pages of the sports section, while the *Examiner* also fills its sports 'news hole' each day with material generated from its sports beats. Accordingly, noncommercial sports often find themselves buried in the back pages. The rationale behind this is straightforward: why would a newspaper make this substantial investment of organizational resources to establish and maintain beats if not to use them to generate the bulk of the news it intends to fill the sports section with? One consequence of the beat system, then, is that the paper's sports news content has a marked commercial sports bias. Indeed, the paper's assignment of beat reporters only to these sports is strong evidence of its commitment to providing extensive coverage of commercial spectator sports as a means of generating a quality audience commodity. In effect, the beat is an institutionalized barrier to the coverage of noncommercial sports (Theberge and Cronk 1986).

In return for the enormous investment of human and financial capital in these beats, the *Examiner* expects its reporters to generate a vast and regular supply of news to be generated from them daily. As the sports editor explained, 'Oh yeah, you bet they'd better produce! We spend a lot of money to have these guys know what's going on with their team and to write about it'. I asked a desker what would happen to a sports reporter who wasn't producing enough news from their beat. His reply is telling: 'He won't have his job for very long'. Responsibility for covering a sports beat entails an obligation to write something every day about its activities. Indeed, the obligation to generate news from the *Examiner's* sports beats is so strong that reporters are expected to do so even if they don't think there is anything newsworthy to report. One reporter explained:

> There's always something to write about, whether it's the previous night's game, a trade rumour, maybe someone isn't playing well and they've been benched . . . In the off-season it's not as bad [the pressure to produce news items every day] because there isn't as much happening day in and day out. But that doesn't mean a beat guy can let up because we don't want to get beat on a story, ever!

Another reporter complained that this need to generate sports news no matter what creates 'bullshit stories' – that lack any real insight or importance. 'There's a lot of pressure to write stories, even if nothing is really going on. To me, that's bullshit'. Lack of activity on a sports beat is thus insufficient grounds for a reporter not to generate any news. As Fishman (1980: 35) notes, 'The sense of how little or how much is happening is largely irrelevant to the normative requirement for reporters to produce these stories'. In short, the journalistic axiom 'no news is news' appears to be a convention at the *Examiner*. There is always something on the beat to write about, even if it's just 'bullshit'. Thus, covering a sports beat for the *Examiner* entails a normative obligation to generate news from it daily. Not only must sports reporters generate expectable quantities of fresh news from their beats, but they must do so under the constraints of fixed deadlines not of their choosing and beyond their control (Sigal 1973; Tuchman 1978; Fishman 1980; Ericson et al. 1987, 1989). At the *Examiner*, sports stories must be submitted no later than the paper's 11 p.m. deadline. This poses a problem for beat reporters because Bytown's commercial sports teams almost invariably play their games in the late evening, often concluding only 45 minutes or so before deadline. The pressure is significant, as reporters have to complete their interviews with players and coaches after the game, and then write the story; all typically within 30 minutes or so. To alleviate some of this pressure, a couple of reporters explained to me that they often write their stories 'on the fly'. As the game progresses, the reporter writes as much of the story as possible, concentrating on big plays, and so on, and after the game reworks the story to correspond to a general theme.

Clearly, the *Examiner's* sports newswork environment is shot through with pressures and constraints. To cope, *Examiner* reporters need sources who can provide them with a steady flow of commercial sports news material. Indeed, reporters depend on routine sources – their 'lifeblood' as one reporter put it. There are two major routine source types: (a) commercial sports organizations, and (b) a network of personal contacts on the beat. Both are routine sources because they facilitate sports newswork – they satisfy reporters' need for fresh news material every day.

## Routine news sources

### Commercial sports organizations

Commercial sports organizations routinely supply reporters with news material through the judicious use of press releases and news conferences. Both are channels through which these organizations pass on potentially newsworthy information to reporters, in effect offering reporters story ideas and the raw materials that they need to write them. The press release is a simple device whereby sources issue statements of current or upcoming events to reporters. Ericson et al. (1989: 229) refer to these as 'knowledge packages', as they typically contain a detailed account of an event, including background information, primary facts and perhaps 'quotable quotes' from source representatives. Press releases, in effect, offer story material to reporters. As one sportswriter noted, 'Press releases give you pretty much all you need in terms of the background you need to write a story'. The Hornets' Director of Media Relations explains that his job is to offer story ideas to sports reporters and to provide them with the raw materials they need to write a news item. He does this primarily with news releases:

> I'm here to help [reporters] do their jobs. It's simply having to know what they want to know. For example, today we signed [names player]. First thing I did was prepare a complete news release on everything he's done and as soon as that was done, we sent it out to the media. Now it's up to them to decide if they want to cover that story; I just made sure they've got the information they need.

This is particularly helpful to a reporter who encounters a slow news day on their beat, and they depend on media relations people to regularly supply them with story material:

I'll send out a press release to [sports reporters] and it's their decision to cover it. *All I can do is let them know about something* . . . . I let them know about something and they'll decide, 'Is there a story in there?' . . . *I'm just basically pitching ideas and stories at them.*

The press release is clearly an important device through which media relations people offer news material to reporters – in effect helping sports reporters do their work – and are also important vehicles that enable noncommercial sports to get some much-needed attention from the press. During my fieldwork at the *Examiner*, the paper was routinely swamped with news releases, its fax machine constantly spitting them out. I asked the paper's editor about this and he said laughing, 'Oh it never stops, that thing is always going. It's mostly junk, but sometimes you get something worth sending someone to cover, or maybe make a couple of phone calls to get the results. We get a lot of our local news that way'. One reporter commented:

Press releases help with some things we don't cover that often . . . say, the Canadian Broomball Association gives us a release saying that some guy has been named to the North American All-Star team and he's from the local area. Well, no one's gonna be covering that as part of any beat, so it's good to know that kind of thing, you know, it's good to get a press release on it. It's the kind of story that might provide for an interesting little sidebar or a small feature or something like that.

Not so long ago, fax technology and the like was a luxury enjoyed almost exclusively by the major commercial sports organizations with ample resources at their disposal. This no longer appears to be the case. Fax machines can be found almost anywhere now, from printing and photocopy shops, schools, even corner stores and shopping malls to most businesses and some homes; thus even the most resource-poor sports clubs and organizations can afford to fax reporters. Ultimately, press releases are used extensively by commercial and noncommercial sports alike in their quest to obtain press coverage, but it is still commercial spectator sport that is privileged in terms of the amount of coverage they enjoy on a daily basis, an advantage reinforced by news conferences.

News conferences are prescheduled news events that have a function similar to press releases; they provide reporters with a wealth of sports news material. Unlike releases, which one reporter explained, 'Maybe

10 per cent of the press releases we get are followed up on', conferences more often constitute a significant news event – sure to garner lots of media attention. The main reason for the *prima facie* news value of conferences lies in the fact that they're held only to announce a significant event, such as a major player trade or signing. This underscores the special nature of the conference as a channel through which reporters can expect especially newsworthy material to flow. Indeed, by tapping into this rich news source, sports reporters often access enough information to generate one and sometimes several news items from a single conference. News conferences arranged by major commercial sports organizations thus provide reporters with a wealth of easily accessible and newsworthy material that moves them one step closer to fulfilling their daily obligation to generate sports news.

Besides news releases and conferences, Bytown's commercial sports organizations also facilitate newswork by providing reporters with various facilities and services at event venues and their corporate offices. The Badgers, Hornets, and Flames all subsidise sports newswork in this manner. Their corporate offices, for instance, have furnished meeting rooms where news conferences are held; these are equipped with all the amenities necessary to accommodate the various media (print, radio, and television), such as electrical outlets, telephones, and so on. Event venues have press boxes fully equipped with video equipment for instant video replays; television monitors that enable reporters to stay on top of other major sports events occurring at the same time as the event they are covering; electrical outlets and telephone jacks, enabling reporters to hook up lap top computers, faxes, and modems – 'the tools of the trade', as one reporter put it. One service provided by both the Flames and Hornets to reporters in the press box is 'runners', who are similar to parliamentary pages or newspaper copy chasers. They distribute information to the press box, mostly game statistics, but also scores and details from the other games around the league that night. For example, reporters covering the Flames' home football games regularly receive updated game statistics, delivered to them in the press box at the end of each quarter. This service provides reporters with the statistical details they need to write their news items as the game progresses and so save scarce time. Yet another service provided by commercial sports organizations is pre-game meals for reporters. The two commercial sports organizations that I closely studied provide reporters with catered meals prior to each home game for a minimal fee ($5 charge by the Hornets) or no fee at all (Flames). This is an especially useful service because, without having to stop for a meal, reporters can drive directly to the event venue, arriving well before the scheduled start of the game, so enabling reporters to do some of the 'legwork' necessary to cover a major league sports event (like pre-game interviews, going over the teams' statistics, and identifying player 'match-ups' to follow during the game). Moreover, it is important for reporters to have plenty of time before a major sports event to roam about. As one beat reporter explained:

> You get some really good stuff this way. Things happen during warm-ups all the time, like a fight might break out among the players . . . And there's a lot of scuttlebutt in the hallways before a big game, you know, there's player agents, league officials, and general managers all over the place and you'd be amazed at the sort of things you overhear them talking about. Really, it's astounding the number of great stories that have been uncovered simply because a reporter overhears a conversation in a hallway before a game . . . You also get some good [information] at the meal because all these same executive types [player agents and team and league officials] are usually there too, talking business or whatever. It's also a good opportunity to corner them for an interview or at least for some comments on that night's game.

Not only are sports reporters assured of a full stomach when covering a Flames or Hornets game but, more importantly, catered meals afford them an opportunity to go about their news gathering virtually from the moment they arrive at the venue. Once again, major league sports organizations facilitate sports newswork, making it easier for reporters to do their job. It's important to briefly consider *why* commercial sports organizations go to all this trouble and expense to facilitate newswork. They do so to secure for themselves regular media coverage of their activities. Essentially, a news item in the paper is akin to publicity – 'publicity-as-news' – and the continued existence of sport as a commodified form of entertainment and spectacle depends on media publicity.

Koppett (1981) posits that when sport is participant-oriented and played simply for fun, there is no urgent need to advertise events, publicise game results, and interpret what happened – the *raison d'être* of the newspaper sports section. However, commercial spectator sport is a unique form of entertainment that draws its very life's blood from media coverage:

> No commercial sport could be economically self-supporting without some coverage from the media .... when a game or match is over, there are numerous things yet to be discussed: Statistics, important plays, records, standings, the overall performances of the players and teams, upcoming games and matches, the rest of the season, next season, and so on ... After games or matches have been played, the scores [and event highlights] become sources of entertainment for fans, regardless of whether they were able to attend the event in person.
>
> (Koppett 1981: 101)

Or, as Leonard Schecter (quoted in Smith and Valeriote 1986: 322) puts it, 'No press, no [public] interest, no baseball, no 22-year-old shit-kicker making 35 grand a year at an animal occupation'. While player wages may have risen, the need remains for major commercial spectator sports for publicity-as-news. Reporters' need for a steady flow of accessible commercial sports news material is well-served, then, by commercial sports organizations' need for publicity-as-news.

### Personal contacts on the beat

The second routine source that reporters depend on for news material is an extensive network of personal contacts (or 'inside sources'). 'The best reporters have the best sources', remarked one beat reporter, and another commented, 'These guys [beat reporters] have a lot of sources, you know, that's why they're so good, they get a lot of good information from their sources'. Athletes and coaches, team trainers and equipment managers, front office staff, player agents, league and individual team executives – are all vital contacts for *Examiner* sports reporters. These sources provide inside information on the world of commercial spectator sport. Arguably, this is the sort of titillating and sensational sports news most appealing to readers, including in-fighting among management and players; star athletes who are demanding they receive exorbitant pay increases or be traded; secret negotiations among owners to impose salary caps; and owners threatening to move their franchise to more lucrative markets in the face of poor attendance. Indeed, a metropolitan daily with a reputation for providing this sort of coverage is likely to have a devoted following of predominantly male readers, clearly making it a prime candidate for businesses looking for a publication in which to invest their advertising dollars (Wenner 1989).

I followed *Examiner* sports reporter Buck Colvin, who works the Hornets beat, through a typical work day to get a better idea of why it is so important for beat reporters to have routine sources, especially personal contacts. As Fishman (1980: 37–44) has demonstrated, studying a beat reporter's routine round of activities – what he calls a 'beat round' – reveals a great deal about the routine nature of news construction. Colvin follows the routine of activities described below on an almost daily basis throughout the Hornets' season, making highly regular, carefully scheduled rounds of the same people at the same locations. He begins a typical day around 9 a.m., first calling his sources to 'see if anything's going on', hoping to get some story ideas from them. As he puts it:

> I'm always looking to see if they've heard any *rumours* because that's how you get your best stories – someone on your beat hears something, they tell you and then you follow it up, see if there's anything to it.

Once he has completed this initial round of telephone calls, he calls the Hornets' media relations director, Gaston Rouge, to see if he has any information. Again, he is looking to find out if anything important has happened with the team since his contact the day before,

> Like, they may have been talking trade with another team the night before, or maybe someone isn't going on the road trip . . . anything that'll make a good story, you know. This is the sort of stuff I'll get from Rouge.

Ideally, Colvin is looking for information to generate two types of news item: stories and briefs. The former tend to be longer items, such as feature-length stories on star athletes, and are usually located in the first couple of pages of the sports section, while the latter are very short items, 'you know, small items, tidbits, like Joe Blow hurt his toe in practice last night and is a doubtful starter for tonight's game'. After completing this initial coverage work – 'I get an idea of what kind of a news day it's going to be' – Colvin goes to the Hornets practice facility at around 11 a.m. Typically, on-ice practice ends at 12:30 p.m., at which time the players head to the gym to continue their workout; 'that's when I start to really dig for something'. Colvin meets with the Hornets' coaches while the players are in the gym, following up on any rumours he's heard or hunches he may have.

> I'll be talking to [names the head coach] and tell him, 'Look, I heard Williams was on the trading block, what's going on with

that?' Or maybe [names player] didn't get much playing time in last night's game, I'll ask Adams or one of his assistants [assistant coaches] if he's been benched or what . . . I'm basically trying to get some stories from them, you know.

After meeting with the coaching staff, Colvin waits in the locker room for the players to return, usually at around 1 p.m. For the next hour or so, he 'hangs out' with the players, talking to different guys, always looking for a potential news item.

If I'm working on a feature that day, I do my interview for that feature; so if I'm doing a feature on, say, [names player] from 1 'til 2 o'clock I'll talk to him. But on most days I'll try to talk to at least four or five players . . .

I'm always asking them about rumours. You always gotta go to the players because the players always know what's going on. They always act like they don't know what's going on, but they always know what's happening.

Having completed his daily round of activities with the Hornets, Colvin goes to lunch and then arrives at the *Examiner's* newsroom at around 3 p.m., when he begins to make more phone calls to his sources. Throughout the day, Colvin is constantly in contact with people who may be able to supply him with potentially newsworthy information about his beat. Typically, this is information he is not able to gather on his own because, as noted earlier, it is financially impossible to do so. Colvin explains:

The *Examiner* obviously can't afford to fly me all over the continent, you know, to every NHL city to write stories about the Hornets. . . . So I always stay in contact with sportswriters in other cities because they've always got something I can use. Like, if the Pittsburgh Penguins are coming into town for a game tomorrow, I may phone Pittsburgh just to, uh, say if a guy is listed as day-to-day, I'll ask the Penguins' beat writer what the guy's injury status is, you know, that's good information because I can work it into a story . . .

I always, always, ask whether they've [other sportswriters] heard any good rumours, you know? I mean, we love rumours, so the big thing here is to get the rumours; they make for good stories.

Colvin indicated that in a typical day he'll easily make upwards of 20 to 30 phone calls. I asked him why he makes so many phone calls, if it is really necessary to spend that much of his work day on the phone.

Oh yeah! I have to do this to know what's happening on my beat, you know, to stay on top of things. If I don't, then I'll get beat on a story, and like I told you, that's my greatest fear . . . For me, meeting deadlines isn't the biggest pressure of my job. The biggest pressure is beating the competition, making sure that you're first . . . I mean, I can meet deadlines. To me, it's bigger to have the story first and the only way you're gonna do that consistently is to have good sources and stay in touch with them.

Colvin usually wraps up this news gathering component of his day around 5:30 p.m. or 6 p.m. with yet another telephone call to the Hornets' media relations people, 'just to see if there's anything else up'. Then he'll set to work on writing his news items, or complete those he has been working on over the course of the day. Otherwise, if he has to cover a Hornets game that night, Colvin will head down to the arena an hour or two before game time and spend the rest of the evening there, covering the game and writing at least one news item for the 11 p.m. deadline.

The most important thing to note about Colvin's beat round is that it enables him to complete a lot of his basic news gathering in one centralised location. Colvin only had to physically be at one place to accomplish much of his basic coverage of the beat – the rest of his news gathering was accomplished over the telephone from his home in the morning and from his desk at the *Examiner* in the late afternoon. This 'idealisation' (Fishman 1980) of Colvin's beat round shows how vital it is for reporters to have a network of sources and to constantly stay in touch with them. As Colvin suggests, without sources, sports reporters wouldn't be able to do their work:

Oh yeah, absolutely I need my sources. There's one guy on the Hornets that I talk to every day during the season; there's a couple I talk to at least three times a week; there's others I talk to once every two weeks . . . I'm looking to see if they've heard any rumours, you know, who the Hornets might be signing, whether they've heard if the Hornets are after a player from another team. You see, I get this kind of information from players because players talk to agents and agents talk to scouts, uh, there's 3 or 4 NHL scouts I talk to every day. I also talk to some other people in the [Hornets] organization every day to find out what's going on . . . Good sources are invaluable! You can't do this job unless you've got good sources.

Without the wealth of news information provided by their sources, *Examiner* sports reporters would not be able to generate the quantities of fresh news demanded of them. Moreover, having these sources centralised in some fashion – such as in a practice facility or accessible by telephone, as we saw with Colvin's beat round – goes a long way toward helping reporters cope with the pressures under which sports newswork is performed, namely, having to produce the expected quantities of fresh news under impending deadlines.

## Concluding remarks

Because it is difficult to convincingly extrapolate general trends from only one case study, I suggest that more institutional studies of the sort I present in this chapter are necessary to develop a more comprehensive theoretical understanding of the production of sports news for the daily press and its broader social implications. It has not been my intention to offer a unidimensional theory of economic rationality to account for the *Examiner's* profound commercial sports bias – market forces do not solely determine newswork routines and ultimately news content in the sports pages. Using this study as a springboard, future research should focus on the 'representational politics' of newspaper work; that is, analyses of how gender, racial, and employment status hierarchies within the sports journalism subculture impact on sports news content.

## References

Bagdikian, B. (1992) *The Media Monopoly* (4th edn.) Boston: Beacon Press.
*Canadian Advertising Rates and Data* (1994, June) 67 (6), Toronto, ON: Maclean Hunter Publishing.
Ericson, R., Baranek, P. and Chan, B.L. (1987) *Visualising Defiance: A Study of News Organization*. Toronto: University of Toronto Press.
Ericson, R., Baranek. R. and Chan, B.L. (1989) *Negotiating Control: A Study of News Sources*. Toronto: University of Toronto Press.
Fishman, M. (1980) *Manufacturing the News*. Austin, TX: University of Texas Press.
Gantz, W. (1985) Exploring the role of television in married life, *Journal of Broadcasting and Electronic Media*, 29: 263–75.
Gantz, W. and Wenner, L. (1991) Men, women, and sports: audience experiences and effects, *Journal of Broadcasting and Electronic Media*, 35: 233–43.

Gantz, W. and Wenner, L. (1995) Fanship and the television sports viewing experience, *Sociology of Sport Journal*, 12: 56–73.

Gelinas, M. and Theberge, N. (1986) A content analysis of the coverage of physical activity in two Canadian newspapers, *International Review for the Sociology of Sport*, 21: 141–51.

Giddens, A. (1982) *Sociology: A Brief but Critical Introduction*. New York: Harcourt, Brace, and Jovanovich.

Gruneau, R. and Whitson D. (1993) *Hockey Night in Canada*. Toronto: Garamond Press.

Jhally, S. (1984) The spectacle of accumulation: material and cultural factors in the evolution of the sports/media complex, *Insurgent Sociologist*, 12(33): 41–57.

Koppett, L. (1981) *Sports Illusion, Sports Reality*. Boston: Houghton Mifflin.

Lever, J. and Wheeler, S. (1984) The Chicago Tribune Sports Page, 1900–1975, *Sociology of Sport Journal*, 1: 299–313.

Parente, D. (1977) The interdependence of sports and television, *Journal of Communication*, 27(3): 131–35.

Rintala, J and Birrell, S. (1984) Fair treatment for the active female: a content analysis of young athlete magazine, *Sociology of Sport Journal*, 1(3): 231–50.

Scanlon, T.J. (1970) *Sports in the Daily Press in Canada*. Unpublished report for the Directorate of Fitness and Amateur Sport, Department of National Health and Welfare.

Sigal, L. (1973) *Reporters and Officials*. Lexington, MA: Heath.

Smith, G. and Valeriote, T. (1986) Ethics in sports journalism, in E. Lapchick (ed.) *Fractured Focus*. Lexington, MA: D.C. Heath.

Sparks, R. (1992) Delivering the male: Sports, Canadian television, and the making of TSN, *Canadian Journal of Communication*, 17: 319–42.

Theberge, N. and Cronk, A. (1986) Work routines in newspaper sports departments and the coverage of women's sports, *Sociology of Sport Journal*, 3: 195–203.

Tuchman, G. (1978) *Making News*. New York: The Free Press.

Wenner, L.A. (ed.) (1989) *Media, Sports, and Society*. Thousand Oaks, CA: Sage.

# 8 | BREAD, BUTTER AND GRAVY: AN INSTITUTIONAL APPROACH TO TELEVISED SPORT PRODUCTION

## Michael Silk, Trevor Slack and John Amis

Excerpt from an article of the same name originally published in
*Culture, Sport, Society*, 2000, 3(1): 1–21.

There has been a paucity of research that has examined the processes involved in the production of televised sport. Frequently, the content of texts has been used to develop arguments about the political and economic context of media production and the labour process involved in creating televised sport (Gruneau 1989). Recent work, however, has maintained that the conditions of production cannot be inferred by merely scrutinizing the programme, that is to say the text (Johnson 1986). The use of text to draw conclusions about the labour process means that much of what has been written has been based upon a narrow understanding of how the images and discourses that are broadcast are actually constructed (Stoddart 1994). Gruneau has maintained that a textual focus is inadequate in understanding the pressures and limits that structure the production of sport for television:

> this perspective has tended to downplay analysis of the political and economic limits and pressures that operate as context for televised sport production, and it has all but ignored analysis of the actual technical and professional practices, the labour process, involved in producing sport for television. In the absence of detailed case studies in these areas, assessments of relationships between televised sport 'texts' and their 'contexts' of production have been speculative at best.
>
> (Gruneau 1989: 135)

Furthermore, the small number of studies that have addressed the labour process are unclear in terms of the agency of production crews or the ways in which their decisions and operations are structured in relation to a wider belief system. Stoddart (1994), for example, attributed a great deal of autonomy to the production crew at live golf broadcasts, suggesting that the crew's decisions were decentralized and consensual rather than imposed by an outside influence. By contrast, MacNeill's (1996) critical observations of the 1988 Calgary Winter Olympic games productions by the Canadian Television (CTV) network did not cede anywhere near as much autonomy to the production crew. She suggested that there was a degree of human agency at the production site, but qualified this statement with the recognition that the production process was highly conventionalised, following historical and cultural televisual codes of practice. Gruneau similarly concluded that the practices used in the Canadian Broadcasting Corporation's coverage of World Cup Skiing comprised a set of unconscious and informal rules and conventions picked up 'on the job' (Stoddart 1994: 82).

It is these televisual codes, or industry held values, and the ways in which they enable and constrain certain practices within the labour process, which need developing and clarifying if scholars are to gain a clearer understanding of the production of televised sport. Specifically, there is a need to determine if there are values and codes endemic to the televised sport industry. Some organizational theorists have suggested that within any industry sector there are certain values that reflect dominant opinions shared by organizations and the actors within them. These values, or 'industrial wisdom', work to inform organization members about how to act; they define the 'rules of the game' (Hellgren and Melin 1992: 180). It is necessary to explain how these codes and values are taken on board by different networks and how actors involved in the labour process in televised sport production operate in relation to them.

This chapter is a start to furthering our understanding of these issues. It presents an ethnographic study of the television production process involved in the 1995 Canada Cup of Soccer. The theoretical basis of the paper is in institutional theory, the basic tenets of which are outlined in the next section of the chapter. This is followed by details of the ethnographic approach that was used to conduct the research. The results of the study are then presented and some conclusions drawn about the ways in which institutional pressures shape the production process.

## Theoretical framework

Writers have long acknowledged that a true appreciation of how an organization operates cannot be grasped without some understanding of the wider environment (the socio-political and economic context) in which it exists. Traditionally, the focus has been on an organization's task environment. Here the emphasis is on the role that markets, resources, and competition play in determining organizational processes and outcomes (Oliver 1997: 99). Other approaches to understanding organization environment relationships have focused on the organization's institutional environment. Here a central role in shaping the processes of an organization is given to values external to the organization (Meyer and Rowan 1977). Organizations are seen as adapting to societal and sectoral values about their appropriate form and mode of operation in order to legitimate themselves. The institutionally prescribed and legitimated values serve as a constraint on an organization's operating processes . . .

Institutional theory has been used to study organizations at both the micro and macro levels (Scott 1995: 55). At the macro level, this perspective gives a central role to cultural belief systems and values that originate outside the organization, and explains how these values and beliefs become appropriate and necessary in legitimating an organization's everyday operations (DiMaggio and Powell 1983; Meyer and Rowan 1983). Others have emphasized the micro-cognitive foundation of institutional theory (Zucker 1983) . . .

Consequently, by applying an institutional approach to televised sport we believe that our understanding of the way in which the production process is shaped can be enhanced. Since the outset of televised sport studies, it has been recognized that there have been codes or values that have framed the action. Whannel's (1992) historical analysis of sport production in the UK, for example, outlined the way in which certain visual conventions became formalised. For example, the halfway line became the institutionally legitimate position from which to cover soccer on television. Similarly, Ryall (1975) noted how, during coverage of the 1974 Soccer World Cup, German television crews employed a simple model that always alternated a 'normal' (long) shot with a 'close' shot. It is important to understand how such modes of operation become immersed within a network, that is, the processes through which they become institutionalised and serve as context for structural and operational dynamics. At a macro level, normative, mimetic and coercive processes work to ensure institutionally legitimated practices are disseminated to organizations within a particular field (DiMaggio and Powell 1983) . . .

It is also important to examine operations and decision-making at the micro level to comprehend the role of institutional values in televised sport production. In an early study, Buscombe (1975) alluded to the role of the individual in relation to pre-existing frameworks and symbolic codes. In his attempt to understand televised sport, he stated that it was impossible to show a sporting event on television without a production team making decisions in accordance with an institutionally prescribed code of practice. This does not necessarily mean that decisions are made consciously. Rather, the values and codes that are perceived to be objective and external to the actors serve to provide guidance and orientation. Decisions about what to cut, whether to move the camera in or out, or which action replay to show need to be taken at speed and must therefore be made with reference to a pre-existing system of codes and values. Thus, while a particular producer or director may not have made exactly the same decision about the rejection or acceptance of a particular shot, a basic logic or structure shapes the actions of the decision-maker (Mintzberg, Raisinghani and Theoret 1976). To sum up, certain legitimated practices may be used by key decision-makers as a context to interpret the task environment of their organizations. These accepted practices, whether cultural or televisual, may not be consciously employed, but rather imbued at the subconscious level. Technical practices thus become naturalised, in the sense that the particular techniques involved are reproduced instinctively as the one and only, the 'natural' way of doing things. It does not necessarily follow that institutionally legitimated values and codes within the televised sport 'community' will be wholly appropriated within a specific firm or television network. However, individual firm or network practices are likely to be heavily influenced by industry norms and conventions. The purpose of this ethnographic study is to try and understand the way in which operating procedures are constructed, and how the meaning of the production is thus determined.

## Method

It has been argued that ethnographies of the television production process are required if the institutional pressures and the mediation of these with the dynamics of human agency that occur in sports broadcasting are to be fully uncovered (MacNeill 1996: 105). Consequently, it was decided to adopt such a research design to examine the televised production of the 1995 Canada Cup of Soccer. Throughout the tournament, the first author became immersed with the television team producing the event. Varying levels of observer status from total to participant were utilized to ensure a well-rounded account of the production process (Atkinson and Hammersley 1994). Observations were made on the conditions and means of production, as well as the 'moment of production itself, the labour in its subjective and objective aspects' (Johnson 1986: 57). This required looking specifically at the practices on which the broadcast drew and the ways in which these were reworked at the production site. The wider range of discursive materials, the ideological themes and problematics that belong to a wider political, social and economic conjuncture, as well as with the lived cultures of social groups, were also considered. A brief outline of the production site is outlined below. This is followed by a consideration of the tools used to determine the role of the micro and macro levels of institutional processes.

### Research site

The Canada Cup of Soccer was one of a series of tournaments played throughout Canada by the national team in 1995. The three-team round robin tournament was used by Chile, Canada and Northern Ireland as a warm up for upcoming World Cup and European Championship qualifying games. The production team was made up of staff from The Sports Network (TSN), a specialised sports cable television network in Canada, supplemented by a local freelance crew. This local crew had worked for TSN on previous occasions, as well as for various other television networks and stations. The main area in which the television production of the event occurred was the mobile production truck. The largest room in the truck was the real 'hub' of activity where the Director, Producer and Switcher were located. This housed four video replay monitors which supplied recordings from the Video Tape Replay (VTR) room; two screens which offered graphics and two larger screens showing the actual programme being aired and the next shot to go out on air, the preview screen. Twelve screens showing the shots being offered by the camera operators, six smaller screens holding still images which were either being shown, in preview or being edited for preview, made up the visual choices for the production team. The Associate Producer and Executive Producer slots were furnished with audio equipment which allowed the first author to listen to all that was said on the head sets. Adjoining the main production area were the audio technicians, who were on headset with the producer and director. Video playback machines and their operators, which created replays and stills for the ongoing program and for the pre-match, post-match and half-time segments, were located behind the audio room. The different cameras fed into different colour coded replay machines (Red, Blue, Green and Yellow). These replays were recorded and sent to the front of the truck where they appeared on the appropriate screen. The Director stated over a headset if the replays were required. If not, they were discarded and the machine was available for the next replay.

The second important area that influenced the production was the press centre inside the stadium. This housed the two main cameras, the commentators and the television suite. In front of the two commentators was a screen showing the image currently on air. The television suite had facilities for all forms of media and was the location for the production meetings. The two main cameras (Camera One and Camera Two) were also positioned here. In all, ten cameras were used for the productions. The floor director was responsible for the rest of the outside areas and the television suite during the pre-match, post-game and half-time segments. Two permanent cameras and a mobile camera were operating on the pitch side. Various crew members were stationed here, including runners, audio technicians and the remaining camera operators. This was also where the communication took place between the crew and the game officials. A mobile camera was placed on the touchline and cameras were high above ground level on the west and south sides of the stadium. In addition, one camera was placed inside each goal. The research site was set up before the first game of the tournament and the temporary facilities dismantled at the end of the final match. In all, four games were produced, two of which were 'live' transmissions and two delayed transmissions. The two games that were not seen live in Canada were broadcast live in Chile, Northern Ireland and other parts of the world. They were therefore produced by the team as if they were live TSN telecasts.

### Observations and content analysis

Observations were focused upon the decision-making processes, negotiations over the content of the broadcasts, the pre-production meetings, the relations between production personnel, the role of human agency and the structure and work routines of the crew. During each broadcast, observations were made from the production truck . . . complemented by an analysis of various historical and contemporary documents to increase understanding of the historical, political, cultural and economic dimensions of the broadcasts. Formal and informal interviews were conducted with key informants at the production site. These included the Director, the Producer, and so forth. Further interviews were carried out with the other members of the crew, such as camera operators, and runners, thus further increasing our understanding of the complex dynamics of production, and of professional codes and ideologies.

The telecasts that went to air were also analysed, so allowing for the key themes and story lines to be easily identified. The interview, observation and textual data were analysed in a number of ways. Common themes were identified and comparisons between the mainstream literature and the theoretical base used in this study were undertaken. These preliminary findings were used as a base for a second period of data collection at the TSN Head office in Toronto. The purposes of this visit were twofold. First, we wanted to fill in gaps in our data that emerged as preliminary analysis was carried out. Second, we wanted to gain a greater understanding of the ways in which institution values and beliefs, the 'industrial wisdom', shaped the production process. Consequently, a further week was spent observing key actors in this production process. This was interspersed with interviews with individuals considered vital to the process. From the observations, interviews and document analyses it became clear that there was a network-held belief system of the 'right way to cover soccer'. Further, this belief system could be traced to an institutionally held, 'legitimate' set of values and beliefs, an industry practice, which served to shape the labour processes of the production team. The following section is thus focused upon the legitimate model of soccer production, the agency at the site of production in terms of each network actor's own desires and choices, and the ways in which the process operated in relation to the fact that the broadcast was produced for a global (as opposed to a completely national) audience.

## Results and discussion

Soccer production in Europe has advanced quickly largely due to the groundbreaking deal in 1992 between the English Football Association and satellite television company BSkyB (Williams 1994). As a consequence of this agreement, the traditional BBC coverage was superseded by more modern broadcasts that utilized new technology and started to bring the principles of market competition into the production. The BSkyB deal revitalised commercial interest in live soccer and created a determining influence over the production of top-level sport. This modernisation can be seen in the manifestations of a 'commercially legitimate' way to cover sport on television. Heavily influenced by a North American style, this commercial approach enhances the excitement/spectacle values of the production. Emphases are determined by the 'cutting and editing of the match, use of camera positions, angle and focus, use of slow motion, use of graphics, interviews and expert analysis' (Maguire 1993: 39–40). This fast-paced approach to televised sport production can be argued to have developed at the American network, ABC, by Roone Arledge, who virtually invented the high production values and technical capabilities of sport broadcasting (Pierce 1995). The marriage of the legacy of Arledge to the corporate values of key players like Rupert Murdoch has 'modernised' televised sport production through the world. Murdoch's television empire consists of BSkyB in Europe, the Fox network in Australia and North America and Star television in Asia. David Hill, now president of Fox Sports (US), has been a key player in ensuring these commercial values are established in televised sport production. Murdoch brought Hill from Australia to Europe to produce Premier League soccer on Sky Sports. Under Hill, according to Vic Wakeling, the head of Sky Sports UK, the Sky philosophy became 'providing a show that will get ratings up so Ford and (other sponsors) will keep their interest in us' (quoted in Silk 1994). These values and labour practices were carried across the Atlantic by Hill when he became president of Fox. Consequently, as Hill explained: 'Fox will have the most replay machines, the slickest graphics, the most efficient production assistants; 12 cameras at every game. In short, biggest, best, most. Each Fox game will have a super-slomo on site and a revolutionary sound system which would bring the bangs, grunts, and the roar of live collisions . . . into every living room' (Drury 1994: 67). Such commercial practices are found across the globe in televised sport production to create a unique and dramatic spectacle (Morris and

Nydahl 1985). Under intense competition and in an attempt to appeal to an audience laden with numerous consumption choices, televised sport has been transformed to include (post)modern representational techniques that emphasise the excitement of the game. The production crew and TSN head office staff involved in this research saw this model as the legitimate and appropriate way to cover sport on television. It will be shown, at least in the confines of the current study, how this model is perceived to be legitimate and how it became appropriated at TSN, contextualising the macro-cognitive level of operations. Specifically, while individual networks operate within their own cultural, political, economic and social landscape, there was a 'new' or 'modern' industry wisdom which framed production decisions and operations in TSN's representation of the Canada Cup of Soccer.

The Canada Cup of Soccer broadcasts were seen by the crew as being a fairly simple process. The crew arrived at the stadium approximately six hours before game time. In addition to putting the final touches to the pre-game show, scripts were finalised, camera operators briefed and rehearsals conducted. During this pre-broadcast time there was considerable interaction amongst the TSN crew. Meetings were held with the local crew where the Director gave feedback on the previous telecasts ('get closer, get more faces guys') and informed camera operators of the players being focused upon in the build-up to the game. The general theme and final script for the day were also determined at this time. During the broadcast, interaction continued amongst the TSN personnel, especially between the Director, camera operators, commentators and audio technicians. From the bank of screens in front of the Director, the Switcher was told by the Director which image to put on air including graphics and archive footage. The Producer offered input ('take a look at camera 2, there's good action in the shot'), yet during the live telecast, the Director was in sole charge. The Producer oversaw the replays and interacted frequently with the VTR operators. During the game segments, there was one guiding convention, as the Director noted when interviewed:

> What's most important is that you take the shot where the action is, that's most important, getting fancy is always the gravy, it's like you've got the bread and butter shot is the guy with the ball, that's your responsibility to the audience, to show them. Anything on top of that is making it fancy, it's the gravy . . .

The non-game segments (pre-game, post-game and half-time) had a similar pattern. At half-time the Director focused on a player who had played a key role during the first half. This was usually a player who had been showcased in the pre-game segment. Following a commercial, the expert announcer offered his selection of highlights and commented on the contribution of those singled out by the production team. This involved normally three slow motion replays of the key incidents. Following another commercial or intermission, the crew came back with a shot of the stadium, a graphic of the score, followed by a close-up of the referee and the beginning of the second half. The post-game wrap was also simple and brief. When the final whistle was blown, the Director chose shots of the game's key performers again, often the designated players from the pre-game and half-time segments. For example, following game one, seven of the 14 post-game shots were of two players focused on during the pre-game segment. A further element of the post-game segment was to show the 'TSN turning point'. This conveys the production team's view of the game's key incident, as well as offering an opportunity to bring commercial interests into the broadcast. In addition, the post-game discussion was used as a platform to promote future TSN presentations.

These guiding conventions of coverage can be defined as bread, butter and gravy. The games were covered by the two main cameras located in the press suite, cameras one and two, which provided 'the bread and butter shots'. Whenever possible, usually during a break in the action for a throw in, corner or free-kick, the Director used the additional cameras to get as close as possible to a particular player, preferably one focused upon in the pre-game story-line. He would then show a replay or a chryon (graphic). In the Director's own words, this was an attempt to make the production 'look fancy'. In other words, these are the 'gravy' shots that add value. These practices were enhanced when there was an incident such as a goal. At these longer breaks in the play more gravy practices were employed. Typically, the goal scoring 'hero' was focused upon, followed by replays of the goal from different angles, normally three owing to the number of VTR machines available in the production truck. This was followed by a shot of the fans and then the celebrating players.

The production team was unified in its assertion that it employed such practices in an attempt to satisfy the audience commodity (Jhally 1989). The TSN crew gave a great deal of credit to their audience and were determined to produce an output that was not only suitable but would also entertain. Owing to a reliance on a textual perspective, scholars have tended to see televised sport as a unidirectional process that involves a production crew choosing images and discourses for consumption by the masses (Blain, Boyle and O'Donnell 1993). Rather than seeing the audience as a mass of cultural dupes who would accept any (symbolic) images and discourses, the TSN team saw the audience as creative, active and skilled consumers and knowledgeable sports fans. This in itself provided an external pressure on the production team that was concerned to produce the best broadcast that they possibly could for the viewers. Like Stoddart (1994), we suggest that craft pride is an important part of televised sport production, a notion that has received little consideration in the mainstream literature. Rather than the everyday operations of the crew being imposed from above, the production team's decisions appeared to be decentralized. That is, there were no direct orders from senior management to try to satisfy the audience commodity. Instead, such practices were the values held as part of the everyday operation of televised sport production by the crew. Of central concern to this chapter is whether these values are institutionalised within the televised sport industry as conventional wisdom and the specific effect that they have on production operations . . .

To understand how these pressures limited agency in the labour process at the Canada Cup of Soccer, we need to go back to the 1994 World Cup hosted by the United States. Although soccer has been covered on television in Europe for many years (the BBC, for example, has broadcast live games since the 1920s), live soccer production in North America is a relatively recent phenomenon. This is particularly true in Canada. The 1994 World Cup hosted by the USA, therefore, was anticipated by staff at TSN with great uncertainty. Consequently, it represented an excellent stage at which to watch mimetic processes at work. DiMaggio and Powell (1983: 149) suggested that firms model themselves on others in their field that are perceived to be successful and legitimate. Before the 1994 World Cup finals a number of teams visited Canada to train and play warm-up games. The Sports Network was responsible for providing coverage for these games. The Network therefore had to quickly learn how to cover live soccer. The Executive Producer decided the best way to do this was to copy the accepted European model of coverage. This caused a change in the labour process of soccer production, a change initiated by the Executive Producer after viewing the style used by European networks in their soccer coverage, who stated:

Before the World Cup, we had a number of European countries over here for training and we were responsible for providing the feed. I've been lucky enough to have been exposed to several Olympic Games where the Olympic organisers have said they'll bring you the best in the world in terms of coverage. So we had the Germans over to show us how they'd like to have us cover it. I learned a lot from that and we changed our coverage. The Germans gave us some ideas so we started covering it like a soccer game, not a hockey game. Our camera positions were fairly conservative, but now we put cameras down on field level at the 16-metre mark. I think now we show the speed and finesse of the game better.

These altered production practices were passed down to the Canada Cup of Soccer Director and Producer in formal production meetings before the 1994 World Cup. Specifically, the Director explained how the Executive Producer had replicated the German and Italian net-works' practices of using more cameras, tighter action and more cuts, and how he had instructed the production team to follow this model . . . As a result of the 1994 World Cup warm up games, the Executive Producer at TSN became exposed to the dominant European model of soccer coverage – the legitimate industry model. We contend that the values that operated as context for the Canada Cup productions had a significant impact on the actions of the production team. These values quickly became institutionalised within TSN and are now the standard TSN approach to producing soccer broadcasts. The Executive Producer's directives were clearly evident at the Canada Cup of Soccer. In other words, the bread, butter and gravy philosophy that was modelled on the European conventions was directly appropriated in the broadcast as the conventions of coverage at the Canada Cup. Thus, the TSN crew's operations at the Canada Cup of Soccer appeared to have been shaped subconsciously (Buscombe 1975: 24) at the cognitive level by an institutionalised set of values and beliefs, the industrial wisdom . . .

The operational logistics of televised sport production make it impossible for a single network to provide every single member of staff for every sport it covers in the broadcast day. While much of this is offset from buying other firms' productions, freelancers make up a significant proportion of production personnel (Tunstall 1993). Indeed, TSN is bound by its licensing arrangements with the policy body, the Canadian Radio and Telecommunications Council (CRTC), to use freelance operators (CRTC 1984). The Associate Producer for the Canada Cup, a freelance operator, explained that wherever she worked, the guiding convention for an Associate Producer was the same: to produce a fast paced opening and story-line that set up the broadcast. In addition, she explained that many of the practices and conventions amongst firms had to be similar owing to technical arrangements. Most networks hire broadcast facilities such as the production trucks which limit the range of operations at a live sporting event. At the Canada Cup, this consisted of camera operators and other technical and manual workers. The Floor Director, the leader of the local crew, explained that they had all worked for different networks in the past and had also done a number of broadcasts for TSN. He explained that each Director wanted something a little bit different and that it was his job to inform his crew of these differences. These individuals apart, the Floor Director outlined how the crew's job is generally the same whoever they are working for, that is 'employing routine practices of television production in order to produce a tight and seamless show'. The local crew and the freelance operator were therefore exposed to a degree of 'on the job socialisation' depending on the individual Director, yet were fully aware of the normative industry values and procedures required for producing good television.

These external production values, legitimised as industrial wisdom in the new competitive global televised sport marketplace, have become part of TSN's internal values for producing soccer. The Director summed up how a more modern, 'younger' style from Europe had become appropriated into the labour process at TSN. Specifically, she stated that TSN's productions were now:

> a little more funky; so we get more cameras, we brought them lower, so it is a much young, a much faster and younger show, I think the younger viewer likes it, but the traditionalist doesn't as it has too many cuts. I know I have to keep the young audience who grew up on video games, channel surfing and the go, go, go and all those flashes channel surfing culture. I'm sure if you just stayed on camera two the whole game, back and forth, they'd be bored.

Through macro-institutional processes such as the filtering of personnel, a cognitive employment base and mimetic pressures from the 1994 World Cup, the industrial wisdom within the field of televised sport production became institutionalised at TSN and operated as context for the Canada Cup of Soccer productions. At the operational level, micro-cognitive institutional processes appeared to act as a reference system for the crew. That is, the TSN crew drew upon the competitive marketplace at the Canada Cup of Soccer. Specifically, the everyday operations and production decisions at TSN appear to have strong cognitive roots that are shaped by how actors categorise and make sense of their organizational world at the same time as being embedded in complex relational networks between firms.

Codes of practice or institutionalised values within the televised sport industry acted as a reference system for actors in production decisions and operations at the Canada Cup of Soccer. That is, a cognitive-belief system acted as context for the crew. The local crew, the freelance Associate Producer and the TSN team all appeared to use a mental model in their everyday production operations. A basic industry logic, one embedded through institutional processes at the TSN network, underlay the choice of discourses and images for production. This 'institutional wisdom', professional ideology or code may not have been made consciously. Such decisions need to be taken at speed and are, therefore, made against a subconscious frame of reference. For example, the Director was usually faced with a choice of ten live shots, together with options from the Replay Operator, the Graphics Operator and the archive. Over the course of the three telecasts over 1500 shots were chosen for broadcast from over 15,000 possible choices. In addition to these choices being offered by the different cameras, replays, archive footage, graphics, statistics and different audio channels were available for the Director. Such an immense task would not have been possible without reference to a subconscious or cognitive 'system', code or industrial wisdom. It thus appears that there are shared assumptions among television directors regarding, for example, the type of shot to choose after a goal has been scored. These assumptions operate as context for actors in their production operations and decision-making. These shared mental representations, language and other cognitive concepts served as a context for camera operators concerning what to shoot and for production personnel in the acceptance or rejection of images and discourses. These data suggest that the institutional values have become part of the cultural belief system of the production team and that collective representations were used to solve everyday decisions. This belief system has thus become ingrained at TSN as a part of their everyday production decisions and operations . . .

However, while technical and manual practices and decisions about shot rejection or acceptance appear to be taken in accordance with an accepted industrial wisdom, it is important to qualify the data. Labour practices may operate under a code, but it should not be overlooked that different networks will attempt to target their broadcasts to different audiences or try to satisfy an advertiser's or sponsor's aim. Television Sport Network's 'strategic choices' were contested at the site of production. While the crew employed an industry model, they also attempted to attend to the environmental conditions of production, specifically the cultural conditions of the broadcasts. The crew initially attempted to produce a broadcast suitable for Canadian viewers that involved a 'Canadianising' of key soccer players in the national team. However, this strategy was soon ceded to both the generic industry model and the logic of capital accumulation.

It was suggested at the outset that institutional belief systems and values would be structured by wider societal structures such as the state (Scott 1995: 41). The labour process at the Canada Cup of Soccer was subject to these external forces. As a state institution, the CRTC directly affected the broadcast and the style in which it was produced. The CRTC regulates TSN in a number of ways. Most significantly, the CRTC licence for TSN is granted under the conditions that the licensee (TSN) cover sports with relatively narrow broadcast appeal and that it commits itself to Canadian programming (CRTC 1984). To some extent these coercive forces reduce the economic pressure on the network. The network has to broadcast programmes of narrow appeal so it does not directly compete with 'conventional' television programming. Further, the style of Canadian programming is directly influenced by the 1991 Broadcasting Act, which stipulates that the Canadian broadcasting style is public property and should 'serve to safeguard, enrich and strengthen the cultural, political, social and economic fabric of Canada' (Broadcasting Act 1991: 4).

The Executive Producer explained that if it was not for such regulations he would broadcast more 'big money' sports like gridiron football and basketball. Furthermore, the CRTC explicitly states that 70 per cent of total programme expenditure should be on the acquisition of or investment in Canadian programming, resulting in a minimum quota of 50 per cent Canadian content over a 24-hour broadcast day. The Executive Producer explained that soccer would probably not even be covered on TSN were it not for these political directives. Therefore, the institutionalised values and practices that TSN utilized to produce the Canada Cup of Soccer were heavily influenced by the CRTC and the 1991 Broadcasting Act. For the crew this meant that the institutionalised micro-cognitive value system which they utilised for production operated in relation to distinct cultural and structural influences . . .

It is important, though, to attend to Stoddart's (1994) warning that the television system is not a single, homogenized mass . . . Recent scholarly attention has been given to the production of media forms, global homogeneity and the conflict with the reinvention and rearticulation of national and local cultures and identities (Rowe, Lawrence, Miller and McKay 1994; Morley and Robins 1995). The televised sport industry operates in a global sphere and the production team at TSN was fully aware that its broadcasts were being carried on a world feed. However, it is logical to expect a cultural production in Canada to appeal to Canadians and to conform to state and other structural influences by choosing images and discourses for broadcast that appeal to this audience. Clearly, not all telecasting of sports will be the same. However, this was always a point of conflict for a crew that was also trying to appeal to their global viewers. Due to the context of the world feed, the TSN crew felt it their responsibility to cut out the majority of their cultural content for the broadcast, notably the promotion of Team Canada. The perceived effect of localised consumption meant that the crew was involved in the telling of stories that to some degree attempted to promote Canadian identity. At the same time, the world feed negotiated and contested any attempt on behalf of the crew to promote Canadian ideologies. Rather, the ideology of the sponsor and of capital accumulation was perceived as more important to the network . . .

We can ascertain from this study that the TSN crew believed that there was a legitimate way within the televised sport field to cover soccer. Further, this institutionalised industrial wisdom operated on the labour process of the Canada Cup of Soccer at the micro-cognitive level of production. Despite this legitimated model, structural and cultural preferences were exerted on TSN and the Canada Cup of Soccer productions, yet these were ceded in favour of creating a product that would be legitimate for a world-wide audience . . .

## Conclusion

An institutional perspective ultimately calls into question the degree of human agency that previous accounts of televised sport production have afforded production crews (Gruneau 1989; Stoddart 1994). It was clear that TSN was also subject to macro institutional processes and that these served as a context for the values/structure relationship at the network . . . This is not to deny that the crew had an amount of craft pride, rather their creativity or agency took place within clearly defined boundaries, an industry prescribed and legitimated model. The network did have a number of strategic choices that were based on political, cultural, economic and social imperatives. However, due to forces from beyond the national state level, the crew's preferred cultural (re)presentations were somewhat taken off the menu and a broadcast that conformed to globally legitimated values within the industry was produced. That is, the televised soccer production analysed operated in a context in which decisions are based on industry held beliefs about the competitive industry environment and the logic of capital accumulation . . . We can conclude, however, 'that the labour process is a site of struggle, resistance and accommodation in which media personnel are able to borrow the ideological and material resources at *hand* to enable the production of privileged meaning and the accumulation of economic capital' (emphasis in the original – MacNeill 1996: 122). By further modifying critical approaches to the study of the labour process and by refining methodologies appropriate for analysis of production, greater understanding can be gained regarding the effect of the institutional context on televised sport broadcasts.

## References

Atkinson, P. and Hammersley, M. (1994) Ethnography and participant observations, in N. Denzin and L. Guba (eds) *Handbook of Qualitative Research*. Thousand Oaks, CA: Sage Publications.

Blain, N., Boyle, R. and O'Donnell, H. (1993) *Sport and National Identity in the European Media*. Leicester: Leicester University Press.

*Broadcasting Act* (1991) *Statutes of Canada 1991*. Ottawa: Minister of Supply and Services.

Buscombe, E. (1975) Cultural and televisual codes in two title sequences, in E. Buscombe (ed.) *Football on Television*, BFI Monograph, 4: 35–7.

CRTC (1984) *Decision 84–339*. Ottawa (2 April).

DiMaggio, P. and Powell, W. (1983) The iron cage revisited: institutional isomorphism and collective rationality in organisational fields, *American Sociological Review*, 48: 7–160.

Drury, B. (1994) Barbarians in the booth: football on Fox, *Men's Journal*, 13 (7): 67.

Gruneau, R. (1989) Making spectacle: a case study in televised sport production, in L.A. Wenner (ed.) *Media, Sports and Society*. Newbury Park, CA: Sage.

Hellgren, B. and Melin, L. (1992) Business systems, industrial wisdom and corporate strategies, in R. Whitley (ed.) *European Business Systems: Firms and Markets in their National Contexts*. London: Sage.

Johnson, R. (1986) What is Cultural Studies Anyway?, *Social Text*, 16: 38–80.

Jhally, S. (1989) Cultural studies and the sport/media complex, in L.A. Wenner (ed.) *Media, Sports and Society*. Newbury Park, CA: Sage.

MacNeill, M. (1996) Networks: producing Olympic ice hockey for a national television audience, *Sociology of Sport Journal*, 13: 103–24.

Maguire, J. (1993) Globalization, sport development, and the media/sport production complex, *Sport Science Review*, 2: 29–42.

Meyer, J. and Rowan, B. (1977) Institutional organisations: formal structure as myth and ceremony, *American Journal of Sociology*, 83: 340–63.

Meyer, J. and Rowan, B. (1983) Institutional organisations, in J. Meyer and W. Seen (eds) *Organisational Environments*. Beverly Hills: Sage.

Mintzberg, H., Raisinghani, D. and Theoret, A. (1976) The structure of 'unstructured' decision processes, *Administrative Science Quarterly*, 21: 246–74.

Morley, D. and Robins, K. (1995) *Spaces of Identity: Global Media, Electronic Landscapes and Cultural Boundaries*. London: Routledge.

Morris, B. and Nydahl, J. (1985) Sports spectacle as drama: image, language and technology, *Journal of Popular Culture*, 18 (4): 101–10.

Oliver, C. (1997) The influence of institutional and task environment relationships on organizational performance: the Canadian construction industry, *Journal of Management Studies*, 34: 99.

Pierce, G. (1995) Master of the universe, *GQ, Special Edition: The Future of Sports*, 180–7.

Rowe, D., Lawrence, G., Miller, T. and Mackay, J. (1994) Global sport: core concern and peripheral vision, *Media, Culture & Society*, 16: 661–75.

Ryall, T. (1975) Visual style in Scotland vs Yugoslavia, in E. Buscombe (ed.) *Football on Television*, BFI Monograph, 4: 35–7.

Scott, R. (1995) *Institutions and Organisations*. Thousand Oaks, CA: Sage.

Silk, M. (1994) 'If There's an Atmosphere Out There We'll Find it': A Case Study of Satellite Television Sports Production. Unpublished thesis, West Sussex Institute.

Stoddart, B. (1994) Sport, television, interpretation and practices reconsidered: televised sport and analytical orthodoxies, *Journal of Sport and Social Issues*, 18: 76–88.

Tunstall, J. (1993) *Television Producers*. London: Routledge.

Whannel, G. (1992) *Fields in Vision: TV Sport and Cultural Transformation*. London: Routledge.

Williams, J. (1994) The local and the global in English soccer and the rise of satellite television, *Sociology of Sport Journal*, 11: 376–97.

Zucker, L. (1983) Postcript: microfoundations of institutional thought, in P. DiMaggio and W. Powell (eds) *The New Institutionalism in Organizational Analysis*. Chicago: University of Chicago Press.

# 9

# MEGA-EVENTS AND MEDIA CULTURE: SPORT AND THE OLYMPICS

## Maurice Roche

Excerpt from *Mega-Events and Modernity: Olympics and Expos in the Growth of Global Culture*. London and New York, Routledge, 2000, Chapter 6: 159–93.

### Olympics and the media

From the 1890s the Olympic movement and the amateur and professional sports movements more generally, were intimately connected with the development of various forms of the press and journalism. This ranged from the elite to the mass press, from literate text-dominated formats to visual photographic formats, from the national to the local press, from the noticeboard/record-keeping function to the event-witness function, and from the generalist press to the sport specialist press. As far as the Olympic movement goes, regarding the revival of the Olympic Games in Athens in 1896 Georgiadis (1996: 12) reports that, at the time, 'the support by the [Greek] press was universal'. Although at times national presses have acted as fora for debate and critique in relation to the politics of hosting expos and Olympics, more often than not they have maintained this affirmative version of the 'Greek chorus' tradition in relation to mega-events. On the other hand, they rarely went to the lengths of being so supportive of these great events as to effectively finance them, or at least not to the extent that television currently does in relation to the Olympics.

The capacity of radio to enable a mass nationwide listening audience to imagine that they are present at a dramatic and important 'live' event received an early demonstration in the USA through broadcasts of the 1932 Los Angeles Olympics. In Britain, in this period, the BBC began to build its central role in British national elite and popular culture in part through its radio broadcasting of major national sport events. The radio broadcasts of other big international sport events in the 1930s, such as heavyweight championship boxing matches between the American Joe Louis and the German Max Schmelling, helped to attest to the dramatic power and international scope of the medium of radio. This involvement of the media in major sport and other cultural events was supplemented by the distribution of news films of such events within the mass market for Hollywood films which had grown up in the 1930s.

These representations of major sport events helped prepare national publics in Western countries for the media and propaganda event of the 1936 Berlin Olympics. This was the first Olympic Games to be radio broadcast 'to the world' as a 'live' event at which an international audience would feel as if they were 'present' as witnesses. It attracted an unprecedented scale of coverage in the press of participating countries and it was immortalised in the visual grammar of Nazi propaganda in Leni Reifenstahl's legendary film 'Olympia'. It was also the first major sport event to be televised, albeit on an experimental basis, via a limited local cable system only available in the city of Berlin. Embryonic elements of the television culture of the post-war period, a mass popular culture that was to impact in different ways on the mega-event genres of expos and Olympics and on their international public cultural roles, were thus already visible in the mega-events of the late 1930s. Specifically, they were visible in the 1936 Berlin Olympics and the 1939 New York expo. We can now turn to consider the nature and role of mega-events, particularly sport and Olympic mega-events in the post-war television era, and particularly in the contemporary late twentieth-century period . . .

### Mega-events, 'media events' and sport: Elihu Katz and Daniel Dayan

Mega-events such as the Olympic Games undoubtedly qualify as examples of 'media-events'. Television organisations typically consider that this kind of event requires a special type of production treatment beyond the ordinary genres and categories of 'news' and 'entertainment'. A wide range of types of event, in addition to the great cultural, commercial and sporting events we have referred to as mega-events, also go beyond news and entertainment, and also can be said to 'make history'. Media-event analysis is, thus, concerned with the media's 'witness-to-history' role in relation to what Dayan and Katz (1992) typify as 'coronations, contests and conquests'. Such 'history-making' events can be exemplified by, in recent times, the death and funeral of Princess Diana, and generally by such things as great state ceremonies (such as Royal Weddings, state funerals, etc.), political/diplomatic events (such as the Pope's first visit to communist Poland, President Sadat's visit to Israel, etc.), and great technological events (such as the first Moon landing). The theoretical frame of reference media-event analysts tend to use to interpret and explain these sorts of events and their social and political effects is one heavily angled towards neo-Durkheimian sociological theory. This is particularly concerned to identify and understand the periodic repro-duction of social integration and solidarity in modern societies through public events (e.g. public ceremonies, rituals and festivities, etc.), regarded forms of (secular) 'civil religiosity' and celebrations of (secular) 'sacred' values and symbols (e.g. Rothenbuhler 1988). This has undoubtedly produced some rich and interesting research into the general culture and, in particular the political culture, of contemporary media-dominated societies. However, the generally functionalist cast of this perspective is open to criticism.[1] Later, in a case study of the 1988 Seoul Olympics as a media event, we will consider the need to counterweight this functionalist emphasis by building in political and critical dimensions to the media-event analytic perspective.

A criterion for qualifying as a media event is that people in many nations feel obliged to watch and feel privileged to be able to witness the event. Typically, these events are viewed in a ceremonial (ritualistic/ civil religious) frame of reference. Where appropriate this is also often a festive or celebratory attitude and viewers typically make efforts to share their viewing with other people and/or to discuss their experience of the event and its significance with other people. In other words, viewers are 'mobilised' by the event. Media researchers in this field argue that people are not 'couch potatoes' in relation to media events. Rather they are typically active in response to the event coverage and experience participation of the event in a way which would not be true for routine TV viewing.

Some key empirical characteristics of media events (Dayan and Katz 1992) are that they are broadcast live, usually sponsored by an agency independent of the broadcasters, marked with a clear beginning and ending that interrupts normal social routines, feature heroic personalities, are highly dramatic or richly symbolic, and they are accompanied by social norms which relate to their special character (obligatory viewing, social viewing, etc.). It is reasonable and useful to conceptualise this type of response to a mega-event – the response of media viewers of the event – as a particular type of popular/citizen mobilization. This is one in which collective ceremonial and, here, festive characteristics of the event itself are participated in by being reproduced in miniature in the ceremonial, festive and social character of home-based viewing. Evidently, mass-media viewing of an event is not the same as 'being there', and the presentational and textual structures of event programming involve what Dayan and Katz (1992) refer to as 'an aesthetics of compensation'. This 'compensates' the viewer for 'not being there' by providing them with information, visual perspectives and commentary distinct from, and in many ways richer than, that available to 'in-person' participants (Dayan and Katz 1992: 92–100). Receiving this media-reworked event in the apparently 'private' sphere of the home effectively transforms the home, temporarily, into a 'public' or quasi-public sphere, and the occasion is used to remember and reaffirm collective values and symbols (127–34).

Dayan and Katz argue that for media events to occur successfully, an informal social contract and a consensus needs to have been, in some sense, 'negotiated' among three 'partners', namely the event organizers, television elites/organisations and the viewing public. We might add – 'at least three'. In this formulation, Dayan and Katz appear to ignore other important potential 'partners' such as the state (i.e. the host politicians, whether at the civic or the national level, or both), and the market (i.e. the world of corporate sponsors and advertisers willing to pay to use the event as their marketing vehicle). Given that mega-event projects occasionally fail, it is worth noting, *en passant*, that understanding the nature of the social contract among media-event partners provides us also with an understanding of the conditions of failure of event projects. Dayan and Katz (in functionalist vein) suggest that we see this as media-event 'pathology', when one or other of the partners fails to deliver on the informal social contract which usually underlies and supports media events and, we can add, mega-events more generally. Dayan and Katz's work made only brief and passing reference to mega sport events such as the Olympics. However, it has been much cited in studies of Olympic TV. As we will see, Larson and Park's (1993) study of the 1988 Seoul

Olympics uses their analysis of media events as a key point of reference even as they also argue for its limitations and for the need for an approach to the study of the Olympic movement and Olympic TV which is more developed in terms of political sociology . . .

## Sport and popular culture in modernity

Marx's legendary dictum that religion is 'the opium of the people'[2] needs to be modified to apply to the ostensibly non-religious culture of late twentieth-century society. In this culture the mass of people claim to be uninterested in religion, but they also have virtually open access to the 'opium' of a vast range of mood-altering legal and illegal drugs. In this context, perhaps it is more appropriate to observe that 'sport is the religion of the people'. That is to say, it provides apparently secular, but (from a sociological perspective) quasi-religious experiences such as those of sacredness and trans-cendence, communal ritual and symbolism, and collective drama and emotionality. Sport is an important sector of popular culture in modern societies both as a quasi-religious institution and also as an industry. Particularly in its professional, spectatorial and media-sport forms, it provides one of the few significant arenas where collective identities, from the local to the national, can be publicly symbolised and emotionally expressed (Roche 1998). Sports calendars and cycles of controlled contests provide rich experiences and forms of participa-tion for mass audiences. Major sport events have compelling dramatic, ceremonial and festive dimensions both as 'live events' in the cathedral-like structures of modern stadia and also as 'media-events', that is as a distinct, compelling and commercially important genre of television programming (Roche and Arundel 1998).

Modern sport has been increasingly globalized since the late nineteenth century, a process driven by, among other factors, the ideological agendas of European empires (Guttmann 1994), the inter-nationalist mission and values of the Olympic movement (Houlihan 1994; Hoberman 1995), the globalisation of consumer markets and the global reach of television.[3] However, it is worth noting, even allowing for the powerful influence of American commercial and media-sport models, that modern sport has a special relationship with Europe's cultures and identities. The cultural institutions of modern sport in most of its forms were largely created in Europe. This was most notably the case in nineteenth-century England where many modern games and the ideology of 'amateurism' were created, and also in late nineteenth- and early twentieth-century France where the Olympic movement and the international dimension of many sports was cultivated. The development of international sport in the late nineteenth and early twentieth centuries evidently provided a potent focus for the cultural mobilisation of the new urban middle classes and industrial working classes around the idea of nationalism and national identity. However, it also helped construct elements of a popular international awareness and helped give some form to ordinary people's conceptions of and interests in the social world beyond the nation-state . . .

## Olympic Games as media events

Understanding the Olympics as a media event, effectively as a TV genre (a 'TV show' or 'mini-series of shows'), means that, as with all media research, we need to explore the three core dimensions of all media processes and genres, namely production, content and audience reception. This is relatively readily achievable in relation to other more mainstream TV genres such as news, soap operas and more routine forms of sport coverage, which have attracted much research in all three of the core dimensions. However, perhaps understandably given the unusually large scale, complexity and rarity of the Olympic TV genre, relatively little substantial and credible research has been undertaken on it. The little research that has been conducted is relatively recent, having mainly been undertaken in the past decade and a half, beginning from studies of the Los Angeles Olympics in 1984.

The 1984 Games was a turning point in what it revealed about the extent to which the American TV networks in particular were prepared to go in bidding up the price of the rights to transmit the Olympics, in terms of income to the Olympic movement and in terms of the threat of the Games being taken over by commercialism. The controversies and public debates that this has engendered around the world concerning the meaning and future of the Olympic Games event and the movement in general has meant that both the International Olympic Committee (IOC), the TV networks and the main commercial sponsors since 1984 ought in principle to have an interest in supporting research on the Olympics as a media event, whether from the point of view of market research for sponsors or the movement, or as a contribution to wider public debates. Consistent with this, and without necessarily carrying implications for their independence and objectivity, the few empirical case studies which have been carried out usually have some connection with one or more of these interest groups. Substantial and systematic empirical media case studies were conducted on the Olympic Games of LA 1984, Seoul 1988 and Barcelona 1992. Less comprehensive and more specialist media studies were conducted on the 1994 Lillehammer Winter Olympics and the 1996 Atlanta Olympics. In addition, the IOC and UNESCO have supported research conferences and colloquies on the topic of the Olympics and the media (e.g. Jackson and McPhail 1989). Each of the main studies indicated has its strengths and weaknesses, not least in terms of their coverage of the three main dimensions of media processes noted earlier. The LA study was mainly a piece of audience research into responses to Olympic TV, while the Seoul and Barcelona studies mainly focused on analyses of the production and content dimensions of Olympic TV, although the Barcelona study also contained a limited amount of audience research. Each of them, but particularly the Seoul study, generated some interesting theoretical interpretations and reflections . . . It is necessary first to briefly review some of the main technical and financial features of the media's general involvement with contemporary Olympic Games.

### TV and the financing of the Olympics

Television income is now crucial to underpinning the huge expenditures on facilities and infrastructures which are needed for cities to be able to stage the Olympic Games in the contemporary period. Since the Los Angeles Olympics, media companies' payments for the rights to broadcast the Games have constituted at least a third of the total income of the event. In aggregate, they are usually the biggest single item as compared with the other main sources of, in descending order of magnitude, sponsorship, ticketing and merchandising. TV income has regularly grown since Los Angeles, sometimes dramatically (see Table 1). In addition, by making the Olympics as a global media event possible, the involvement of television underpins the other main income sources. That is, by carrying advertising within the 'Olympic TV show' it indirectly encourages significant income from sponsorship, for instance through the TOPS programme (i.e. the licensing of the use of the Olympic symbols in international marketing by a select group of multinational companies). And it stimulates public interest internationally and thus encourages tourists and visitors to attend the event, thereby boosting ticketing income.

*Table 1*   TV rights income for Summer Olympics 1960–2000 (in US$millions)*

| Year | City | USA TV | Euro TV |
|------|------|--------|---------|
| 1960 | Rome | 0.39 (CBS) | 0.66 (EBU) |
| 1964 | Tokyo | 1.5 (NBC) | no data |
| 1968 | Mexico City | 4.5 (ABC) | 1.0 (EBU) |
| 1972 | Munich | 12.5 (ABC) | 1.7 (EBU) |
| 1976 | Montreal | 24.5 (ABC) | 4.5 (EBU) |
| 1980 | Moscow | 72.3 (NBC) | 5.6 (EBU) |
| 1984 | Los Angeles | 225.0 (ABC) | 19.8 (EBU) |
| 1988 | Seoul | 300.0 (NBC) | 28.0 (EBU) |
| 1992 | Barcelona | 416.0 (NBC) | 90.0 (EBU) |
| 1996 | Atlanta | 456.0 (NBC) | 247.0 (EBU) |
| 2000 | Sydney | 715.0 (NBC)** | (333.0) (EBU)*** |

*Sources*: *Adapted from Spa et al. (1995: 19 – NB figures include payments for technical services and other more minor payments); also IOC (1996: 170–3), ACOG (1997: 67), Rowe (1999: 71).
** Rowe (1999: 71).
*** Author's rough estimate. The EBU's payment for the set of three Summer Games and two Winter Games 2000–2008 is $1.442 million (Culf 1996-P). Estimate is based on $221 million per Winter Games and $333 million per Summer Games.

The biggest single source of TV fee income has always been one or other of the major USA TV networks. At Los Angeles this was ABC, but since Seoul it has been NBC. However, there are signs that this situation is beginning to change. The Atlanta Olympics showed the biggest ever total TV income, which was $900 million (all figures in US dollars unless otherwise stated). It is worth noting that the local organisers (ACOG), kept $568 million of this to help cover event expenditures, while the rest went to the IOC to help fund the movement's global activities. The $900 million represented a major increase from the $635 million total TV revenue at the Barcelona Games only four years earlier. The main reason for this overall TV income growth was the massive growth in the European Broadcasting Union's (EBU's) payments, namely a rise from $66 million at Barcelona to $250 million at Atlanta (or, including additional payments for technical services, from $90 million to $255 million). In 1996 the IOC introduced a new system of broadcast rights payments, in which the rights to the set of Summer and Winter Olympic Games, from 2000 to 2008 inclusive, were sold in one package. The EBU paid $1.442 billion for this package and NBC paid $3.57 billion. This system considerably increases the power of the IOC in relation to the national Olympic committees and the local organising committees of Games events it covers.[4] . . .

## The 1988 Seoul Olympics as a media event

One of the most systematic studies of the Seoul 1988 Olympics as a media event was that of James Larson and Heung-Soo Park in association with Nancy Rivenburgh (1993, see also Rivenburgh 1992; Gratton and Taylor 1988; Seh-Jik 1991). Their main theme is that of analysing the Olympic event as a form of political communication by the Korean hosts, addressing the world about their nation through 'global' TV. More generally, they used the Seoul case study to assess Katz and Dayan's media-event analysis. The research consists of a set of interrelated studies of the production, content and impacts of the event on the Korean public, introduced by an account of post-war Korean political history. Their historical account rightly emphasises the Olympic event's role in the rapid economic modernisation of Korea in the 1980s and also, more questionably, emphasises its role in the often very fraught and conflict-ridden process of political modernisation and democratisation in the country over this time. To put the event in context it is important to briefly sketch this history. Recent revelations about Korea's politics (Higgins 1996a,b,c) and the IOC's sport politics (Hill 1992; Simson and Jennings 1992; Jennings 1996) in this period casts more political shadows around the Seoul Games than Larson and Park found in their study. Olympic Games events have always been capable of being used by national political elites to promote their own power and ideologies. This has been particularly so for authoritarian purposes, as with the Nazi's use of the 1936 Berlin Olympics, and as also happened in the 1968 Mexico City Olympics and the 1980 Moscow Olympics. The Seoul Olympics to a certain extent can be said to have fitted this pattern. After the 1952 Korean War, partition of the country and US hegemony in the South, South Korea became an undemocratic military dictatorship in 1961, and effectively remained so until at least 1988, arguably until 1993. As assumed bulwarks against communism, South Korean leaderships were supported by the USA and by the presence of the US army throughout this period. South Korean leaders were changed, if at all, by assassination and *coup d'etat*, and the political system became increasingly corrupt, with politicians accepting huge bribes in exchange for contracts from some of the country's leading multi-national companies.

The three presidents during the relevant period were Presidents Hee (1961–79), Chun (1980–8) and Roh (1988–93), all of whom were ex-generals. Chun and Roh were implicated in a massacre of protesters in 1980 after the coup which brought Chun to power. In 1996 both of them were convicted and jailed for accepting bribes throughout their careers (Chun £180 million/$280 million and Rob £240 million/$380 million). The dictator Hee had been impressed with Japan's use of the Tokyo Olympics in 1964 to mark its entry as a nation on to the world stage. He took the decision that Korea should bid for the 1988 Games in 1979 and assigned one of his secret service chiefs, Kim Un Yong, to assist with winning the bid from the IOC. Although Hee was assassinated later in 1979, Kim brought back the positive IOC decision to the new dictator Chun in 1981. In 1986 Kim led the Seoul organising committee, notably in pressuring the record price of $309 million out of NBC for the US TV rights, and in 1986 he also became a member of the IOC.

During the Games event itself, Korea's Olympic project may, ultimately, have been very popular with the huge international audience which watched it on global TV. However, like the dictators and 'strong men' who promoted it, it was not popular with the Korean people. Partly this was because Western sport culture was little known in the country in the early 1980s. Chun, therefore, created a new sport ministry to propagandise sport culture and the Olympics project and to build the necessary sport facilities and telecommunications infrastructures in Seoul. As a result Larson and Park (1993) note that, in this period building up to and actually staging two sport mega-events, the Asian Games in 1986 and the Olympics in 1988, Korea's national image was often seen as being that of a 'Sports Republic' (Grayson 1993). However, the unpopularity of Chun's dictatorship meant that a national political crisis built up in which the people (workers, students, new middle class) could exert pressure on government by threatening chaos during the Olympic event 'when the world would be watching'. This culminated in Chun's resignation shortly before the Games, with Roh taking over provisionally, getting an 'Olympic truce' with his own citizens, and offering to hold presidential elections after the Games.

This background indicates why the Korean government, its media and the Korean people were all, for various reasons, very sensitive during the Games about the information and images conveyed in the world's media, particularly US TV. Koreans could receive US TV because of the presence of the US army and its broadcasting system. Two of the main stories carried to the world by Olympic TV, and by which the Seoul Olympics are remembered by the general public probably above all else, were the disqualification of the Canadian sprint star Ben Johnson for drug use and the 'riot' which occurred during a boxing match, both of them stories with a negative slant. Larson and Park (1993), making reference also to Rivenburgh's (1992) content study, provide a substantial content analysis of those elements of the TV coverage which reflected most on Korea's national image. This included in particular the Opening Ceremony and also the boxing match incident.

The Opening Ceremony was watched by an estimated 1 billion people worldwide, double the predicted audience and a new record for Olympic TV. Korean nationalism was built into the Opening Ceremony through the use of a veteran marathon runner as the torch bearer. The runner was the legendary Korean athlete and Olympian Sohn Kee Chung. In the 1930s Korea was dominated by Japan and was part of its Empire. As an outstanding athlete, Sohn Kee Chung had only been able to compete in international sport under the Japanese flag, and at the 1936 Berlin Olympics he had become the Olympic marathon champion. Back in Korea, Chung had become a symbol of the anti-imperial, anti-Japanese struggle in this period. Generations later he remained a powerful symbol of national independence and this was the significance to be attached to his participation in the Opening Ceremony of the Seoul Olympic Games. Korean-American relations suffered somewhat during the Games because of US TV's treatment of the Opening Ceremony and of the boxing match incident. On the one hand, there was NBC's apparent act of disrespect to the Korean hosts when it edited out much of the Korean culture section of the Opening Ceremony in its broadcast to the US audience. On the other hand, there was its allegedly 'anti-Korean' coverage of the boxing incident. In this case a Korean boxer had lost a dubious decision on points. Protesting against the decision Korean officials entered the ring and assaulted the referee, and the boxer staged a one-hour 'sit in' in the ring. The officials and the boxer were clearly guilty of a breach of the rules and were subsequently banned from the sport. However, at the time, NBC's negative news coverage of the event was deemed to be intrusive and arrogant towards the host country, and led to a wave of anti-American feeling in the Korean media and public.

Larson and Park use the Seoul case to assess the overall soundness of Katz and Dayan's (1992) media-event analysis. They judge that the Seoul Olympics produced a wave of pro-Korean and anti-American nationalism together with apparently significant democratic concessions from the military dictatorship, namely post-Games presidential elections. As it happened, Chun's protégé Roh won in these elections. Larson and Park note that Katz and Dayan's view of media events was that they tended to be among other things, 'salutes to the *status quo*' and 'legitimations of elites' (quoted in Larson and Park 1993: 245). However, they feel that Korea's experience with the Olympics was 'a notable exception to the rule' and 'Political liberalization and democratization in South Korea quite literally framed or enveloped the Seoul Olympics'. The Olympic media event seemed 'to signal change . . . of the status quo' and 'delegitimation . . . of military dictatorship'. However, this judgement seems to overestimate the reality of the political changes which accompanied President Roh's successful election. As it turned out, he was effectively little more than an acceptable face of rule by the same corrupt political, economic and military establishment which had ruled Korea since the 1970s. Katz and Dayan's 'status quo' endorsing media-event analysis probably has more applicability to the Seoul case than Larson and Park suggest.

Beyond Katz and Dayan's analysis, Larson and Park argue for perspectives on media events which are more consistent with the approach taken in this chapter. Thus they propose that media-event analysis should take a long-term 'Socio-Political Process' view of media events rather than just a short-term event-centred view. In the Korean case, the Seoul Olympics was an eight-year project connected with economic and political processes and not just an isolated two-week event and TV show. Also they advocate a 'political' view of event production. That is, the Olympic Games event is effectively cultural 'theatre' in the world political system, and the Olympic movement is an important transnational actor in its own right in this system (MacAloon 1984; Hoberman 1986). Finally, given the evident and enduring inequalities in the world political system, they recommend that poor countries and world regions such as Africa should be provided with much improved access to global TV. In addition, they suggest that in the future the global cultural and political system could be interestingly represented using global TV technology to create multi-site global events, including a new multi-site version of the Olympics . . .

## Olympic movement problems: nationalism and commercialism in Olympic TV

Two criticisms are often made of the Olympic movement and its main games event in the contemporary period. The idealistic meanings and values distinctive of the Olympic sport worldview are notionally internationalist rather than nationalist. Also, while the hightide of its 'amateurist' anti-commercial vision of sport is long gone, there remains at least an idealistic indifference to commercial gain in the meaning of 'Olympism'. On both of these fronts the contemporary Olympics can be argued to have lost touch with these values and even to be subverting them. Whatever the Olympic movement can be said to have done for the cause of internationalism since their creation, the Games have, in addition, also evidently provided a platform for competitive nationalisms. This was clear, for instance, in the Greek nationalism of the 1896 event, the American-British nationalist conflicts at the 1908 event, the German nationalism of the 1936 event, and the American–USSR conflicts of the post-war period which effectively turned the 1980 and 1984 Games events into nationalistic celebrations of Soviet communism and American capitalism respectively. Such things as the IOC's formal recognition of participating athletes only as members of national teams and its rule that national flags and anthems are to be used as part of victory ceremonies underscore the nationalist reading of Olympic Games events. So, too, does the long-standing and informal but influential practice in the media of ranking and comparing national performance and success in winning medals. The advent of the Games as a global media event arguably has only served to provide a bigger stage for competitive nationalisms. Also and equally evidently, the Olympic Games, particularly in its post-amateur global media-event incarnation, and particularly since the accession of Juan Samaranch to the IOC's Presidency in 1980, has become inextricably bound up with commerce . . .

### The commercialism problem in Olympic TV

The 1984 LA Olympics represented a first wave of intensive commercialisation of an Olympic event. However, less than a decade later, the Olympic movement was already beginning to get into difficulties in its new relationship with the consumer culture world of big corporate sponsors and global TV. The Los Angeles Olympic Organising Committee was the first to demonstrate the extent to which, and the practical ways in which, the Games event could attract income from sponsors. Drawing on that experience since that time, the IOC selects a special group of major corporate sponsors for its Games events (the TOPS programme), often including global multinationals like Coca-Cola and Kodak. For a high price this group is granted the sole rights to use the Olympic symbols in advertising their products, including in particular the five rings which appear on the Olympic flag (Hill 1992). On its part, the Olympics, which Spà et al. (1995: 187) call the 'world's largest athletic and media event', needs the finance provided by this group of sponsors and (because of them) by TV if it is to be staged on an appropriate scale. On their part, the sponsors need the prestige of association with the meanings and values of the Olympic movement, and the dramatic attraction of the Olympic event to keep an edge over their competitors in the marketplace. The relation between commercial and Olympic (non-commercial) meanings and values in Olympic TV is increasingly becoming as difficult a problem for the Olympic movement and the IOC as the issue of athlete's professionalism once was. The IOC insists on keeping the Olympic stadium, and thus TV images of it, clear of explicit advertising. The result of this is that, to achieve marketing value for the Olympic symbol advertising rights they have bought at high cost, and to prevent counter-advertising by their competitors, the main sponsors have to seek as much exposure as possible through multiple advertising breaks in the TV transmission of events like the Opening Ceremony. This in turn necessarily interrupts and intrudes upon the integrity of the Olympics images and messages the IOC is seeking to present through Olympic TV (Spà et al. 1995: 204).

In the Barcelona case, the use of Olympic symbols and themes by advertisers and by sponsors (e.g. rings) and also by non-sponsors (e.g. in the verbal use of word 'Olympic'), risked hijacking the unique experience and special values associated with the Olympic Games event (193–4). Coca-Cola adverts associated their drink with 'that special Olympic feeling'. Kodak inserted its advertising images and messages during the torch ritual in the US broadcast. Sponsors' logos were superimposed on TV screens and, more insidiously, were present on athletes' clothing and equipment. 'Star' athletes who, outside of the Olympics, might appear in adverts and associate themselves with products and brands, whether they intend to or not, implicitly carry those associations with them in the context of an Olympic TV broadcast. As John Langer has observed: 'Select athletes themselves become corporate signs. They stand in for advertising' (quoted in Spà et al.

1995: 203). Spà et al. (1995) recommend that the IOC should at least seek to control the design and extent of advertising interruptions in relation to the key images and 'moments' they aim to communicate through the televising of events like the Opening Ceremony. However, they conclude that 'It is apparent from the evidence in this study that the mixing of commercial and Olympic messages' is a process at work in the contemporary Olympic movement and in Olympic TV in particular, and that this process is 'headed for increasingly murky waters' (205) . . .

## Notes

1  Katz and Dayan were by no means unaware of the gaps and problems in their analysis and of the strengths of alternative and more critical approaches, see the Appendix of Dayan and Katz (1992). For a general critical review of Katz's contribution to the study of the media's address to ritual and identity, see Curran and Liebes (1998); Liebes and Curran (1998); Eastman and Riggs (1994).

2  Excerpt from 'Toward the Critique of Hegel's Philosophy of Right', in Marx and Engels (1969: 303).

3  For relevant analyses of global television, see Barker (1997), Herman and McChesney (1997), McChesney (1998). On the media globalisation of the Olympics, see Larson and Park (1993); Spà et al. (1995). On the media globalisation of sport in this context, see Whannel (1992), Rowe et al. (1994), Sugden and Tomlinson (1998), Whitson (1998), and Rowe (1999).

4  See ACOG (1997) on television in relation to the Atlanta Games and on the event's finances. For information on broadcast rights fees for Sydney and subsequent Games, see Spà et al. (1995), IOC (1996) and Culf (1996-P). Within NBC's block deal for American broadcast rights to the 2000–2008 Winter and Summer Games, it is claimed that the prices for the rights to the three Summer Games of Sydney 2000, Athens 2004 and the 2008 event were $715 million, $793 million, and $894 million respectively (Rowe 1999: 71).

## References

ACOG (1997) *The Official Report on the Centennial 0lympic Games*, Vol. 1. Atlanta: ACOG.

Barker, C. (1997) *Global Television*. Oxford: Basil Blackwell.

Culf, A. (1996) £961m bid wins the Olympics for BBC, *Guardian*, 31 January.

Curran, J. and Liebes, T. (1998) The intellectual legacy of Elihu Katz, in T. Liebes and J. Curran (eds) *Media, Ritual and Identity*. London: Routledge.

Dayan, D. and Katz, E. (1992) *Media Events: The Live Broadcasting of History*. London: Harvard University Press.

Eastman, S. and Riggs, K. (1994) Televised sports and ritual: fan experiences, *Sociology of Sport Journal*, 11: 249–74.

Georgiadis, K. (1996) The press and the first Olympic Games in Athens, *Olympic Review* XXV–8, 11–12.

Gratton, C. and Taylor, P. (1988) The Olympic Games: An economic analysis, *Leisure Management*, 8 (3): 32–4.

Grayson, J. (1993) Sport in Korea: tradition, modernization and the politics of a newly industrialized state, in C. Binfield and J. Stevenson (eds) *Sport, Culture and Politics*. Sheffield: Sheffield Academic Press.

Guttmann, A. (1994) *Games and Empires: Modern Sports and Cultural Imperialism*. New York: Columbia University Press.

Herman, E. and McChesney, R. (1997) *The Global Media: The New Missionaries of Global Capitalism*. London: Cassell.

Higgins, A. (1996a) Humbled Roh 'ready for punishment', *Guardian*, 16 January.

Higgins, A. (1996b) Politics exploits past sins, *Guardian*, 20 January.

Higgins, A. (1996c) Graft at the heart of Seoul miracle, *Guardian*, 24 January.

Hill, C. (1992) *Olympic Politics*. Manchester: Manchester University Press.

Hoberman, J. (1986) *The Olympic Crisis: Sports, Politics and the Moral Order*. New Rochelle: Aristide D. Caratzas.

Hoberman, J. (1995) Toward a theory of Olympic internationalism, *Journal of Sport History*, 22 (1):1–37

Houlihan, B. (1994) *Sport and International Politics*. London: Harvester Wheatsheaf.

IOC (1996) *The International Olympic Committee – One Hundred Years, Vol. 3: 1972–1996*. Lausanne: IOC.

Jackson, R. and McPhail, T. (eds) (1989) *The Olympic Movement and the Mass Media*. Calgary: Hurford Enterprises.

Jennings, A. (1996) *The New Lords of the Rings*. London: Simon & Schuster.

Larson, J. and Park, H-S. (1993) *Global Television and the Politics of the Seoul Olympic*. Oxford: Westview Press.

Liebes, T. and Curran, J. (eds) (1998) *Media, Ritual and Identity*. London: Routledge.

MacAloon, J. (ed.) (1984) *Rite, Drama, Festival, Spectacle*. Philadelphia: The Institute of Human Issues.

McChesney, R. (1998) Media convergence and globalization, in A. Thusu (ed.) *Electronic Empires: Global Media and Local Resistance*. London: Arnold.

Marx, K. and Engels, F. (1969) *Marx and Engels: Basic Writings on Politics and Philosophy*, L. Feuer (ed.) London: Fontana.

Rivenburgh, N. (1992) National image richness in US-televised coverage of South Korea during the Seoul Olympics, *Asian Journal of Communication*, 2 (2): 1–39.

Roche, M. (ed.) (1998) *Sport, Popular Culture and Identity*. Aachen: Meyer and Meyer Verlag.

Roche, M. and Arundel, J. (1998) Media sport and local identity: British Rugby League and Sky TV, in Roche (ed.) *Sport, Popular Culture and Identity*. Aachen: Mayer and Meyer Verlag.

Rothenbuhler, E. (1988) The living room celebration of the Olympic Games, *Journal of Communication*, 38 (4): 61–81.

Rowe, D. (1999) *Sport, Culture and the Media: The Unruly Trinity*. Buckingham: Open University Press.

Rowe, D. et al. (1994) Global sport? Core concern and peripheral vision, *Media, Culture & Society*, 16: 661–75.

Seh-Jik, P. (1991) *The Seoul Olympics: The Inside Story*. London: Bellew.

Simson,V. and Jennings, A. (1992) *The Lords of the Rings: Power, Money and Drugs in the Modern Olympics*. London: Simon & Schuster.

Spà, de Moragas M., Rivenburgh, N., and Larson, J. (1995) *Television in the Olympics*. Luton: John Libbey Media.

Sugden, J. and Tomlinson, A. (1998) *FIFA and the Contest for World Football*. Cambridge: Polity Press.

Whannel, G. (1992) *Fields in Vision: Television Sport and Cultural Transformation*. London: Routledge.

Whitson, D. (1998) Circuits of promotion: media, marketing and the globalization of sport, in L.A. Wenner (ed.) *MediaSport*. London: Routledge.

## Part I: Further reading

Bairner, A. (2001) *Sport, Nationalism, and Globalization: European and North American Perspectives*. Albany: State University of New York Press.

Bernstein, A. and Blain, N. (eds) (2003) *Sport, Media, Culture: Global and Local Dimensions*. London: Frank Cass.

Boyle, R. and Haynes, R. (2000) *Power Play: Sport, the Media & Popular Culture*. Harlow, UK: Pearson Education

Brookes, R. (2002) *Representing Sport*. London: Arnold.

Maguire, J. (1999) *Global Sport: Identities, Societies, Civilizations*. Cambridge: Polity.

Martin, R. and Miller, T. (eds) (1999) *SportCult* Minneapolis: University of Minnesota Press

Miller, T., Lawrence, G., McKay, J. and Rowe, D. (2001) *Globalization and Sport: Playing the World*. London: Sage.

Rowe, D. (1995) *Popular Cultures: Rock Music, Sport and the Politics of Pleasure*. London: Sage.

Rowe, D. (2004) *Sport, Culture and the Media: The Unruly Trinity*, 2nd edn. Maidenhead: Open University Press.

Wenner, L.A. (ed.) (1998) *MediaSport*. London: Routledge.

Whannel, G. (1992) *Fields in Vision: Television Sport and Cultural Transformation*. London: Routledge.

# Part II

# MEDIA SPORT DECONSTRUCTION: READINGS, FORMS, IDEOLOGIES AND FUTURES

The previous section provided a wealth of information about how media sport is brought to our screens, speakers and pages. It also revealed several of the media's assumptions about the appeal of sport and the people to whom it appeals. What it did not concentrate on are the 'ways of reading' various modes of media sport, the manner in which they come alive and, in the process, may be modified or even transformed in the hands of the human subjects to whom they are directed. The second part of the book is concerned, then, with the meanings, interpretations and uses of media sports texts.

Miquel de Moragas Spà et al. (Chapter 10) open the section by taking one of the most global of all media sports spectacles – the Olympics – and present perspectives from those other than 'the usual suspects'. Thus, while the Anglo-American media may dominate the production of global sport (providing the visual 'feed' for all other countries), their images are 'brought to earth' by people in very different contexts, such as Africa, Russia, the Balkans, China and South America, all of which are discussed here. Ketra Armstrong (Chapter 11) also looks at the different ways in which media sports texts can be read, but in her study considers how Nike, the sport and leisurewear brand that has prominently featured African American athletes like Michael Jordan in 'pitching' to white markets, also represents itself to black consumers. She uses a symbolic interactionist approach in analysing Nike's techniques of adapting and speaking to the different characteristics of African American culture. The images of masculinity generated by Nike resonate to some degree with Michael

Messner et al.'s (Chapter 12) appraisal of television sports shows and their accompanying advertisements. Their textual analysis of 23 hours of sports programming and the 722 commercials that took up almost a quarter of this time generated 10 recurrent themes that comprise what they describe as the Televised Sports Manhood Formula that instructs boys how to recognize and emulate 'hegemonic masculinity'. Laurel Davis (Chapter 13) then examines another side of 'hegemonic masculinity' through a case study of the high-profile swimsuit issue of *Sports Illustrated* in which the relationship between sport and femininity renders women as predominantly decorative. Davis addresses texts, producers, photographic models and consumers in probing the framing of the media sports text and its reception and impact. In this case the readership is positioned as predominantly young to middle-aged males, the crucial demographic category governing Messner et al.'s Televised Sports Manhood Formula. Kyle Kusz (Chapter 14) then develops, also using *Sports Illustrated* as case material, a critical analysis of the ideological linkage of youth, masculinity, and race through the media sports text. He locates media sport within a wider context of trends in popular culture (including popular music and film) in which white youthful masculinity is problematized and affluent white males are represented as victims. This is an example of how media sports texts may make potent interventions in cultural politics while appearing to be 'innocent' and de-politicized.

Deborah Stevenson (Chapter 15) then shifts the focus from the United States to Australia in considering questions of the media, globalization and gender. Through a study of media coverage of the 1999 Australian Tennis Open, she explores the contradictory ways in which women players are represented, including the temporary national 'adoption' of some foreign players and media-fuelled disputes over sexuality, the body, fashion and performance-enhancing drugs. Stevenson reveals the polysemic nature of media sports texts and the provisional nature of readings of them. David McGimpsey (Chapter 16) analyses a rather different kind of media sports text – baseball writing (with passing reference to film and television) – but finds gendered and class discourses running through its élitist hostility to football and, by association, to television and 'mass', male working-class culture and feminized popular culture. Robert Rinehart (Chapter 17) then appraises a phenomenon likely to be even more objectionable to the baseball writer in the form of the postmodern television spectacle of *The eXtreme Games*, a sporting innovation with an 'MTV' look designed for 'Generation X'. Rinehart's reading of 27 hours of

ESPN's coverage of *The eXtreme Games* teases out the contradictions of a radical sport that must find sponsors, media and audiences in order to prosper, producing a much more conservative media sports text and apparatus than at first appears. The section concludes by mirroring Rinehart's concern with the representation of new forms of TV sport with two chapters on the new sports media that are now registering a significant impact on the representation and experience of sport. Brian Stoddart's (Chapter 18) discussion of convergence and its consequences for media sports texts and textual relations is instructive in that it was written before many of the recent organizational and technological changes described elsewhere in the Reader (such as the AOL Time Warner merger) took place. He argues that 'the Net offers the potential for an alternative sports communication system, the first in a long time, if not for the very first time in the history of the modern communications industry'. Michael Sagas et al. (Chapter 19) test an aspect of this promise of the Internet in the most seemingly propitious of settings – intercollegiate sport. Their examination of coverage of softball and baseball in a sample of 52 university websites reveals the persistence of gender inequality (baseball receiving more coverage than softball) and of regional variations. New media sports texts, therefore, even when non-commercial and located within 'enlightened' institutions governed by anti-discrimination legislation, are seen here to replicate some of the sins of the old. This reminder of the need for theoretically informed and empirically grounded critical textual analysis of all the corners of the media sports cultural complex is an appropriate concluding point for the Reader. There is clearly a continuing need for strong research and scholarship in Cultural and Media Studies that explores, disentangles and assesses the multifarious relationships between sport, culture and the media. The sample of published work presented here offers some guidance for those with new ideas and perspectives to engage with this most compelling of research fields.

# 10

# LOCAL VISIONS OF THE GLOBAL: SOME PERSPECTIVES FROM AROUND THE WORLD

## Miquel de Moragas Spà, Nancy K. Rivenburgh and James F. Larson

Excerpt from *Television in the Olympics*. London: John Libbey, 1995, Chapter 12: 223–40 (currently available through University of Luton Press, London).

Visions of the Olympic Games, in professional and academic circles, have largely come from western, developed countries. These views have shaped, and somewhat confined, modern images of the Olympic Games. Yet, most serious observers of the Games realize this and know that, for many cultures around the world, the Olympics create more a sense of participating in the festival of 'others' than of participating in a universal event. This chapter is from a book based on a large international comparative content analysis of 28 Olympic television broadcasts from around the world of the 1992 Barcelona Olympic Games, combined with reports about their respective Olympic 'experiences' from cooperating researchers in 25 countries. The chapter reproduced here is based on those correspondents' reports, with each section drawing primarily upon the contributions of the study correspondents from those countries (the sections of this chapter concerning Africa and Latin America draw upon contributions from Carmen Gómez Mont, whose cooperation the authors gratefully acknowledge). It offers just a few different perspectives from around the world, and even has the audacity to combine the views of several countries into more regional overviews. The limitations of such ventures are obvious and, while for each area a more in-depth analysis could certainly have been conducted, the idea here is just to offer a sense of how different countries and geographic regions live the Olympics, largely through the eyes of the study correspondents.

## Africa

The old adage that from where one sits determines what one sees is particularly pronounced in the interpretations of Africa nations looking at the Olympic Games. The analysis of some selected African perspectives on Olympic Games highlights the diversity in the forms of interpreting and experiencing the Olympic Games. It also underscores the pervasive theme of hierarchy (or haves and have nots), as well as issues concerning ways in which identity is manifested through televised images.

### Limitations in television production and reception

The different technical conditions of television reception and production colour every aspect of the presentation and understanding of the Olympic Games in Africa. When referring to the African continent one cannot speak of 'universal coverage' let alone viewer 'choice' in selection of television programs. Although this study did not collect specific audience data across Africa, it is clear that the Olympic Games were mainly of interest to literate sectors of the population who have higher access to television and speak the primary languages (English and French) used in broadcasts. Of the countries involved in this study, Cameroon has a literate population above 15 years of age of 46 per cent, Ghana 40 per cent, Egypt 52 per cent and South Africa 24 per cent (UNESCO 1993). As expected, however, it was the radio, and not the television, that allowed much of the population to keep in touch with the Games. Within African society the radio has a considerable audience and broadcasts the most popular modern sports on the continent, mainly soccer and long distance running.

### Second hand broadcasts

The most significant characteristic of television coverage of the Olympics in Africa is the virtual absence of images of Africans or images produced by Africans on objects of local interest to television viewers:

From beginning to end nothing was shown or said about the participation of Cameroon on the television, except when the country was identified during the Parade of the Nations in the Opening Ceremony.

(Wete 1992)

Even in the Opening Ceremony, however, Cameroon only appeared on camera for 16 seconds during the athletes' parade. The broadcasting of the Barcelona '92 Olympic Games reached the majority of African countries by means of European international networks produced for very different 'home' audiences. For example, Cameroon Radio TV (CRTV), via an arrangement through URTNA, used Canal France International as an intermediate broadcaster. As a consequence of this the viewers in Cameroon saw an Opening Ceremony narrated by French commentators for French television viewers. The presence of Cameroon broadcast personnel during the Opening Ceremony was limited to the participation of two commentators situated in their own television studio in Cameroon and not in Barcelona. These commentators, one speaking French and the other speaking English among themselves, were only able to intervene in the presentation during the brief advertising breaks destined for the French audience:

> J.L.: We're going to return to Barcelona in a few moments. Perhaps we need to explain the reason for these brief interruptions in this ceremony that has to last three hours. We are receiving the images from TF1 and this channel cuts the ceremony in order to introduce their advertising and we cannot pass on an advert that comes from France (. . .)
>
> (CRTV, Cameroon, Opening Ceremony)

The dependency on foreign television channels not only had consequences for broadcast attention to African countries but also, in a more general manner, for programming and quality of reception. Karikari points out in his report that:

> In Ghana the majority of the broadcasts were carried out by people other than Ghanaians, in English and in French, the broadcast was in black and white (due to the lack of technical link-up), and there were constant interruptions in order to improve the image. The timetables were not published in advance and many of the major events of most interest for Ghana were excluded.
>
> (Karikari 1992)

Wete says something similar in relation to the experience of television in Cameroon:

> The programming of the Games wasn't announced in advance (. . .) they were simply discovered on the television. Cameroon television coverage was fragmented and irregular (. . .) The commentators were French and spoke of France, the European Union and the West in order of importance.
>
> (Wete 1992)

Local commentaries were added to the end of the programs or, as mentioned, during advertising breaks in the original broadcasts, spaces in which the local commentators quickly referenced issues of most relevance to the local viewers.

### The Olympic host seen from the South

Looking south to north, the African countries saw the Olympic host – in this case Barcelona – as a land of development, wealth and modernity. In this sense, the Olympic Games represented for African countries the chance to contrast their position in relation to the modern world, a world that uses economic development as its primary evaluative standard. These types of comparisons are not necessarily made in a negative sense. As Awatef Abd El-Rahman from Egypt said, Spain is seen as 'a developed country with a heritage of civilization and modern technology' and that 'the Egyptians see a synthesis of East and West in the Olympic Games'. These observations are interesting in that they project an idea of symbiosis between the ancient and the modern, between tradition and technology, the central idea around which the new African identity is trying to be constructed. Yet other observers of the Barcelona Games were less accepting of the displays of wealth bundled up into the Opening Ceremony when considering North/South comparisons. Other study correspondents expressed it in this way, and in the process implicate television in this display of world economic disparity:

> A ceremony of this kind is designed to depend on extravagant spectacle and thus it also sharply conveys a celebration of conspicuous wealth. This is no doubt a by-product of the fact that television coverage is dominated by requirements of audiences in the world's richest nations. But the gigantism of the whole event has the inadvertent consequence that the arrival of the world's

poorer nations in the great parade of athletes with only a handful of people looks almost embarrassing – as if they cannot [pay to send] a hundred or more lusty youths.

(Izod et al. 1992)

### Non-national African identity

Although an event based in the philosophy of internationalism, the design of the Games ceremonies and competition is such that the concept of the nation-state is central to identity differentiation. Yet for African participants in the Games whose identity was linked to different types of membership groups such national symbols were not highly relevant or were too new in their formation to be very meaningful. In other words, the central role of 'nation' found in the Olympic concept of identity is more compatible with western forms of identity representation, where symbols such as national flags, national anthems, the presidency or royalty have strongly reinforced historical, legal and cultural representation functions. That is not to say, however, that there wasn't an acute interest and pride, on the part of Africans, in being at the Olympic Games.

### Uniforms instead of flags

This interest in African self identity was most deeply expressed in what for some western countries could be interpreted as a trivial question: the clothes worn by the athletes in the Opening Ceremony parade. At the time of choosing their attire some African countries were equally divided between those who opted to show off their traditional style of dressing and those who opted to dress in the 'western' style, with a majority of the Arab delegations opting for the traditional style of dressing. Various reasons can be put forward for this difference in choices. On the one hand those who chose to wear western style clothes seemed to do so just to adopt symbolic forms of the modern world. On the other hand, it is possible that those who opted for the traditional form of dressing did so as a consequence of attributing to the athletes' clothes and uniforms even greater importance than their own flags and national symbols. The choice of athletes' uniforms was clearly more than a fashion statement. It was seen as a sign of identity that referred to the most ancient of their traditions, as well as contrasting with western ways.

The analysis of the coverage of the Opening Ceremony on Cameroon television underscores the importance of this choice. The athletes of Cameroon appeared in the Barcelona stadium wearing elegant western style suits. This circumstance went unnoticed by the French commentators who were broadcasting the ceremony for France – and also for Cameroon. However, it was noticed by the commentators situated in the television studio in Cameroon, and in their brief appearances during French commercial breaks, that the main theme commented on was, precisely, the merits of the western style attire worn by the Cameroon athletes:

> Yes, it has to be said that large sports events are also great opportunities for cultural and even political propaganda because each country that participates wants to announce a message (. . .) And we thought that Cameroon would wear the national dress (. . .) We paraded wearing typical dress in the African Games, and now we are unfortunately parading wearing (western) suits (. . .) When the people in charge from the Ministry of Youth and of Sport return they will be asked why they allowed Cameroon to portray a cultural image that isn't theirs (. . .) The Africans are becoming westernized, the Arabs are becoming westernized, Egypt too (. . .) Traditional dress is culture and isn't that all we have left when we have lost everything. This is what we will be left with (. . .)
>
> (CRTV, Cameroon, Opening Ceremony)

Despite the reference in the quote to Egypt, the Egyptian ERTU2 commentator noted literally every team that entered the Olympic stadium, African or not, wearing traditional attire.

### The athlete, the hero and personification of the nation

African athletes, as representatives of popular identity and associated with strength and success, are highly important in the construction of African identity. More than political representatives, flags or national anthems, it was the athlete-hero who took centre stage for the Africans. This has not just been the case during the Olympics. As Baker affirms, when the victorious athletes returned home from any sports events:

> They were received with full honours, they went on national and international tours, their photographs appeared in many public places, troubadours sang of their exploits and public works and streets were named after them. In 1970 African athletes became important symbols of national identity (. . .) and, more

than political heroes, it was the athletes who represented for a
large number of young Africans a chance of success within their
reach

(Baker 1987)

But these idols are not 'national' ones as is understood in western
countries, where they are linked to the performance of the nation state
and wrap themselves in the national flag upon victory or cry on the
medal stand at the playing of the national anthem and the raising of
their national flag. The idol of an African nation is an African idol.
'With Kenya we're also hoping for a handful of gold medals, above all
in the long distance races' (CRTV, Cameroon, Opening Ceremony).
As in the case of Latin America, it is not just the pride of the country
(nation state) that is at stake when being represented in a sport, but
rather the identity of the whole continent. The idea that a sportsperson or a team has a chance of winning strengthens the whole of
Africa against everyone else.

> We think that the African countries who went in traditional dress
> are the pride of Africa in these Olympic Games (. . .) Ghana,
> Egypt, Morocco, I'm convinced that one of these countries will
> bring back gold from the Games.
>
>   As for the football which began yesterday with the Republic of
> Qatar and Egypt, one-nil, it was a poor beginning for Africa on
> this occasion (. . .) I hope that all will be put right in the name of
> Africa.
>
> (CRTV, Opening Ceremony)

This idea of collectivity and importance of identity is even stronger in
the case of the Arab countries, as was evidenced by Egyptian television's keen attention to every entering Arab delegation, as well as
explicit praise (noted above) for any team dressed in a traditional
costume. In fact, it was the commentators from these countries who
expressed the biggest reservations about and criticisms of the cultural
forms of the event's spectacles (for example, opera) and even the
costumes of the spectators caught by the television cameras (such as
bikini tops). A special attitude of rejection was perceived by the
researchers towards western cultural forms, attitudes and lifestyles
that contrasted with religious and, above all, moral, principles.

## South Africa: an identity crisis

The South African media faced an enormously difficult task when it set about dealing with the Barcelona Olympic phenomenon. On the one hand, South Africa's return to the Olympics after 32 years was generally seen as a cause for celebration. But on the other hand, South Africa's participation became yet another site of politico-cultural conflict in an already tense society.

(Louw and Nkosi 1992)

Re-admittance to the Games was, for many South Africans, an important symbol of having re-joined the world community and 'being normal again' as a nation (De Beer et al. 1992). Yet at the same time South Africa in 1992 had no national identity to bring to this signifi-cant event, demanding that teams come with a suitcase of national symbols (anthem, flag, uniform). The South African team performed under a specially designed National Olympic Committee of South Africa (NOCSA) flag explicitly to avoid conflicts which would most likely arise using the blue, white, and orange flag identified with the apartheid era. Ironically, RTO '92, as host broadcaster, unwittingly served to spoil the positive intent of this by showing South African spectators at the Olympics wildly waving the flag of 'white South Africa'. South African athletic officials at the Games even tried to stop, to no avail, the spectators from waving the flags.

Other apartheid era national symbols, the official anthem and the springbok logo (long associated with South African sport), were also dropped, leaving the team and country with little to speak of in terms of meaningful identity, yet much to argue about between groups as a consequence of those moves. In addition, there were several other areas of turmoil related to athlete selection, the leading white politician de Klerk not receiving an invitation to the Games (although Nelson Mandela sat with other heads of state), and other events which served to disillusion some audiences only days into the Games. The result was that, rather than being a unifying experience, the Games provided one after another reminder of the painful transition that the country had been going through and, as such, become enveloped in the domestic crisis, including the struggle among groups to, in fact, define just what South Africa should be. In this sense, South Africa's return to the Games was ultimately very bittersweet. This was accentuated by the fact that the team performance was disappointing, causing 'much soul-searching' in the press during and after the Games. While the Olympics did not serve, in any way, to construct a sense of national unity in

South Africa during this period, it is suggested that the Olympic broad-cast, which occurred during one of the most politically violent periods of South Africa's history, at least offered an escape (De Beer et al. 1992). Ironically, the international media offered a chorus of celebration for the return of South Africa and demise of apartheid in their commentaries without any reference whatsoever to the continuing domestic crisis in that country. Rather, the presence of South Africa was presented – and symbolized by commentators through the stadium presence of Mandela – as a victory already won. The SBC 12 commentator from Singapore exemplified this sentiment when he said, upon entrance of the South African team, 'What a moment for those athletes, [visual of Mandela] Nelson Mandela, I'm sure with a tear in his eye'. Or the Australian commentator who noted the dove symbol on their track suits 'to demonstrate their commitment to peace and democracy'.

The South African experience, as with other African nations, was another reminder of the skewed nature of the international Olympic audience, and of other television reception in general on the African continent. As Louw (1992) noted, not all South Africans could participate in the Olympics as a television event because only about 25 percent of South Africans own, or have access to, a television set, effectively skewing Olympic audiences in favour of middle-class whites, coloureds (people of mixed blood) and Indians (people whose ancestors came from India). Black TV viewing, according to Louw (1992), is mostly concentrated in the 'formal' black townships. This viewership was also reflected in the television coverage. Of the five SABC presenters, all were middle-class and four were white, two of the latter speaking Afrikaans. Yet the white-Afrikaans-speaking population constitutes only 9 per cent of the total South African population and only 18 per cent of the population use it as their language at home. Only 6 per cent of the South African population is English speaking, with about 20 per cent of the population speaking Xhosa, although 46 per cent of the population can understand Xhosa (Zulus, Swazis, and Ndebeles). This meant that just 36 per cent of South Africans used the three languages of the broadcast presentations during the Barcelona Olympics as a primary language (English, Afrikaans, Xhosa). None of the SABC presenters catered to the Sotho-speakers (about 23 per cent of the population) and the black presenter used mostly English in his commentaries. In this sense, the Barcelona Olympics was for a 'westernized' South Africa. Not to be daunted by some of the problems accompanying this first foray back into the Olympics, the cities of Cape Town, Durban, and Johannesburg began to work on applications to host a 2004 Olympics shortly after the Barcelona Games. If successful South Africa would have been the first African nation to host an Olympic Games (instead Athens and Beijing were selected to host, respectively, the 2004 and 2008 Games).

## Russia

The Barcelona 1992 Olympics represented a special case in the history of Russian participation in the Olympics due to the disintegration of the Soviet Union. Nearly every aspect of the television coverage of the Games – the production quality, the commentary, the audience, the broadcast scheduling, and even the criticisms of the coverage – reflected in some way the changes and problems going on in Russia and the former Soviet republics at that time. In the Barcelona Games, Russian athletes, as well as those from other former Soviet republics, participated as part of the 'Unified Team'. Although they marched into the Olympic stadium together, each republic had its own identity and if a medal was won – and there were many – it was the anthem of the newly independent republic or Russia that was played. For audiences, the Barcelona Games represented a transition from the old to the uncertain new. As the study correspondents from Russia put it, 'In a certain way the attitude of the Russian public towards the Barcelona Olympics was unique in its mixture of nostalgic images of the victories of the powerful Soviet team in the past and . . . of the appreciation of the achievements of Russian athletes still in the framework of the Unified Team' (Zassoursky 1992).

### A difficult time for media in Russia

For broadcasters, Barcelona also represented a new way of doing things, reflecting both the structural changes and financial hardships of the media inside the former Soviet Union. The two main Russian channels 1 and 2, although still owned by the Russian state, now sported new identities. Channel 1 'Ostankino' broadcast to Russia and practically all other former Republics, and Channel 2 had become the Russian Television and Radio Broadcasting Company (RTR) broadcasting almost exclusively to Russia. However, the two broadcasters competed for audiences within Russia. For the coverage of the Barcelona Olympics both channels were hampered by a lack of resources that seriously affected their abilities to provide quality commentary. The two channels were able to send only 34 people to Barcelona for television and radio operations (compared with 1300 broadcast personnel brought by NBC of the USA). They occupied a small, two-room office without a television studio. This was a significantly smaller operation than had attended the Seoul '88 Games. Russian print media, although now flourishing within a new post-censorship atmosphere, was suffering from similar financial hardships as broadcasters, resulting in very few journalists travelling to Barcelona. This put the main burden for covering the Games on television. The two Russian broadcasters had come to Barcelona having agreed to share coverage of the Games by alternating the days on which each channel would broadcast the most 'popular' sports. However, given a new atmosphere of competition within Russia, it was not long before one accused the other of 'breaking' the agreement and soon they both ignored any prior complementary programming agreement. By the Closing Ceremony, Russian viewers could watch two versions of the ceremony, each with its own commentator, on two different channels. In a related sign of the times, for the first time ever in Russian coverage of the Olympics, the Games were interrupted by commercial breaks.

### The Games as a distraction from domestic problems

At first the Olympics seemed neglected in relation to domestic media coverage of the difficult political situation within Russia and tensions with the former republics. However, ultimately there were significant amounts of daily television attention devoted to Olympic coverage, with RTR broadcasting close to 9 hours a day (including summaries) for much of the Games. One RTR commentator in Barcelona confessed that he thought the amount of Olympic television coverage was excessive given all that was going on in Russia. He quipped that the government actually wanted it that way, suggesting that the long hours of Olympic broadcasting kept people from going outside to protest about the domestic situation. He said, 'the government is happy the Olympics are in August . . . it keeps everyone inside watching TV' (Gomelsky 1992).

### Post-Cold War commentary

The television coverage itself was criticized by the Russian press and viewers for the poor quality of both sports and cultural commentary.

That aside, the commentary did exhibit several important features also reflective of the changes that were going on in Russia. There was a distinct absence of confrontational, Cold War style rhetoric that had characterized prior Olympic broadcasts. If there was any rhetoric apparent it related more to the beauty of sport and notions of international friendship and peace – both concepts were brought up repeatedly during the ceremonies. At one point in the Opening Ceremony, commentators reminded audiences that in ancient Greece war had always stopped during the Olympic Games. For the war-torn [then] Commonwealth of Independent States (CIS) this value seemed of special importance. Further, the commentary reflected a transition period in the national identity of Russia. For example, when the Unified Team entered the stadium during the Opening Ceremony, very little was said by the commentators, and what was said seemed routine, matter of fact, and disjointed:

> Here is the team of CIS. You know, of course (name of co-commentator) that all former republics of the Soviet Union, with the exception of the Baltic states, are suppose to perform as one team. And in case of victories, the flag of their country will be flown and the corresponding anthem will be played in their honour. So, the team of the Commonwealth of the Independent States: representatives from Azerbaijan, Armenia, Belarus, Georgia, Russia, Tadjikistan, Turkmenistan, Uzbekistan and Ukraine. The largest delegation is from Russia. The Olympic flag is carried by Alexsandr Kerelin, the champion of the Olympics in Seoul, our famous wrestler.
>
> (Ostankino 1, Russia, Opening Ceremony)

As Zassoursky et al. (1992) noted, 'In some respect we watched a disunified team of a disunited nation . . . [in that sense] "national identity" was adequately portrayed'. Interestingly, twice as much was said about the next team that entered – the United States. It seemed easier for commentators to talk about the US athletes:

> EV: Just at this moment you see the delegation as a whole. The delegation of the USA – one of the most numerous – has just entered the field.
>
> AS: To be precise, they are the largest.
>
> EV: Yes, 591 athletes will go to the starting line in the competitions that are part of the compulsory program. But overall the

American delegation here in Barcelona includes 365 people who are coaches, doctors, managers, participants of the demonstration sports, and, of course, the most numerous team – track and field – numbering 141 athletes. They have the most realistic chances for Olympic medals. In swimming 52 people will go to the starting line and Americans suggest that in this Olympics they expect to achieve the highest results in all of history, and win the most medals.

AS: We'll note that Americans . . . have brought fantastic basketball led by Magic Johnson, a legend of American basketball, the strongest . . . in the world today. And that's exactly why, perhaps, the tickets to the final game cost enormous amounts of money, and are, of course, all already sold out. Everybody will watch the performance of the wonderful sprinter Carl Lewis. . . and many, many other athletes from the United States of America.

(Ostankino 1, Russia, Opening Ceremony)

At the same time, the sports coverage of the Russian broadcasters was also generous in its recognition and applause of the achievements of athletes from the newly independent Baltic States (Lithuania, Latvia, and Estonia) and former Soviet athletes now on the Israeli team. It is also interesting to note that the Russian commentators offered an extremely favourable portrayal of the Spanish Royal Family. During the Closing Ceremony, the Spanish horse-riding skills were compared to those of the old Russian guard. As Zassoursky et al. (1992) suggested, 'This description of Russian traditions may set a future model of a nation's portrayal'. More generally, the Russian perspective is one that has been consistent in its support of the Olympic movement. As one of many examples throughout the broadcast commentary, toward the end of the Opening Ceremony, the Ostankino 1 commentator said, in an impromptu outburst:

And now we say good luck to all the participants of the Games and to the Olympic Games as a whole. We want this unique festival that has lasted on our planet for almost 100 years not to end, ever, but become more wonderful and bring joy to all of us.

(Ostankino 1, Russia, Opening Ceremony)

## Slovenia

The Barcelona Olympics were the first time that Slovenia participated in the Olympic Games as an independent state. Thus, the playing of the Slovene national anthem, *Zdravlijica*, upon the entrance of the Slovene athletes held a very special meaning for the Slovenian people. For the media, it also provided a 'natural' interpretive framework within which to view the Games: as a promotion of nationhood. For the commentators of Slovenia's second channel, the Slovenian athletes marching behind the national flag represented an 'historic' moment of national and international recognition of Slovenia as a legitimate nation-state. Through the course of the Games Slovenian athletes were repeatedly presented as national symbols and, as such, incorporated into a dialogue of national promotion. When Slovenian rowers won two bronze medals, they were portrayed as 'heroes' in Slovenian eyes.

### The Olympics and war

However, only 200 kilometres south of Slovenia, in another newly independent state of Bosnia and Herzegovina, civil war was raging. Each day the media were flooded with horrific pictures of refugees, concentration camps, and war. The proximity of this tragedy was to dominate the media agenda and overshadow the pure joy of seeing Slovenian athletes compete for the first time under their national flag in an Olympic Games. Unfortunately, 'for the Slovene audience the reality of war was closer than the reality of the Olympic Games' (Splichal et al. 1992). In a telling cartoon published in *Delo*, a Bosnian athlete is waiting to start a race, listening to the starter saying, 'it is important to participate', while the starter points his pistol at his head. These two realities would meet briefly in the commentary of the Games. For example, it was stressed repeatedly that both Serbia and Montenegro were absent from the Games' roster of countries. While Slovenian news and sport commentary isn't known for rhetoric or hyperbole, the dual interpretive frameworks of proximity of war and of new nationhood also seemed reflected in the distinct lack of broadcast discourse about Olympic and universalistic values of peace and internationalism common to other broadcasts. Here was one isolated reference:

> Peace and friendship through the world is symbolized with 15,000 doves released from the stadium. In ancient Greece, during the

Opening Ceremony all the wars came to a stop. Unfortunately, today's reality does not follow the old Greek habit.

(2nd Channel, Slovenia, Opening Ceremony)

And, later in the Opening Ceremony, at the sight of the Olympic flag, the commentator added:

Unfortunately, the world is not at peace today. While we have the Olympic Games in one part of the world . . . in other parts we have wars and destruction . . . Let this unfolding of the Olympic flag be a symbol of the Olympics, peace, friendship, love . . .

(2nd Channel, Slovenia, Opening Ceremony)

## China

Late July was extraordinarily hot along the coastal areas of China. This did not deter an estimated 500 million Chinese from watching the Opening Ceremony of the Olympic Games (Li 1992), although this CCTV figure seems somewhat exaggerated. If not at home, they watched in courtyards, restaurants, night markets, and stores, or in the village centres. Li (1992) states that, according to a newspaper report, there were 'thousands of people . . . watching outside on the street' during the Opening Ceremony in the cities of Nanjing, Shanghai, and Wuhan. Further, he said that the Barcelona Games was a significant topic of daily conversation as viewers commented and argued about various events and outcomes (Li 1992). The roots of this interest can be found in the broad, government supported integration of sport in society, the tremendous growth and reach of television, and the very social nature of Chinese TV viewing as a form of entertainment.

### Setting television broadcast records

The broadcasting of the 1992 Olympics did disrupt the routines of daily life across China. Because of an awkward time delay between Barcelona and Beijing, live Olympic programs aired during the middle of the night, well after CCTV's normal broadcast hours. Although an extreme rarity in Chinese broadcasting history, CCTV extended its hours past its normal sign off time of 23:00 to broadcast an unprecedented 276 hours of Olympic broadcasting, replacing much regular programming (setting CCTV records for both hours of pro-gramming and reach for a televised event). People readily stayed up to watch, as both sport and television viewing in China are very important parts of public life. In a 1986 study of 367 urban Chinese, sports programs were found to be second only to drama as a favourite program type, with men favouring sport over women (Lull 1991). In a 1987 *China Daily* poll of TV viewers, 50 per cent said that sports programs are 'an indispensable part of their lives' (Brownell 1993). For the Barcelona Games, men and women's basketball, table tennis and track events – all popular school sports – were the most watched sports events for Chinese audiences. For students, the Olympics were held during summer vacation, so viewing the Games became a popular activity. Given this favourable public attitude toward both sports and the integral nature of television viewing as entertainment in China, it is not surprising that television and print coverage of the Barcelona Games was both comprehensive and positive in China. Stimulating this high level of audience attention has been a steady increase in Chinese worldwide sports accomplishments since the early 1980s that was reflected in the performance of the Chinese team at the Olympics.

### International sport as linked with stature

Media coverage of the Games portrayed China's very successful participation in the Games as proof of Chinese prominence and incorporation within the Olympic Family and, by extension, in world affairs (a philosophy made clear by the Chinese government's avid promotion of China as an international sports competitor). The Chinese team clearly carried the full burden of national identity with them to Barcelona. In this sense, international sports are inextricably linked with national prestige in China. So it was little surprise when Olympic gold medal Chinese diving champion Gao Min announced shortly after the Barcelona Olympics that she wanted to sell another gold medal that she had won at the world swimming and diving championships (earlier in the year) so that the proceeds could go to Beijing's campaign to host the 2000 Olympics. Brownell (1995) explains this attitude in terms of the type of 'face' work that has much more moral force than western or Olympic ideals of fair play and friendly competition. For example, she says that the Chinese keep a point system concerning Olympic performance (not simply a medal count as in other countries) and they talk about one country 'beating' another in the very specific sense of point tallies. According to Brownell (1995), China's performance in the world of international sport is not just participation in a game, but is as 'real as military defeat, economic accomplishments, or political reversals'. Possibly as a result of this attitude, the broadcast of the Olympic Opening Ceremony tended to be solemn and grand, presented with an attitude of the team on a serious mission, rather than endowed with any character of Olympic festival. This is reflected in Kong Xiangan's (1992) observation that the Chinese athletes entering the stadium in Barcelona were 'lined up neatly and their spirit inspiring' and that the visual attention given to China by the international signal (much longer than the 30-second average) 'was correct given China's due place in the Olympic Family'. The commentary was formal, poetic, inexact, and full of common sports slogans ('The torch symbolizes the bright future; it lights up all corners of the globe' CCTV, China, Opening Ceremony). It also was atypical for this kind of event in that it was very sparse. This was largely due to a combination of language barriers and the late-arriving media script for the ceremonies not allowing the Chinese commentators to follow their usual pattern for this type of event, and prepare and rehearse an elaborate script. As a result, the commentary offered little flavour of the host city culture

### The Beijing Olympic bid

It was also of no small consequence that Beijing was in 1992 still in the running to host the 2000 Olympic Games. China's bid was discussed frequently in the media along with a campaign of sorts for convincing the Chinese people of the importance of this effort. For example, the media gave accounts of the positive impacts of hosting for Barcelona's urban development. Newspapers praised the 'miracle' of Barcelona's supposed transformation from an old to a modern city in just a few years. Newspapers also wrote admiringly of the wide participation of Barcelona's citizens in the Games, suggesting that China could learn from the 1992 Games in terms of both development and volunteerism. More generally, the Games were defined in terms of not just peace and friendship, but progress. Olympic spirit was explicitly linked with economic modernization. One article in *Liberation Daily* headlined, 'Let the Olympic Spirit Spread in China', advocated that China's economic reform and modernization would benefit from some Olympic spirit (Li 1992). Conversely there was virtually no attention to any of the usual problems identified with the Olympics, such as drugs, professionalism, and encroaching commercialism. As such the Olympics from the Chinese perspective is a very serious business. In fact, one Chinese study correspondent even lamented this fact. When discussing the obvious joy, frivolity, and friendship among the Olympic athletes dancing together at the end of the Closing Ceremony, he wrote:

> Regrettably, since at the time of the Closing Ceremony most of the Chinese athletes had already returned home . . . one could not see any Chinese athlete. This was not due to the bias of the [television] director, but was the inevitable result of the traditional Confucian teachings learned by Easterners . . . In the free activities of the Closing Ceremony, the defects in the personalities of Eastern youth were easy to see. If Beijing's bid for the 2000 Olympic Games is successful, simply having the smiles of the city residents is not enough; the national character still ought to change towards openness.
>
> (Kong 1992)

## Latin America

In order to analyse the significance that the Barcelona Olympic Games had for Latin America it must be remembered that 1992 was the year of the 500th anniversary of Columbus' voyage, the year that Latin America met Spain once again, in a new atmosphere dominated by the region's democratization and economic modernization processes. It is not difficult to imagine that this self-image of transformation would link to heightened, and even unrealistic, expectations of sporting triumph. It is in this context – a continent looking for some acknowledgment and reward as players in a changing global environment – that Latin America approached the Barcelona Games:

> More than a parade of sport teams this could be an example of the new world map, the new geopolitical distribution.
>
> (TV Globo, Brazil, Opening Ceremony)

But instead of playing as equals through sport with the imaginary west as it had hoped, Latin Americans experienced the emotional highs and lows of a local television drama.

### Sport, television, and soap opera

Across many parts of Latin America, sport provides the 'ordinary' people with a space in the open air that they do not have at their disposal in their homes. There are abundant football clubs in the neighbourhoods where playing and organizing matches becomes a question of identity and territory. Football is played anywhere, even in the middle of the street, but within the neighbourhood. Sundays, and in certain cases, the end of the working day, are organized around this activity. Big sports stars such as Pele, Maradona and Romario have emerged from the common people, from the street. In another aspect of life, the majority of homes have videocassette recorders, cable television or satellite dishes. Audiovisual technology is now part of the urban and rural landscape. For a Latin American, the television is a terminal from which they establish contact with the outside world out of simple curiosity, entertainment or a desire for news. However, it is also the medium through which is created fantasies as forms of escape. The creation of fantasies finds its perfect television format in the 'telenovela', an extremely popular Latin American form of soap opera. The telenovela is a story that allows the viewer to come in contact with lifestyles in which success is one of the key values. The Olympic Games, in the Latin American context, adapts perfectly to the telenovela structure. It embodies festivity, drama, spectacularity, suspense, reward, punishment, heroism, anti-heroism, tears, laughter, embraces and more. Its sports competitions are like episodes condensed into sixteen days during which the viewer is passionately involved. The characters suffer, cry, laugh, cherish victory and are turned into heroes and anti-heroes. If they take shape as winners part of their lives appears glorious. The element of surprise comes into play, hope for the victory of one of 'ours' keeps the people glued to the television screen. Identification is sought with the hero of the telenovela: the athlete. Such was the case of Ximena Restrepo, the first woman to win an Olympic medal in the history of Colombia. In the Barcelona Olympics all the above elements converged: the hopes and needs of Latin America for international recognition; the channelling of these hopes through sporting expectations; and the playing out of these expectations through the Olympic broadcast as a dramatic story. In true telenovela style, the story contained some peak experiences, but ultimately ended with dashed expectations and self-examination.

*A proud start*

Latin America has been falsely understood as a quasi-homogeneous region. In fact, it is a complex mosaic of historical and cultural diversity, in which races, languages and various historical levels co-exist. Strong nationalist feelings exist, but they do not exclude the idea of belonging to the same region. Latin American first introduced itself during the Barcelona '92 Opening Ceremony through the athletes' parade, with its broadcasters noting the appearance of each Latin American nation, and by drawing attention to the large presence of Latin American political figures in the Royal Box (due to the celebration in Madrid of the Summit of Latin American States in the days before the Games). Commentators emphasized national pride by evoking their neighbours as both fellow countries and rival countries, but always as belonging to a common 'group':

> The first representative that appears from South America is Argentina. There is President Menem.
> (TV Bandeirantes, Brazil, Opening Ceremony)

> And here is . . . Brazil, a big power, without doubt, on the American continent.
> (Canal 13, Mexico, Opening Ceremony)

> Argentina, not many possibilities to win . . . Brazil, a South American giant . . . Chile, the first Latin American country to win a gold medal in 1896 and first to participate in the Olympic Games . . . Mexico, a brother country.
> (Tele-Rebelde, Cuba, Opening Ceremony)

> After 12 years, Cuba returns to an Olympic Games . . . Here is President Fidel Castro applauding the entrance of Cuba.
> (RCN, Colombia, Opening Ceremony)

> Get Belho who is the shot-putter of South America . . . And don't forget that we made the Australian basketball girls cry when Brazil won the pre-Olympic match . . . In Seoul, when Cuba was not there, only two medals went to South America . . . Our eternal sports rival, thank God, Argentina.
> (TV Bandeirantes, Brazil, Opening Ceremony)

> Without taking into account the US, Cuba has won 14 gold medals and the rest of the continent 8; Cuba has won 6 silver and the rest of continent 11, Cuba has won 11 bronze and all America 13. That is what gives superiority to Cuba.
> (Tele-Rebelde, Cuba, Opening Ceremony)

*But soon to be disappointed*
Realistically, Latin America knows that its sports potential, in contrast to other countries, is particularly poor. The United States and the

Unified team won large amounts of medals. Cuba, the exception, was in fifth place in the medal table, Brazil was in 25th place, Jamaica 35th and the rest of the countries were positioned between 50th and 60th place. For these countries winning a medal seemed to be more the result of a 'miracle' than the consequence of sports planning.

> Large countries, powerful . . . with good teams . . . sports powers . . . high levels of literacy . . . favourable economic conditions, the United States, a team that will fight for all.
> (Canal 13, Mexico, Opening Ceremony)

> But the truth is that the people know that victory is taken by the richest countries.
> (TV Globo, Brazil, Opening Ceremony)

> But there are no countries that can equal what the United States is ready to do, that is to sweep all the metal in the Olympic Games.
> (Canal A, Colombia, Opening Ceremony)

*Moments of festival*
In Latin America a victory immediately led to a popular celebration – for the Games are, above all, 'a fiesta'.

> All is joy in this moment . . . nice, colourful spectacle . . . the tears, the emotion, happy faces . . .
> (RCN, Colombia, Opening Ceremony)

> And finally, it is evident that the Olympics is the true fiesta of humankind.
> (Canal 13, Mexico, Opening Ceremony)

When Brazil won the volleyball 'the fiesta became Brazilian'. Television images would show how the people threw themselves onto the court, forming piles of people with some on top of others, embraces, tears of joy, praying on their knees and the coach asking the television not to ask him anything else about the victory so as to allow him to get back to the festivities. The rest of the Olympic Games were forgotten, as if there were no other medals nor other countries nor other competitions.

*Attempts at 'luck'*
These moments, however, were few. In fact, most Latin American countries had little hope of widespread victory at the Games, since to achieve it a sustained sports policy over a long period of time is

required. Such an effort was not possible for Latin American children and youth who trained in the 1980s, the crisis years, and precisely those who participated in Barcelona '92. For this reason in the television commentaries there was insistent talk of luck or faith in God as the things that could bring about success, other factors not being considered by the media.

> China . . . it's good to remember that they can give us a headache in women's basketball . . . but Brazil, here, was lucky to win the game. Because of that we hope to win a medal for Brazil.
> (TV Bandeirantes, Brazil, Opening Ceremony)

*But ultimately the face of disappointment*
In the context of Latin American success and failure tread a fine line and, when hope disappears, the festivities can turn into mourning and the expression of disillusionment can be great. Marijosé Alcalá, the Mexican jumper, raised hopes too soon – two days after the beginning of the Games. In Mexico the morning news bulletins were cancelled, there was a reduction in traffic in the city and the people held their breath. In the end the press were saying that 'the medal slipped through our hands'. The athlete stated: 'My tears are not of sadness, but of courage, sport is one of the most beautiful activities, but sometimes is really very cruel' (Xicotencatl 1992). This lack of winning athletes ultimately seemed a painful thorn in the side of a region that saw itself gaining prominence on a world stage. A few days before the Closing Ceremony the press was once again complaining that 'the Olympic Games go and the Olympic Games come and we always write the same story of frustration. Oh, it's a horrible feeling to specialize in the chronicle of defeat' (Gutiérrez Pérez 1993).

### Playing with the imaginary west

Not to be put off by athletic defeats, Latin American broadcasters still found ways to join with the imaginary West in other ventures and show the extent of the changes that Latin America had undergone.

> . . . united by the technology, around the beauty, around the drama of each sports competition.
> (TV Globo, Brazil, Opening Ceremony)

> The biggest Olympics in the modern era . . . Catalonia is in heaven . . . its capital, beautiful and cultured . . . demonstrated by

the fact that inside of the stadium you can get music, culture, sport, everything.

(TV Bandeirantes, Brazil, Opening Ceremony)

Barcelona and the Olympic Games is associated with modernity, here will stay the Colombians . . . Through sport, Latin American television shows reach to high levels of organization. Projecting efficiency, precision, coordination, professional and sports spirit.

(RCN, Colombia, Opening Ceremony)

In 1992 the Olympic Games seemed an opportunity for Latin America to construct a new self-image in the presence of the world using television and the Olympic Games. The Latin American countries approached the Olympic Games with realism, recognizing their competitive limits against the world sports powers. However, television's commercial and dramatic interests led them to build up their hopes by creating stories inviting success. Unlike soap opera, where the outcome can remain in the fantasy realm, the results of the Games are written into history. The medals table has direct implications for the image that a country offers in the face of international and national scrutiny. For all these reasons sport is seen as an element of identity for the peoples of Latin America. It is for this reason that the Olympics are so dramatically charged, celebrated, and felt within Latin American culture.

## References

Baker, W. (1987) Political games: the meaning of international sport for independent Africa, in W. Baker and J.A. Mangan (eds) *Sport in Africa: Essays in Social History*. Africana Publishing.

Brownell, S. (1993) The Olympics and television: the Chinese perspective. Paper presented at the International Symposium on Television and the Olympic Games, Olympia, Greece, July.

Brownell, S. (1995) *Training the Body for China: Sports in the Moral Order of the People's Republic*. Chicago: University of Chicago Press.

De Beer, A.S., van Vuuren, D. P. and Steyn, E. (1992) Correspondent report for South Africa, *Television in the Olympics Project Archive*. Barcelona: Centre d'Estudis Olimpics i de l'Esport, Universitat Autònoma de Barcelona.

Gomelsky, V. (1992) Interview, 3 August.

Gutiérrez Pérez, F. (1993) Hay que decirlo . . ., *Exelsior*, 4 August.

Izod, J., Meech, P. and Hornicroft, T. with the collaboration of R. Kilborn (1992) Correspondent report for United Kingdom, *Television in the Olympics Project Archive*. Barcelona: Centre d'Estudis Olimpics i de l'Esport, Universitat Autònoma de Barcelona.

Karikari, K. (1992) Correspondent report for Ghana, *Television in the Olympics Project Archive*. Barcelona: Centre d'Estudis Olimpics i de l'Esport, Universitat Autònoma de Barcelona.

Kong, X. (1992) Correspondent report for China, *Television in the Olympics Project Archive*. Barcelona: Centre d'Estudis Olimpics i de l'Esport, Universitat Autònoma de Barcelona.

Li, L. (1992) Correspondent report for China, *Television in the Olympics Project Archive*. Barcelona: Centre d'Estudis Olimpics i de l'Esport, Universitat Autònoma de Barcelona.

Louw, E., with Nkosi, N. (1992) Correspondent report for South Africa, *Television in the Olympics Project Archive*. Barcelona: Centre d'Estudis Olimpics i de l'Esport, Universitat Autònoma de Barcelona.

Lull, J. (1991) *China Turned On: Television, Reform, and Resistance*. London: Routledge.

Splichal, S., with Basic, S. and Luthar, B. (1992) Correspondent report for Slovenia, *Television in the Olympics Project Archive*. Barcelona: Centre d'Estudis Olimpics i de l'Esport, Universitat Autònoma de Barcelona.

UNESCO (1993) *Statistical Yearbook*. Paris: UNESCO.

Wete, F.N. (1992) Correspondent report for Cameroon, *Television in the Olympics Project Archive*. Barcelona: Centre d'Estudis Olimpics i de l'Esport, Universitat Autònoma de Barcelona.

Xicotencatl, A. (1992) Mis lágrimas no son de tristeza, sino de coraje, *Exelsior*, 28 July.

Zassoursky, Y. with Kolesnik, S. and Richter, A. (1992) Correspondent report for Russia, *Television in the Olympics Project Archive*. Barcelona: Centre d'Estudis Olimpics i de l'Esport, Universitat Autònoma de Barcelona.

# 11

# NIKE'S COMMUNICATION WITH BLACK AUDIENCES: A SOCIOLOGICAL ANALYSIS OF ADVERTISING EFFECTIVENESS VIA SYMBOLIC INTERACTIONISM

## Ketra L. Armstrong

Excerpt from an article of the same name published in *Journal of Sport & Social Issues*, 1999, 23(3): 266–86.

In light of the growing sociological and economic importance of African American (used interchangeably with Black) consumers in the marketplace, many organizations have begun to increase their under-standing of how to communicate with them effectively to facilitate a favourable marketing exchange (Mallory 1992). One approach of marketing to Black consumers is premised on the notion that communications are most effective when their elements (that is, the channel or medium used to transmit the information, the content of the message, the icons and symbols used to convey the message, values portrayed in the message) refer to African American culture (Pitts, Whalen, O'Keefe and Murray 1989; Simpson 1992; Hecht, Collier and Ribeau 1993). 'Communication is meaningful because of the culture that frames it . . . all communication exists in a cultural context' (Hecht et al. 1993: 1). As a result, marketing communications have been carefully designed to contain promotional messages with content that is relevant to Black consumers and presented in a culturally appropriate manner. More than US$700 million (all following figures in US dollars) was spent in one year on advertisements targeted to African Americans (Mabry 1989).

'African-American culture is constituted through communicative forms such as the use of code switching from Black English to Mainstream American English, an assertive, stylized communication manner, and rituals such as "playing the dozens" and "jiving" ' (Hecht et al. 1993: 19). Communications become a critical vehicle whereby African Americans construct their social worlds, create, interpret, validate, and substantiate their cultural identities. Although Blacks may be reached by mainstream media, many of them respond more favourably to culturally-based communications that acknowledge their heritage and respect their culture. In fact, many Blacks often ignore messages that are perceived to be irrelevant to them personally or void of appeal to their culture or reference group. What is noteworthy for marketers to understand is that a multiplier effect is created when Black consumers see a Black lifestyle in a print or television advertisement at the same time they see a general market advertisement for the same product in mainstream media (Boggart 1990; Rossman 1994).

Sport organizations are not exempt from responding to the importance of Blacks in the marketplace and should therefore increase their understanding of how culture influences effective sport marketing communication strategies. For the sport industry (at large) to improve its marketing and communication efforts to secure Black consumers, it must also understand the sociocultural implications of doing so. For sport to continue to grow and prosper as a business entity (that is, maximizing the usage of its products and services among consumers who have the interest and resources to do so), sport organizations must (a) develop an understanding and appreciation of the functional and symbolic usefulness of their products and services to certain target markets and (b) devise appropriate channels by which to communicate the salient product market features to the desired markets. Herein lies the focus of this study.

## Sport advertising

Advertising is one vehicle marketers use to convey information about their products. It includes verbal and nonverbal cues, images, and printed and spoken words (Mullins, Hardy, and Sutton 1993; Stotlar 1993). Advertising is 'paid, nonpersonal communication through various media by business firms, non-profit organizations, and individuals who are identified in the advertising message and hope to inform or persuade members of a particular audience' (Boone and Kurtz 1992: 532). It is usually constructed around a message that has been designed to build an audience and promote an increase in sales (Shilbury, Quick, and Westerbeek 1998) . . .

Advertising is often carefully crafted to be a conduit of culturally transmitted meanings. It works as a potential method of meaning transfer by bringing the consumer good and a representation of the culturally constituted world together within one comprehensive frame (Shilbury et al. 1998). Some organizations devise specific advertisements with messages for particular ethnic groups, communicating with them in a culturally-attuned manner (targeted marketing communications). Others try to find a universal or common (cultural) denominator among the masses and use it as a communication technique (mass marketing communications). Regardless of the approach, persuasive communications that ignore the influence of culture are rarely successful . . .

As suggested by Altheide and Snow (1991), sport is rife with elements that subject it to media formats and media logic. Sport events are very entertaining and they have a massive appeal. Because they provide an effective medium for reaching large audiences, they are popular electronic and print communications vehicles for networks and advertisers (Gorman and Calhoun 1994) . . . In addition to the use of electronic media such as television, advertisers also use sport as a communication vehicle in the print media. The increasing number of culturally-based magazines and newspapers make them viable vehicles whereby advertisers can target messages to specific cultural/ethnic groups.

Notwithstanding the popularity of sport, the advent of electronic technology (remote controls, split screens, picture in a picture, and so on) has made zapping (the means by which viewers change the channels to avoid watching a commercial) a critical challenge to television advertisements. The amount of clutter in magazines and newspapers has also limited the effectiveness of print advertisements, making them susceptible to being rapidly scanned by the readers. Although advertisers cannot prevent zapping or scanning from occurring, they can infuse their advertisements with elements to ensure that viewers are motivated to watch their commercials and read their printed messages. It is therefore imperative that advertisers understand which product market features and communications strategies will be attractive to their target audience.

## Blacks' sport media consumption

According to a report by Humphrey ('Black Spending Power' 1998), Black power is on the rise in the marketplace, making them an important segment to advertisers. The Black population is growing at a rate of 14 per cent, compared with a 9 per cent growth rate for the nation as a whole. Shimp (1997) suggests that the Black population is expected to reach 39 million by 2010. Humphrey reports that Black spending power is also growing faster than the national average and is projected to increase from $308 billion in 1990 to $533 billion in 1999 (reflecting approximately a 73 per cent increase in less than one decade, compared with the national increase of approximately 57 per cent). Humphrey's study forecast that Black consumers would account for 8.2 per cent of the total buying power in 1999 (compared with the 7.4 per cent they accounted for in 1990). The study concluded that capturing Black consumers can make the difference between many businesses making a profit or suffering a loss. Not only is the Black consumer market sizable, it is one that places much significance on sport. Research has indicated that sport is more salient to Blacks than to Whites. Blacks are more likely than Whites to incorporate sport into their daily lives and to be more strongly affected by the sport outcome involving a favourite team or athlete (Rudman 1986). Spreitzer and Snyder (1990) also revealed that Blacks were more involved in sports than Whites in their operationalization of passive sport involvement as a measure of the following seven dimensions: watching sports on television, listening to sports on the radio, reading the sport pages of the newspaper, watching/listening to sport news on radio or television, reading sport books, reading sport magazines, and talking about sports with friends. Black men scored higher than White men (60 per cent and 40 per cent, respectively), and Black women scored higher than White women (27 per cent and 14 per cent, respectively). Sachs and Abraham (1979) reported that the sport of basketball, in particular, was more salient and had a more symbolic meaning to the Black culture than to Whites.

Advertisers and corporations who are seeking to use sport as a vehicle to communicate with Black consumers must be mindful of Blacks' noteworthy media habits. Blacks (particularly Black females) watch more television than the general population, and the shows they watch are more apt to be those about Black people; listen to the radio approximately 3.5 hours daily, which is about 30 minutes longer than White listeners; prefer Black-owned radio stations and listen to

AM stations more than Whites do; can be reached with some general magazine publications, but prefer to read Black magazines; and are more affected by advertising than Whites, particularly when the advertisements contain elements that reflect their lifestyles (Boone and Kurtz 1992; Hawkins, Best, and Coney 1992; Johnson 1995).

With regard to Blacks' viewership of televised sport events, Blacks comprised 14.6 per cent of the viewing audience of post-season professional basketball games, 12.1 per cent of the viewing audience for post-season college basketball games, 10.2 per cent of the viewing audience of professional baseball games, 12.9 per cent of the viewing audience of college baseball games, 10.2 per cent of the viewing audience of postseason college football games, 8.3 per cent of the viewing audience of post-season professional football games, 15.7 per cent of the viewing audience of boxing events, 7 per cent of the viewing audience of tennis matches, and 16.7 per cent of the viewing audiences of track and field events (Simmons Market Research Bureau 1994). Thus, the three most popular sports among Black television viewers are track and field, boxing, and basketball. However, the sport with perhaps the largest appeal for advertisers (given its popularity in the United States) is basketball. The sport of basketball was the most popular sport to watch on television for the subscribers of the Black magazines that were included in Simmons' 1994 Market Research Study. For example, post-season professional basketball was watched, respectively, by 17.8 per cent of *Jet*, 17.7 per cent of *Ebony*, and 16.1 per cent of *Essence* subscribers. Thus, basketball appears to be a popular sport for the print and electronic media consumption of Black consumers.

## Theoretical and methodological framework

To examine effective means of communicating with Black consumers, it is imperative that the theoretical underpinning employed allows for a manifestation of the effects of African American culture. Hecht et al. (1993) present some sensitising constructs that are critical to a basic understanding of communication effectiveness. They refer to sensitising constructs as the elements that enable people to create ethnic culture and identity and to reinforce commonalities. The sensitising constructs they deemed important were core symbols (symbols of cultural beliefs, views, central ideas, and expressed behaviours that are identified through recurrent patterns that are verbal and nonverbal) that depict their interpretation of 'what is', prescriptions (evaluative aspects and notions of what should be), whether communication is problematic (because of the transient nature of multiple identities and assigning multiple meanings and interpretations), code (broad system of beliefs, values, and images of the ideal reflected in language patterns), conversation (a patterned representation of a people's experience involving exchange of rituals), and community (a grouping of persons where communality is derived from shared identity).

Hecht et al.'s (1993) sensitising constructs are embedded in the theory of symbolic interactionism, a sociological perspective based on the following three premises: human beings act toward things on the basis of the meanings that the things have for them; the meaning of the things arises out of the social interaction one has with others; and the meanings of things are handled in and modified through an interpretive process used by the person in dealing with the things he or she encounters (Prus 1989; Patton 1990; Hewitt 1994) ... The tenets of symbolic interaction (which also subsume the sensitising constructs mentioned by Hecht et al. (1993)) are necessary for understanding African American communication. As such, they collectively offer an appropriate perspective from which to evaluate the effectiveness of advertisements in their attempts to communicate meanings to Black audiences, allowing them to establish and maintain a sense of identity and affiliation with the product/service being endorsed. Because research suggests that sport in general and basketball in particular are salient to the Black culture, basketball appears to be a viable vehicle whereby sport advertisers may communicate with Black audiences. As such, sport marketers should note the premise (logic), grammar/packaging/contextualisation, and overall presentation and delivery of the messages contained in electronic and print advertisements associated with the sport of basketball that Black consumers may be exposed to. Thus, the purpose of this study was to examine the advertisements that used basketball as a communication tool and placed in media that had high visibility among Black consumers. This study sought to examine the manner in which one sport organization, Nike, Inc., communicated with Black consumers from the sociological perspective of symbolic interactionism. The methodology of symbolic interactionism is naturalistic, descriptive, and interpretive...

Using the 1994 Simmons Market Research Study as a backdrop, the researchers analysed and contextualised the meanings portrayed and interaction episodes depicted in Nike advertisements. To examine Nike's use of electronic media, a total of five different commercials aired during the Saturday and Sunday games of the 1994 NBA playoffs was videotaped. For an examination of Nike's usage of print media, random issues of Black magazines (*Essence, Jet, Ebony,* and *Black Enterprise*) were surveyed to locate different Nike advertisements. Data for the print analysis were found in a 1992 and a 1993 issue of *Black Enterprise* magazine. Each transcription was then coded by three independent African American researchers. The researchers performed a qualitative content analysis using a coding sheet to assess the premise of the message, the grammar/packaging/contextualisation of the message, and the overall style of presentation and delivery of the message as suggested by symbolic interactionism. To establish coder reliability, the researchers combined their analyses and discussed any discrepancies before arriving at a consensus for each category. The objectives of the methodology were to examine the intentions of Nike as the communicator, as well as the speculative effects on Black consumers as the receivers of the communication.

## Data

Following is a transcript of the electronic (television commercials) and print (magazine) advertisements examined for this study.

### Electronic media: television commercial 1

The commercial setting begins with Dennis Rodman (a Black male professional basketball player) walking into a barber shop. The Nike logo flashes across the screen, and music is playing. The setting quickly flashes to Rodman inside the barber shop sitting in a chair to get his hair done. The people in the barber shop are Rodman, Tim Hardaway and David Robinson (also Black male professional basketball players), and a Black lady who is preparing to cut Rodman's hair. As Rodman begins to talk, the viewers are shown a television with a live flashback of him playing (the commercial allows the viewers to see Rodman in real life action). The camera then zooms in on the shoes Rodman is wearing (which are Nike's). He begins, 'I wanna go out there and test it, you know? The money don't mean anything to me, you know? I can go out there and play for free'. Hardaway replies, 'See he got them two rings, that's what it is'. Laughter is heard in the background along with 'yeah that's what it is'. Hardaway repeats louder, 'Them two rings!' Robinson adds, 'Yeah they can't do nothing to him now!' Hardaway jumps in, 'Before he had them two rings he was like . . . [gesturing humbleness]'. The group responds with laughter and hand gestures. Rodman replies, 'Aw them rings don't mean anything really'. Hardaway interrupts, 'Oh them rings don't mean nothin'?' Rodman replies, 'Naw they're a part of history'. Hardaway continues, '[Well] can I have one?' Rodman is speechless initially, yet replies with a smile 'Oh no, no!' The people in the barber shop burst into laughter as they jive and joke with Rodman. The Nike logo flashes across the screen and the commercial goes off.

### Electronic media: television commercial 2

The commercial setting begins with David Robinson (as mentioned in the previous commercial) walking down a sidewalk with George Gervin (a Black man who was formerly a professional all-star basketball player for the San Antonio Spurs, and their current assistant coach). They are laughing and smiling as they are about to enter a barber shop. Music is playing as they are walking along. The audience sees flashes on a television screen of Gervin playing basketball in the NBA. Then the viewers see Gervin sitting in the barber shop spinning a basketball on his fingertips. The people in the barber shop include Tim Hardaway (as previously mentioned), Robinson, Gervin, a Black barber, and a couple of other Black men. Hardaway opens up, '1977, butterfly collar' (the camera focuses on a poster of Gervin in a silk warm-up suit with a butterfly collar and 'ICE' inscribed on it, hanging on the wall of the barber shop). 'Walk outside with that on in San Antonio now, and you'll burn up!' The people in the shop respond with laughter and hand/body gesturing. The footage of Gervin shooting his finger roll appears on the television (in the barber shop). Hardaway continues, 'George, tell us about that finger roll from the free throw line'. Gervin responds, 'Oh yeah, that was my patented, that was my patented shot. One thing I could do was finger roll'. The people in the shop respond with an outburst of laughter, the viewers then see footage on the television screen in the barber shop of Gervin performing a finger-roll shot in an actual NBA game. The camera then gets a total picture of all of the men in the barber shop. The Nike logo flashes across the screen, and the commercial goes off.

### Electronic media: television commercial 3

Charles Barkley (a Black male professional basketball player) appears on the screen with a black background (the picture is in black and white). A clipping from a newspaper appears on the split screen to the side of Barkley, and he begins to read:

> Teens Held in Death of Four Year Old. Phoenix – Two teenagers were charged with second degree murder for the April drive by shooting of a four-year old girl. The girl was in her living room getting ready for bed when a bullet pierced the front window and struck her in the head. She died instantly. This murder marks the 10th homicide in Phoenix this year involving juveniles.

Appearing on the screen is 1-800-929- P.L.A.Y paid for by Nike. A voice-over is heard saying: 'Participate in the lives of America's youths'. Barkley comments, 'if not now, when?' The commercial then goes off. While Barkley was reading, he was continuously shaking his head in disbelief as he was emotionally bothered by this incident and related occurrences.

### Electronic media: television commercial 4

The setting of this commercial begins with Chris Weber (a Black rookie professional male basketball player) walking into a barber shop. The Nike logo flashes across the screen as the music to a hit rhythm and blues song of the past, 'Strawberry Letter 23', is playing in the background. The commercial immediately flashes to Weber inside the barber shop sitting in the chair to get his hair done. Weber says, 'The first person I ever dunked on was LaJuane Pounds, Detroit, Michigan! And he used to talk about my mother, talk about my shoes, my shorts . . . (the commercial flashes to Weber shooting baskets outside on a playground) . . . so I dunked on him! And I said nah! There! There you go! Nah! Nah!! And by that time they had gone down and scored a lay-up' (the camera flashes back to him sitting in the chair in the barber shop reflecting). 'But that's all I remember from that game!' The people in the barber shop laugh. The only other visible person is the Black lady who is doing Weber's hair. The camera flashes on the Nike shoes Weber is wearing and footage of Weber dunking appears on the television in the barber shop. Weber continues, 'He was the only kid who used to dog me and talk about me – but I wonder where he is now? Cause I wanna just say I dunked on 'em!' (more footage of Weber dunking in an NBA game appears on the television in the barber shop). Weber sits in the chair smiling. A voice, presumably that of Tim Hardaway, says, 'He's probably bragging in the parks, he dunked on me, man Chris Weber dunked on me'. Weber repeats, 'He's bragging yeah, he dunked on me!' The commercial goes off.

### Electronic media: television commercial 5

A rhythm and blues song 'Express Yourself' is playing. The commercial opens up with two Black male youngsters peeking into the window of a barber shop. The commercial then flashes to the inside of the barber shop. One Black male who was sitting in the barber shop with a small Nerfbasketball in his hand (Person 1) says, 'Did you see Chris dunk on Barkley?' At this time the camera shows footage of Weber on the television in the barber shop coming down the court in an NBA game. At the bottom of the television in the barber shop is the Nike logo and an advertisement for a local radio station (K-FUNK 1450 AM). A flash of the Nike shoes Weber is wearing appears on the screen. A second person replies (Person 2), 'Naw, I didn't see it'. Person 1 replies, 'Well, it went something like this' (he gets out of his chair to demonstrate what happened). Weber interrupts, 'Here, put this cape on [Weber hands Person 1 the cover that was on him to prevent hair from covering him to use as a cape], because I was super man!' Person 1 replies, 'Oh yeah you were' (as Weber puts the cape around him). The camera flashes to footage of Weber playing in the NBA on the television in the barber shop. Person 1 gets up to demonstrate how Weber dunked on Barkley, Weber assumes the role of Barkley. Person 1 says, 'Okay, catch it like this [footage of Weber catching the ball in an actual game against Phoenix's Barkley appears on the television] around the back' [footage of Weber taking the ball around his back flashes on the screen]. 'Barkley comes over here to try to block it' (Weber and Person 1 imitate the action while footage of the actual move appears on the television). Weber (in his Barkley imitation) replies, 'Wait, he's too high – he's too high!' Then Person 1 dunks the Nerfball in the basketball hoop in the barber shop. The actual footage of Weber dunking on Barkley appears on the television. Person 1 asks Weber, 'Then what did Barkley say?' Weber replies, 'He said I don't believe in role models, but uh, you mine'. The place erupts in laughter and high five gestures and handshakes. The Nike logo flashes across the screen as Weber and Person 1 engage in a brotherly embrace, and the commercial goes off. Throughout the commercial, the words of the rhythm and blues song 'Express Yourself' are heard.

### Print media: magazine advertisement 1

The advertisement is in colour. It features a silhouette of two young-sters playing basketball, presumably on a dilapidated playground court. Vertically, along the left side of the picture, appears the following script:

> My dad's a gangster. My dad's a father. My dad runs around. My dad runs 4 miles a day. My dad says women are only good for one thing. My dad says Black women are living jewels. My dad sent me money. My dad sent for me. My dad says school's for fools. My dad says knowledge is power. Like father, like son? Scold him. Mold him. Love him. Don't let him quit. If he's third string, go to his games, anyway. If he can't hit a curve ball, don't sweat him. If he's not doing well in school, give him hell. If he can recite a rap, word for word, he can memorize a history lesson, date for date. Be there for him. And he'll be there for his brother. JUST DO IT. NIKE. (The Nike logo appears at the bottom left corner of the advertisement.)

### Print media: magazine advertisement 1

This advertisement is in colour. It features a huge view of the top of a dilapidated rim, one that has pieces of a net attached to it with different types of tape. The setting is one of a local playground, in a not-so-affluent neighbourhood. Appearing vertically along the right side of the rim is the following script:

> Goals. Some are realistic. Some aren't. You gotta bust your butt to find out. One thing's for sure. Life preys on one dimensional players. Those who put everything in one basket. It's not fair. But you realize, it's not your ball. So you've set many goals. Earn a Ph.D. Finish a marathon. Write a screenplay. Own an N.F.L. team. Run for President. Yeah, you're shooting for the stars. But that's cool. If you don't make one, you take what you've learned and alter your shot. JUST DO IT. (The Nike logo appears in the upper left corner of the advertisement.)

## Analysis and discussion

The content of the advertisements was analysed according to the following three domains: the premise (logic) of the message, the grammar/ packaging/contextualisation of the message, and the overall style of message presentation and delivery.

### Premise/logic of the messages

The premise of the Nike advertisements included in this study represented the historical and mythological foundation for Nike, Inc. Nike is the winged goddess of victory in Greek mythology. Her domain was Olympus, where she sat at the side of Zeus, the ruler of the Olympic pantheon. A mystical presence, characterising victorious encounters, Nike presided over history's earliest battlefields. A Greek would say 'when we go to battle and win we say it is Nike' (Nike Publications 1993). A swoosh is Nike's symbol of performance excellence. As such, the media logic in the advertisements reflects their slogan of 'Just Do It!' The 'Just Do It' mentality was conveyed in the manner in which the advertisements spoke to the social ills plaguing America and the means by which people may overcome them with the support of, and through interactions with, their significant others (reference group, community). The logic of the Nike advertisements emanated from the premise of symbolic interactionism: meanings in their advertisements arose out of social interaction and human emotions and experiences. This was depicted in the interaction episodes displayed in the casual behaviour of the men in the barber shops in the television commercials as they interacted to celebrate the accomplishment portrayed. This logic was also conveyed in the words of the print advertisements.

Be it winning two NBA world championship rings, having a distinctive stylish move such as a patented finger roll, taking an active role to stop teen violence, remembering getting even in a nonviolent, sport-related manner with a bully or someone who picked on you, dunking a basketball over a very prominent athlete to establish yourself and your turf, setting goals, or looking out for sons or brothers, Nike advertisements rewarded athletic prowess, yet also contained messages of hope and encouragement to overcome social, physical, and psychological barriers that may seem insurmountable. Thus, the premise of the Nike advertisements posited Nike as a brand that goes far beyond its functional product attributes (in athletic excellence), but also has some symbolic usefulness to Black consumers as it endorses and celebrates nuances, emotions, and interactions that occur within the African American culture.

### Grammar/packaging/contextualisation of the messages

A language is critical to group membership and contact with the group via abstract and concrete objects (Hewitt 1994). Effective grammar must contain a language that is appropriate for the intended audience. The grammar and means by which Nike advertisements contextualised the language in which they communicated meanings and messages to their audiences were contained in a number of core symbols included in the advertisements. The conversational pattern of expression was perhaps one that Blacks could relate to because they included patterned verbal and nonverbal representations of the Black participants' experiences. The participants in the commercials spoke to the audience in slang, jive-talking, with their codes, and with their jargon to 'express themselves' (which was the title of one of the songs playing in the background). Such an inclusion of rhythm and blues music was another strategic ploy, given that music is also a critical context for communication and many Blacks have an affinity to rhythm and blues music in particular. Also, in one of the barber shop scenes, the viewers saw an advertisement for an AM radio station (which was also strategically placed given Blacks' listening habits). The exchange of rituals and nonverbal gestures depicted in the commercials such as handshakes, hugs, high fives, body gestures, and so forth that the participants engaged in conveyed a special meaning and were also a critical part of the language being spoken. The print advertisements were also packaged to speak a language containing the grammar and reflections of some of the elements of inner-city life as depicted in the silhouettes of dilapidated playground basketball facilities and equipment. The grammar in the print advertisements was culturally constructed and presented in a dichotomous manner (for example, 'gangster/father', 'don't sweat/give him hell').

Both the electronic and print advertisements contained a number of core symbols, codes, and conversations that were an integral part of the packaging of the message being communicated. Perhaps they served as sensitising constructs, and allowed for the creation of cultural identities and the reinforcement of commonalities as the Black participants communicated with one another (in the electronic advertisements) and as Black readers were being spoken to (by the print advertisements). Thus, the grammar/packaging/contextualisation of Nike advertisements was constructed with an appeal to some aspects of African American culture.

### Overall style of message presentation and delivery

The Nike advertisements did not present blatant product endorsements. The placement of its logo/brand symbol was secondary to the interactions and symbolic settings captured and portrayed in their advertisements. The focus of the Nike advertisements was on the culture of the participants in the commercials and social interactions they (as consumers of Nike products) engaged in. The theme of each advertisement was conveyed through human interaction, experience, and emotion. Although the advertisements allowed for the participants' frame of reference to be conveyed (perspective-oriented), they also may have allowed Black consumers to engage in self-referencing techniques because they could either see themselves or significant others in the settings portrayed. The advertisements were also processual, in that they drew the audience into the message (with live footage of the actual NBA games) and enabled them to be a part of the interaction episodes. Contributing to the processual nature of the Nike advertisements was the circular, fast-paced motion in which the commercials were produced and the print messages were written. The verbal and visual inflections of the advertisements allowed for the audience to naturally be a part of the setting. The commercial action and flow of the text allowed for spontaneous expressions because they did not have a very rigid or structured format. For example, the electronic advertisements began with a scene depicting the athlete entering the barber shop, then flashed back to the athlete competing in a real basketball game, then came back to the barber shop. This format was also depicted in the flow of the text of the printed ads: 'My dad sent me money. My dad sent for me . . . Write a screenplay. Own an N.F.L. team'. The action/message jumped from idea to idea and from person to person, fostering a contagion effect of communication which fostered interaction among the viewers and readers.

Perhaps the most critical element of the Nike advertisements in communicating with Black audiences, however, was their relational characteristic. The frame of reference for Nike advertisements is not only the immediate situations or individual circumstances, but rather a collectivity that many Black consumers may relate to. Hewitt (1994) refers to the community as the set of real or imaginary others with whom the person feels a sense of similarity and common purpose. Marketers often utilise the reference group influence, and Nike marketing was no exception. The Nike advertisements contained real-world settings like barber shops that did not have to be manipulated or artificially contrived or reproduced for television or magazines. The advertisements also contained real people speaking to an audience rather than at them. Even though Nike employed professional Black male athletes as their spokespeople, the athletes were portrayed in such a manner that reduced their celebrity status and made them believable people, as opposed to larger-than-life or privileged characters. Thus, the overall style of the presentation and delivery of the messages were constructed in a manner that contained characteristics that symbolic interactionism would posit as appealing to many Black consumers.

It has often been said that people will always tune into television/radio station WIIFM (What's in it for Me). Because of their relevance to African American culture, the emotional content of the Nike advertisements may become a salient product market feature (speaking volumes to the African American culture) that will capture the attention of Black consumers thereby preventing commercial zapping and magazine scanning. The meanings of the messages were modified and interpreted through the code, conversation, presentation, and style of the advertisements that may be appealing to Black culture. Thus, it appears that Nike's electronic and print advertisements contain the sensitising constructs as mentioned by Prus (1989), Hecht et al. (1993), and the tenets of symbolic interaction to create relevant and symbolic meanings that are conveyed via plots, language/dialogues, messages, images, people, and interactions that are drawn from the culturally constituted world of many Black consumers. In so doing, Nike has created advertisements that are very symbolic in their non-product attributes. Such symbolism may result in the association of culturally-salient meanings being a perceived attribute of the Nike product being endorsed. The swoosh, therefore, may be an external stimulus that represents the total packaging of the Nike experience that evokes a positive feeling (cultural affect) within Black consumers.

## Conclusion

Merely including culturally salient elements in a communication is by no means a guarantee that viewers who culturally identify with them will respond in a favourable manner. However, research (Pitts et al. 1989) has revealed that Black consumers do respond favourably to advertisements that are culturally targeted to them. Nike has packaged and presented its advertisements in a culturally appropriate manner that perhaps may promote optimal communication with Black consumers. As mentioned at the outset of this article, effective communication is largely dependent on shared values and meanings conveyed in symbolic verbal and nonverbal signs and symbols. Nike advertisements contain such symbolic features and also communicate something symbolic about its consumers.

Schudson (1986) contends that advertising does not really change people's minds about a product, rather it is most effective when it celebrates the product, reinforcing existing attitudes. Nike advertisements do just that because they are drawn from the naturally occurring culturally constituted worlds of their consumers. In addition to the content of the message that may heighten viewer's interest in an advertisement, a person's conception of self is a driving motivational force and may have grave implications in determining the effectiveness of the advertisement. From a symbolic interactionist perspective, Nike has been effective in including a number of sensitising constructs that convey cultural meaning and may tap into the self-concept and consciousness of Black consumers, allowing them opportunities to relate, refer, establish, and maintain positive identities through the symbols used and images created and communicated via the Nike electronic and print advertisements.

Perhaps Nike's effectiveness in communicating with Black consumers contributed to Blacks' patronage of Nike products. Whereas Operation PUSH (People United to Serve Humanity, a Chicago-based civil rights organization) reports that Black purchases constituted 30 per cent or $669 million of Nike sales, Nike reports that minorities accounted for only 13.6 per cent or $303 million of its sales (Woodard 1990). Operation PUSH claims that Nike has a poor record of hiring Blacks at the executive level and has limited investment in the Black communities. But even during this race-oriented controversy, Nike experienced a 42 per cent increase in sales (Grimm 1990). So, it must be noted that Nike has received its share of charges for not being culturally sensitive to (and even being somewhat exploitative of) the

Black culture as a result of their intense, effective marketing efforts that are attractive to and reflective of Black lifestyles. Nike rejected the attacks and increased its hiring of Black employees (including at the executive level), its engagement in cause-related/social marketing activities, and its investments in the Black youth and in Black communities via projects such as inner-city boys' and girls' clubs, United Negro College Fund, Urban League, and education-oriented basketball camps (Grimm 1990).

Nike is not the only sport entity that has employed a cultural approach to marketing communications. For example, the National Basketball Association has advertisements that are rife with elements reflective of African American culture that may be a response to Blacks' affinity with basketball. Also, Major League Baseball (MLB) launched a commercial advertisement that featured Black rhythm and blues singer Aretha Franklin and rapper L.L. Cool J endorsing MLB. It also placed some print advertisements celebrating Blacks' contribution to baseball in a number of popular Black magazines such as *Ebony*. The National Football League had a commercial advertisement depicting some young, Black male youths playing football on inner-city playgrounds. Major League Soccer (MLS) also employed the talents of popular Black musicians in their advertisement that featured rhythm and blues rap group Run D.M.C. promoting the MLS. Each of these ventures illustrates the need for sport organizations to address the cultural implications of communicating with Black audiences. Advertising is a critical facet of marketing. When people buy products, they are also purchasing experiences that often become an extension of their psychosocial selves. Because of the increased cultural diversity America is undergoing, sport marketers and advertisers must be cognisant of the challenges of presenting advertisements to consumers who do not want to give up their racial, cultural, and ethnic uniqueness in their consumption and purchase behaviours, but instead want their identities validated and their uniqueness acknowledged and respected (Wilson and Gutierrez 1985). Thus, advertisements (along with other elements of the marketing promotional and communications mix) should be carefully crafted to speak to the intended audiences in a culturally appropriate manner, highlighting the functional and symbolic usefulness of the product to the consumers. Nike has apparently sought to communicate with Black consumers by focusing their advertisements on human interaction and emotion, with an inherent social/cultural message accompanied by a peripheral product endorsement. Yet, care must be taken to convey messages that are not exploitative, but instead promote the establishment of long-term positive relationships with consumers. Although Nike may forever be at the forefront of controversy regarding its marketing practices, their advertisements provide an illustration of the importance of understanding and applying a sociological grounding to the construction of marketing communications. In this regard, Nike knows how to 'Just Do It!'

## References

Altheide, D.L., and Snow, R.P. (1991) *Media Worlds in the Post Journalism Era*. New York: de Gruyter.

Black spending power on rise, survey reports (1998) *Columbus Dispatch*, 30 July.

Boggart, L. (1990) *Strategies in Advertising: Matching Media and Messages to Markets and Motivations*, 2nd edn. Chicago, IL: NTC Business Books.

Boone, L.E., and Kurtz, D.L. (1992) *Contemporary Marketing*, 7th edn. Orlando: Dryden.

Gorman, J., and Calhoun, K. (1994) *The Name of the Game: A Business of Sports*. New York: John Wiley.

Grimm, M. (1990) PUSH comes to shove as Nike defends its image, *Adweek*, 19 August.

Hawkins, D.I., Best, R.J., and Coney, K.A. (1992) *Consumer Behavior: Implications for marketing strategy*, 5th edn. Homewood, IL: Irwin.

Hecht, M.L., Collier, M.J., and Ribeau, S.A. (1993) *African American Communication: Ethnic Identity and Cultural Interpretation, Language and Languages Behavior* (Vol. 2). Newbury Park, CA: Sage.

Hewitt, J.P. (1994) *Self and Society: A Symbolic Interactionist Social Psychology*, 6th edn. Needham Heights, MA: Simon and Schuster.

Johnson, P. (1995) Black radio's role in sports promotion: sports, scholarships, and sponsorships, *Journal of Sport & Social Issues*, 19(4): 397–414.

Mabry, M. (1989) A long way from Aunt Jemima, *Newsweek*, 14 August.

Mallory, M. (1992) Waking up to a major market, *Business Week*, 23 March.

Mullins, B., Hardy, S., and Sutton, W. (1993) *Sport Marketing*. Champaign, IL: Human Kinetics.

Nike Publications (1993) *Informational Packet: Participate in the Lives of America's Youth*. Beaverton, OR: Author.

Patton, M. Q. (1990) *Qualitative Evaluation and Research Methods*. Newbury Park, CA: Sage.

Pitts, R.E., Whalen, D.J., O'Keefe, R., and Murray, V. (1989) Black and White responses to culturally targeted television commercials: a values based approach, *Psychology and Marketing*, 6(4): 311–28.

Prus, R.C. (1989) *Pursuing Customers*. Newbury Park, CA: Sage.

Rossman, M.L. (1994) *Multicultural Marketing: Selling to a Diverse America*. New York: American Management Association.

Rudman, W. (1986) The sport mystique in Black culture, *Sociology of Sport Journal*, 3: 305–19.

Sachs, M.L. and Abraham, A. (1979) Playground basketball: a qualitative, field examination. *Journal of Sport Behavior*, 2: 27–36.

Schudson, M. (1986) *Advertising, the Uneasy Persuasion: Its Dubious Impact on American society*. New York: Basic Books.

Shilbury, D., Quick, S., and Westerbeek, H. (1998) *Strategic Sport Marketing*. St. Leonards, Australia: Allen and Unwin.

Shimp, T.A. (1997) *Advertising, Promotion, and Supplemental Aspects of Integrated Marketing Communications*, 4th edn. Orlando, FL: Dryden.

Simmons Market Research Bureau, Inc. (1994) Study of media and markets, *Sports and Leisure*, 10(9): 278–300.

Simpson, J. (1992) Buying Black, *Time*, 31 August.

Spreitzer, E., and Snyder, E. (1990) Sports within the Black subculture: A matter of social class or distinctive subculture, *Journal of Sport and Social Issues*, 14(1): 48–58.

Stotlar, D.K. (1993) *Successful Sport Marketing*. Dubuque, IA: Brown and Benchmark.

Wilson, C.C. II, and Gutierrez, F. (1985) *Minorities and Media: Diversity and the End of Mass Communication*. Newbury Park, CA: Sage.

Woodard, W.M. (1990) It's more than just the shoes. *Black Enterprise*, September.

# 12

# THE TELEVISED SPORTS MANHOOD FORMULA

## Michael A. Messner, Michele Dunbar and Darnell Hunt

Originally published in *Journal of Sport & Social Issues*, 2000, 24(4): 380–94.

A recent US survey found 8- to 17-year-old children to be avid consumers of sports media, with television most often named as the preferred medium (Amateur Athletic Foundation of Los Angeles 1999). Although girls watch sports in great numbers, boys are markedly more likely to report that they are regular consumers of televised sport. The most popular televised sports with boys, in order, are pro football, men's pro basketball, pro baseball, pro wrestling, men's college basketball, college football, and Extreme sports.[1] Although counted separately in the Amateur Athletic Foundation (AAF) study, televised sports highlights shows also were revealed to be tremendously popular with boys. What are boys seeing and hearing when they watch these programs? What kinds of values concerning gender, race, aggression, violence, and consumerism are boys exposed to when they watch their favourite televised sports programs and their accompanying commercials? This chapter, based on a textual analysis, presents the argument that televised sport consistently presents boys with a narrow portrait of masculinity, which we call the Televised Sports Manhood Formula.

## Sample and method

We analysed a range of televised sports (in a study funded by Children Now) that were identified by the AAF study as those programs most often watched by boys. Most of the programs in our sample aired during a single week, May 23–29, 1999, with one exception. Because pro football is not in season in May, we acquired tapes of two randomly chosen National Football League (NFL) *Monday Night Football* games from the previous season to include in our sample. We analysed televised coverage, including commercials and pre-game, half-time, and post-game shows (when appropriate), for the following programs:

1. two broadcasts of *SportsCenter* on ESPN (2 hours of programming);
2. two broadcasts of Extreme sports, one on ESPN and one on Fox Sports West (approximately 90 minutes of programming);
3. two broadcasts of professional wrestling, including *Monday Night Nitro* on TNT and *WWF Superstars* on USA (approximately 2 hours of programming);
4. two broadcasts of National Basketball Association (NBA) play-off games, one on TNT and the other on NBC (approximately 7 hours of programming);
5. two broadcasts of NFL *Monday Night Football* on ABC (approximately 7 hours of programming); and
6. one broadcast of Major League Baseball (MLB) on TBS (approximately 3 hours of programming).

We conducted a textual analysis of the sports programming and the commercials. In all, we examined about 23 hours of sports programming, nearly one quarter of which was time taken up by commercials. We examined a total of 722 commercials, which spanned a large range of products and services, collecting both quantitative and qualitative data. Although we began with some sensitising concepts that we knew we wanted to explore (such as themes of violence, images of gender and race), rather than starting with preset categories we used an inductive method that allowed the dominant themes to emerge from our reading of the tapes. Each taped show was given a first reading by one of the investigators, who then constructed a preliminary analysis of the data. The tape was then given a second reading by another of the investigators. This second independent reading was then used to modify and sharpen the first reading. Data analysis proceeded along the lines of the categories that emerged in the data collection. The analyses of each separate sport were then put into play with each other and common themes and patterns were identified. In one case, the dramatic pseudosport of professional wrestling, we determined that much of the programming was different enough that it made little sense to directly compare it with the other sports shows; therefore, we only included data on wrestling in our comparisons when it seemed to make sense to do so.

## Dominant themes in televised sport

Our analysis revealed that sports programming presents boys with narrow and stereotypical messages about race, gender, and violence. We identified 10 distinct themes that, together, make up the Televised Sports Manhood Formula.

### White males are the voice of authority

Although one of the two *SportsCenter* segments in the sample did feature a White woman co-anchor, the play-by-play and ongoing colour commentary in NFL, wrestling, NBA, Extreme sports, and MLB broadcasts were conducted exclusively by White, male play-by play commentators. With the exception of *SportsCenter*, women and Blacks never appeared as the main voices of authority in the booth conducting play-by-play or ongoing colour commentary. The NFL broadcasts occasionally cut to field-level colour commentary by a White woman but her commentary was very brief (about 3.5 minutes of the nearly 3 hours of actual game and pre-game commentary). Similarly, one of the NBA broadcasts used a Black man for occasional on-court analysis and a Black man for pre-game and half-time analysis, whereas the other NBA game used a White woman as host in the pre-game show and a Black woman for occasional on-court analysis (see Table 1 below).

*Table 1*   Race and sex of announcers

| White men | White women | Black men | Black women |
|-----------|-------------|-----------|-------------|
| 24 | 3 | 3 | 1 |

Although viewers commonly see Black male athletes – especially on televised NBA games – they rarely hear or see Black men or women as voices of authority in the broadcast booth (Sabo and Jansen 1994).

In fact, the only Black commentators that appeared on the NBA shows that we examined were former star basketball players (Cheryl Miller, Doe Rivers, and Isaiah Thomas). A Black male briefly appeared to welcome the audience to open one of the Extreme sports shows but he did not do any play-by-play; in fact, he was used only to open the show with a stylish, street, hip-hop style for what turned out to be an almost totally White show.

### Sport is a man's world

Images or discussion of women athletes is almost entirely absent in the sports programs that boys watch most. *SportsCenter's* mere 2.9 per cent of news time devoted to women's sports is slightly lower than the 5 per cent to 6 per cent of women's sports coverage commonly found in other sports news studies (Duncan and Messner 1998). In addition, *SportsCenter's* rare discussion of a women's sport seemed to follow men's in newsworthiness (for example, a report on a Professional Golfers' Association [PGA] tournament was followed by a more brief report on a Ladies Professional Golf Association [LPGA] tournament). The baseball, basketball, wrestling, and football programs we watched were men's contests so could not perhaps have been expected to cover or mention women athletes. However, Extreme sports are commonly viewed as 'alternative' or 'emerging' sports in which women are challenging masculine hegemony (Wheaton and Tomlinson 1998). Despite this, the Extreme sports shows we watched devoted only a single 50-second interview segment to a woman athlete. This segment constituted about one per cent of the total Extreme sports programming and, significantly, did not show this woman athlete in action. Perhaps this limited coverage of women athletes on the Extreme sports shows we examined is evidence of what Rinehart (1998) calls a 'pecking order' in alternative sports, which develops when new sports are appropriated and commodified by the media.

### Men are foregrounded in commercials

The idea that sports is a man's world is reinforced by the gender composition and imagery in commercials. Women almost never appear in commercials unless they are in the company of men, as Table 2 shows:

*Table 2*    Sex composition of 722 commercials

| Men only | Women only | Women and men | No people |
| --- | --- | --- | --- |
| 279 (38.6%) | 28 (3.9%) | 324 (44.9%) | 91 (12.6%) |

That 38.6 per cent of all commercials portray only men actually understates the extent to which men dominate these commercials for two reasons. First, nearly every one of the 91 commercials with no visual portrayals of people included a male voiceover. When we include this number, we see that more than 50 per cent of commercials provide men-only images and/or voiceovers, whereas only 3.9 per cent portray only women. Moreover, when we combine men-only and women and men categories, we see that men are visible in 83.5 per cent of all commercials and men are present (when we add in the commercials with male voiceovers) in 96.1 per cent of all commercials. Second, in the commercials that portray both women and men, women are often (although not exclusively) portrayed in stereotypical, and often very minor, background roles.

### Women are sexy props or prizes for men's successful sports performances or consumption choices

Although women were mostly absent from sports commentary, when they did appear it was most often in stereotypical roles as sexy, masculinity-validating props, often cheering the men on. For instance, 'X-sports' on Fox Sports West used a bikini-clad blonde woman as a hostess to welcome viewers back after each commercial break as the camera moved provocatively over her body. Although she mentioned the show's sponsors, she did not narrate the actual sporting event. The wrestling shows generously used scantily clad women (e.g., in pink miniskirts or tight Spandex and high heels) who overtly displayed the dominant cultural signs of heterosexy attractiveness[2] to escort the male wrestlers to the ring, often with announcers discussing the women's provocative physical appearances. Women also appeared in the wrestling shows as sexually provocative dancers (for example, the 'Gorgeous Nitro Girls' on TNT).

In commercials, women are numerically more evident, and generally depicted in more varied roles, than in the sports programming. Still, women are under-represented and rarely appear in commercials unless they are in the company of men. Moreover, as Table 3 illustrates below, the commercials' common depiction of women as sexual objects and as 'prizes' for men's successful consumption choices articulates with the sports programs' presentation of women primarily as sexualised, supportive props for men's athletic performances. For instance, a commercial for Keystone Light Beer that ran on *SportsCenter* depicted two White men at a baseball game. When one of the men appeared on the stadium big screen and made an ugly face after drinking an apparently bitter beer, women appeared to be grossed out by him. But then he drank a Keystone Light and reappeared on the big screen looking good with two young, conventionally beautiful (fashion-model-like) women adoring him. He says, 'I hope my wife's not watching!' as the two women flirt with the camera.

*Table 3*   Instances of women being depicted as sexy props or prizes for men

|  | *SportsCenter* | *Extreme* | *Wrestling* | *NBA* | *MLB* | *NFL* |
|---|---|---|---|---|---|---|
| *Commercials* | 5 | 5 | 3 | 10 | 4 | 6 |
| *Sport programs* | 0 | 5 | 13 | 3 | 0 | 4 |
| *Total* | 5 | 10 | 16 | 13 | 4 | 10 |

Note: NBA = National Basketball Association, MLB = Major League Baseball, and NFL = National Football League.

As Table 3 shows, in 23 hours of sports programming, viewers were exposed to 58 incidents of women being portrayed as sexy props and/or sexual prizes for men's successful athletic performances or correct consumption choices. Put another way, a televised sports viewer is exposed to this message, either in commercials or in the sports programme itself, twice an hour on average. The significance of this narrow image of women as heterosexualised commodities should be considered especially in light of the overall absence of a wider range of images of women, especially as athletes (Duncan and Messner 1998; Kane and Lenskyj 1998).

### Whites are foregrounded in commercials

The racial composition of the commercials is, if anything, more narrow and limited than the gender composition. As Table 4 shows, Black, Latino, or Asian American people almost never appear in a commercial unless it also has White people in it (the multiracial category below).

*Table 4* Racial composition of 722 commercials

| White only | Black only | Latino/a only | Asian only | Multi- racial | Undeter- mined | No people |
|---|---|---|---|---|---|---|
| 377 | 28 | 3 | 2 | 203 | 18 | 91 |
| (52.2%) | (3.9%) | (0.4%) | (0.3%) | (28.1%) | (2.5%) | (12.6%) |

To say that 52.2 per cent of the commercials portrayed only Whites actually understates the extent to which images of White people dominated the commercials for two reasons. First, if we subtract the 91 commercials that showed no actual people, then we see that the proportion of commercials that actually showed people was 59.7 per cent White only. Second, when we examine the quality of the portrayals of Blacks, Latinos, and Asian Americans in the multiracial commercials, we see that people of colour are far more often than not relegated to minor roles, literally in the background of scenes that feature Whites, and/or they are relegated to stereotypical or negative roles. For instance, a Wendy's commercial that appeared on several of the sports programs in our sample showed White customers enjoying a sandwich with the White owner while a barely perceptible Black male walked by in the background.

### Aggressive players get the prize; nice guys finish last

As Table 5 illustrates, viewers are continually immersed in images and commentary about the positive rewards that come to the most aggressive competitors and of the negative consequences of playing 'soft' and lacking aggression.

*Table 5* Statements lauding aggression or criticising lack of aggression

| SportsCenter | Extreme | NBA | MLB | NFL |
|---|---|---|---|---|
| 3 | 4 | 40 | 4 | 15 |

Commentators consistently lauded athletes who most successfully employed physical and aggressive play and toughness. For instance, after having his toughness called into question, NBA player Brian Grant was awarded redemption by *SportsCenter* because he showed that he is 'not afraid to take it to Karl Malone'. *SportsCenter* also informed viewers that 'the aggressor usually gets the calls [from the officials] and the Spurs were the ones getting them'. In pro wrestling commentary, this is a constant theme (and was therefore not included in our tallies for Table 5 because the theme permeated the commentary, overtly and covertly). The World Wrestling Federation (WWF) announcers praised the 'raw power' of wrestler 'Shamrock' and approvingly dubbed 'Hardcore Holly' as 'the world's most dangerous man'. NBA commentators suggested that it is okay to be a good guy off the court but one must be tough and aggressive on the court: Brian Grant and Jeff Hornacek are 'true gentlemen of the NBA ... as long as you don't have to play against them. You know they're great off the court; on the court, every single guy out there *should* be a killer'.

When players were not doing well, they were often described as 'hesitant' and lacking aggression, emotion and desire (such as for a loose ball or rebound). For instance, commentators lamented that 'the Jazz aren't going to the hoop, they're being pushed and shoved around', that Utah was responding to the Blazers' aggression 'passively, in a reactive mode', and that 'Utah's got to get Karl Malone toughened up'. *SportsCenter* echoed this theme, opening one show with a depiction of Horace Grant elbowing Karl Malone and asking of Malone, 'Is he feeble?' Similarly, NFL broadcasters waxed on about the virtues of aggression and domination. Big 'hits'; ball carriers who got 'buried', 'stuffed', or 'walloped' by the defence; and players who get 'cleaned out' or 'wiped out' by a blocker were often shown on replays, with announcers enthusiastically describing the plays. By contrast, they clearly declared that it is a very bad thing to be passive and to let yourself get pushed around and dominated at the line of scrimmage. Announcers also approvingly noted that going after an opposing player's injured body part is just smart strategy. In one NFL game, the Miami strategy to blitz the opposing quarterback was lauded as 'brilliant' – 'When you know your opposing quarterback is a bit nicked and something is wrong, Boomer, you got to come after him'.

Previous research has pointed to this heroic framing of the male body-as-weapon as a key element in sport's role in the social construction of narrow conceptions of masculinity (Messner 1992; Trujillo 1995). This injunction for boys and men to be aggressive, not passive, is reinforced in commercials, where a common formula is to play on the insecurities of young males (that they are not strong, tough, smart, rich, attractive, decisive enough, and so on), and then attempt to convince them to avoid, overcome, or mask their fears, embarrassments, and apparent shortcomings by buying a particular product. These commercials often portray men as potential or actual 'geeks', 'nerds', or passive 'schmucks' who can overcome their geekiness (or avoid being a geek like the guy in the commercial) by becoming decisive and purchasing a particular product.

### Boys will be (violent) boys

Announcers often took a humorous 'boys will be boys' attitude in discussing fights or near-fights during contests, and they also commonly used a recent fight, altercation, or disagreement between two players as a 'teaser' to build audience excitement, as Table 6 records.

*Table 6*   Humorous or sarcastic discussion of fights or near-fights

| SportsCenter | Extreme | NBA | MLB | NFL |
|---|---|---|---|---|
| 10 | 1 | 2 | 2 | 7 |

Fights, near-fights, threats of fights, or other violent actions were over-emphasised in sports coverage and often verbally framed in sarcastic language that suggested that this kind of action, although reprehensible, is to be expected. For instance, as *SportsCenter* showed NBA centres Robinson and O'Neill exchanging forearm shoves, the commentators said, simply, 'much love'. Similarly, in an NFL game, a brief scuffle between players is met with a sarcastic comment by the broadcaster that the players are simply 'making their acquaintance'. This is, of course, a constant theme in pro wrestling (which, again, we found impossible and less than meaningful to count because this theme permeates the show). We found it noteworthy that the supposedly spontaneous fights outside the wrestling ring (what we call unofficial fights) were given more coverage time and focus than the supposedly official fights inside the ring. We speculate that wrestling producers know that viewers already watch fights inside the ring with some scepticism as to their authenticity, so they stage the unofficial fights outside the ring to bring a feeling of spontaneity and authenticity to the show and to build excitement and a sense of anticipation for the fight that will later occur inside the ring.

*Give up your body for the team*

Athletes who are 'playing with pain', 'giving up their body for the team', or engaging in obviously highly dangerous plays or manoeuvres were consistently framed as heroes (see Table 7 below).

*Table 7* Comments on the heroic nature of playing hurt

| SportsCenter | Extreme | NBA | MLB | NFL |
| --- | --- | --- | --- | --- |
| 9 | 12 | 6 | 4 | 15 |

Conversely, those who removed themselves from games due to injuries had questions raised about their character, their manhood. This theme cut across all sports programming. For instance, *SportsCenter* asked, 'Could the dominator be soft?' when a National Hockey League (NHL) star goalie decided to sit out a game due to a groin injury. Heroically taking risks while already hurt was a constant theme in Extreme sports commentary. For instance, one bike competitor was lauded for 'overcoming his fear' and competing 'with a busted up ankle', and another was applauded when he 'popped his collarbone out in the street finals in Louisville but he's back on his bike here in Richmond, just 2 weeks later!' Athletes appear especially heroic when they go against doctors' wishes not to compete. For instance, an X Games interviewer adoringly told a competitor, 'Doctors said don't ride but you went ahead and did it anyway and escaped serious injury'. Similarly, NBA player Isaiah Rider was lauded for having 'heart' for 'playing with that knee injury'. Injury discussions in NFL games often include speculation about whether the player will be able to return to this or future games. A focus on a star player in a pre-game or half-time show, such as the feature on 49ers' Garrison Hearst, often contain commentary about heroic overcoming of serious injuries (in this case, a knee blowout, reconstructive surgery, and rehabilitation). As one game began, commentators noted that 37-year-old 'Steve Young has remained a rock . . . not bad for a guy who a lotta people figured was, what, one big hit from ending his career'. It's especially impressive when an injured player is able and willing to continue to play with aggressiveness and reckless abandon: 'Kurt Scrafford at right guard – bad neck and all – is just out there wiping out guys'. And announcers love the team leader who plays hurt:

Drew Bledso gamely tried to play in loss to Rams yesterday; really admirable to try to play with that pin that was surgically implanted in his finger during the week; I don't know how a Q.B. could do that. You know, he broke his finger the time we had him on Monday night and he led his team to two come-from-behind victories, really gutted it out and I think he took that team on his shoulders and showed he could play and really elevated himself in my eyes, he really did.

### Sport is war

Commentators consistently (an average of nearly five times during each hour of sports commentary) used martial metaphors and language of war and weaponry to describe sports action (battle, kill, ammunition, weapons, professional sniper, depth charges, taking aim, fighting, shot in his arsenal, reloading, detonate, squeezes the trigger, attack mode, firing blanks, blast, explosion, blitz, point of attack, a lance through the heart, and so on):

*Table 8* Martial metaphors and language of war and weaponry

| SportsCenter | Extreme | Wrestling | NBA | MLB | NFL |
|---|---|---|---|---|---|
| 9 | 3 | 15 | 27 | 6 | 23 |

Some shows went beyond commentators' use of war terminology and actually framed the contests as wars. For instance, one of the wrestling shows offered a continual flow of images and commentary that reminded the viewers that 'RAW is WAR!' Similarly, both NFL *Monday Night Football* broadcasts were introduced with explosive graphics and an opening song that included lyrics 'Like a rocket burning through time and space, the NFL's best will rock this place . . . the battle lines are drawn'. This sort of use of sport/war metaphors has been a common practice in televised sports commentary for many years, serving to fuse (and confuse) the distinctions between values of nationalism with team identity and athletic aggression with military destruction (Jansen and Sabo 1994). In the shows examined for this study, war themes also were reinforced in many commercials, including commercials for movies, other sports programs, and in the occasional commercial for the U.S. military.

### Show some guts!

Commentators continually depicted and replayed exciting incidents of athletes engaging in reckless acts of speed, showing guts in the face of danger, big hits, and violent crashes:

*Table 9*  Depictions of guts in face of danger, speed, hits, crashes

| SportsCenter | Extreme | NBA | MLB | NFL |
|---|---|---|---|---|
| 4 | 21 | 5 | 2 | 8 |

This theme was evident across all of the sports programmes, but was especially predominant in Extreme sports that continually depicted crashing vehicles or bikers in an exciting manner. For instance, when one race ended with a crash, it was shown again in slow-motion replay, with commentators approvingly dubbing it 'unbelievable' and 'original'. Extreme sports commentators commonly raised excitement levels by saying 'he's on fire' or 'he's going huge!' when a competitor was obviously taking greater risks. An athlete's ability to deal with the fear of a possible crash, in fact, is the mark of an 'outstanding run': 'Watch out, Richmond', an X-games announcer shouted to the crowd, 'He's gonna wreck this place!' A winning competitor laughingly said, 'I do what I can to smash into [my opponents] as much as I can'. Another competitor said, 'If I crash, no big deal; I'm just gonna go for it'. NFL commentators introduced the games with images of reckless collisions, and during the game a 'fearless' player was likely to be applauded: 'There's no chance that Barry Sanders won't take when he's running the football'. In another game, the announcer noted that receiver 'Tony Simmons plays big. And for those of you not in the NFL, playing big means you're not afraid to go across the middle and catch the ball and make a play out of it after you catch the ball'. Men showing guts in the face of speed and danger was also a major theme in 40 of the commercials that we analysed.

### The televised sports manhood formula

Tens of millions of US boys watch televised sports programs, with their accompanying commercial advertisements. This study sheds light on what these boys are seeing when they watch their favourite sports programs. What values and ideas about gender, race, aggression, and violence are being promoted? Although there are certainly differences across different kinds of sports, as well as across different commercials, when we looked at all of the programming together, we identified 10 recurrent themes, which we have outlined above. Taken together, these themes codify a consistent and (mostly) coherent message about what it means to be a man. We call this message the Televised Sports Manhood Formula:

> What is a Real Man? A Real Man is strong, tough, aggressive, and above all, a winner in what is still a Man's World. To be a winner he has to do what needs to be done. He must be willing to compromise his own long-term health by showing guts in the face of danger, by fighting other men when necessary, and by 'playing hurt' when he's injured. He must avoid being soft; he must be the aggressor, both on the 'battle fields' of sports and in his consumption choices. Whether he is playing sports or making choices about which snack food or auto products to purchase, his aggressiveness will net him the ultimate prize: the adoring attention of conventionally beautiful women. He will know if and when he has arrived as a Real Man when the Voices of Authority – White Males – say he is a Real Man. But even when he has finally managed to win the big one, has the good car, the right beer, and is surrounded by beautiful women, he will be reminded by these very same Voices of Authority just how fragile this Real Manhood really is: After all, he has to come out and prove himself all over again tomorrow. You're only as good as your last game (or your last purchase).

The major elements of the Televised Sports Manhood Formula are evident, in varying degrees, in the football, basketball, baseball, Extreme sports, and *SportsCenter* programs and in their accompanying commercials. But it is in the dramatic spectacle of professional wrestling that the Televised Sports Manhood Formula is most clearly codified and presented to audiences as an almost seamless package. Boys and young men are drawn to televised professional wrestling in great numbers. Consistently each week, from four to six pro wrestling shows rank among the top 10 rated shows on cable television. Professional wrestling is not a real sport in the way that baseball, basketball, football, or even Extreme sports are. In fact, it is a highly stylised and choreographed 'sport as theatre' form of entertainment. Its producers have condensed – and then amplified – all of the themes that make up the Televised Sports Manhood Formula. For instance, where violence represents a thread in the football or basketball commentary, violence makes up the entire fabric of the theatrical narrative of televised pro wrestling. In short, professional wrestling presents viewers with a steady stream of images and commentary that represents a constant fusion of all of the themes that make up the Televised Sports Manhood Formula. This is a choreographed sport where all men (except losers) are Real Men, where women are present as sexy support objects for the men's violent, monumental 'wars' against each other. Winners bravely display muscular strength, speed, power, and guts. Bodily harm is (supposedly) intentionally inflicted on opponents. The most ruthlessly aggressive men win, whereas the passive or weaker men lose, often shamefully. Heroically wrestling while injured, rehabilitating oneself from former injuries, and inflicting pain and injury on one's opponent are constant and central themes in the narrative.

## Gender and the sports/media/commercial complex

In 1984, media scholar Sut Jhally pointed to the commercial and ideological symbiosis between the institutions of sport and the mass media and called it the sports/media complex. Our examination of the ways that the Televised Sports Manhood Formula reflects and promotes hegemonic ideologies concerning race, gender, sexuality, aggression, violence, and consumerism suggests adding a third dimension to Jhally's analysis: the huge network of multi-billion-dollar automobile, snack food, alcohol, entertainment, and other corporate entities that sponsor sports events and broadcasts. In fact, examining the ways that the Televised Sports Manhood Formula cuts across sports programming and its accompanying commercials may provide important clues as to the ways that ideologies of hegemonic masculinity are both promoted by – and in turn serve to support and stabilise – this collection of interrelated institutions that make up the sports/media/ commercial complex. The Televised Sports Manhood Formula is a master discourse that is produced at the nexus of the institutions of sport, mass media, and corporations who produce and hope to sell products and services to boys and men. As such, the Televised Sports Manhood Formula appears well suited to discipline boys' bodies, minds, and consumption choices within an ideological field that is conducive to the reproduction of the entrenched interests that profit from the sports/media/commercial complex. The perpetuation of the entrenched commercial interests of the sports/media/ commercial complex appears to be predicated on boys accepting – indeed glorifying and celebrating – a set of bodily and relational practices that resist and oppose a view of women as fully human and place boys' and men's long-term health prospects in jeopardy.

At a historical moment when hegemonic masculinity has been destabilised by socio-economic change, and by women's and gay liberation movements, the Televised Sports Manhood Formula provides a remarkably stable and concrete view of masculinity as grounded in bravery, risk taking, violence, bodily strength, and heterosexuality. And this view of masculinity is given coherence against views of women as sexual support objects or as invisible and thus irrelevant to men's public struggles for glory. Yet, perhaps to be successful in selling products, the commercials sometimes provide a less than seamless view of masculinity. The insecurities of masculinity in crisis are often tweaked in the commercials, as we see weak men, dumb men, and indecisive men being eclipsed by strong, smart, and decisive men and sometimes being humiliated by smarter and more decisive women. In short, this commercialised version of hegemonic masculinity is constructed partly in relation to images of men who don't measure up. This analysis gives us hints at an answer to the commonly asked question of why so many boys and men continue to take seemingly irrational risks, submit to pain and injury, and risk long-term debility or even death by playing hurt. A critical examination of the Televised Sports Manhood Formula tells us why: the costs of masculinity (especially pain and injury), according to this formula, appear to be well worth the price; the boys and men who are willing to pay the price always seem to get the glory, the championships, the best consumer products, and the beautiful women. Those who don't – or can't – pay the price are humiliated or ignored by women and left in the dust by other men. In short, the Televised Sports Manhood Formula is a pedagogy through which boys are taught that paying the price, be it one's bodily health or one's money, gives one access to the privileges that have been historically linked to hegemonic masculinity – money, power, glory, and women. And the barrage of images of femininity as model-like beauty displayed for and in the service of successful men suggests that heterosexuality is a major lynchpin of the Televised Sports Manhood Formula, and on a larger scale serves as one of the major linking factors in the conservative gender regime of the sports/media/commercial complex.

On the other hand, we must be cautious in coming to definitive conclusions as to how the promotion of the values embedded in the Televised Sports Manhood Formula might fit into the worlds of young men. It is not possible, based merely on our textual analysis of sports programs, to explicate precisely what kind of impact these shows, and the Televised Sports Manhood Formula, have on their young male audiences. That sort of question is best approached through direct research with audiences. Most such research finds that audiences interpret, use, and draw meanings from media variously, based on factors such as social class, race/ethnicity, and gender (Whannel 1998; Hunt 1999). Research with various subgroups of boys that explores their interpretations of the sports programs that they watch would enhance and broaden this study.

Moreover, it is important to go beyond the preferred reading presented here that emphasises the persistent themes in televised sports that appear to reinforce the hegemony of current race, gender, and commercial relations (Sabo and Jansen 1992). In addition to these continuities, there are some identifiable discontinuities within and between the various sports programs and within and among the accompanying commercials. For instance, commercials are far more varied in the ways that they present gender imagery than are sports programs themselves. Although the dominant tendency in commercials is either to erase women or to present them as stereotypical support or sex objects, a significant minority of commercials presents themes that set up boys and men as insecure and/or obnoxious schmucks and women as secure, knowledgeable, and authoritative. Audience research with boys who watch sport would shed fascinating light on how they decode and interpret these more complex, mixed, and paradoxical gender images against the dominant, hegemonic image of the Televised Sports Manhood Formula.

## Notes

1 There are some differences, and some similarities, in what boys and girls prefer to watch. The top seven televised sports reported by girls are, in order, gymnastics, men's pro basketball, pro football, pro baseball, swimming/diving, men's college basketball, and women's pro or college basketball.

2 Although images of feminine beauty shift, change, and are contested throughout history, female beauty is presented in sports programming and commercials in narrow ways. Attractive women look like fashion models

(Banet-Weiser, 1999): They are tall, thin, young, usually (although not always) White, with signs of heterosexual femininity encoded and overtly displayed through hair, makeup, sexually provocative facial and bodily gestures, large (often partially exposed) breasts, long (often exposed) legs, and so forth.

## References

Amateur Athletic Foundation of Los Angeles (1999) *Children and Sports Media.* Los Angeles: Author.

Banet-Weiser, S. (1999) *The Most Beautiful Girl in the World: Beauty Pageants and National Identity.* Berkeley: University of California Press.

Duncan, M.C. and Messner, M.A. (1998) The media image of sport and gender, in L. A. Wenner (ed.) *MediaSport.* New York: Routledge.

Hunt, D. (1999) *O.J. Simpson Facts and Fictions.* New York: Cambridge University Press.

Jansen, S.C. and Sabo, D. (1994) The sport/war metaphor: hegemonic masculinity, the Persian Gulf war, and the new world order, *Sociology of Sport Journal,* 11:1–17.

Jhally, S. (1984) The spectacle of accumulation: material and cultural factors in the evolution of the sports/media complex, *Insurgent Sociologist,* 12(3): 1–52.

Kane, M.J. and Lenskyj, H.J. (1998) Media treatment of female athletes: issues of gender and sexualities, in L.A. Wenner (ed.) *MediaSport.* New York: Routledge.

Messner, M.A. (1992) *Power at Play: Sports and the Problem of Masculinity.* Boston: Beacon.

Rinehart, R. (1998) Inside of the outside: pecking orders within alternative sport at ESPN's 1995 'The extreme Games', *Journal of Sport & Social Issues,* 22: 398–415.

Sabo, D. and Jansen, S.C. (1992) Images of men in sport media: the social reproduction of masculinity, in S. Craig (ed.) *Men, Masculinity, and the Media.* Newbury Park, CA: Sage.

Sabo, D. and Jansen, S.C. (1994) Seen but not heard: images of Black men in sports media, in M.A. Messner and D.F. Sabo (eds) *Sex, Violence and Power in Sports: Rethinking Masculinity.* Freedom, CA: Crossing Press.

Trujillo, N. (1995) Machines, missiles, and men: images of the male body on ABC's *Monday Night Football, Sociology of Sport Journal,* 12: 403–23.

Whannel, G. (1998) Reading the sports media audience, in L.A. Wenner (ed.) *MediaSport.* New York: Routledge.

Wheaton, B. and Tomlinson, A. (1998) The changing gender order in sport? The case of windsurfing subcultures, *Journal of Sport & Social Issues,* 22: 252–74.

# 13

# THE BASIC CONTENT: 'IDEALLY BEAUTIFUL AND SEXY WOMEN FOR MEN'

## Laurel A. Davis

Excerpt from *The Swimsuit Issue and Sport: Hegemonic Masculinity in Sports Illustrated*. Albany: State University of New York Press, 1997, Chapter 3: 19–32.

Interestingly, consumers, for the most part, agree with each other in regard to the basic content of the swimsuit issues and the type of people who are most likely to consume these issues. Some elements of the swimsuit issue texts, production, consumption, and the sociocultural environment help to create this agreement.

### The basic content: ideal women's bodies

Consumers clearly feel that producers design the swimsuit issue to display women's bodies. As one interviewed consumer expresses it, the swimsuit issue is about 'women showing off their bodies'. Consumers believe that the swimsuit issue does not just focus on *any* women or *any* bodies, but on feminine women and their ideally beautiful and sexy bodies. That consumers declare beauty to be an essential component of the swimsuit issue is illustrated by one interviewed consumer's statement that the issue consists of 'beautiful girls in swimwear'. Most consumers assume mainstream or dominant definitions of beauty, and they rarely articulate critiques of these socially created beauty standards. Only two of the interviewed consumers, both people of colour, critique these standards in any way. Most consumers also name sexuality as a central element of the swimsuit issue content.

One interviewed consumer calls the swimsuit issue 'cheesecake', while another describes it as 'soft-core pornography'. Most of the interviewed consumers immediately and forthrightly articulated this meaning, yet other interviewed consumers waited until part way into the interview to suggest this meaning and seemed nervous in stating it. Societal taboos regarding open conversations about sexuality likely contributed to the hesitancy on the part of these consumers to freely discuss sexual meaning, especially with an unknown person.

Finally, consumers view the swimsuit issue models as symbols of femininity, womanhood, or women's difference from men. For example, in the February 22, 1982 issue of *Sports Illustrated*, a letter writer states that the swimsuit issue is a relief from the winter outfits he currently sees, which he complains do not help to distinguish between men and women: 'Do you realize it's 20° below zero here in Colorado . . . and we can't even tell women from men because of the multilayers of clothing we're wearing . . . I love [the swimsuit issue]' (72). A 1984 letter writer declares that, 'In an age of transvestite rock stars, bisexuality and drug abuse in sport, I find it wholesome to see that boys can still be boys, and girls can still be girls' (March 12: 86). Later I will discuss the role that perceived physical gender difference plays in legitimating the current gender order.

## The ideal readers: men

Consumers consensus goes beyond the basic content of the swimsuit issue, as they also concur about who reads the swimsuit issue. Most consumers maintain that men and boys constitute the primary con-sumers of the swimsuit issue, and that women either do not consume the issue much at all or represent less significant consumers. For example, the interviewed consumers describe the swimsuit issue as 'geared towards men', 'a draw for men', and 'male-oriented'. By the 1970s consumers whose letters appear in the Letters to the Editor section of *Sports Illustrated* began to explicitly define the swimsuit issue as a form of representation for men. For example, one writer describes the swimsuit issue as something '. . . that sons hide under mattresses' (February 19, 1979: 78), while another claims that the issue features pictures of 'girlie stuff to leave our sports-loving men with their tongues hanging out' (February 22, 1982: 72).

## Denotative versus connotative level meaning

Awareness of antagonistic opinions concerning the swimsuit issue, and the recently-produced academic literature that claims that audience members create divergent interpretations of all media texts, led me to anticipate that there would be little agreement among consumers regarding the meaning of the swimsuit issue. Thus, I was surprised to find consensus among consumers regarding the basic content and ideal readers of the issue. To explain such a finding, Celeste Michelle Condit (1989) maintains that it is useful to distinguish between denotative and connotative level meanings. The distinction between these two levels of meaning is purely analytical (Hall 1984; Heck 1984). Heck explains that:

> Denotation 'simply refers to the first system of signification which generates a second system "wider than the first" (which is the plane of connotation)' . . . In this sense 'denotation' is nothing more than a useful rule for distinguishing, in any particular instance or operation, those connotations which have become naturalized and those which, not being so fixed, provide the opportunity for more extensive ideological representations.
>
> (Heck 1984: 125–6)

As Hall (1984: 132) observes, at the level of denotation, encodings and decodings often have an 'achieved equivalence'. Most struggle over meaning takes place at the connotative level (Hall 1984). Condit argues that it is probably common for an audience to create similar interpretations of denotative level meaning, or the basic content of a media text, but then to evaluate this text in different ways, thus producing different connotative level interpretations:

> Polyvalence occurs when the audience members share understandings of the denotations of a text but disagree about the valuation of these denotations to such a degree that they produce notably different interpretations . . . Different respondents may similarly understand the messages that a text seeks to convey. They may, however, see the text as rhetorical – as urging positions upon them – and make their own selections among and evaluations of those pervasive messages.
>
> (Condit 1989: 106–7)

Here, Condit (1989) is talking about oppositional readings. Justin Lewis (1991) contends that some audience members do challenge denotative level meanings, thus producing resistant readings. My findings regarding consumer interpretations of the swimsuit issue reaffirm the findings of Condit (1989) that, within a given culture, different interpretations of meaning occur primarily at the connotative level. Within a common culture, the different sub/countercultural discourses understood by various categories of consumers mainly influence how they evaluate the basic content of a media text, not what they define as this content. Certainly, consumers create resistant readings of many media texts, where the reading does not rest upon the same denotative level meanings as dominant, negotiated, and oppositional readings. Yet, I did not discover any such resistant readings of the swimsuit issue.

## Factors that encourage denotative level consensus

Many factors help to produce relative consensus among consumers regarding the basic content and ideal readers of the swimsuit issue. Although I do not have room to document all of these factors and the relationships between them, here I provide some examples of how these factors contribute to the consensus.

### The ideas of producers

Most of the interviewed producers indicate that they design the swimsuit issue to highlight the models' bodies. Some of the interviewed producers point out that the backgrounds and the swimwear are secondary to the models' bodies. For example, an interviewed model argues:

> Usually if you're in a fashion shoot, what people are interested in is having the clothes look good. In this case, it's really making sure that your body looks good . . . I don't think there's anyway of getting around the fact that what you're really showing is not bathing suits, it's bodies . . . it's about bodies.

Some of the interviewed producers imply that they design the swimsuit issue to express femininity and/or ideal beauty. An interviewed photographer says he hopes that the reader will 'see that he's got a really beautiful woman in front of him'. An interviewed model states that the producers try to capture 'the essence of woman'. One interviewed photographer notes that when he works on the swimsuit issue he tries to convey 'a lot of sensuality as well as sexuality'. Although almost all of the interviewed producers named sexual meaning as central to the swimsuit issue, some neglected to name or discuss this meaning. I asked these producers why many consumers interpret the issue as expressing sexual meaning. They responded in two ways, arguing that the standpoint of the consumers prompts this interpretation, and asserting that 'There's a component of erotic appeal in almost every way that people appreciate other people for their physical skills'. Since much of the controversy surrounding the swimsuit issue relates to sexual meaning, it is not surprising that some of the producers deny that they intentionally produce this meaning.

When asked about the audience they address when they create the swimsuit issue, some of the interviewed producers claim that they do not shape the issue with any specific types of reader in mind. A few remark that they consider their colleagues from the media industry, while others say that they keep the demographic data of *Sports Illustrated* in mind. Most of the interviewed producers imply or directly state that they fashion the issue primarily for men and boys. For example, one interviewed producer declares that the issue is 'clearly for a male audience'.

### The production process

A variety of production practices helps to create the consensus among consumers regarding the denotative level meaning of the swimsuit issue. These practices include: the small number of influential producers; the communication practices used by producers; body management and posing techniques; picture modifications; and the criteria employed during selection of pictorial background, photographers, models, swimwear, and the pictures themselves. The small number of influential producers, and the power these producers have to select other producers that agree to shape the issue in the desired manner, enable them to create texts that convey little ambiguity. Only a few producers make decisions that directly and substantially impact on the meanings encoded into the text. The senior editor and managing editor have the most significant impact, while the design director and photographer(s) also exert a considerable influence. Other producers contribute to the encoded meanings in a much less consequential way. The managing editor occupies the position with the most power over the content of *Sports Illustrated*, and possesses final authority over the content of the swimsuit issue. As the interviewed managing editor notes, 'I contribute a lot in that I express my desire and my concern for a certain kind of story, and it's the responsibility of the senior editor . . . to deliver that for me'. The senior editor and the assistant(s) to the senior editor hold the only jobs at *Sports Illustrated* that solely involve duties related to the swimsuit issue. The senior editor manages the daily work on the swimsuit issue and makes most of the decisions related to the issue. For example, the senior editor selects the swimwear, hires the models, directs the shoot, helps to choose the pictures, and creates the written text for the spread.

The communication that takes place between the producers increases the degree of agreement among them regarding the meanings that they attempt to express during the encoding phase. Producers insist that those who work on the swimsuit issue possess the ability to work well together. In the 1990 swimsuit issue calendar, the senior editor writes that there must be chemistry, 'Between the model and me, the photographer, the rest of the crew and, most of all, the reader'. Producers require that those who work on the swimsuit issue commit themselves to the mission of the issue, which seems to mean that they must submit to those who most understand this mission. In the 1990 swimsuit issue calendar, the senior editor writes that the models need 'a ready recognition of the nature of the assignment, and a willingness to commit to it'. An interviewed producer argues that *Sports Illustrated* selects photographers that 'they can push around'. The senior editor communicates her conceptions regarding meaning to others involved in the production of the issue. As one interviewed model describes it:

> Basically, when you do your first issue and your first shoot, and throughout the shooting, the [senior editor] . . . is constantly coaching you . . . as to what image they would like you to bring across . . . I sat down and sort of had an interview with *Sports Illustrated* before I even did the issue, and they told me what it was all about.

This model continued to note that if she was not 'capturing' sensual meaning, producers 'would say something'.

The criteria producers use to select the backgrounds, swimwear, and models contribute to the consensus regarding the content of the issue. Some of the interviewed producers state that the locations for the pictures should include beaches, water, rocks, sky, and sunrises/sunsets. This routinisation of the background encourages consumers to view the models as the most important part of the picture rather than the setting. Some of the interviewed producers note that *Sports Illustrated* often selects swimwear that 'reveals' the models' bodies, and thus expresses sexual meaning. For example, one interviewed producer asserts that one of the 'most important' criteria for selecting the swimwear is 'sexuality'. Producers consider 'physical beauty' an important criterion when selecting the models. The interviewed producers believe that the beauty of the models is enhanced when they are thin, tall, 'good' for swimwear, and adept at posing. In the modelling world, 'good' for swimwear means more curvaceous than bodies used for most other forms of clothing. As one interviewed producer describes it:

> *Sports Illustrated* does portray itself, and sells itself, on a tits-and-ass type issue. As a result, they're looking for curvy, curvaceous bodies, girls with good bodies, with tits and ass . . . They're looking for a model who is sexy, a model who can make a bathing suit look great.

Producers of the swimsuit issue use various posing, body management, and adornment techniques to create images which suggest meanings of ideal beauty to consumers. According to one interviewed producer, prior to the shoots the models tan in the nude and remove pubic hair. Letters from the Publisher indicate that the models use bleach to lighten their hair (1978) and cosmetics (1984). One of the interviewed models comments on the posing techniques:

> You just always have to be very conscious of how your body looks and how to sit and how not to sit, and how not to have your stomach out, and how not to have your thighs look too big in this position or that position . . . There's a definite technique as far as body movements.

Producers use the criteria of beauty to reduce the large number of photographs they take to the small number actually published. As one interviewed producer expresses it:

> You have to look for a flawless picture. [Flaws are] things like focus or a bad expression. Sometimes the flaws just happen to be the way a knee looks, or an arm looks, or an elbow, or just something that appears to be a blemish on the photograph, whether it's a shadow or one hair blowing in front of her eye.

Finally, the producers encourage interpretations of ideal beauty by touching up the pictures to remove signifiers (that is, objects or symbols) that run counter to the current beauty ideal. Some inter-viewed producers cite examples of aspects of swimsuit issue pictures that producers 'touch up', including hair, wrinkles on a model's hip, colour, dark shadows, and 'funny positioning'.

### Features of the text

Many components of the swimsuit issue texts encourage consumer consensus regarding the content and ideal readers of the issue. Of course, consumers need to attend to, and have particular under-standings of, these features of textual structure for this process to work. Some elements of the swimsuit issue texts suggest to the con-sumer that they should attend to the models' bodies. For example, the captions describe the models as alluring (1980; 1990), attracting attention (1986; 1987; 1989), and an eyeful (1989). The producers usually locate the models in the centre of the pictures, and their bodies typically fill a large percentage of the space in the picture. Producers rarely crop the pictures above the model's mid-thigh. The swimsuit issues typically include pictures that do not present the swimwear in prominent ways. The backgrounds behind the models look very routinised, and sometimes one cannot even see this background. The posing styles and expressions also suggest that consumers should focus on the bodies of the models. Many times the lower bodies of the models face one way, while their upper bodies and/or heads are twisted toward the spectator. In almost all of the pictures, the models pose with a head cant to the side and/or down, and eye aversion. Scholars argue that these conventions invite the spectator's guiltless gaze (Goffman 1976; Dyer 1982; Kuhn 1985).

Many elements of the swimsuit issue texts urge consumers to view the models as ideally beautiful. For example, captions commonly suggest that the models epitomise beauty (1970; 1976; 1984), with the title for the 1984 swimsuit spread being, ' "A" You're Adorable, "B" You're . . .' (64–65). The models featured in the swimsuit issue resemble the current feminine beauty ideal. For the most part, they are young, thin and curvaceous, lack blemishes, muscular definition and visible body hair (except on the scalp, eye area, and occasionally on the forearms), and show no signs of disability. The fact that the beauty ideal demands youthfulness and lack of disability is evidence that it reflects and reinforces ageism and 'ableism'. Given the racism embedded in the dominant beauty ideal, it is not surprising that models of colour have been under-represented in the swimsuit issues over the years, almost all of the white models possess blonde or light brown, long and straight hair, and blue eyes prevail. Many parts of the swimsuit issue texts encourage consumers to interpret the models as valid representatives of ideal femininity defined as clear difference from the masculine: women are or should be markedly dissimilar to men. The contrast between how women appear in the swimsuit issue and how men appear as athletes in *Sports Illustrated* accentuates such difference. On three occasions, the Letter from the Publisher has featured pictures of men posing like the women models (February 9, 1981; February 10, 1986; February 9, 1987). Producers suggest that viewers perceive these pictures as humorous, probably because the pictured men represent a contrast to the models' femininity. The swimsuit issue texts commonly direct attention to the gender of the models. For example, a producer writing in the 1970 issue describes the swimwear as feminine, '. . . proving that girls can still resemble girls' (34).

The physical characteristics of the models, described above, correspond with the current feminine appearance ideal. The fact that the models tend to resemble each other intimates that there is a single standard of ideal womanhood. The use of jewellery, cosmetics, and fashions with features such as lace and flowers also suggests that the models look feminine. Since emotionality, connection to nature, lack of power, youthfulness, and (female) heterosexuality signify femininity in contemporary United States culture, the many features of the swimsuit issue texts that suggest these meanings encourage the consumer to associate the models with femininity. Some emotional activities attributed to the models in the captions are 'smouldering' (1975), 'musing' (1982), and being 'downcast' (1989). When the written texts in the swimsuit issue feature a discussion of the models' status as wives and girlfriends (of men), these texts suggest that the models are heterosexual, a central component of the contemporary feminine ideal.

Poses, appearance management techniques, and swimwear featured in the swimsuit issue link the models to nature. Since the late 1970s, the swimsuit issues sometimes picture suits that resemble animal skins or plants. A recurring pose for models is a crawling position with the buttocks thrust upward, similar to the way many animals appear. Often in the 1980s, and occasionally in the 1970s, the swimsuit issue captions suggest that the suit or model resembles or blends in with parts of nature. Some routine appearance management or body decoration techniques insinuate meanings related to nature. For example, sometimes the hair of the models looks messy, suggesting natural freedom or disarray due to immersion in nature. Many features of the swimsuit issue texts convey femininity by signifying in various ways that the models lack physical power because of their thinness and lack of muscular definition. The models also commonly pose in ways that express a lack of power (Goffman 1976; Berger 1982; Masse and Rosenblum 1988). They rarely directly face the camera and often appear in a lying or crawling position, peering out from behind something, with their heads canted down and/or to the side, and with their eyes averted. Although most of the swimsuit issue pictures are shot from the same level as the model, the magazine published a significant number of pictures, especially in the 1980s and early 1990s, photographed from above the model.

Childhood also signifies a lack of power, and thus femininity. The lack of body hair on the models suggests that they resemble children. Poses that display immature movement patterns, silliness, and simple gymnastics moves encourage viewers to perceive the models as childlike. Other symbols of childhood, such as pigtails or ponytails, a childlike expression such as pouting, or a suit with a childlike theme, frequently accompany these poses. Childlikeness is also conveyed through written texts in the swimsuit issue. For example, the Letter from the Publisher often portrays the models as innocent and frightened. One publisher writes about a model bringing a stuffed animal along for security (1985); another describes a model as bridging 'the gap between the innocent little girl look and the sophisticated woman look' (1976: 6). Femininity is not a politically neutral construct. The notions that women are vastly different from men, overly emotional, childlike, physically weak, dependent on men, and connected to nature (rather than civilization) have been used to limit women's power. Thus, when *Sports Illustrated* publishes images that reinforce these ideas about women, they reinforce sexism.

Many parts of the swimsuit issue texts encourage consumers to think that the issue conveys sexual meaning. Youthfulness, thinness, curvaceousness, hairless bodies, long blonde scalp hair, and cosmetics are widely accepted contemporary signifiers of a woman's (passive) sexual appeal. In the West, due to the racist stereotype that people of colour are licentious, dark skin signifies unrestrained sexuality; therefore the tanned skin of the white models increases the perception that they are sexy (Lurie 1981; Urry 1990). Many consumers think that the swimwear pictured in the swimsuit issue contributes to the sexual meaning of the issue. For example, one interviewed consumer calls the swimwear 'erotic'. Although diverse styles of bathing suits appear in the swimsuit issue, suits with features that suggest sexual meaning appear regularly. Since people in the United States generally perceive breasts, buttocks, and the pubic area as erogenous zones, and nudity itself as sexual, they associate outfits which expose most of the body or these parts of the body with sexuality. The material, style, and size of the suits appearing in the swimsuit issues reveal the contours and edges of these erogenous zones, especially since the 1970s. Some examples of swimwear featured in *Sports Illustrated* that suggest nakedness include: [white] flesh coloured suits, suits without tops, suits with see-through parts, suits with minimal material, and suits with large v-cut openings down the middle of the chest. Written texts in the swimsuit issue commonly reinforce this sexual meaning. For example, captions from the 1970s and 1980s intimate that the models are 'stripped' (1977; 1985), 'wearing no top' (1971; 1979; 1982; 1983), and 'almost wearing or barely wearing' a suit (1979; 1980; 1982; 1983).

Many consumers feel that the posing featured in the swimsuit issue conveys sexual meaning. For example, one interviewed consumer describes the poses as 'sexually oriented'. The models usually arch and cant their bodies, which creates a curvaceous look, thus signifying sexuality. In the 1980s and early 1990s, the models sometimes hold parts of their suits in ways that reveal more of their bodies or suggest that they might reveal more. Two facial expressions that signify sexual meaning, the come-on and autoerotic look, often appear in the swim-suit issues. Models create the come-on look by slightly parting their lips, looking at the camera with narrowed eyes, and tilting their heads to the side (and perhaps downward) so that they glance at the camera in a slightly angled way. When constructing an autoerotic look, the model tilts her head fully backwards, slightly parts her lips, and closes or narrows her eyes (Millum 1975; Coward 1985; Kuhn 1985). Finally, the swimsuit issue texts suggest that the ideal readers of the issue are men and boys. For example, the Letter from the Publisher in 1976 implies that the swimsuit issue models appeal more to men than women; the publisher states that one of these models '. . . may not be the girl all women want to look like, but she has a quality that makes her the way most men think a woman should look' (6). The author of an article in the 1989 anniversary swimsuit issue discusses how young men use the swimsuit issue pictures as pin-up material.

### Schooling the reader

Through their references to the swimsuit issue in media texts other than the spread itself, *Sports Illustrated* producers encourage the denotative level meaning consensus, and thus end up schooling readers about 'appropriate' interpretations of the issue. For example, some recent television advertisements for *Sports Illustrated* that are explicitly aimed at men highlight the swimsuit issue, linking it with male consumers. The titles producers place above the published letters of reader response to the swimsuit issue nurture the consensus. These titles commonly suggest that consumers should direct their attention to the bodies of the models, such as 'Fore and Hindsight' (January 26, 1969), to the beauty of the models, such as 'Bathing Beauties' January 30, 1978), or to the sexuality of the models, such as 'Uncover Girl' (February 1, 1965). Several parts of the 1989 swimsuit issue video encourage consumers to define the content of the issue as ideally beautiful and sexy women's bodies. For example, the producers describe one model as sexy, and then the video pictures her stating that models need to 'flirt with the camera'. The producers highlight body parts that signify sexuality by focusing the camera on these parts and zooming slowly up or down the body. For example, in one segment, a model pulls a tank top up to reveal the lower part of her breasts as the camera operator zooms in on her chest and the photographer says, 'Come a little closer to me, Elle. Now pull it over your head. Go for it'.

### The social context

In order for consumers to see women's bodies, femininity, ideal beauty, and sexuality as the central content of the swimsuit issue, they must be familiar with the signifiers of these meanings that appear in the swimsuit issues. For example, one must understand the normative signifiers of women's sexuality, such as curvaceousness and the come-on facial expression, to interpret the swimsuit issue as conveying sexual meaning. Since normative signifiers of beauty, femininity, and sexuality regularly appear in the mass media in the United States, consumers typically have learned the common meaning of these sig-nifiers. The social context also encourages consumers to believe that the swimsuit issue is designed for men. In United States culture *Sports Illustrated* magazine itself is typically associated with men, and this bolsters the notion that the swimsuit issue is aimed at them. One interviewed consumer explicitly calls *Sports Illustrated* a 'men's magazine', while another consumer explains:

> I think that mainly men are probably interested in [*Sports Illustrated*]. I would guess they would be [the] main subscribers.

And, therefore, [with the swimsuit issue] they're gearing more toward them by putting out an issue they would be interested in.

The wider societal context also socialises people to believe that hetero-sexuality is natural, universal, and compelling, and thus most people in the United States take this belief for granted. If consumers assume that the issue signifies sexual meaning and that all readers are heterosexual, then they often deduce that producers make the issue for men. For example, one interviewed consumer notes, 'The male audience would be attracted to women in swimsuits . . . The issues I've seen, they didn't have any men in bikinis. Therefore, they're definitely not catering to a female audience'. Another interviewed consumer argues:

> The whole idea behind *Sports Illustrated* [swimsuit issue] is sexual . . . A man probably . . . would not be as likely to pick up a [women's] fashion magazine and look at [their] swimsuit issue . . . [But] they would [look at] *Sports Illustrated* [swimsuit issue].

## Recognising the power of producers and the text

Although audience members hold a variety of disparate opinions about the swimsuit issue, it is clear that the intentions of producers, production practices, the swimsuit issue texts, media texts other than the swimsuit issue, and the wider sociocultural context all contribute to consumer consensus regarding the denotative level meaning of the swimsuit issue. These findings illustrate the point that there are many factors that affect the audience during the process of interpretation. The intentions of producers and various parts of the production pro-cess clearly influence the structure and content of media texts. The structure and content of media texts just as clearly influence the meanings that consumers produce when they interact with the texts. Yet, textual structure alone cannot prompt a consumer to decode a media text in a manner that matches the producer's intentions. The cultural knowledge/perspective that the consumer employs during decoding must, to a large degree, correspond with that of the pro-ducers for consumers to create a dominant/preferred reading of the text (Morley 1980; Woollacott 1982; Wren-Lewis 1983; Lewis 1991). In fact, effective communication depends on some correspondence between encoded and decoded meanings (Hall 1984). It appears that a common cultural setting often provides producers and consumers with a similar understanding of many symbols, and this similar understanding limits the potential for resistant readings on the part of consumers.

Justin Lewis (1991) argues that the ideological power of the mass media does not depend on producers' intentions because consumers may not interpret a media text in ways that producers prefer, but are encouraged by the combination of textual structure and their own cultural knowledge to create particular interpretations. Also, the ideological power of some media texts depends on their ability to appeal to different audience groups in different ways. But the ability of consumers to create particular interpretations does not necessarily involve free choice, because consumers are limited by the ideological environment in which they are enmeshed. Lewis maintains that the polysemic nature of media texts does not diminish the ideological power of the media. I have no reason to doubt these claims. But, the results of my scholarship on the swimsuit issue lead me to conclude that producers' intentions and practices, and textual structure, do influence the ideological power of the media. The way that producers shape the content and structure of media texts does influence consumer interpretations. Within a given cultural context, textual content and structure set the stage for debates over meaning. As the normative meaning of signifiers change, interpretations of content will change. But, the consumer still must work with texts that represent a limited number of signifiers. The findings of this study provide a crucial warning against the recent trend in media studies to grant practically unlimited power to the audience and dismiss the producers and texts as barely relevant. The fact that producers influence the interpretations of many consumers, through the ways they shape textual content and structure, suggests that attempts to critique and change media texts may be one useful strategy for affecting wider social change.

## References

Berger, A.A. (1982) *Media Analysis Techniques*. Beverly Hills, CA: Sage.

Condit, C.M. (1989) The rhetorical limits of polysemy, *Critical Studies in Mass Communication*, 6(2): 103–22.

Coward, R. (1985) *Female Desires: How They are Sought, Bought and Packaged*. New York: Grove.

Dyer, R. (1982) Don't look now, *Screen*, 23(314): 61–73.

Goffman, E. (1976) *Gender Advertisements*. New York: Harper Colophon.

Hall, S. (1984) Encoding/Decoding, in S. Hall, D. Hobson, A. Lowe and P. Willis (eds) *Culture, Media, Language: Working Papers in Cultural Studies, 1972–79*. London: Hutchinson

Heck, M.C. (1984) The ideological dimension of media messages, in S. Hall, D. Hobson, A. Lowe and P. Willis (eds) *Culture, Media, Language: Working Papers in Cultural Studies, 1972–79*. London: Hutchinson.

Kuhn, A. (1985) *The Power of the Image: Essays on Representation and Sexuality*. Boston: Routledge & Kegan Paul.

Lewis, J. (1991) *The Ideological Octopus: An Exploration of Television and Its Audience*. New York: Routledge.

Lurie, A. (1981) *The Language of Clothes*. New York: Random House.

Masse, M.A. and Rosenblum, K. (1988) Male and female created they them: the depiction of gender in advertising of traditional women's and men's magazines, *Women's Studies International Forum*, 11(2): 127–44.

Millum, T. (1975) *Images of Woman: Advertising in Women's Magazines*. Totowa, NJ: Rowman and Littlefield.

Morley, D. (1980) *The 'Nationwide' Audience: Structure and Decoding*. London: British Film Institute.

Urry, J. (1990) *The Tourist Gaze: Leisure and Travel in Contemporary Societies*. Newbury Park, CA: Sage.

Woollacott, J. (1982) Messages and meanings, in M. Gurevitch, T. Bennett, J. Curran and J. Woollacott (eds) *Culture, Society and the Media*. New York: Methuen.

Wren-Lewis, J. (1983) The encoding/decoding model: criticisms and redevelopments for research on decoding, *Media, Culture & Society*, 5: 179–97.

# 14

# 'I WANT TO BE THE MINORITY'[1]: THE POLITICS OF YOUTHFUL WHITE MASCULINITIES IN SPORT AND POPULAR CULTURE IN 1990s AMERICA

## Kyle W. Kusz

Excerpt from an article of the same name published in *Journal of Sport & Social Issues*, 2001, 25(4): 390–416.

*I'm talking about the disadvantages of being a white guy in America.* I'm sick of minorities hogging the good complaints. Whitey's been silent for too long ... whitey's been getting a constant pounding. I've been taking so many lefts I'm begging for rights.

(Spade 1998: 52, emphasis added)

It is also the era of the multicultural. And the challenge of this multicultural era is the challenge of living in a world of difference. It requires generating a mythology of social inter-action that goes beyond the model of resentment that seems so securely in place at these times ... *Indeed, as the purveyors of 'white reign' assert themselves, they simply underscore their own vulnerabilities and fragilities.*

(McCarthy 1998: 339, emphasis added)

As I search the radio for background music to facilitate my writing process, I tune into Green Day's (a West Coast punk band whose music was surprisingly embraced by the pop music mainstream in 1995) latest release, 'Minority'. Characteristic of punk music, Green Day's music is fast, hard, and defiant. Yet, many of its songs, particularly those that have received airplay on mainstream radio stations and MTV, are also distinguished by great melodies and infectious choruses. 'Minority' has regularly appeared on MTV's show, *Total Request Live*, an unofficial measuring stick of what's popular with America's teens. The seemingly peculiar popularity of a punk song performed by three young, White guys proudly proclaiming a desire to be 'the minority' requires analysis. 'Minority' was preceded in the 1990s by the popularisation of 'alternative' music, a malleable label used to describe a variety of music (grunge rock, indie rock, and 1990s punk, to name a few). Perhaps the most notable and unifying elements of alternative music are its performance and consumption by Whites, particularly White males, and its appropriation of language and imagery associated with 'working class and underclass white cultures' (Newitz 1997: 146). Green Day's anthem can be located within this 1990s popular music context in which we hear a number of songs by White male artists who express a desire for alterity and make claims of being disadvantaged and victimised. But as the alternative music trend lost some of its momentum in the late 1990s, the popularity of Green Day's 'Minority' demonstrates that, in the new millennium, there is still a market and demand for songs by White male bands expressing sentiments of being victimised and ill treated.

Alternative music represents just one of several sites of contemporary American popular culture in which one encounters images and narratives of victimised young White males. In this chapter, I examine such images and narratives of disadvantaged young White males as they are produced in . . . a 1997 *Sports Illustrated* cover story titled, 'Whatever Happened to the White Athlete?', which forwards a panic-driven tale about the declining position of White male athletes in American professional and high school sports (Price 1997). My aim is to offer a contextualised cultural analysis of these discourses that explains how their representations of 'youthful' victimised White males are not only constituted by, and constitutive of, the representational strategies of 1990s White male backlash politics, but signal a new inflection of these representational strategies.

My project draws on David Savran's (1998: 4) observation that the 1990s marked 'the ascendancy of a new and powerful figure in US culture: the white male as victim'. But unlike Savran's work, which ignored the context of American sport and focused on older White masculinities that largely conform to the biographical dimensions of the baby boom generation, my study examines more youthful White masculinities produced both within and outside of the context of American sports. Building on Savran's work, I contend that these representations of disadvantaged and victimised youthful White masculinities signify a new representational strategy of White male backlash politics – the 'youthification' of the 'White male as victim' trope. . . .

At first glance, these seemingly unrelated sites of American popular culture – the discourse on the development of adolescent boys and a *Sports Illustrated* report about the disappearance of a White majority within American professional sport – would not seem to share very much in common. But, through my analysis, I articulate these sites as localities of the national popular involved in the production of images and narratives of victimised and disadvantaged young White males that both reflect, and reproduce, the discursive logics of the contemporary White male backlash. By making connections between these popular sites – one that exists outside of sport and the other within sport – I highlight the pervasiveness of this strategy of representing young White males as vulnerable, victimised, or otherwise disadvantaged subjects. I am interested in these seemingly banal sites of popular culture (what Berlant [1997] called the 'waste material of everyday communication': 12) because they are the places where conservative backlash ideologies that seek to re-conceal, protect, and re-secure the representational and material privileges of White masculinity are being translated into a 'non-ideological' and 'common sense' viewpoint and where they are learned and mobilised by real social actors to make sense of their everyday lives (Kellner 1995) . . .

### *Sports Illustrated*'s crisis of the young white (male) athlete: American sport as a site of the white male backlash

> The white athlete – and here we speak of the young men in team sports who ruled the American athletic scene for much of the century – doesn't want to play anymore . . . the playing field [American professional sports arena] had become the nation's common ground, the one highly visible stage on which blacks and whites acted out the process of learning to live, play and fight together as peers. Today fewer whites stand on that common ground.
>
> (Price 1997: 32–3)

*Sports Illustrated*'s December 6, 1997 issue offered readers a special report titled, 'What Ever Happened to the White Athlete?' (Price

1997). The article is represented as a 6-month long inquiry into the subject of race and sport that included 'dozens of interviews with coaches, athletes, executives and academics and a nationwide poll of 1,835 middle school and high school kids' (33). Despite its best efforts to give this article the gloss of an objective and soundly researched scientific report, the end product of *Sports Illustrated*'s work is a panic-driven news story focused on the increasing absence of the White athlete in contemporary American professional sports. In my analysis, I implicate this article about the declining position of White (males) in sport as another site of 1990s America in which the representational strategies and discursive logics of White male backlash politics are deployed and disseminated for public consumption. Then, I make visible how *Sports Illustrated*'s report uses representations of youthful White males, configured by the logics and strategies of the White male backlash, as opposed to adult White males. These young White masculinit(-ies) first get figured as suffering and victimised minority subjects and then get contradictorily refigured, by the article's end, as having an extraordinary will and self-determining agency as well as a restored confidence. In addition, through critically interrogating the functions and contradictions of the article's depictions of youthful White masculinities, we gain insight into how the article's conflicting and seemingly incongruous representations of White masculinity work to reproduce the hegemonic power of Whiteness.

The first evidence of how *Sports Illustrated*'s special report on race and sports is produced by, and reproduces, the White male backlash ideologies is the magazine's conspicuous choice for the cover photo that accompanied the report. The cover displayed a nostalgic-laden, black-and-white image of four high-school-aged, clean-cut, affable White male basketball players whose uniforms and hairstyles unmistakably code them as pre-1960s figures. Each player has a con-servative, closely cropped haircut; big ears, and inviting boy-next-door smile. Each dons Chuck Taylor sneakers and playing uniforms that are notably white. The players could easily be mistaken for the all-White high school basketball team featured in the 1986 blockbuster film *Hoosiers*. Each player is shown kneeling with one hand extended forward touching a single basketball resting in the centre between them. This positioning of the athletes, each with a hand on the basket-ball, signifies them as a team that presumably works together toward a shared goal rather than as a group of individuals. Their smiling faces, oozing with optimism and innocence, and their unifying pose invite

(White male) readers to nostalgically identify with them and a set of traditional values that they project – teamwork, competition, camaraderie, winning, hard work, and playing for the love of the game. Of course, these are the values that many sports pundits and fans resentfully decry as having been lost in today's professional athletes and sports. So, then, this 1950s team-oriented, sacrificial White male athlete constructed in *Sports Illustrated*'s article is implicitly defined over and against the African American NBA or NFL player who is said to be more concerned with making money and achieving celebrity status than with winning championships and being a solid role model.

*Sports Illustrated*'s decision to use a picture of pre-1960s White male youths rather than an image of contemporary youths is quite noteworthy for a number of reasons. Like other texts framed by White male backlash ideologies, *Sports Illustrated*'s decision to use this image evokes a pervasive nostalgia (invested in by many adult White males) for an historical moment imagined as a less complicated and innocent time, particularly for White males. A moment absent from such things as the 'annoying' sensitivities of political correctness and affirmative action, the increased public marking of Whiteness, and directives to emphasise and celebrate multiculturalism and cultural diversity. This recollection of 1950s America, embodied in these smiling and wholesome young White males, invokes a longing for imagined good old days – prior to the 'disrupting' events of the 1960s – when the centrality and pre-eminence of the White male was taken for granted, when the position of White males was rarely publicly challenged. The nostalgic longing for a pre-1960s America expressed in this *Sports Illustrated* cover photo is a variation of the backlash strategy in which populist rhetoric that does not explicitly mention race, gender, or class is deployed to reproduce social practices, institutional arrangements, and ideologies that centre and normalise the position of White masculinity. In this case, by invoking these backlash ideologies through the photo without actually expressing them, nostalgia (with its racial and gender implications) can be conveyed in a seemingly innocent and inconspicuous manner.

*Sports Illustrated*'s cover image also begs the question: what audience would be interpellated by this image and special report on the plight of the professional White (male) athlete? *Sports Illustrated*'s nostalgic black-and-white choice rather than a contemporary colour photo of White youth may signal an effort to appeal to middle-aged White men who recognise themselves in the image. But *Sports*

*Illustrated*'s repeated framing of the crisis of the White athlete as a contemporary crisis of *young* White male athletes suggests that the intended audience is a young White male who is allegedly turning away from sport. Rather than arguing that the article is intended to appeal to either older or younger White males, I contend that the article's framing – its choice for the cover image, use of statistics collected from a national survey of current high school athletes, and stories of contemporary young White male professional athletes – invites the interpellation of White males across different generations. On one level, the article's focus on young White (male) athletes signals how representations of unfairly disadvantaged youthful White masculinities, in this case within sport, are increasingly being employed as symbols to serve the ideological ends of White male backlash politics – generating anxiety, resentment, and a sense of crisis about the supposed declining position of White males within American society and culture. On another level, the interweaving of these images and stories about both former young White (male) athletes and current White (male) athletes suggests an effort to construct a narrative that interpellates younger White males to invest in the White male backlash imaginary.

Henry Giroux (1997a) has noted that, during the 1990s, 'whiteness' was increasingly made visible at times when Whites were constituted as victims. *Sports Illustrated*'s special report exemplifies Giroux's observation. In bold white letters that stand out in relation to the black-and-white photo, the question, 'What Ever Happened to the White Athlete?' is posed. The word White appears in a much larger font; its prominence demonstrates how, in the late 1990s, Whiteness is often made visible and marked in popular culture at those times when the practices of a White-skinned person or group do not conform to, or fit within, the dominant meanings associated with Whiteness. Stated differently, Whiteness is often made visible in the national-popular when particular performances of White-skinned subjects or historical events (such as the changing racial configuration of athletes within certain professional sports in the United States) potentially challenge, and threaten to disrupt, our 'naturalised' ideas about the cultural meanings of Whiteness (its invisibility and/or normativity) or its centred social positioning. Even further, Whiteness is not only made visible in the article to signify the disruption of its naturalised meanings or the social position of Whites in society, but it is paradoxically made visible to restore the invisibility of Whiteness and, thus, to re-secure its normative and central sociocultural position.

Moving to the text of *Sports Illustrated*'s special report, the article begins and ends with a story about a 29-year-old White male American sprinter named Kevin Little. We are first introduced to Little recalling a recurring incident in his life in which, to his dismay, he has to explain to disbelieving others (Whites and Blacks) that he is a professional sprinter. Little laments how he commonly receives a look of surprise, a slight chuckle, and the words, 'But you're white?' when he identifies himself as a sprinter (Price 1997: 32). We are told that Little is tired of the disbelief and scepticism he encounters when he tells others that he is a sprinter. Next, we learn that, in March 1997, Little not only tied the American indoor record in the 200 metres at the world championships in Paris, but he was the first White American since 1956 to win a major international sprint title (Price 1997).

This story about Little is not mobilised simply to highlight his remarkable on-track performances (although his athletic success is an important facet to his story). Rather, Little's story gains its currency because it figures him as a young, White male athlete who is 'suffering' from self-doubts brought about by fans, friends, and (Black) competitors stereotyping him as an inferior athlete because he is White. In the typical manner of a backlash text, Little is initially rendered visible to the reader as a victim. In this case, Little is constituted as a victim of the negative stereotypes about White athleticism. Here, the increased public marking of Whiteness by others is represented as having unfairly caused Little much suffering and unfairly constrained him by erecting social and psychic forces (people's unsupportive comments and his own self-doubts) that constrain his efforts to fulfil his aspiration of being the best sprinter he can be. In contradistinction to the arguments that White conservatives often proffer that race does not affect a person's life outcomes (usually applied in cases in which people of colour speak of disadvantages that are the result of their racial identity), Little's story asserts that the recent public marking of Whiteness – particularly, the limiting stereotypes of White athleticism – produces significant debilitating effects that unfairly restrict his actions and aspirations. Thus, within *Sports Illustrated*'s report, race is deemed important in those moments when the public marking of Whiteness negatively affects the life possibilities of White males. Furthermore, through its exposition of the way in which making Whiteness visible has had derogatory effects on Kevin Little, *Sports Illustrated*'s story implicitly endorses a desire to make Whiteness once again invisible.

It should be no surprise that *Sports Illustrated* begins its report by featuring an athlete like Kevin Little. As a White person participating in a sport commonly understood as being dominated by Black athletes (200-metre run), he is the perfect figure to play the role of the unprivileged, minority White male subject within contemporary American sports. By making Little's story the lead, *Sports Illustrated* presents him as 'Exhibit A' in its crisis narrative about the ground that the White (male) athlete has unfairly lost. Through its survey of middle school and high school youth's attitudes about sport participation, *Sports Illustrated* attempts to show that Little is not alone; that he is just one of many young White (male) athletes who have either turned away from sport or whose confidence in their athletic abilities has waned due to the disappearance of White (male) athletes on the national athletic stage. Young White males are represented as dropping out of the 'big three' American sports (football, baseball, and basketball) at a rapid rate or as being unfairly deterred from participating in these sports by parents, coaches, and the media, all of whom see African American males as a dominating athletic presence that impedes White male athletes' chances to compete at either the youth or professional levels. These young, White male athletes are figured as being unfairly subjugated (having their agency constrained), not only because of the debilitating effects of negative stereotypes about White athleticism but because of the overwhelming success of Black males in American professional sport. Within this story line, Black male athletes are depicted as a dominant, discriminatory, and exclusionary force whose success unfairly constrains the life possibilities of White male youths by forcing them to abandon their dreams of being a professional athlete. This narrative of Black dominance and White male disadvantage in sport enables the U.S. racial hierarchy to be turned on its head so that White males can be positioned as a seemingly legitimate unprivileged subject. But by inverting the social order, this story of White male disadvantage represents an attempt to forget or render inconsequential the long histories of racial inequalities, institutional racism, and White privilege that have existed in the past and that still persist in the present, both within and without sport (Rodriguez 1998).

*Sports Illustrated*'s special report, then, alleges that perhaps the most alarming effect of the disappearance of the White male professional athlete is that it has caused 'a spreading White inferiority complex' for young White males (Hoberman, cited in Price 1997: 44). Although *Sports Illustrated* makes this claim, it does not support this allegation with evidence. In fact, it actually provides evidence that contradicts such a claim. The article provides pie charts with shocking titles like 'White Flight' and 'Feeling Inferior' that catch readers' eyes and reinforce its thesis of White (male) athletes being in crisis. But closer inspection of these graphs and charts reveals that only 34 per cent of the White male youths surveyed agreed with the statement, 'African-American players have become so dominant in sports such as football and basketball that many Whites feel they can't compete at the same level as blacks', whereas 45 per cent of the White male youths surveyed disagreed with the statement (Price 1997: 34). Although short on evidence, these graphs and statistics, with their veneer of scientific objectivity and their prominent titles, create the impression that *Sports Illustrated* has sufficiently supported its hyperbolic claims of White male victimisation within sport.

The articulation of this White inferiority complex is also important because it shows how youthful White males, as opposed to middle-aged White men like a Promise Keeper or Rush Limbaugh listener, or the celluloid figure D-Fens, are being mobilised within this back-lash politics. The relative 'youthification' of the White male backlash figure within this narrative about sport is significant because it is his youth – a traditionally subordinate subject position – that, in part, facilitates the production of his victimised identity. In *Sports Illustrated*'s narrative, constructing American professional sport as a site of African American dominance and White inferiority requires that one selectively forgets two things. First, that the commercialised and mediated American sports formation also includes sports like tennis, golf, extreme sports, professional wrestling, and soccer, which are (numerically) dominated by Whites. Second, professional sports are almost exclusively administered (coached, owned and operated) by White males. But, by focusing on relatively young White athletes (whether at the professional or youth levels of sport) within its narrative of White athletic crisis, such irrefutable evidence can be conveniently forgotten or overlooked.

In addition, as in the discourse of boys' development (for example, Gurian 1998; Pollack 1998; Garbarino 1999), the connotation of 'the future', which is often articulated with the category of youth, implies that the 'spreading inferiority complex' being felt by these White males is not merely a problem of today but could escalate into a potential problem of the future. The unspoken anxiety that underwrites this claim of a spreading White inferiority complex among young White male athletes is, 'If young White males feel inferior to African-American men in sport will this sport-specific inferiority complex translate into feelings of inferiority in other spaces and practices unrelated to sport?' Suddenly, what is at stake is not simply the cultural position of White males in sport but the cultural and social position of White masculinity in American culture as a whole.

Similarly, the category of youth is also frequently articulated with notions of 'hope' and 'limitless opportunities'. Consequently, the alleged African American dominance in sport becomes a force that unfairly limits the life possibilities of White male youths afflicted by this supposed inferiority complex, which it is claimed influences young White male athletes to give up their optimistic dreams of athletic stardom and effectively arrest their athletic development. The notion that taking away a young person's dreams is equivalent to arresting their development is subtly at play within this articulation of White male crisis to youthful White males, especially as sport is under-stood as providing youths with valuable lessons about the merits of hard work, perseverance, meritocracy, and optimism that transcend their sporting experiences. Thus, the youthfulness of the victimized White male athlete intensifies what is at stake in the African American dominance of American professional sport. Not only is the alleged growing White inferiority complex of young White males implicitly cast as a symptom of the eroding position of White masculinity within American culture in the present, its articulation with youthful White males further suggests that it may have deleterious effects on them in the future.

Meanwhile, the article also produces another important image of White masculinity through a story about the athletic success of White NBA player, Brent Barry. Although Barry garners much attention as the son of NBA legend, Rick Barry, his story is important for *Sports Illustrated*'s narrative because he defied conventional racial logic when he won the 1996 NBA Slam Dunk Championship. Thus, Barry is intro-duced into the article's narrative because he represents a young White male who has achieved a relatively high level of athletic success in a sport dominated by Black athletes in the 1990s (basketball). He is valorised for his strong will to succeed and his ability to be a self-determining agent who is not constrained by forces outside of himself (such as Black dominance in basketball, derogatory stereo-types of White athleticism). This representation of a youthful White masculinity as an unconstrained, self-determining agent is needed within *Sports Illustrated*'s special report to counter its initial image of White masculinity as a suffering, disadvantaged, minority subject within American sports. In addition, this counterimage of White masculinity functions to re-secure the normative way in which it is imagined within American sports culture (as sovereign, individualistic, self-determining agents), thus providing an imaginary solution to any possible anxieties the article might have created in White male readers.

The construction of Barry as possessing an extraordinary will relies on the stereotype of Whites' athletic inferiority to Blacks and is enabled by the depiction of suburban culture (implicitly coded as White) as a social barrier for White (male) athletic success because it is overwrought with comforts and distractions like video games and abundant opportunities outside of sport. In addition, the supposed lack of community-wide support of White athletes is used to constitute suburban culture as a social constraint on White (male) athletes. Quite ironically, suburban comfort is cast in *Sports Illustrated*'s narrative as a gigantic social barrier that young White male athletes have to overcome to become professional athletes. This peculiar representation of 'suburban comfort as constraint' is necessary to constitute youthful White male athletes, like Barry, as possessing an extraordinary will. Coupled with its reliance on the stereotypical notion of White athletic inferiority, this depiction of suburbia allows young, White male athletes to be represented as having to work harder than the inner-city Black athlete. A testimonial from Barry is used within the article to legitimate this representation of suburban culture:

> 'It almost takes more effort to get out of a situation where you could sit back and be comfortable' he says. 'If you're struggling you could say, "I don't need to do this anymore. My parents have great jobs, I could go to any college I want".
>
> 'It's a much different set of social barriers; the pressure on you to perform isn't so great. If you're the white kid and you've got glee club after school, the ski trip on the holidays and Stratomatic baseball in the spring, well, that's what you're going to do. I pride myself on the fact that I had to have a lot of desire and will and competitiveness to get out of white suburban America and make it in a game dominated by great black athletes'.
>
> (quoted in Price 1997: 50)

Through his comment, Barry offers an amazing inversion of the customary sporting upward-mobility tale usually associated with basketball and African American, inner-city males in the 1990s. Within Barry's statement, the dire economic and social conditions (de-industrialisation, drugs, rampant crime, institutionalised racism) that often leave economically disadvantaged, inner-city Black males few viable avenues for success other than sport are trivialised and rendered incomparable to the alleged social barriers facing the suburban White male athlete. In fact, these bleak social and economic conditions are constituted as advantages for the Black athlete because they produce pressure to succeed in, and community-wide support for, athletics in the Black community. Incredibly, *Sports Illustrated* does not merely equate the social conditions of the suburban White male athlete and the inner-city Black male athlete. It constitutes the plight of the White male suburban subject who has to overcome the 'distractions' of suburban comfort and a White community that does not fully support his athletic investments as being more difficult than the condition of his Black male counterpart. The economic and social privileges of being White, male, and from the suburbs are reconstituted to become social barriers hampering White males' athletic success. *Sports Illustrated*'s contradictory narrative of White male athletic disadvantage (a variation of the construction of the 'White male as victim' trope) represents a unique and troubling attempt to disavow White male privilege. Yet, its framing of Barry's story also enables White masculinity within the *Sports Illustrated* article to be rendered visible not just as a social victim, but also to be figured as a self-determining agent whose strong will and determination propelled him to overcome the social and psychological barriers necessary to achieve athletic success.

The configuration of Barry as a White male with an extraordinary will is reinforced by a final story about the lone White sprinter, Kevin Little. In the closing two paragraphs, Little re-enters the narrative and is much different than the Kevin Little the reader met in the opening of the article. He is constituted as no longer being afflicted by feelings of self-doubt and defensiveness brought about by the negative stereotypes of White athleticism. Instead, Little is represented as using his newly visible Whiteness to gain an advantage on his Black competitors:

> No one [African American] wants to lose to him. 'Then the edge goes to me', he says. 'I can look into their eyes and their faces, and if they have a little fear of losing to a white sprinter, I've won right there. *I'm holding the cards.*
>                    (Little, quoted in Price 1997: 51, emphasis added)

Little's quote is employed to both reaffirm the need to make Whiteness once again invisible while also serving to reassure the (White male) reader through this fabrication of White men as self-determining subjects who are not and will not be constrained by social conditions (like stereotypes, Black dominance, and lack of social support for their athletic endeavours). Little re-emerges at the end of the article as a pedagogical figure – an example of an unfairly disadvantaged White male who not only proves their superior will but has even learned to use 'black dominance as his weapon' (Price 1997: 51). Thus, by the article's end, White masculinity is reconfigured not as a suffering and constrained social victim but as many White American men would like to imagine themselves – as self-determining subjects of history (rather than its objects) who author their own life outcomes and who are not constrained by social forces beyond their control.


## Conclusion

> Forms of media culture induce individuals to identify with dominant social and political ideologies, positions, and representations. In general, it is not a system of rigid ideological indoctrination that induces consent to existing capitalist societies, but the pleasures of the media and consumer culture . . . [that] seduce[s] audiences into identifying with certain views, attitudes, feelings, and positions.
>
> (Kellner 1995: 3)

Several other cultural critics, influenced by the critical work being done on Whiteness, have illuminated how a number of popular culture sites like Hollywood films (Clover 1993; Kennedy 1996; Giroux 1997b; McCarthy 1998; Savran 1998), AM radio (Giroux 1997a), television (Newitz and Wray 1997), and grunge music (Newitz 1997) have been instrumental in not only disseminating but also generating the representational strategies and logics of this White male backlash politics. Surprisingly little work has examined how contemporary discourses involving sport, as a site of popular culture, have been influential in the production and dispersal of the logics of this White male backlash politics. My interrogation of *Sports Illustrated*'s special report is an initial effort in this direction. Such critical attention to contemporary discourses and developments in sport can illuminate how it has become an important site of the White male backlash. This is because the over-representation of African American males in these sports enables the fabrication of a crisis narrative about the vulnerable cultural position of White males that can be seemingly defended through a quick glance at the 'empirical' evidence of the contemporary racial makeup of American professional athletes.

Furthermore, my analysis provides evidence of how images of more youthful White masculinities are increasingly being employed within White male backlash texts. This 'youthification' suggests that an effort is being made to interpellate younger White males to the White male backlash ideologies. Such an effort might produce a cross-generational investment by White men of various ages in these ideologies that would facilitate the continuation of the White male backlash's political goals in the future. Or, the 'youthification' of the White male backlash figure might also be symbolically useful as it enables the popular acceptance of backlash ideologies that seek to re-secure the hegemonic position of White masculinity within American culture in the name of such things as improving the lives of boys or in the name of enabling young White males an opportunity to pursue their interests in traditional sports, like basketball or football or track. Nonetheless, what can be said with some reasonable certainty is that the production of these representations of disadvantaged and victimised young White males within popular music, popular literature, and popular sport operates, as Kellner (1995) stated, as sources of cultural pedagogy that attempt to seduce (White male) audiences to 'deny what is most obvious: the privileged position of whiteness' (Kincheloe and Steinberg 1998: 15).

## Note

1 Title taken from Green Day's song, 'Minority'.

## References

Berlant, L. (1997) Introduction: the intimate public sphere, in *The Queen of America Goes to Washington City: Essays on Sex and Citizenship*. Durham, NC: Duke University Press.

Clover, C. (1993) 'Falling Down' and the rise of the average White male, in P. Cook and P. Dodd (eds) *Women and Film: A Sight and Sound Reader*. Philadelphia: Temple University Press.

Garbarino, J. (1999) *Lost Boys: Why Our Sons Turn Violent and How We Can Save Them*. New York: Free Press.

Giroux, H. (1997a) Rewriting the discourse of racial identity: towards a pedagogy and politics of Whiteness, *Harvard Educational Review*, 67(2): 285–320.

Giroux, H. (1997b) White noise: racial politics and the pedagogy of Whiteness, in *Channel Surfing: Race Talk and the Destruction of Today's Youth*. New York: St. Martin's.

Gurian, M. (1998) *A Fine Young Man*. New York: Jeremy T. Parcher/Putnam.

Kellner, D. (1995) *Media Culture*. New York: Routledge.

Kennedy, L. (1996) Alien nation: White male paranoia and imperial culture in the United States, *Journal of American Studies*, 30(1): 87–100.

Kincheloe, J. and Steinberg, S. (1998) Addressing the crisis of Whiteness: reconfiguring White identity in a pedagogy of Whiteness, in J.L. Kincheloe, S.R. Steinberg, N.M. Rodriguez, and R.E. Chennault (eds) *White Reign: Deploying Whiteness in America*. New York: St. Martin's.

McCarthy, C. (1998) Living with anxiety: race and the renarration of public life, in J.L. Kincheloe, S.R. Steinberg, N.M. Rodriguez and R.E. Chennault (eds) *White Reign: Deploying Whiteness in America*. New York: St. Martin's.

Newitz, A. (1997) White savagery and humiliation, or a new racial consciousness in the media, in M. Wray and A. Newitz (eds) *White Trash: Race and Class in America*. New York: Routledge.

Newitz, A. and Wray, M. (1997) What is 'White trash'? Stereotypes and economic conditions of poor Whites in the United States, *The Minnesota Review*, 47: 61–77.

Pollack, W. (1998) *Real Boys*. New York: Owl.

Price, S.L. (1997) Whatever happened to the White athlete? *Sports Illustrated*, 87(23), 6 December 6: 32–51.

Rodriguez, N. (1998) Emptying the content of Whiteness: toward an understanding of the relation between Whiteness and pedagogy, in J.L. Kincheloe, S.R. Steinberg, N.M. Rodriguez and R.E. Chennault (eds) *White Reign: Deploying Whiteness in America*. New York: St. Martin's.

Savran, D. (1998) *Taking It Like a Man: White Masculinity, Masochism, and Contemporary American Culture*. Princeton, NJ: Princeton University Press.

Spade, D. (1998) White man blues, *George*, April.

Wray, M. and Newitz, A. (1997) *White Trash: Race and Class in America*. New York: Routledge.

# 15 | WOMEN, SPORT AND GLOBALIZATION[1]: COMPETING DISCOURSES OF SEXUALITY AND NATION

## *Deborah Stevenson*

Excerpt from an article of the same name published in *Journal of Sport & Social Issues*, 2002, 26(2): 209–25.

### Introduction

The Russian Anna Kournikova and French woman Amelie Mauresmo did not play each other at any stage during the Australian Tennis Open in January 1999. One can only speculate as to the media and crowd responses if they had. Arguably, such a contest would have exposed even more starkly than the actual final between Mauresmo and the player who has come to be known as 'the Swiss Miss' (Masters 1999a: 38), Martina Hingis, the contradictory discourses of femininity and sexuality that underpin women's sport in general, and which are perhaps most evident in professional tennis. In contrast to other high profile sports like athletics and swimming, where such an image has never been hegemonic, the image of the fit, yet feminine tennis player persists, with players such as Kournikova the modern embodiment of the ideal. It would be misleading, though, to suggest that there is only one acceptable physical form for female athletes (or tennis players) and that Mauresmo stands completely at odds with the hegemonic idea of the contemporary woman tennis player. On the contrary, within women's tennis today there are several competing versions of femininity and body shape being 'played out' that defy simple polarised explanations in terms of 'good' and 'bad' femininity.

As an aspect of a bigger research project into globalization, regional sports culture and the media, this chapter examines issues associated with women and global sport. Using the media coverage of the 1999 Australia Tennis Open as a touchstone, it considers the tension between gender expectations, representation, and imagery in one of the few sports where women's competition matches that of men in terms of media coverage, spectator interest and, increasingly, prize money and sponsorship. The chapter considers the ways in which the Australian print media dealt with issues of gender, femininity and sexuality to illuminate some of the processes framing women and global sport. Working from the premise that an understanding of the gender dimension of global sport will contribute to more general academic knowledge of globalization processes, I thus seek to contribute to current debates over global sport, media and gender.

## Globalization, sport, and the media

In little more than a decade the rhetoric of globalization and its implications have come to dominate academic, political and popular discourse as many cultural and economic trends and exchanges seem unconstrained by the geographic and administrative boundaries of nation-states. These trends effectively operate with few opportunities for the mediations of national governments and scant regard for the local consequences of decisions that have been made not just elsewhere in the world, but often in no one specific place (Stevenson 1999). There is a logic to the discourses of globalization that marginalises and disempowers communities and regions. As individuals and collectivities, people seem unable to intervene effectively either to prevent change or direct its trajectory. Moreover, those who dare to challenge the assumptions underpinning globalization face accusations of conservative parochialism. Globalization is now, simultaneously, the unchallengeable explanation and rationale for unemployment, de-industrialisation and the emergence of 'rustbelt' cities and regions (Stevenson 1998), whilst, in sport, globalization frames community resignation to the amalgamation and often disintegration of long-established local sporting clubs, the reshaping of sports competitions, the disappearance of many premier tournaments from free-to-air television, and the serial movement of teams and players between regions and clubs (Rowe and Lawrence 1998). Those localities that are frequently most affected by such changes to the structure and delivery of sport are also often the very places negatively affected by the impacts of 'global' economic and industrial change. The imperatives of globalization are reconfiguring social, cultural and regional inequality to such an extent that it is very hard to dispute Wenner's (1996: 235) observation that globalization (in all its guises) is 'hard to like'.

In sport, globalization is being driven by the entwined quest for increased corporate profits and the global media audiences deemed necessary to achieve such levels of profitability. The electronic media increasingly frames sporting imagery, narratives and competitions for the consumption of existing and new fans. But national, metropolitan and regional newspapers also play important roles in the promotion of different sports, the construction of local and global sporting heroes, the interpretation of events, and the delivery of sporting images to local consumers. Although frequently entwined in a web of ownership that spans media forms and continents, the print media play a very different, albeit complementary role in the global-media-sport nexus. It is the print media that is in a position to provide an arena for the expression of local resistance (including the sports of women). Lacking the immediacy of the electronic forms, it can be a space for analyses and the presentation of considered images and ideas.

Sport and the associated images of sporting bodies that are routinely packaged in all media for the consumption of local and international audiences are heavily gendered. High-profile male sports, such as the football codes, are amongst the most lucrative globally marketable sports and sporting events. Although the under-representation of women's sport in the media is well-established (Hargreaves 1994; Brown 1995; Lenskyj 1998), scant attention has been paid to the implications of this bias for women with specific regard to the process of globalization (Rowe 1996). Academic analyses have rarely considered the situation of women and their relationships as participants or consumers in global sport and its imagery. Even a cursory glance at the literature on sport and globalization (and indeed globalization generally) provides evidence of the masculinist nature of the debate to date. For example, Donnelly (1996) in his overview of the field at no stage mentions women or gender equity as significant issues. Hargreaves (1994: 182–85), on the other hand, gives some attention to the internationalisation of women's sport and the potential of policy, organisational and networking developments to foster gender equity in sport. She also pays considerable attention to women, globalization and the Olympics. However, she does not explore these gender/sport issues in terms of general globalization debates, nor does she consider whether globalization may significantly be shifting the terms of gender inequality in sport.

Arguably, there are many reasons for such omissions. Not least of these is the reality that, with a few high profile exceptions, such as international tennis and the Olympic Games, women's sporting contests rarely receive the media coverage required to enter the national, let alone the global, sporting marketplaces. Furthermore, although women are increasingly targeted in audience development campaigns, these seek to appeal to them either as mothers, family decision-makers, or through sex. However, women occupy complex, often contradictory positions in relation to the global-sport nexus that require investigation not just through an analysis of the sports they play, but also in terms of the high profile men's sports of which many are avid fans (Sargent, Zillmann and Weaver 1998). International tennis is one example where women and their sport have achieved a global media profile. Indeed, the women's final of the US Open for the last three years of the 1990s received higher television ratings in the United States than that of the men (Associated Press 1999). This profile has made it possible for top women's players to receive substantial endorsements and prize money. In the history of women's sport and of women as athletes, it is fair to say that tennis was the 'game which inaugurated women's entry into top-level competition and has remained prominent as *the* sport in which women have excelled' (Hamer 1994: 62 – emphasis original). Media coverage has also ensured that a number of women tennis players has been afforded the status of either hero or villain (Birrell and Cole 1994) – an essential element of the globalization of sport. Tennis has been a site where debates on women and sport have flourished and, as Hamer and others (such as Rowe 1995) suggest, it is a sport where assumptions about hegemonic femininity have been challenged – an arena where the media negotiate sexuality, image and the sporting woman.

## Women, sport and sexuality

The body, and hegemonic notions of femininity and masculinity, are central to the discourses and representation of both men's and women's sport: 'Sport, especially at the elite level, plays an integral role in the assemblage and projection of the engendered and sexualized postmodern bodies' (Rowe, McKay and Miller 2000: 247). For men, sport provides opportunities where, as spectator and/or player, they can affirm their identity and status as heterosexual males and their physical, symbolic and economic dominance over women. As has been repeatedly demonstrated, the media have considerable difficulty dealing with sporting women who challenge hegemonic ideas about femininity (Hargreaves 1994). Media references to a sportswoman's feminine credentials, such as to boyfriends, husbands and children, are commonplace and reassure audiences of gender priorities. Moreover, there has been considerable discussion in the literature about the importance of sexuality to the promotion of women's sport (Heaven and Rowe 1990), and frequently the (hetero)sexuality of women has been exploited as a catalyst for obtaining media coverage for women's sport. There are countless examples of sports where the competitors have adopted 'sexy' outfits (either as teams in national competitions or as individuals) in an effort to attract media attention, or have posed for makeover or soft pornography features (such as calendars) (Lenskyj 1998). This sexualisation occurs in opposition to the construction of masculinity and as an antidote to the discourse of sexual ambiguity that frames female athletes. Women as athletes and sporting fans are 'Other'. Some sociologists of sport have argued that sport as a social institution is an arena of male control over women (McKay 1997). This control extends to controlling the bodies of women. Women who breach the boundaries of sports femininity and appear too muscular, powerful – or, indeed, too good – are subjected to subtle forms of discipline which ensure they and their sport do not threaten the superiority of men:

> . . . the presence of physically powerful female bodies poses a threat to 'hegemonic masculinity' thus precipitating male 'hysteria' and attempts by men to contain women's aspirations and resistance.
>
> (Rowe, McKay and Miller 2000: 247)

The media are central technologies controlling hegemonic notions of the ideal non-threatening female athlete. Nevertheless, it is important to acknowledge that the situation of women as athletes and their relationship to their sports and their bodies, and the role of the media in these processes, are far more nuanced than a purely structural analysis will allow. In particular, there is no one acceptable female sporting body. Body form and discourses of the body vary not only from sport to sport but also within sports. Some of these contradictions emerged in January 1999 when the unseeded French woman,

Amelie Mauresmo, became the 'surprise' finalist in the Australian Open, where she played Swiss World Number 2 (and one of tennis's self-labelled 'spice girls') Martina Hingis.

Mauresmo's sexuality and body shape were the subjects of considerable discussion in the Australian media and elsewhere. Openly lesbian and visibly strong, Mauresmo's body provided a sign around which a range of signifiers clustered. At the same competition, television viewers witnessed the unprecedented displays of (male) fan adoration that accompanied every appearance of the hyperfeminine Russian Anna Kournikova. Indeed, crowd and media interest in Kournikova's body shape and sexuality equalled that shown in Mauresmo's. These contradictory images provided the impetus for this study into the complexities of the women-global sport-media nexus, including media reactions to and reportage of the women players at the Australian Open, and the ways in which a global women's sport is 'localised' for a specific audience.

The analysis is based upon a detailed study of the Australian print media's coverage of the Australian Tennis Open in January 1999, supported by a complementary study of the television coverage. The analysis focused on four daily papers – *The Age* (Melbourne), *The Sydney Morning Herald*, *The Newcastle Herald*, and *The Australian* (national), and one Sunday paper, *The Sun Herald* (Sydney). Television coverage of the final between Mauresmo and Hingis was also studied. The examination tracked the words and images that reported the women's competition over the two weeks of the Open, along with some consideration of the coverage in the period leading up to this tournament. From this analysis three dominant themes in the reportage emerged as important in the context of the study: women as (honorary) Australians; women as hyperfeminine; and women as powerful. The high profile players (including Mauresmo) were situated differently (and often contradictorily) in terms of each of these discourses, and it is in the context of this broader discursive framework that the media response to Mauresmo must be considered.

## Narratives of nation

Media coverage of two high profile sports – men's international cricket (both one-day and test matches) and men's and women's international tennis – dominate summer in Australia. These sports receive saturation coverage on competing free-to-air television networks –

cricket on the Nine Network and tennis on Seven – as well as filling the sports pages of the national, metropolitan and regional print media across the country. Both sports also receive considerable international media coverage. As one of the few truly global women's sports, the media attention given to the women's tennis competitions during January is significant. At this time there are several premier men's, women's and mixed tennis tournaments played in Australia prior to the Grand Slam event in Melbourne. Each of these minor tournaments also receives extensive print and electronic media attention.

Australia revels in its image as a sports-loving nation. Indeed, that sport is 'life' to many Australians is an orthodoxy entrenched in cultural commentary. Sport, it is popularly argued, upholds the nation and builds the national character (Horne 1964; Rowe 1999). The majority of the nation's heroes are sports stars and the ideal of the fit (male) sportsperson is central to discourses of national image and identity. Despite the individualism of the modern game, tennis has a central place within these discourses of Australian nationhood. The idea of a 'golden age' of Australian tennis has become part of national mythology. This was a time (especially in the 1950s and 1960s) when Australian players dominated international men's tennis, in particular. Indeed, Australia's success in the Davis Cup, a tennis competition between players representing nations rather than themselves, was pivotal initially to establishing tennis, along with cricket, Olympic sports and rugby, as integral to the definition of the national type. Of the 88 times the Davis Cup has been held over the last 100 years, Australia has won it 26 times, a success rate that has been described as the nation's 'greatest sporting achievement' (Hooton 1999: 24).

Despite its historical dominance, Australian tennis suffered something of a decline in the 1980s and early 1990s, generating little public interest as a result and cementing the 'golden age' in myth. At the time of the 1999 Australian Open two Australian male tennis players were ranked in the top ten in the world – Patrick Rafter (winner of the US Open in 1997 and 1998) and Mark Philippoussis (runner up to Rafter in the US Open in 1998). As a result of the profile of these two players (and of the highly successful doubles combination of Mark Woodforde and Todd Woodbridge), there was heightened media and public interest in the 1999 Australian Open. Australia has not had a woman consistently ranked in the top ten for several decades, although the nation's best known former champion players – Evonne

Goolagong-Cawley and Margaret Court – continue to be acclaimed as national sporting icons. In a country that values champions and winning, women's tennis has become almost a source of national shame.

Whilst in 1999 media coverage of the men's competition slightly exceeded that of the women's, it would be misleading to explain this imbalance solely in terms of gender. One newspaper report underlined the national significance of the men's competition as follows:

> Can we do it? As they sweated it out at Melbourne Park yesterday, Mark Philippoussis, bare-chested under a baking sun, and Pat Rafter, controlled and fluent in centre-court practice, the hope of a nation hung heavy in the air.
>
> (Walker and Haslem 1999: 1)

In other words, any privileging of the men's competition over the women's in the Australian media should be seen in the first instance as an outcome of a nationalist agenda rather than as evidence of an intrinsic bias in favour of men's sport and sporting heroes. National identification is fundamental to gaining maximum audience interest in global sporting competitions. The audience-global sport nexus is dominated by competitions between nations (and to a lesser extent regions). Mega-events, such as the Olympic Games and the various football World Cup competitions, pit nation against nation. So competitions seemingly structured by the placelessness of the global are, in fact, centrally about place defined in terms of local and national identification. Elite sport may be technically interesting but to generate global audiences must be grounded in a place-centred tribalism. Of course, just as the media are the motor for the development of global sport, they also play a pivotal role in framing audience identification with the competitors and in fuelling the local allegiances necessary for successful competitions.

In the case of a sport like tennis, however, except at the Olympic Games and Davis and Federation Cups, players are representing themselves, not nations. The media must report the performances of individuals in a way that is relevant to audiences used to supporting local and national teams or representatives. In an attempt to establish a relationship between the players, the competition and a potential (in this case Australian) audience, the media emphasise the localness of the competition and the links between player and nation. Obviously, the Australian players (in particular, Rafter and Philippoussis) were privileged in this regard. The performances of promising teenagers

Lleyton Hewitt and Jelena Dokic also attracted the interest of the Australian media. In the absence of any high-profile Australian women players and in an attempt to generate interest in the women's competition, the Australian media set out to position several high profile players, if not as honorary Australians, then in terms of their 'special' relationship to Australia and the Australian Open. Of note here were Martina Hingis, Steffi Graf and Monica Seles, who between them had won 10 out of the 11 championships held at Melbourne Park (the current venue). Seles, for instance, was described as having 'an affinity with the Australian Open' (Agence France-Presse 1999: 28) because, until defeated by Hingis in the 1999 semi-final, she had won her last 33 Australian Open matches. With veterans Graf and Seles the association with Australia was nostalgic, while Hingis, as defending champion, was positioned as part of a present involving a 'new breed' of high profile 'glamour' player. There was also a suggestion that Hingis's connection with Australia was deeper that that of the others. For Hingis, winner of the previous two titles, Melbourne was 'home'. One columnist called her a 'homing bird' (Masters 1999a: 38) and there were several other reports describing favourably Hingis's connection with Melbourne/Australia. The following illustrates the tenor of the articles:

> ... [Hingis] loves Melbourne and not just because the centre court is like her one at home. The Swiss Miss, Martina Hingis, declared Melbourne 'home' yesterday.
>
> (Masters 1999a: 38)

When she won the final against Mauresmo, Hingis's connection with Melbourne was again highlighted: '. . . she felt at home on the centre court, which she describes as "my territory"' (Hinds 1999b: 28). This 'home court' advantage was apparently a factor contributing to her victory. When Hingis played (and defeated) young Australian aspirant Dokic in an earlier round, it was 'big sister' playing 'little sister'. There were also several reports of the encouraging advice given by Hingis to Dokic. It was also pointed out that in Perth several weeks earlier Hingis had asked to practise with Dokic, after which they apparently exchanged 'girls' talk' (Hinds 1999a: 32). The media also eagerly reported Hingis's pre-and post competition pastimes (such as rollerblading in Melbourne, going to Manly Beach in Sydney, and shopping in Perth) which connected her more strongly with place than any other non-Australian player. The establishment of this 'hometown' connection automatically placed her in symbolic opposition to her high-profile opponents. Thus, whoever she played in the final was going to be, symbolically, the outsider. When it emerged that Hingis would play French woman Mauresmo, though, another set of oppositions was grafted onto the hometown/outsider dualism. Now the 'hometown', heterosexual, hyperfeminine 'princess of grace' was to be opposed by an outsider who was not only 'foreign' but also lesbian, overly muscular and wearing masculine clothing.

## The power and the passion

Despite 'whispers' about her throughout the tournament, it was not until Mauresmo made the final rounds of the Australian Open that the Australian print media began overtly to notice and comment on her. Overall she received only passing mention and her victories were routinely reported. A *Sydney Morning Herald* report interestingly entitled 'Girl-Powerplay' made no overt mention of Mauresmo's physicality (despite the name of the article) when it referred to her in relation to Australian Nicole Pratt. On the contrary, the report seems to view her with admiration:

> Her third-round opponent is rising Frenchwoman Amelie Mauresmo, who eliminated Australian women's hardcourt champion and eighth seed Patty Schnyder ... the talented Mauresmo ... shot up 80 places to No. 29 on the WTA rankings last year.
>
> (Pearce 1999a: 40)

In the context of later reportage and media interest, it is possible to suggest that a report such as this one contains a subtext – Mauresmo's unexplained meteoric rise through the ranks – something which was referred to repeatedly in later articles. In the television coverage of Mauresmo's participation at the Open the situation was slightly different. No doubt because of the immediacy of the medium, television match commentators seemed to have greater difficulty ignoring both Mauresmo's sexuality and her appearance. Here the subtext was indisputable and considerably closer to the surface. For example, *Sydney Morning Herald* journalist Richard Hinds (1999d: 50) argued that the Channel 7 commentary on Mauresmo's semi-final match against Lindsay Davenport was 'salacious', with 'much of it [was] done in the customary wink-wink, nudge-nudge style ... commentators were tying themselves in knots trying to work out how to refer to

Bourdon [Mauresmo's partner] during the Davenport match . . .' The tenor of the reportage and television coverage would have been expected to continue if not for the comments of leading players Martina Hingis and Lindsay Davenport (as mediated and presented by the media). These comments made Mauresmo the object of unrestrained television and print media interest and speculation, licensing the media to comment directly on her sexuality, appearance and the reasons for her spectacular rise from apparent obscurity. First, Davenport in a press conference immediately after being defeated by Mauresmo suggested:

> A couple of times, I mean, I thought I was playing a guy, the girl was hitting it so hard, so strong . . . I would look over there and she's so strong in those shoulders, and she just hits the ball very well. I mean, she hits the ball not like any other girl.
>
> (Pearce 1999b: 1)

Soon after Davenport made these remarks, Hingis, in an interview with a German newspaper, was reported to have said of Mauresmo, 'she's here with her girlfriend. She's half a man' (Pearce 1999b: 1). Mauresmo's being likened to a man by the two top players in the world resonated in the media in two, self-reinforcing ways. First, she was judged male because of the way that she played tennis (both her style and her physical strength) and, second, because of her overt lesbianism. These two forms of 'maleness' became indivisible – it mattered not that she wasn't the hardest hitting player in modern tennis, nor the only lesbian. The player, media and public interest in Mauresmo unleashed following the comments of Hingis and Davenport pivoted on three related issues which confirmed her as male: her clothes; her sexuality; and her body. In other words, because she wore unfeminine clothes, was openly lesbian and muscular, Mauresmo was different (an outsider) and dangerous – indeed, she now threatened actually to win the Grand Slam competition.

In the history of women's tennis the assertion that the top players 'play like men' is well established. According to Hamer (1994: 62), 'In tennis history it has often been considered that top women players play like men, a belief which began with French champion Suzanne Lenglen in 1919 . . .' The term 'playing like a man' can be a negative comment on the woman's sexuality. This connotation certainly applied when used to describe lesbian players Billie Jean King and Martina Navratilova. On the other hand, it can be a comment made in admiration, or a reference to a particular style of play that is deemed masculine (in modern times, this relates to such features as the amount of top-spin put on the ball). Either way, the notion contributes to the sexual ambiguity of women tennis players that is central to the reportage of women's tennis and the representation of its players. During the Australian Open this sexual ambiguity extended also to the coverage of the so-called 'glamour girls'. For instance, Martina Hingis is described in one feature article as being '. . . more Sundance Kid than Annie Oakley' (Masters 1999a: 38). Such a comment disrupts the finely crafted Hingis image of obvious femininity and introduces notions of the masculine – the archetypal sexually ambiguous, unruly tomboy. Significantly, the masculine here is boy not man – not only do boys not threaten male dominance, but the notion de-sexualises Hingis without constructing her as a freak. In fact, less than two weeks before the furore over Mauresmo, the term 'playing like a man' had reportedly been used by one high-profile women tennis player to describe the game of another. Ironically, Hingis and Davenport were the players involved. On being defeated by Davenport at White City in Sydney the week prior to the Australian Open, Hingis reportedly said that playing Davenport 'felt like she was playing a man' (Evans 1999: 32), a description of Davenport that was not new having been 'ventured unkindly by others back in the days when Davenport carried an extra 14kg. Davenport used to lumber in front of her rivals like a road block. Now the 1.89m Amazon menacingly towers over them all, including Hingis . . .'

It is made clear, however, that Hingis was being admiring in her comment, and the report stressed that Davenport and Hingis are friends, and that the two 'Girls have a reputation for just wanting to have fun and these two top seeds confess they don't mind downloading together' (Evans 1999: 32). To be described by another player as playing like a man, therefore, is not necessarily negative or a reference to sexuality. It would seem that when Davenport made her remarks about Mauresmo it was with reference to her playing style, as much as to her physicality rather than a comment on her sexuality: 'While some women may take comparisons with a man as an insult, from Davenport – the US Open winner and world No 1 – it is high praise'. (Hinds 1999c: 32). Davenport also claimed in the same interview that Mauresmo was 'acting like a champion' (Hogan 1999b: 63) – a point almost totally ignored in the ensuing media debate. The 'spin' put on the story generally by the media slid from 'playing like a man' to not being a real woman as evidenced by her lesbianism and her body, as well as her confidence and strength:

> Before this tournament, most felt no woman could beat her
> [Davenport]. No ordinary woman, anyway. Mauresmo is cer-
> tainly not that. From her incredible physique to her frankness
> about her relationship with girlfriend Sylvie Bourdon, she exudes
> strength and confidence on and off the court . . .
>
> (Hinds 1999c: 32)

This view was reinforced by Hingis's (later denied) suggestion that
Mauresmo was 'half a man'. Hingis subsequently claimed that, like
Davenport, she was not referring to anything other than Mauresmo's
playing style. The temptation is to see the media speculation about
Amelie Mauresmo solely as a reworking of the lesbianism/Martina
Navratilova crises of earlier times – and, certainly, issues associated
with sexual preference were important here. However, the centrality
of the lesbianism discourse has to be considered in the broader context of widespread lesbianism in women's tennis and the increased
prominence (indeed, fashionability) of lesbianism in popular culture.
Moreover, Mauresmo is not the strongest player on the circuit
(assessed in terms of serve speed). Surely, other issues are at stake here,
one relating to insider/outsider narratives within women's tennis,
and the other to a series of tensions which emerged most famously
in tennis with the controversy over the eligibility or otherwise of
transexual Renee Richards to play against women (Birrell and Cole
1994), but repeatedly also in sports like swimming and athletics. In
other words the Mauresmo case – both the players' comments and
the media interest generated – should be considered in the context of
debates over the use of performance-enhancing drugs in tennis which
raise questions about whether a competitor is (biologically) part man
and, thus, cheating.

### Enhancing performance? Drugs and clothes

Player and media debate over drug use in international tennis was of
central concern during the Australian Open. Czech player Petra Korda
had tested positive to anabolic steroids during the 1998 Wimbledon
tournament and subsequently received only a fine. This decision,
allowing him to play in the Australian Open, caused considerable
anger amongst players, with several players' meetings held during
the tournament and considerable speculation about player boycotts.
Significantly, senior players like Jim Courier and Todd Martin were

particularly outspoken and there were suggestions that many current (unnamed) players were cheating. There is now an established precedent in elite sports for competitors to make comments which generate speculation about another competitor's possible substance abuse. For example, the American swimmers openly questioned the improvement of Irish swimmer Michelle Smith (de Bruin), and Australian swimmers have repeatedly used the media to raise doubts about the Chinese women's swimming team. The comments of Davenport and Hingis, and the subsequent emphasis on Mauresmo's body shape and rapid improvement, can be seen in the context of speculation about cheating and steroid abuse in international tennis. Mauresmo's open lesbianism, albeit a significant issue, articulated with a powerful discourse that already challenged her biological 'completeness'. The subtext that can be discerned from the words and imagery featured in the media underline this connection. A hazy photograph of a younger, slimmer and considerably smaller Mauresmo taken in 1996 often appeared next to photos of her current physical form. These photos accentuated both her physicality and, in particular, her ('masculine') jaw-line. Usually, too, she was featured in aggressive poses, in almost all cases with a clenched fist and warrior-like open mouth. Alongside these photographs were repeated references to her 'remodelled physique', 'granite jaw' with headlines such as 'Pumped up' (*Newcastle Herald* 1999: 112).

As Angela Ndalianis (1995: 14) suggests, despite the recent emphasis on 'working out' there are well established limits within mainstream culture to the muscularity of both men and women – including sportsmen and women, and especially for the latter, as 'the female form must be toned and fit without revealing the denser, harder muscle which tampers with her "femininity"'. She also argues that the overly muscular female form disrupts binary notions of male and female – especially when the possibility of steroids is introduced. Sportswomen, however, frequently breach the boundaries of accepted female muscularity. The media generally seek to reassure people of their 'femininity' and sportswomen themselves frequently adopt a range of dress and adornment tactics to divert attention from their muscularity and to conform to hegemonic notions of femininity. Notable here is the late American athletics champion Florence Griffith Joyner, whose flamboyant use of overtly sexual clothes, hairstyles and adornments, such as colourful false fingernails (Kane and Greendorfer 1994), was an effective counterpoint to her muscularity and to any questioning of its origins. Nobody challenged Griffith Joyner's sexuality. Notably, Mauresmo chose not to employ such tactics.

Hamer (1994: 62), in her discussion of the controversy over the sexual ambiguity of women tennis players in 1919, points out the importance of clothes, with Suzanne Lenglen being the first player to wear knee-length culottes instead of a full-length skirt: '[t]he ambiguous gender status of these women has been compounded by the women themselves who have donned increasingly less feminine modes of dress for play'. In 1993, Martina Navratilova became the first woman to wear shorts in international competition (Hamer 1994: 63). Navratilova, however, like Graf and other champion tennis players, often also appeared in makeover 'glamour' spreads for women's magazines, a move not very different from soft porn calendars featuring sporting stars. Clothes and adornments featured heavily in the media representation of the women players at the Australian Open – notably, Hingis shopping for shoes and jewellery and wearing a red miniskirt and high heels after her win; Mary Pierce's yellow (Nike) dress; everything worn by Anna Kournikova; the Williams sisters' beads and flashy jewellery (as much statements of Afro American identity as femininity), and, of course, Mauresmo, who according to one columnist: 'presented a formidable and intimidating image on court dressed in a navy blue T-shirt and shorts, resembling a council worker bundying on for an afternoon's navvying' (Masters 1999b: 32).

Davenport suggested that Mauresmo's 'huge' shoulders might be an illusion caused because she was 'wearing a tank top' (Masters 1999b: 32), a view apparently reinforced by comments made by French journalist Yannick Cochennec of *Tennis Magazine*, who was reported as saying, 'I think the problem is the ways she dresses'. Cochennec was one of several commentators to suggest that Mauresmo's tight black shorts and top with cut-off shoulders only accentuated her size and upper body bulk (Yallop 1999: 5). Prior to the Mauresmo controversy, the glamour versus power binary already structured media coverage of women's tennis. However, once the players had drawn attention to her body in a climate framed by innuendo about performance enhancing drugs, Mauresmo could no longer be contained within the media's established discursive distinction between strength and beauty. Glamour and sex appeal are pivotal to the marketing of women's international tennis. This packaging of glamour seeks to balance so-called (controlled) power players like Davenport and the 'grace' of Hingis, Kournikova and others:

> . . . the arrival of the 'tude brood' as the US press dubbed the bejewelled self-motivated teen queens [such] as the Williams

sisters, Hingis and Kournikova, allowed the sport to land a $US120m ($AUS190m) deal for worldwide TV rights with Regency Enterprises, a US film conglomerate . . . While Regency didn't have Mauresmo and Davenport in mind when they made their bid, there will be plenty of 'lights, camera, action' ahead when the Hingis-led style players meet the power hitters.

(Mottram 1999: 50)

Elsewhere in media reports, Martina Hingis is credited with acknowledging the role of the media and marketing in framing women's tennis: 'It's business that wants this from us, and we're playing the game – me and Anna and Venus. We're the Spice Girls of tennis' (Hogan 1999a: 25).

It is ironic that African-American Venus Williams (who with her sister Serena is perhaps the biggest and most powerful player on the circuit) is bracketed with Kournikova and Hingis as part of a women's tennis glamour package. Arguably, race (an important variable outside the parameters of this chapter) is an issue here, but her inclusion also serves to highlight the importance of dress, adornment and sexuality in the marketing, promotion and media coverage of international women's tennis – underlining the nexus of global consumer culture and celebrity.

## Conclusion

In the reportage of women's sport the issue of sexuality is never far from the surface. This is especially so in international tennis – one of the few truly global women's sports. However, as it is a global sport, discourses of nation are necessarily also central, so connecting sexuality and nation. In this study of the discourses framing the media coverage of the 1999 Australian Tennis Open, three, often contradictory, themes emerged as significant – Australianness, hyperfemininity and power. These themes combined in reinforcing and contradictory ways – creating an interplay of insider/outsider oppositions. First, they coalesced to localise a global event played between individuals rather than nations. In the absence of a high-profile female Australian players, the Australian media emphasised the special relationship a number of overseas players had with Australia. Of note here was the then World Number 2 Martina Hingis, who was repeatedly positioned as having a home court advantage because of her unique attachment to Australia/Melbourne. When it emerged that Hingis was to play Mauresmo, the muscular, lesbian Frenchwoman in the final, these discursive oppositions intersected with another set of framing oppositions which were centred on sexuality and hegemonic femininity. Now the 'hometown', heterosexual, hyperfeminine player was being challenged by the outsider who was not only 'foreign' but also lesbian, overly muscular and wearing masculine clothing.

The body and identity of Mauresmo presented the media with a number of challenges. She emerged at a championship where media discourses were dominated by the hypersexuality of Kournikova and Hingis, and by a subtheme that emphasised the physicality and power of other players. The championship was also caught up in the Korda drug controversy and accusations by leading players that performance-enhancing drugs were rife in international tennis. It is tempting to explain the media response to Mauresmo's appearance and sexuality as being a conservative tactic to discipline the female athlete, but the situation is far more complex. In order to understand the media coverage of Mauresmo one has to look also to the general representation of women tennis players in the media during the competition and the discourses of nation, athleticism, the body and femininity that framed this representation. There is, then, a need for caution when reading media coverage of sporting events in the presence of a number of competing and coalescing discourses. These pivot on gender, sexuality, nation, and identity. In this regard, the reading of media texts serves to highlight the contradictions and ambiguities that frame the women-global sport nexus.

## Notes

1 This research was conducted as part of the 'Globalization and Local Impacts Project' funded by an Australian Research Council Large Grant.

## References

Agence France-Press (1999) Seles's record run can't be beaten', *The Australian*, 18 January.
Associated Press Women top TV ratings (1999) *http://sport.newcas.com.au*, 16 September.

Birrell, S. and Cole, C. (1994) Double Fault: Renee Richards and the construction and naturalization of difference, in P. Creedon (ed.) *Women, Media and Sport: Challenging Gender Values*. Thousand Oaks, CA: Sage.

Brown, P. (1995) Gender, the press and history: coverage of women's sport in the *Newcastle Herald*, 1890–1990, *Media Information Australia*, 75: 24–35.

Donnelly, P. (1996) The local and the global: globalization in the sociology of sport, *Journal of Sport & Social Issues*, 20 (3): 239–58.

Evans, L. (1999) Glamour girls don't faze determined Davenport, *Sydney Morning Herald*, 18 January.

Hamer, D. (1994) Netting the press: playing with Martina, in D. Hamer and B. Budge (eds) *The Good, the Bad and the Gorgeous: Popular Culture's Romance with Lesbianism*. London: Pandora.

Hargreaves, J. (1994) *Sporting Females: Critical Issues in the History and Sociology of Women's Sport*. London: Routledge.

Heaven, P. and Rowe, D. (1990) Gender, sport and body image, in D. Rowe and G. Lawrence (eds) *Sport and Leisure: Trends in Australian Popular Culture*. Sydney: Harcourt Brace Jovanovich.

Hinds, R. (1999a) Dokic to meet Hingis: but fear is not a factor, *Sydney Morning Herald*, 22 January.

Hinds, R. (1999b) Gifts for the gifted: chilling champion, *Sydney Morning Herald*, 1 February.

Hinds, R. (1999c) Mauresmo sizes up Martina, *Sydney Morning Herald*, 29 January.

Hinds, R. (1999d) This could be the start of something big, *Sydney Morning Herald*, 30 January.

Hogan, J. (1999a) Battle of the sexes, *The Australian*, 18 January.

Hogan, J. (1999b) 'Man' taunts fire up Mauresmo – Hingis upsets French rival, *The Weekend Australian*, 30 January.

Hooton, A. (1999) A case of white line fever, *Good Weekend The Sydney Morning Herald Magazine*, 11 September.

Horne, D. (1964) *The Luck Country*. Ringwood: Penguin.

Kane, M. and Greendorfer, S. (1994) The media's role in accommodating and resisting stereotyped images of women in sport, in P. Creedon (ed.) *Women, Media and Sport: Challenging Gender Values*. Thousand Oaks, CA: Sage.

Lenskyj, H. (1998) 'Inside sport' or 'on the margins'? Australian women and the sport media, *International Review for the Sociology of Sport*, 33 (1): 19–32.

Masters, R. (1999a) Homing bird, *Sydney Morning Herald*, 28 January.

Masters, R. (1999b) Queen Lindsay guillotined in an open revolt, *Sydney Morning Herald*, 29 January.

McKay, J. (1997) *Managing Gender: Affirmative Action and Organizational*

*Power in Australian, Canadian and New Zealand Sport*. Albany: State University of New York.

Mottram, W. (1999) Grace v power: an eternal struggle, *Sydney Morning Herald*, 30 January.

Ndalianis, A. (1995) Muscle, excess and rupture: female bodybuilding and gender construction, *Media Information Australia*, 75: 13–24.

*Newcastle Herald* (1999) Pumped up, 30 January.

Pearce, L. (1999a) Girl-powerplay, *The Sydney Morning Herald*, 21 January.

Pearce, L. (1999b) Volleys fly after final loss, *The Age*, 29 January.

Rowe, D. (1995) *Popular Cultures: Rock Music, Sport and the Politics of Pleasure*. London: Sage.

Rowe, D. (1996) Editorial, *Media, Culture & Society*, 18 (4): 523–26.

Rowe, D. (1999) *Sport, Culture and the Media: The Unruly Trinity*. Buckingham: Open University Press.

Rowe, D. and Lawrence, G. (1998) Framing a critical sports sociology in the age of globalization, in D. Rowe and G. Lawrence (eds) *Tourism, Leisure, Sport: Critical Perspectives*. Melbourne: Cambridge University Press.

Rowe, D., McKay, J. and Miller, T. (2000) Panic sport and the racialized masculine body, in J. McKay, M.A. Messner and D. Sabo (eds) *Masculinity, Gender Relations and Sport*. Thousand Oaks, CA: Sage.

Sargent, S., Zillmann, D. and Weaver, J. (1998) The gender gap in the enjoyment of televised sports, *Journal of Sport & Social Issues*, 22 (1): 46–65.

Stevenson, D. (1998) *Agendas in Place: Urban and Cultural Planning for Cities and Regions*. Rockhampton, QLD: RESRC Central Queensland University Press.

Stevenson, D. (1999) Reflections of a 'great port city': the case of Newcastle, Australia, *Environment and Planning D: Society and Space*, 17 (1): 105–19.

Walker, J. and Haslem, B. (1999) Hope springs eternal, *The Australian*, 18 January.

Wenner, L. (1996) One more 'ism' for the road: Dirt, globalism, and institutional analysis, *Journal of Sport & Social Issues*, 20 (3): 235–39.

Yallop, R. (1999) Mauresmo out in the Open, *The Australian*, 30–31 January.

# REPRESENTATIONS OF FOOTBALL IN BASEBALL LITERATURE: THE LYRIC FENWAY, THE PROSODY OF THE DODGERS, AND ARE YOU READY FOR SOME FOOTBALL?

## David McGimpsey

This chapter is predominantly unpublished but contains some passages from *Imagining Baseball: America's Pastime and Popular Culture*. Bloomington and Indianapolis: Indiana University Press, 2000.

### Introduction: my apologies

One of the most characteristic gestures in the critical appraisals of baseball literature is the apology. Highly sensitive to the dismissals products of popular culture often receive in academic circles, baseball literature's enthusiasts often offer detailed surveys that hope to demonstrate the intellectual worthiness of their subject. Proleptically dealing with a variety of perceived detractions, baseball's readership has developed its own critical rhetoric, insisting upon the sport's specialness and its unique literary claims.

A subsequent trope of baseball literature then, perhaps even its most common, is the proposition that baseball is the very best sport, maybe even possessed of some sublime integrity or mystical quality that makes it, among all sports, most appropriately suited for literary exercise. And true to this proposition, baseball has, in fact, gained a literary reputation that no other American sport, and very few objects of American popular culture, enjoy. Marianne Moore's (1967: 221) lines 'baseball is like writing/you can never tell with either/how it will go/or what you will do' are often quoted in anthologies of base-ball writing, rarely on the premise of interrogating the accuracy of Moore's statement, but mostly as an example of the game's literary suitability and cultural pedigree (how could anything that is like writing be bad?)

Because it is unlikely that authors would write baseball books if they were not also fans of the game, an author's declaration that baseball has a specialness which makes it well-suited for art is perhaps to be expected. But in baseball literature the compatibility of writing to sport is not solely a light-handed aside to acknowledge the author's leisure-time tastes. The connection between writing and baseball is made both poetically and analytically, motivating an influential dis-course. Cordelia Candelaria (1989: 2), the author of the first book-length study of baseball fiction, characteristically declares that 'the rules and object of the game, coupled with its rich social texture, make it especially serviceable as literary subject'. This and like declarations are repeated throughout baseball literature's evaluations, earnestly proposing that the understanding of baseball naturally reconciles with the study of literature. One may likely read or hear that the game's leisurely pace, its open timing, what Thomas Boswell (1989: 9) called its 'fecund pauses', have naturally attracted the interest of those with literary skills. As Canadian poet George Bowering (1990: 7) puts it: 'Have you ever heard a writer complain that baseball is too slow? Not a chance'. The compatibility of baseball and the literary is something that is believed in by many baseball writers, and this belief has been the source of some laudable inspiration. Bart Giamatti's (1989: 95) idealistic summary that 'Baseball is the Romantic Epic of homecoming America sings to itself' is in some ways a ridiculous conflation, but it's also a strong example of how baseball's literary enthusiasts have been able to make their case in creative ways with a passion not easily dismissed. But, of course, there is nothing about the sport of baseball itself that makes it uniquely amenable to literary representation.

There is nothing special about baseball that makes it a fruitful subject for a novel, poem or play. There is nothing to say that a novel about *jai alai* or the Canadian Football League could not be every bit, or even more artistically successful, than a novel about baseball. Literary representation is capable of capturing the worlds of fast sports, slow sports, stupid sports and spoiled sports with equal accuracy and flair. The artistic imagination, even when cruising in the world of American professional sports, is not limited to the leisurely or the contemplative. Nevertheless, the idea that baseball is 'the writer's game' has, I think, become the Doubleday myth of sport literature – something said so often that it has become, regardless of its short-comings in truth, a constitutive element of the sport's cultural allure and thus part of the real truth. There is also nothing to say that a nightingale is a better subject for an ode than a Grecian urn, but if one is speaking to the 'Society for Grecian Urn Appreciation' one should know what poem to read – and there's the rub. Baseball literature has the tradition of baseball literature. My starting argument here may sound frustratingly circular, but what I mean is that baseball's longstanding popularity, its constancy on the American scene, and its standing as popular culture is the source of its literary enrichment, not its so-called inherent poetic properties. This declaration does not diminish baseball. Obviously, certain pop-cult objects like baseball or Coca-Cola have acquired a cultural weightiness that 'frolf' (the mixture of frisbee and golf) and Diet Squirt have not. Though many writers believe that there is something writerly about the way the game of baseball is played, it is baseball's cultural weightiness which is the origin of its relatively newfound status as serious literature. Say what you will about 'the writer's game' (Orodenker 1996), there probably won't be a Kevin Costner movie about curling next summer, but if 'the faith of fifty million people' were invested in curling you could expect to see Bonspiel of Dreams at a theatre near you.

One might note, though, that baseball is no longer America's most popular sport, and its literary forms are also deeply marked by a nostalgia that is highly conscious of the game's decline in market share, and 'the national pastime' is a metaphor for alienation from much of contemporary American culture. Romantically aligning the sport with imagined pastoral virtues of the past, baseball literature has strong Luddite, anti-TV pretensions; a conservative undercurrent that is loathe to recognize the sport as part of the American entertainment industry. Baseball's essence is somehow uncomfortable in the modern world. But baseball is still a thriving billion-dollar business and base-ball's literature thrives, in part, as a satellite industry to Major League Baseball (MLB). As such, the cultural capital of baseball may be strategically important to the sport's greying fan base. Ignored by the commercial culture aimed at American youth, baseball's literary devotees often emphasize the sport's 'timeless' formal aesthetics and 'Platonic' tradition. So, for scholar George Grella (1975: 550), baseball 'is a game for poets and priests and philosophers and scholars, worthy of contemplation and rich in wonder', and, according to W.P. Kinsella, author of *Shoeless Joe/Field of Dreams*, other American pastimes are simply 'not conducive to quality' writing (in Horvath and Palmer 1987: 188).

Hence in many baseball books, the sport of football has become provocatively scapegoated as the bad 'gladiator's sport' that a feared, post-literate, TV-obsessed America can't help but love. As such, football, arguably the most popular sport in the United States, is almost always present in baseball's critical discourse. From George Carlin's famous comedy sketch on the differences between the two pastimes, to Thomas Boswell's (1989) popular essay '99 Reasons Why Baseball is Better Than Football', the metonymy of the gridiron is thoughtfully constructed by baseball writers as a measure of comparison to the metonymy of the ballpark. This dialectic ostensibly argues over the differing aesthetic qualities of the games, but structures the antagonism to declare a position in a wider cultural context. 'Baseball vs. football' becomes an obliquely gendered dispute between high culture and popular culture, particularly as it is manifested in the tensions between literature and television. In constructing the meaning of football as connected to its own 'essences' (clock-enslaved, TV-driven, martially encoded, muscle bound), baseball's 'literary' lustre is increased, allowing football to claim the sins of the present so that baseball can declare the virtues of the past. The existence of such a 'bad sport' unlikely to inspire quality writing is a crucial *leitmotif* in baseball's claim to its place in the proper University. Unloved by the TV crowd of the National Football League (NFL), baseball's perceived ratings decline is reformed as a significant part of its 'literariness'. Baseball can be imagined to have somehow 'escaped' the tawdriness of American popular culture, where it exists separately in the green fields of Walt Whitman and W.P. Kinsella. In this context, to prefer baseball to football is also a sign of taste, class and education. For Luke Salisbury (1995: 236), author of the fine baseball novel *The Cleveland Indian*, recognizing the advanced literary status of baseball is akin to making the 'obvious' recognitions that make '*Madame Bovary* a better novel than *Valley of the Dolls*' (1995: 236).

While I'd like to believe I am quicker than most Canadian academics to defend the honour of Jacqueline Susann, I am not arguing for football's or baseball's superior aesthetic value. I simply argue that 'football' exists in baseball texts as another apology for writing about baseball and as a commentary on the problems of all spectator sports in American society. This contentious good sport/bad sport dialectic informs ideas of baseball's literary pre-eminence. By appreciating the impact of a gendered social metonymy of the 'literariness' of baseball meets the 'TVness' of football, we might form a more complex picture of baseball literature's place in modern American culture.

## Good game/bad game

In October 1997, the deciding game of a divisional playoff between the New York Yankees and the Cleveland Indians was television's highest rated baseball game since the start of the new 'wild card' playoff format. The game, however, was handily beaten in the Neilson ratings by ABC's *Monday Night Football*, just six weeks into the new season, with a match between the Denver Broncos and the New England Patriots. ABC and football had a 13.9 rating and a 23 share, while FOX and baseball had a 9.8 rating and a 16 share (Monday Night 1997: C15). While the ratings for both broadcasts are significantly lower than an average audience for a hit TV drama like *ER*, the disparity between the two sports informs some of the rationale of baseball literature. Though Boswell (1989: 86) assures us, with his reason number 78, that 'nothing in baseball is as boring as the four hours of ABC's *Monday Night Football*', an apparently increasing number of Americans do not agree. The major factor in baseball's ratings decline has been the relative inability of the sport to appeal to younger viewers and to reactivate its fan base. In a *Variety* article that tries to delineate FOX's new strategy to deliver baseball to advertisers interested in younger viewers, the current baseball television demographics are analysed:

> baseball is – and will be for the near term – one of the oldest skewing TVsports, right up there with bowling and golf. With a demographic profile heavy on 50ish, modest income men, baseball has simply proved less attractive than the NBA and NFL to the core athletic shoe and auto advertisers that networks covet.
>
> (Levin 1996: 1)

Yet, for baseball's purists there exists a kind of catechism which affirms baseball's unique qualities and transcendental value. The claims of baseball's singular difficulty, its historical integrity, mathematical formulae, release from time-clocks, green fields, defence-with-the-ball, strategy, mirror of republican democracy, ratios of failure, and so on, are sublimated as exclusive claims to 'timeless' virtues and as 'a daily reminder of our rapidly disappearing past' (Grella 1975: 555). Importantly, many of these claimed virtues of baseball harken to a golden era and an idealised space where, according to poet Baron Wormser (1985: 14), 'neither forces [n]or actions equivocate'. The reactive list of baseball's sins: its Astroturf, domed stadia, free agents, and designated hitters, are all signs of the game's modern corruptions; selling out to 'the mindless, commercial credo of the NFL' (Salisbury 1995: 245).

For acclaimed poet Donald Hall (1985: 30), the superior status of baseball is a critical lesson for the moral health of American society: 'Baseball is fathers and sons', he writes, 'Football is brothers beating each other up in the backyard, violent and superficial. Baseball is the generations . . .'. Hall, as another literary Red Sox fan and a prominent talking head from Ken Burns' TV documentary *Baseball*, is though emblematic of baseball's cultural capital, his book of essays *Fathers Playing Catch With Sons* contains many unpretentious insights into baseball and other sports. Looking back to football's roots, Hall offers an important reminder:

> It was all very collegiate. It is not much remembered that in this country football originated as the gentleman's sport; baseball belonged to the working classes. Football was like tennis, not bowling; it was like rugby, not soccer.
>
> (1985: 179)

Though 'popularity' can be quantified in other ways besides TV-ratings and magazine covers, there is little doubt that baseball does not enjoy as exclusive a relationship with the working-class audience as it did up until the television era. Ironically, the expressed disdain for football is closely linked to the working class's current preference. Describing football fans' faces as 'meaty with liquor' (1985: 192), Hall expresses a palpable disgust over the importation of uncouth football rituals like 'tail-gating' or shouting 'Go!' at baseball games. Beginning with a well-accepted connotation (football = violence), Hall's rhetoric spirals into a kind of associative nightmare where football's popularity is entwined with an image of the 'fury (of the) underclass' (193). Looking specifically at the cartoon image of the football player on the transformed logo of the NFL's New England Patriots, Hall is overwhelmed with anticipatory horror:

> . . . thick-necked, leering with mayhem, giggling with sadism, brow furrowed not by thoughts of his tiny dinosaur-brain but by anabolic steroids – an image of the decline of the republic's hero

from enlightenment ectomorph, spiritual with endeavour and guilt, to sadistic, hulking mesomorph, and apelike Homo Footballus, the object of our weekend attention and obsession, squatting before the goalposts of a diminished life.

(198)

It's a long way from 'Drop Kick Me, Jesus' to be sure, but it does represent a pattern of a feared historical degeneration. In passing from baseball to football, the whole country somehow passes from Ralph Waldo Emerson to Hank Williams Jr. Fearing. Such a passage into uncivilized brutality has long been a fascination of the American literary imagination and is an informing distress in baseball writing. In *The Cleveland Indian* the revelation that the title character loves 'that gladiator's game' (Salisbury 1992: 98), football, is a prelude to his envelopment by the white man's crude West. The novel's narrator goes so far as to blame the Indian's final depredations on a lack of love for the good game: 'he didn't love baseball' (284) he says as a kind of autopsy. It is as if to not love baseball, and to prefer football, is to be subsumed by the nation's coarser hegemonies.

Of course, the violence associated with professional football may indeed be anathema to prose idealists who see in baseball a peaceful image vaguely associated with the American heartland or a New England University's quad. Even though the essential action of base-ball (pitching the hardball) is fraught with the potential for menace, football is a more violent game. But there is little or no evidence to suggest that the violence of an admired sport is of such direct bearing on the 'fury of the underclass' (Hall 1985: 193). Otherwise, how would Americans explain the relationship of soccer hooliganism to a game that they find even more boring than baseball? How can the 'law and order' establishments of Canadians be squared with the intense violence of their national game of hockey? For the baseball purist, the slow deliberateness of baseball is not just a simple consideration of play, it aligns baseball within the discriminations of taste and class. In Eric Rolfe Greenberg's (1983) admired novel *The Celebrant*, baseball is a crucial test for the son of an immigrant's desire to truly belong to America. In the course of the novel, the standard anti-football rap is subtly disguised as an idealised Christy Mathewson sermonizes on the Middle-Eastern game known as *bushkazi*, a medieval polo/lacrosse mix that involves severed goats' heads. The novel's Mathewson indicates that all such games are part of monstrous pre-American identities before the more prudent beauty of baseball revealed itself.

Football, like *bushkazi*, or as it is often represented by baseball's celebrants, is essentially an atavistic enthusiasm considering the more republic-friendly charms of baseball. 'The Christian Gentleman' declares, 'Games of possession, games of targetry – they're all as obvious as *bushkazi* ... Baseball is the most intellectual of the physical sports. It is totally artificial, creating its own time, existing within its own space. There is nothing real about it' (Greenberg 1983: 85). This declaration, that baseball is somehow propelled outside of its cultural contexts while football/*bushkazi* remain inside the obvious worlds of savage conquest and greed, is one of the most provocatively repeated tropes of baseball's purists.

I would imagine that most people who care enough about baseball to focus part of their writing career on the subject could probably be described as 'purists' – people who would be fairly happy with the dimensions of the game as they are, and who would reasonably be suspicious of the innovations designed to please a new era of less-informed fans. Salisbury (1995: 237), in a fire-and-brimstone speech titled 'Baseball Purists Purify', claims that the purist is out to preserve the form of baseball itself, the 'crucial' thing which maintains the sport's integrity. In standing up to declare baseball's pre-eminence, he declares that the purist must be morally resolute in the face of all NFL-like alterations: 'If we all stood up like Christ facing the money lenders, Major League Baseball would be as receptive to our message as humanity has been to HIS' (241–2). While many authors would not be as evangelical as Salisbury, baseball's transgressions like the wild-card playoff system are nonetheless frequently invoked by 'lay-men' as impurities that the 'perfect, separate' corpus of baseball can do without.

For novelist (and purist) W.P. Kinsella the magical and quasi-religious essentialness of baseball is frequently the inspiration for his heartfelt and comedic work. Rather than see baseball as an explicitly social engagement, Kinsella keeps returning to the imaginative possibilities inherent in the game's aesthetic qualities. For example, the absence of a clock in regulating the duration of the game and the extension of baseball's foul lines become the basis for an obscure globalism:

> The other sports, football, basketball, hockey are twice enclosed, first by time and second by rigid playing fields. There is no time limit on a baseball game. On the true baseball field the foul lines diverge forever, the field eventually encompassing a goodly

portion of the world, and there is theoretically no distance that a great hitter couldn't hit the ball.

(Horvath and Palmer 1987: 188)

His poetry is appreciable, but Kinsella's statement ignores the theories by which physics are usually understood. By this fabulation (recast in Kinsella's novel *The Iowa Baseball Confederacy*), the infinitely extending line would also be shared by 'the plane' of the football's goal line. Theoretically, if Emmitt Smith jumped a mile high and broke 'the plane', it's still a touchdown. As baseball fans may have a long wait to see 700-foot home runs or 40-day games, just as they might be waiting on any number of unlikely miracles, these occurrences are in Kinsella's highlight-reel primarily to draw attention to baseball's interesting conventions. By extending the boundaries of baseball's rules, Kinsella turns them into myths of spirit and further emphasises the rightness of their more quotidian equivalences. The 40-day game of *The Iowa Baseball Confederation* (1986) is not just an American satire on the great flood, but a witty elaboration on the saying 'it ain't over till it's over'. By believing in the pure essences of baseball, the fan may be brought to more imaginative possibilities. 'There are no limitations', Kinsella has said, 'at least in baseball fiction' (Horvath and Palmer 1987: 188).

But even in the world of the matter-of-fact, the baseball enthusiast will still discover that their sport is the superior reserve for intellect and craft. George Will's bestseller *Men at Work* (a title that thoughtfully distinguishes itself from the sentiments of *Boys of Summer, When It Was A Game* etc.) goes to great lengths to establish baseball's superiority on more empirical grounds. Paraphrasing San Francisco general manager Al Rosen, Will writes that the football 'receiver has to learn his routes, the defensive ends his zones, or man-to-man coverage. But these skills do not compare in difficulty with the skills required to hit a baseball' (1990: 309). Indeed, for many observers the cliché that a great hitter 'fails 7 out of 10 times' is part of the testimony to baseball's ascendancy. Hitting is extremely difficult, I'm sure, but it is a mistake in logic to equate one evaluative system for another. A 300 hitter has put in an 'A' performance as has a football receiver with 9 touchdown catches, but in the terms of the baseball/football comparison the 'difficulty' of hitting a baseball is problematically translated into cultural exclusivity. Similarly, regardless of claims of equal difficulty, earning a PhD at an Ivy League university is not quite the same thing as earning it at one of lower status. It's hard then not to notice some of the anxieties of class stratification hidden in Will's declaration that 'the best baseball people are [...] Cartesians' (1990: 324) – a stylish reworking of the classic 'it's a game of inches'.

Defining the aesthetic differences between professional sports is a free, honest enterprise, and there is nothing wrong with the fan of one sport or another making a claim for it. That's half the fun. However similar the organizational structures of professional football and baseball, these sports are quite different to see. When the Henry Wiggen character of Mark Harris's (1953: 67) *The Southpaw* says, 'I did not think much of basketball. Actually I consider it pretty nearly as dreadful as football', this is not necessarily unconscious social climbing. Nevertheless, the persistence of baseball lit's unease with the popularity of football is expressed in curiously stratified ways. The biased attribution of positive moral qualities to one sport at the expense of others (sportism, perhaps) has a currency that is important in the cultural formation of baseball literature. There are grounds on which one can compare the moral universes of, say, cockfighting and badminton, but even these comparisons may also revolve around stereotypes of class and the rarefied authority of 'the literary'. It would be hard to imagine a better sports novel than Charles Willeford's instructive thriller *Cockfighter*, where the protagonist claims an integrity for his chosen sport which is often mourned in baseball fiction: 'Cockfighting is the only sport that can't be fixed, perhaps the only fair contest left in America. A cock wouldn't throw a fight and couldn't if he knew how' (1972: 51). What is being criticised or obscured by such 'sportist' statements about good and bad sports?

### 'Effete snobs'

Despite the side-taking partisanship of some writers, most baseball fans have an appreciation of football as most football fans have an appreciation of baseball. The commercial structures and methods of consumption for both products are practically identical. The literary discussion between the two sports depends upon the popularity of their styles of play and the knowledge of their rules. Ironically, when some of football's literary enthusiasts defend their sport they do not claim football's literary credentials, but allow baseball's recent association with East Coast intellectuals to speak for itself. In a familiar anti-intellectual gesture, football enthusiasts are also glad to say that baseball is 'the poet's game'. An anti-baseball response also becomes coded in the mythos of baseball-as-erudition, satirising the pretensions of the literary and unapologetically celebrating football's machismo. Dan Jenkins, the author of the classic sport novel *Semi-Tough* (1972), and an outspoken critic of baseball's 'literary types', describes a 'typical' baseball book:

> Dave McWords is primarily known for his deep-thinking political books, such as the lavishly praised *What I Grasped and You Didn't About 1957 and Part of 1958*, but his loyal fans were rewarded when he focused his attention on sports the past year. The result was *Why Me?*, a sympathetic look at the Chicago White Sox slugger Zack Thrasher; who makes only $8 million a year, [but] coped with the baseball strike while overseeing the construction of his new home, a 19,000-square-foot mansion in Rodendo del Taco el Pinto, California. In the first 968 pages, McWords discusses the political ramifications, both domestically and globally, of an intentional walk Thrasher received from a New York Yankee reliever at 4:17 p.m. on August 22, 1989.
>
> (1995: xviii–xix)

Rather than claim the intellectual respectability of 'football novels' like Harry Crew's (1976) *A Feast of Snakes* or Frederick Exley's (1968) *A Fan's Notes*, baseball is left to suffer with the unmasculine connotations of its literary 'respect'. It's not surprising, then, that reviewer Will Manley (1993: 24), in a column titled 'Why I Hate Baseball', declares 'the real threat to baseball comes from the effete snobs who want to emasculate the sport. I never thought it was possible, but academic intellectuals are ruining baseball like they have ruined many great books'. In a *Newsweek* article called 'Why Don't Eggheads Love Football?', Greg Easterbrook (1994: 64) writes, 'For decades American writers and intellectuals of all stripes have been producing paeans to baseball, while nearly ignoring football'. The oddity, for Easterbrook, is that baseball's plays are relatively simple in comparison to the complex and secretive play formations associated with football: 'The complexities of football make it almost impossible to bluff an understanding of the game. And if there's one thing intellectuals hate, it's not being able to bluff their way to apparent mastery of something' (64).

If 'writerliness' is thought to be in conflict with 'manliness', an argument between baseball and football fans has some significance for female sport writers who are already negotiating the maleness of American sport culture. In some women's baseball writing the fact that baseball isn't as discernibly male as football is part of the sport's allure. In her poem 'Why I Love It', Mary Leary (1994: 128) writes that baseball is 'not like football, where they'd eat you for breakfast and really/mean it, or work awful hard to,/that's a sport for men'. Imagining baseball's space as more gender-neutral, however, does invite another series of placating stereotypes. In his essay 'Expansion Draft: Baseball Fiction of the 1980s', Christian K. Messenger (1991: 70) claims that one sign of baseball's pre-eminence among literary sports is that it 'appears to be the team sport most congenial to women athletes, with its lack of aggressive physical contact and premium on attributes other than size and strength. Competition and heroic striving are present in the fiction but are integrated with the team's other potentials: nurture, family growth'. Assurances that women couldn't really be primarily interested in 'size and strength' may sound familiar, and this kind of certainty underwrites much of the anxiety about women in the world of sport. But to date there have been the same number of women in the NFL as in MLB, while as spectator sports go, exaggerated masculinity can also be of interest to female fans and, at times, female writers. It seems that those who are arguing for baseball's natural suitability to literature may also want the existence of women's baseball texts to serve as further evidence of the game's ability, unlike football, to transcend its physical and corporate realities (and to represent audiences outside the traditional male base).

As Bowering (1986: 119) writes 'We know football is as referential as can be to war, to business, to sex life, to the years filled more and more with injuries and failing health'. That is, football refers to the compromised subjectivity of the American male. By analogy, baseball is thought to have a less sexually-restricted metaphorical province, where its literary quarters can be thought as welcoming as another 'lady's day'. As Boswell (1989: 31) imagines in his reason number 24, 'Marianne Moore loved Christy Mathewson. No woman of quality ever preferred football to baseball'. Though I may be accused of drawing too much serious attention to articles written for gentle amusement, this kind of discrimination is a rather curious form of extolling the virtues of baseball. Unchallenged, these systematic poetic linkings lead to the most spurious kinds of gendered speculation, like Hall's (1985: 112) sex'n'violence theory that football and basketball 'encourage penis-envy prose: envy of meat violence, splintered bone, and cleat marks on the eyeball; in basketball, grey-boy envy of black cool'.

## The red, white and blue glow of the TV

Whatever the similarity of their professional institutionalization, the metaphorical comparisons of baseball and football obviously trace the fault lines of some of America's greatest controversies: North vs. South, tradition vs. progress, city vs. country, and even PBS vs. MTV [public service broadcasting versus commercial music television]. In a compelling essay which tracks the development from 'the local rooted-ness' of fan support to the TV era in football audiences, Michael Oriard writes:

> The change has not been simply one of loss. Nostalgic golden-agers too easily forget, for example, that segregation – Jim Crow baseball and football – was one consequence of tribal identifi-cation with sports. Television and the integration of sports advanced together and are more than coincidentally related. I would hesitantly suggest that television has by this time nearly deracinated the Black athletes who dominate football and basket-ball for young viewers such as my son.
>
> (1996: 38)

The 'globalizing' effect of television broadcasts helped bring baseball past its more embarrassing traditions and helped create a more com-prehensive readership for it. While technology and television are often cast as the moustache-twirling villains in baseball texts, it is through technology and television that most of us have been able to 'read' and 're-read' baseball's great moments collectively, and this textual resource reconfirms its defining moments and recontextualizes their drama. Most of the great baseball moments 'we' share, like Willie May's catch and Carlton Fisk's home run, are so because everybody can see them on TV. Yet, the hard-to-believe complaint that baseball does not work well on TV is worn like a badge by baseball's literary elite. In *Men at Work*, George Will (1990: 324) assures us that 'a base-ball game is an orderly experience – perhaps too orderly for the epi-sodic mentalities of television babies'. It would perhaps take too much time to historicize what is wrong with Will's statement, but clearly, baseball's debasement through television is an important part of the rationale for turning it into a literary monument. Boswell (1989: 37) lets that equation speak for itself in his reason number 91: 'Baseball is vastly better in person than on TV . . . Football is better on TV'.

The proposition that television is the great enemy of all things literary is a thought with a great deal of socio-political energy and importance in American culture. Even television is a reliable source to receive the message that the most significant cultural hobby of Americans (TV watching) is, like junk food, bad for you. The scope of this chapter is too narrow to properly address the value and abuse in this rhetoric. But, while the role of television in popularising the once collegiate sport of football with the working class can't be underestimated, a reified image of television consciousness has emerged in baseball literature's more idealistic forms as a true source of villainy. Football's TV appeal becomes a self-evident example of the positive qualities associated with baseball; football's relationship with television becomes linked to a coming cultural apocalypse where 'I Love Lucy' will be deemed too difficult to teach in University. When Peter C. Bjarkman (1991: xvii) writes that 'baseball is the foremost game among acute thinkers, intellectuals and, above all, storytellers and poets', there is a conscious effort to talk baseball up to where the beer-drinking tube jockey is thought better off waiting for Sunday. When Bart Giamatti Miltonically dubs television as 'all-falsifying' (Valerio 1991: 1) or George Will (1990: 224) complains that today's clubhouses have 'been swallowed by MTV', they are both canvassing baseball's place in a sports caste system. It is hard, for example, to miss the authority placed on the literary in Boswell's (1989: 35) reason number 63, 'The baseball Hall of Fame is in Cooperstown, New York, beside James Fenimore Cooper's Lake Glimmerglass; the Football Hall of Fame is in Canton Ohio, beside the freeway'. Baseball is thus geographically distanced from the class sorrows of America's off-ramp culture and left to luxuriate in its bookish pasture. Being 'pastoral' tacitly declares the sport's cultural relationship with great, improving works such as Marvell's poetry or Shakespeare's *As You Like It*. Even Harold Bloom (1994: 31), whose hostility to televised popular culture is fairly complete, allows the discourse of greenspaced ballparkerie to slip beneath his radar, declaring that if teams represented political ideologies 'that would give us a form of baseball into which we could not escape for pastoral relief, as we do now'.

Sportswriter Peter Golenbock (1988: 6) may see a paradigmatic Fenway Park [in Boston, home of the Red Sox] where 'Harvard professors sit and talk the same language with the fans with blue collars'. However the seating arrangements in the real Fenway are organized with class consideration in mind and the heavy book-buyers may not exactly be working on their sunburns in the bleachers. Baseball literature's premier essayist Roger Angell talks about seeing a Mets game with Giamatti, who launches into a kind of hallelujah for authentic baseball fans; blaming the television era for a failure amongst less gifted fans and fractiously evoking an unpleasantly elitist differentiation between 'us' and 'them':

> 'You and I are traditional fans. We come here in a ceremonial fashion. We don't exactly kneel, but we're interested only in that stuff' – he gestured at the diamond and the outspread field before us – 'for our basic information we come to testify. We're not participatory fans. For them, that object' – he pointed to the towering Diamond vision board in left center – 'is more important than anything that happens on the field. For them, it's the videos and the dot races and the commercials, which are probably all connected to rock music anyway'.
>
> (in Angell 1991: 322)

Apparently, it wasn't enough that they paid to see the Mets.

## Conclusion

As long as football remains popular it will continue to be an important signifier in baseball literature. Where baseball is sanctified as tempered and transcendent, football can be baseball's evil cousin. Matthew Goodman and Stephen Bauer, after admiring the metaphorical elasticity of terms like 'gopher-ball' and 'o-fer', then despair:

> Football, that aggressive pretender to the title of National Game, has plenty of distinct expressions – such as blitz, sack, bomb, slant, crackback, nickel back, or more evocatively, button hook; but the difference is that these are technical terms; they are not genuinely metaphoric, for they call to mind nothing other than the specific action they mean to represent. Rather than being outward and open to the world, the language of football remains mired in the blood and dirt of the football field.
>
> (1993: 229)

The *jouissance* in the words of sports is appreciable but betrays the predisposition to never test the potential of metaphor beyond its most likely application. Or to put it another way, because research into sport literature isn't exactly a fourth-and-goal situation, it's understandable that scholars don't read the defence properly and are forced to utter an untested option. Naturally, the endless comparisons between the two sports are made because they evoke opinions in an excitedly contested arena of familiar terms. Nobody is going to write an essay called '99 reasons why baseball is better than lacrosse'. But in its repeated references to football, some baseball writing unfairly attempts to draw their sport outside of the negative aura surrounding American sport culture, where it can be more like writing. Marianne Moore's lines, quoted in the Introduction, are, after all, deeply inaccurate. The writer does, to a certain extent, know how it will go and can always start over again and revise if they don't like what they've done. Referring to Moore's slogan, Bart Giamatti (1989: 82) wonders if baseball could not be considered 'a form of writing' as 'serendipity is the essence of both games'. But, as anybody who has prepared a chapter for a book could tell you, serendipity is not the essence of writing – editing is.

## References

Angell, R. (1991) *Once More Around the Park: A Baseball Reader*. New York: Random House.

Bjarkman, P.C. (1991) Introduction, in P.C. Bjarkman (ed.) *Baseball and the Game of Life: Stories for the Thinking Man*. New York: Vintage.

Bloom, H. (1994) *The Western Canon: The Books and School of the Ages*. New York: Riverhead.

Boswell, T. (1989) *The Heart of the Order*. New York: Penguin Books.

Bowering, G. (1986) Baseball and the Canadian imagination, *Canadian Literature*, 108: 115–24.

Bowering, G. (1990) Introduction, in G. Bowering (ed.) *Taking the Field: The Best of Baseball Fiction*. Red Deer: Red Deer College Press.

Candelaria, C. (1989) *Seeking the Perfect Game: Baseball in American Literature*. Westport: Greenwood.

Easterbrook, G. (1994) Why don't eggheads love football? *Newsweek*, 5 December.

Giamatti, A.B. (1989) *Take Time for Paradise: Americans and Their Games*. New York: Summit.

Goldstein, W. (1989) *Playing for Keeps: A History of Early Baseball*. Ithaca: Cornell University Press.

Golenbock, P. (1988) Preface, in M. Shannon (ed.) *The Best of Spitball*. New York: Pocket.

Goodman, M. and Bauer, S. (1993) From Elysian fields: baseball as the literary game, *The Sewanee Review*, 101 (2): 226–39.

Greenberg, E.R. (1983) *The Celebrant*. New York: Viking.

Grella, G. (1975) Baseball and the American dream, *The Massachusetts Review*, 16 (4): 550–67.

Hall, D. (1985) *Fathers Playing Catch with Their Sons: Essays on Sport (Mostly Baseball)*. San Francisco: North Point Press.

Harris, M. (1953) *The Southpaw*. Lincoln: University of Nebraska Press.

Horvath, B.K. and Palmer, W.J. (1987) Three on: an interview with David Carkeet, Mark Harris, and W.P. Kinsella, *Modern Fiction Studies*, 33 (1): 183–94.

Jenkins, D. (1995) Foreword, in D. Jenkins (ed.) *The Best American Sports Writing of 1995*. Boston: Houghton Mifflin.

Jenkins, D. (1972) *Semi-Tough*. New York: Signet.

Kinsella, W.P. (1986) *The Iowa Baseball Confederacy*. Toronto: HarperCollins.

Leary, M. (1994) Why I love it, in E. Nauen (ed.) *Diamonds Are A Girl's Best Friend: Women Writers On Baseball*. Boston: Faber and Faber.

Levin, G. (1996) FOX baseball pitch targets rookie Auds, *Variety*, 1–7 April.

Manley, W. (1993) The manly arts: why I hate baseball, *Booklist*, 1–15 June.

Messenger, C.K. (1991) Expansion draft: baseball fiction of the 1980s, in W. Umphlett (ed.) *The Achievement of American Sport Literature: A Critical Appraisal*. Toronto: Associated University Presses.

Monday night NFL game outdraws Indians-Yanks (1997) *The Montreal Gazette AP*, 8 October.

Moore, M. (1967) *The Complete Poems of Marianne Moore*. New York: Viking.

Morris, T. (1997) *Making the Team: The Cultural Work of Baseball Fiction*. Urbana and Chicago: University of Illinois Press.

Neal-Lunsford, J. (1992) Sport in the land of television: the use of sport in network prime-time schedules 1946–50, *Journal of Sports History*, 19 (1): 56–76.

Oriard, M. (1996) Home teams, *The South Atlantic Quarterly*, 95 (2): 471–500.

Orodenker, R. (1996) *The Writer's Game: Baseball Writing in America*. New York: Twayne.

Salisbury, L. (1992) *The Cleveland Indian: The Legend of King Saturday*. New York: The Smith.

Salisbury, L. (1995) Baseball purists purify, *Nine: A Journal of Baseball History and Social Policy*, 3 (2): 235–47.

Valerio, A. (1991) *Bart: A Life of A. Bartlett Giamatti By Him and About Him*. Orlando: Harcourt, Brace Jovanovich.

Willeford, C. (1972) *Cockfighter*. New York: Vintage.

Will, G. (1990) *Men at Work: The Craft of Baseball*. New York: HarperCollins.

Wormser, B. (1985) *Good Trembling*. Boston: Houghton Mifflin.

# 17 | SPORT AS CONSTRUCTED AUDIENCE: A CASE STUDY OF ESPN's *THE EXTREME GAMES*

## Robert E. Rinehart

Excerpt from *Players All: Performances in Contemporary Sport.*
Bloomington and Indianapolis: Indiana University Press, 1998,
Chapter 7: 98–110.

> Spectacularism: A fascination with extreme situations.
> (Douglas Coupland, *Generation X:*
> *Tales for an Accelerated Culture*)

Ethnography, popular culture, critical studies, and cultural studies work have all examined the media's logic of spectatorship and audience formation. Cultural studies in particular has interrogated the ways in which the media contribute a certain logic of sense-making, yet examination of the sport media's contribution to this logic is largely lacking (a rare exception being Gruneau 1989). An overriding goal of this chapter is to deconstruct, ethnomethodologically, some of the electronic media's logic of sports production. The 'scientific project of ethnomethodology', as defined by Alain Coulon (1995: 2), is an attempt 'to analyse the methods, or the procedures, that people use for conducting the different affairs that they accomplish in their daily lives'. Thus, in this chapter I will co-opt ethnomethodology and turn it to an examination of one of ESPN's 1995 sport programming ventures, *The eXtreme Games*.[1] More specifically, I seek to discover how ESPN has framed production of *The eXtreme Games* so that it will gain acceptance and power in the larger culture and yet promote a sense of diversity, appearing to remain true to the internal logics of the individual athletes, audience, and practitioners. What are the overriding themes that ESPN uses to draw in an audience for this spectacle? Additionally, how does ESPN create verisimilitude – a 'you are there' feel and a sense of participation – for the viewer?

According to ESPN announcers Suzy Kolber and Chris Fowler, *The eXtreme Games*, a made-for-cable-TV sports event, includes nine sports, with 30 different events, played by 400 athletes from six continents, representing 25 countries. With so many different sports, and varied events within each sport, the micro-logics of shooting the sports obviously must vary. But, as with programming for the Olympics (with its multitude of sports), the electronic media have learned consistent ways (macro-logics) to 'tell the stories' so that viewers can understand the logics of the sports as they are presented for viewer consumption.

### Dominant metanarratives

*The eXtreme Games* is a postmodern, self-consciously constructed, result-driven form of sport. The viewer has learned a common television sports language from other sport productions, so that, when watching, she anticipates a short introduction to each game or sport (Morgan 1994). She also expects to see one or more of the key athletes profiled, with a story that emphasises the athlete's individual uniqueness but also contextualises them within the larger logics of the sport and within the collectivity of fellow sportspersons. This individual/collective dynamic, in which individuals' agency and belongingness are both privileged, is termed 'universal singularity' (see Denzin 1991). The viewer, moreover, expects to see multinational corporate advertisements specifically designed for and intertextually linked to this *eXtreme Games*. Thus, she easily consumes advertisements for Taco Bell and the movie *Congo*, Chevy trucks, and Mountain Dew, with catchy, smarmy, self-effacing Madison Avenue-driven tones and sound bites evocative of the constructed, made-for-television nature of *The eXtreme Games*. In many cases, the most memorable portion of televised sport for the television viewing audience is the commercials – especially around Super Bowl and Olympics time.

For example, the following advertisement for Mountain Dew aired during the run of *The eXtreme Games*. It depicts four mountain bikers, and begins with a voiceover (sports) announcer, in super-hype mode, proclaiming various progressively difficult, progressively absurd mountain-biking tricks:

Announcer: 'Extreme mountain biking . . . 45 miles an hour'.
Biker #1: 'Did it'.
Announcer: '. . . 65 miles an hour'.
Biker #2: 'Done it'.
Announcer: '. . . blindfolded'.
Biker #3: 'Been there'.
Announcer: '. . . then, a 4000-foot vertical drop'.
Biker #4: 'Tried that'.
Announcer: 'All while slamming a Dew'.
All bikers: 'Whoa'.
Announcer: 'Nothing's more intense than slamming Mountain Dew. Oh, Yeah – while watching *The eXtreme Games* on ESPN'.
Biker #3: 'Decent'.

(Mountain Dew commercial 1995)

At the same time ESPN has constructed a sport-familiar terrain for viewers, the producers of *The eXtreme Games* have promoted the theme that this is unusual, cool, exceptional, extreme sport. The advertisers have learned that intertextuality – simply put, the combining of formerly disparate cultural signifiers – sells. Thus, using '. . . while watching *The eXtreme Games* on ESPN' seems appropriate in a Mountain Dew commercial, and easily elides into another commercial or the show itself. The viewer, although she may not know it, thus expects to be told certain logics of the sporting show. She fully expects to be informed, at some level, how to 'read' this televised text. Thus, the idea of themes, or metanarratives, enters into the logic of sports programming which is on the modernist/postmodernist cusp. Sports programmers, using what has formerly worked while still attempting what *might* work, continue with a largely modernist strategy, a comfortable logic that is, for the most part, sequentially (or temporally) 'logical'. At various times, innovations that might seduce sponsors are attempted, even though readers (television sports viewers) seem content with most familiar methods of presentation. Thus, the viewer learns to expect some kind of theme(s) to the show. The dominant themes, or mythoi, of these *Games* include the normalcy of the athletes; the paradoxical uniqueness of the players; the inextricable link between all players of all sports; the historical link among all sports, and the basic fact that ESPN's *The eXtreme Games* is sport.

One of the themes/mythoi of ESPN's *The eXtreme Games* is the ideological paradox of this sporting event being done by normal people who perform extraordinary feats:

These are Marines, bankers, engineers, even a window cleaner. Teams of regular folks from all over the world attempting something very irregular: hiking, peddling, and paddling, from ancient Indian hunting grounds in the isolated wilderness of Maine, all the way here to Fort Adams on a course that they have to help chart themselves.

(*The eXtreme Games* Preview Show, 24 June 1995)

The paradox is that anyone can do it, despite the fact that the viewer is reminded that these are professionals who have spent years perfecting their athletic skills.

A second dominant theme of *The eXtreme Games* is the uniqueness of its players: the audience is informed that many of the athletes and spectators, even the two announcers, are members of Generation X. This marker of generational individuality at once creates a space for and defines a target market for ESPN. As co-anchor Chris Fowler says, emptily, it 'helps to explain why, when it comes to sports, Gen X is Gen eXtreme' (Fowler 1995). In line with an advanced capitalistic logic 'in which the relationship to consumption seems to have at least slightly displaced the relationship to production' (Springwood 1996: 22), *The eXtreme Games* television programming encourages consumption (indeed, that is a fundamental and perhaps ultimate purpose of any television programming). It does so through an ideological logic of the 'American values' of rugged individualism, perseverance, egalitarianism, cooperation, fairness, and deservedness. The viewer is told that 'Fort Adams represents New Age sports values', (Scott 1995) yet the same modernist consumer values, hypertrophied, are presented to the audience.

As with most ideology, there is some basis for the claims – and for counterclaims. Certainly the generation of people born in the 1960s and 1970s, with their training and facility with computers, computer simulations, digitising for biomechanical analysis, and use of electronic/cybernetic software, has leapt forward into an arena of sports innovation and technological construction which may rival that of the mid- to late 1800s. In fact, during *The eXtreme Games* in 1995, television viewers were encouraged to 'become interactive' with the sky surfing event on the World Wide Web. As in-line skater Arlo Eisenberg says, 'it's really exciting to be a part of something and to know that you're the first ones to do it, that you're pioneering it, that you're the ones that are in control' (*The eXtreme Games*, 25 June 1995). He might see himself as a sort of avant-garde artist. But then Alf

Imperato, a windsurfer, in the same place says, 'Everyone wants their own identity. And specific tasks and specific identities sometimes make a lot of money. And that's what a lot of the people are looking for'. A statement of kitsch.

Tied in with the uniqueness of its players is the third theme of *The eXtreme Games*: that the players are inextricably linked to other players in other times. ESPN airs interviews that generally reinforce this idea. Thus Chris Fowler, speaking of the former outlaw status of many of the sports that have first been shown on television as part of *The eXtreme Games*, says of barefoot water skiing, 'This is a great moment for guys in the sport. This is a sport searching for a sponsor, without a pro tour: these guys are used to just jumping for fun and the cheers of the crowd' (*The eXtreme Games*, 25 June 1995). As with the growth of professional beach volleyball (and the status of its athletes), many of the 'extreme' sports and some athletes involved in *The eXtreme Games* are seeking sponsorship, big-money tournaments, recognition, and power. They are modelling themselves after other professional sports: 'You know, athletes in alternative sports have been craving a stage where they can prove, just like football and basketball players, they are serious competitors who leave as much sweat on the playing field as anyone' (Scott 1995). It is a tenuous balance, working between the allure of the professional sports model and the idealised purity of the amateur sports model.

Another example links athletic generations. In case the viewer is not clear on the historical and thematic ties between the Olympics and *The eXtreme Games* (and the athletes of each), Suzy Kolber makes it explicit:

> There's more history to many of these sports than you might think. Quite a bit of evolution along with the revolution . . . Yes, we will concede that the Olympics carry unmatched prestige, but they've been around since 1896. We must say, though, in our first go-round, we're not lacking in international flavour.
> (*The eXtreme Games* Preview Show, 24 June 1995)

Postmodern technological advances, while seen as innovative, are also a link to the previous modernist technological advances in the ongoing process that is sport. As Fowler says,

> Technology here is another story. You're gonna see some high-tech coverage never used on any sport before. Our cameras and mikes are going to be everywhere: on helmets and handlebars,

an inch off the street at 60 miles an hour, and free falling from 13,000 feet.

(Fowler 1995)

Thus the technological theme becomes a subtheme; it serves to connect athletes with their predecessors. For example, in order to properly judge the performance of a sky-surfing combination, the judges look at a video shot by the sky surfer's partner. Via a 'Sony Jumbotron™ and microwave hookups', the television viewer is told, the audience on the ground can see the generated performance as it occurs. Thus the cameraperson and the sky surfer combine to generate the performance, which is then conveyed, via videotape, to the judges. The performance is judged on the technique and artistic merit of both the surfer and the cameraperson. Simultaneous use of cutting-edge technology (like helmet cams), technological jargon and name-dropping (Sony Jumbotron™), and a subtle link to familiar scoring methods (technical and artistic merit) provide the viewer with an acceptable stretch to his sporting imagination.

The fourth dominant theme of *The eXtreme Games* is its historical linkage to other sports. Appreciation of a significant historical sporting past – and *The eXtreme Games'* justifiable place in that past – becomes a constant, overriding theme. The event itself is packaged to represent, in hyperbolic ESPN language (with announcers hawking loudly, reminiscent of WWF announcers' work), a 'sports revolution' in that athletes are only part of the 'story'; technology and technological advances in equipment and communications have combined to create specific ways of documenting the performances, and in some cases have become integral to the generation of new sport forms.

It is useful to contrast and compare the utilisation of this specific historical myth for *The eXtreme Games* (for example, the Eco Challenge, which traces a course along 'ancient Indian hunting grounds') with the televised construction of other celebrated, massified sport. In the 1993 Ironman Triathlon, the opening framing theme advanced by NBC Sports is one of a stereotypic Polynesian native (who, incidentally, looks like Hulk Hogan) picking his way across the lava fields of the Big Island. This visual is accompanied by text that sets up the viewer's understanding of the Ironman Triathlon as an epic struggle between the human spirit and the harsh Hawaiian elements. In hushed, solemn, reverent, and evenly cadenced tones (until the final sentence, which is an echo of the 'Let the games begin!'

of *The American Gladiators*, or the 'Play ball!' of major league base-ball after the National Anthem), the announcer introduces this abiding theme:

> Ancient Hawaiian religion tells us of the unbreakable chain: how Man, along with sky, land, and sea, are inextricably One, forever united and interdependent. The early Hawaiian sought to mesh with the forces of nature, not fight them. He'd be a fool to upset the threads that bind him together with nature and the gods. In Hawaiian culture, spirit and matter are one in themselves, but, like the gods, matter is truly just as powerful, fully capable of thinking . . . and willing. It is, indeed, alive, conscious, and receptive to human communication. The modern triathlete talks to it, exists with it, not against it. This big island is all-powerful, imposing, and treacherous. But the successful athlete will never challenge it, knowing the race with nature is never won. It is only carried on.
>
> Today, the world's greatest athletes perpetuate the everlasting bond . . . The rules of the island were cast thousands of years ago, and the teachings of ancient Hawaii still tell us today that the chain shall never be broken. Welcome to the Gatorade Ironman Triathlon World Championships.
>
> (NBC-TV, 20 June 1993)

The shift from the secularism of playing the sport ('Play ball!' or 'Let the games begin!') to celebration of a multinational corporate sponsorship ('Gatorade') is, I think, significant. The historical con-nection is tenuous at best, with the nostalgic purity of a bygone era linked with a plug for Gatorade. Similarly, NCAA college foot-ball bowl games, whose corporate sponsors unashamedly have incorporated their names into the very titles of the bowls, hawk those sponsors' products every time the event itself is announced. However, in the links with historical discourse, there is an attempt to establish and reify cultural myths, societal tropes that inform and establish standards by which members of societies (a televisual sports audience society) can enact their lives. By reaching out to multiple audiences with such culturally significant tropes, ESPN's pro-ducers have keyed in on multivocal representations, none of which is necessarily privileged over the other (Tuchman 1994). In generating the themes and mythos of *The eXtreme Games*, the ESPN producers and writers have (re)constructed a sport-familiar metalanguage for viewers, which consciously promotes and assumes dominant, oppositional, and consensual readings. These readings are not discrete, but rather fluid, with the readers moving in and out of the positions as they and the producers co-produce the event. In this way, a kind of reader identification – and a television viewing audience – is created.

The use of modernist strategies (such as establishing certain themes and stories that the viewer can see reach a satisfactory closure) is, of course, not excluded by a postmodern sensibility. If, in fact, we 'live in an age of transition' between modernism and postmodernism (Rojek 1995: 6) these logics may coexist. Thus, the athletes are said to be 'not daredevils, . . . not weekend warriors, they're hardcore professionals', yet they are also common people, 'regular folks'. The 'culturally literate' audience may identify with the athletes along a continuum rather than in a bipolar fashion. The 'sports-savvy' viewer sees not a continuous event, shown in real time from start to finish, but one constructed in MTV style, with quick cuts, increasingly familiar logos of *The eXtreme Games*, and thematically seamless advertising. The difference might be compared to viewing a Greek tragedy, in which characters deliver long, uninterrupted speeches, versus watching almost any (post)modern drama on film, in which characters interrupt, make assumptions, speak to each other and the situation, and demonstrate indexicality (that is, specific contextual meaning). Given the modernist use of cultural myth, it is important to remember that one of the key elements of televised sports (indeed, of television) is its major emphasis on selling products. Quick viewer recognition and identification (generally on a sensory level) is one of the keys to successful product marketing. Identification – and simulated participation – of the audience helps accomplish this goal.

The opening sequence of *The eXtreme Games* shows a spinning Games symbol, which, over the course of ten days, two cable stations (ESPN2 and ESPN), and 30-plus hours of coverage, will become easily and quickly identifiable. In many cases, of course, with pre-publicity on ESPN and ESPN2, the symbol has already become a signifier of *The eXtreme Games*. Its red 'X', crossed dramatically like two skis, is 'logoed' onto everything – and, in fact, incorporated into the very name of the event itself. Similarly identifiable to the viewer is the MTV-style, quick-cut, split-screen visual 'bites' that accompany the Games' identifier. Included in the 'in-your-face' visuals (that is, helmet-cam visuals in which the footage is shot from the close-up point of view of a co-participant or of someone who is in peril of collision from a participant) are rapid shots of a bungee jumper cascading toward the camera, a sky surfer wheeling in midair, an in-line skater 'pulling a 360', a barefoot water skier spinning on his back, a mountain biker somersaulting, a street luger pulling a hard corner, and a rafter digging in for control in frothing white water. These hyperactive clips all serve to entertain – and to educate the viewer about just what these *eXtreme Games* might be. Additionally, there is a global symbol, a sort of elongated line drawing of longitudinal and latitudinal frames, which subtly serves to remind the viewer that this is an international competition. This fact will be reinforced to the viewer over time. A key subtheme of *The eXtreme Games* that is foreshadowed in the opening frames is that they rely on cutting-edge technology: thus we hear the creak of metal on metal, and we see computer-generated graphics of fragmented, generic wheels and gears coexisting with humans propelling themselves through space.

The symbol of *The eXtreme Games*, the red elongated 'X', becomes quickly recognizable – much like the five Olympic rings, the Olympic flame, or the colours of Olympism (Slowikowski 1991). If *The eXtreme Games* are eventually successful, of course, a whole historical ethos will develop around and surround them. Much as with the 30-year-old Super Bowl, 'traditions' will be invented and, eventually, reified (Hobsbawm and Ranger 1983). But the 'alternative' sports themselves must gain credibility. Thus, the most dominant, overriding theme, which often coexists simultaneously with and recursively informs the other themes – that athletes are normal people, that the players are unique but linked to all sports players, and that sports links historically with other sports – emerges: *The eXtreme Games* is real sport. According to Kolber, though, it is a new form of sport (with obvious historical links):

> This is an attitude toward life; passion that comes from the soul. From its beginnings, Rhode Island has been distinguished by its support for freedom, its rebellious, authority-defying nature. Fort Adams, built to defend, looms large this week as a new generation makes its stand. It's an opportunity to redefine the way we look at sports.
>
> (Kolber 1995)

The next section will examine how these five themes are specifically enacted, and how the enactments serve to construct audience(s) for ESPN and its sponsors.

## Logics of *The eXtreme Games*

The two news anchors – they call themselves 'hosts' – of the event have been placed in a set overlooking Fort Adams in Newport, Rhode Island. Clearly, ESPN's producers have overtly replicated much of the successful formulae of the Summer and Winter Olympic Games. But they have also imitated on another level: they have doled out story segments, framed in certain ways familiar to culturally literate viewers. The segments can be analysed by the ways they work on viewers. The producers and directors provide the audience with a simplified entry into each new sport form, via explanation and/or demonstration; they personalise the players through the use of biographical sketches or profiles, and foster viewer identification with those athletes; they create suspenseful drama by cutting, mid-event, to other events; they ground the event in a constant returning to the sports anchors for reiterative commentary and summation of what just happened; and they preview what is to come.

Throughout, though the narrative is not cloying, the viewers receive reinforcement and confirmation that what they are seeing is real sport – in fact, 'EXTREME' sport. The announcers emphasise the word 'extreme' nearly every chance they get; interviewees do the same (the term 'extreme' is as omnipresent as is 'NFL' in the Super Bowl, 'American Gladiators' in *The American Gladiators*, or 'WWF' in the World Wrestling Federation presentations). Not just anyone can do these sports, and yet most of the athletes are proclaimed as true amateurs. For most of *The eXtreme Games'* sports, the first type of segment, explanation/demonstration, is fairly straightforward. Prior to each event, there is a 'What It Is' segment, with a rough explanation of the goals and scoring. But, as with *The American Gladiators*, the examples that ESPN's programming uses link these events to other sports – or segments of sports – that the viewer already knows. With in-line skating (vert), for example, the television audience is informed that 'each skater will attack the wall for two 45-second rips, while Your Honor grades on a 100 point scale'. (*The eXtreme Games*, 25 June 1995). As well, the audience is told that the subjective scoring ('judging') for sky surfing is based on 'a hundred total points on a 50-second performance. Half goes toward the technical, half toward the artistic portion of the performers' routine' (Smith 1995). Chris Fowler explains sky surfing: 'These are two-man teams, both judged on their artistry, one with a board, the other with a helmet cam, while falling at a hundred twenty miles per hour'. Suzy Kolber adds that sky surfing 'is a timed event, but there isn't much importance put on the time, much like figure skating or gymnastics. You don't really think about how much time they're out there, just what they do with that time' (*The eXtreme Games*, 25 June 1995). The links to mainstream, and in this case 'legitimate', sport are obvious.

The second type of segment is the personalisation of athletes. Both in the show previewing *The eXtreme Games* and in the Games itself, ESPN has taken great pains to familiarise viewers with individual sport practitioners. There is a segment that profiles Bob Pereyra, who, the viewer is told, 'is street luge' (Kolber 1995). The story is that Pereyra is generous of spirit, a street luger whose greatest concern is for the sport. However, in setting up for ESPN (in a trial run) for *The eXtreme Games*, the first ever major event for a formerly 'outlaw' sport, Pereyra cracked a bone in his left heel. Can he compete with a broken bone? The cameras roll as *The eXtreme Games'* orthopaedic surgeon suggests that competing would be a major risk for Pereyra. Nevertheless, at the eleventh hour, Pereyra is allowed to compete in the duals, but not in the mass event. A sense of tension, identification with Bob Pereyra and his troubles, and hope for a judicious result creates viewer involvement, which leads to a larger viewership. There are similar profiles of potential champions in every event. As in the televised broadcasts of the Olympics, the Hawaiian Ironman Triathlon, and countless other events, human interest stories frame the events so that viewer identification with the athletes – thus a doubly reflective participation, by both audience and athlete – is assured. Bob Pereyra represents Integrity: a hardworking blue-collar type who might attract an audience grounded in the 'American values' of rugged individualism, hardy perseverance, and reliance on the rightness of rules (much like Shane). Chris Edwards, a young in-line skater, is called '"The Air Man", because he believes in big tricks. [He is] the ultimate pioneer of aggressive in-line'. He is also, by his own statements, a 'psycho skater', attempting innovative moves that have never even been thought of before; a dedicated and loyal father and husband (the audience sees him holding his infant son), and a youth pastor for the local ministry whose goal is to become a minister. He, like Pereyra, has great integrity, but he represents a more clean-cut, youthful image. With two different profiles, ESPN has managed to target at least two segments (and undoubtedly more) of its demographic market. This strategy echoes – or is echoed by – the Nike campaign for NBA stars, in which different mediated images solidify different segments of the market for Nike products.

The third way that ESPN's directors and producers have utilised production techniques is in their segmentation and fragmentation of the actual sporting events. As with the presentation of professional football on television, the choice is up to the directors (Gruneau 1989). Only intermittently does the television audience see an event from start to finish. Instead, viewers are given a taste of the EcoChallenge, then switched to sky surfing, on to sport climbing (bouldering), and so on. The frustration level may mount, but the director's ability to complete events intermittently generally gives the viewer enough purchase to feel almost satisfied. Choosing to put already taped results in a following segment of ESPN's broadcast of *The eXtreme Games* similarly accomplishes the goal of creating suspense. Viewers are pre-viewed with expectations – teasers – of upcoming events, and this works to increase tension and anticipation, and to heighten the sense of drama for especially undramatic events. Linked with stories of years-long rivalries (such as the barefoot water-skiing rivalry tracing back to the 1970s between Ron 'The Raging Bull' Scarpa and Mike Seipel, the first man to invert a barefoot jump), the technique is to find symbolic difference between contestants wherever possible. If the 'rivalries' do not pan out, it matters little: segments have been completed, the continuing story that is *The eXtreme Games* has been furthered, sponsors have reached an audience. Furthermore, the stories stand alone: to always follow the winner would make the production seem canned. The fact that ESPN has not gotten every winner only adds to the seeming 'uncertain outcome' – the apparent verisimilitude – for attentive viewers of the events, and further legitimates *The eXtreme Games* as real sport.

A fourth technique that is used to enhance story segments is the centralised set. By using a set overlooking Fort Adams in Rhode Island, ESPN has sited *The eXtreme Games* in place – but also in history. Canned pieces that 'educate' the viewer about the cultural and historical placings of Newport, Fort Adams, and *The eXtreme Games* provide a justifiable linkage with 'legitimate' televised sport. After this justification has taken place (it is continual), the audience touches base with the hosts at the central set. This serves several purposes: it allows for review of events 'just' completed, lends ultimate authority to Suzy Kolber and Chris Fowler, makes for summative commentary, provides a stabilising force, creates smooth transitions to and from com-mercials, and aids in self-promotion of *The eXtreme Games*. Finally, the fifth technique that producers utilise for segments is the preview. Before each commercial 'break', visual 'bites', accompanied by supporting narrative, inform viewers about what to expect. Producers seem to think that expectations – as part of complete fulfilment – are what drive viewer loyalty. This 'preview' logic also carries over from show to show, as in the Olympics. Thus the audience is told to tune in for the later show if they expect to see the finals of a specific event.

## Constructing the audience

In both the use of a historical mythos and the use of celebrated, massified sport, the hoped-for outcome by ESPN is a legitimation of the new sport itself; the electronic medium is, not unlike any other medium, an arena replete with power struggles. Grounding sport in something that someone has already done justifies someone doing it again. Imitation – with only slight homage to innovation – is the dominant model in television. The hoped-for result of the hoped-for outcome, of course, is further massification, which in turn will most likely lead to increased sponsorship and receipts. Has this imitative strategy been successful for ESPN's *The eXtreme Games?* According to Joan Wilson, ESPN's director of marketing for affiliate sales, *The eXtreme Games'* ability to promote local ad sales has meant that they have slightly exceeded the number of affiliates that the NFL carries on ESPN. They have followed the Olympic and World Cup terminology: 'ESPN signed Advil as its "official pain reliever" and sold six "gold-level sponsors"' (Forkan 1995: 11). Those sponsors, whose one or two spots specifically designed for *The eXtreme Games'* coverage continually bombard the viewer, are Miller Lite Ice, Taco Bell, Mountain Dew, Nike's ACG brand, AT&T, and General Motors. But even this co-opting by corporations appears paradoxical: in *The eXtreme Games*, the television audience is told that, until recently, many of the games were 'outlaw' sports, and so most decidedly not sanctioned by a governing body or given sanctions by the established corporate world. Now, with ESPN promoting and selling the sports in a packaged form, the 'cutting-edge', 'outlaw' nature of the sports themselves becomes problematised.

Thus audiences see a BMX dirt bike rider sneering into the camera before his event, only to state during the post-ride interview, 'I thank HYPER for sponsoring me'. Another athlete thanks Schwinn Bikes. We discover that yet another athlete, a street luger who is celebrated by his fellows as being a nonconformist, is 'president of RAIL, a sanctioning organization for [street] luge'. Co-opting by conformity standards is everywhere. It is not unlike the co-opting that has occurred in the art world, of the so-called 'cutting edge' artists whose work is seen as *avant-garde*, yet whose commercialisation far exceeds their artistic output (Gablik 1984). Of course, introductions to sports events always work on several levels. The audience is made to understand the (produced) theme of the event and is directed to the key points of the 'story' to come, told how and what to watch. But the audience is also given access to identity-making with the athletes, with a potential for hero(ine) worship. The producers' ultimate object is not just to tell a good story, but also to create a broad-based market that is receptive to the commodities being sold. To that end, they produce segments that amplify the audiences' individuality while creating links to a larger collective. This is done intertextually, so that the target audiences identify with four mountain bikers sucking down Mountain Dew, so that viewers listen patiently to an explanation of what makes them unique and what their generation – Generation X – may have to offer. The target audiences, therefore, are not really unlike any market created by businesspeople, except in kind: they must buy into the vertiginous aspects of these 'new' kinds of sports, as offered by ESPN, yet they must remain true to their own lived experiences (see also Beal 1995).

For some – like in-line skaters or skateboarders – the experience is similar, but not identical, to that portrayed by ESPN. Thus, subscribers to *InLine: The Skate Magazine* were informed that *The eXtreme Games* has promoted 'aggressive skating more in the public eye. I don't know if that's good or bad. It has created a whole professional class of rock-star-like people' (McComb, quoted in Densmore, 1995: 37). There are possibly some good outcomes from increased exposure, this magazine for in-line aficionados seems to say, but with growth comes a certain loss of innocence. The skateboarders' reaction to *The eXtreme Games* (as evidenced in a less mainstream magazine, *Thrasher*) was less ambivalent. The title says it all: 'For Love or Money? Extreme Showcase Predictably Network' (*Thrasher*, October 1995). But many other viewers' lived experiences are simply not even close to duplicates of *The eXtreme Games'* athletes' experience. So their ideal lived experiences are reconstructed, reconstituted seamlessly for their visual consumption. Throughout the ESPN-produced extreme Games, the use of intermittent 'teases', drawing from a kind of folk behaviouralism, creates a reward system of flashing lights and colour, jolting sound, and satisfying recognition of the intersections of popular culture for the attentive viewer. This 'MTV look' shapes some viewers' loyalty just as the action at Las Vegas might shape the fixated gambler. It serves to create a divide between people by demonstrating difference – for example, generational difference – at the same time that it protests their similarity. There is diversity, but there is also power, agency, and strength in being part of a group.

The 'MTV look' is a strategy that segments the audience, parcels them out into neat demographic units, while insisting on their community. The object, of course, is to create a larger audience, reaching parts of each potential viewer. The rhetoric of the show – that is, the narrative of the anchors and reporters, the visuals of what is portrayed – reinforces this seeming paradox: witness Chris Fowler, who says of the sport events to be shown, 'We're not going to treat them like music videos'. But that is exactly what ESPN has done, and in so doing, they have created a new, mutated sport form, a televisual, simulated sport form that is just as highly fragmented and segmented as many music videos. The non-linearity of the sports, the use of techniques that tell stories but tell them in chunky segments, assumes reader involvement. Thus these techniques ensure audience co-opting and participation.

## Note

1 This chapter is a study of the ESPN coverage of *The eXtreme Games*, broadcast 24 June–July 1995. Both ESPN and ESPN-2 aired the event. I examined 27 hours of ESPN's coverage.

## References

Beal, B. (1995) Disqualifying the official: An exploration of social resistance through the subculture of skateboarding, *Sociology of Sport Journal* 12 (3): 252–67.

Coulon, A. (1995) *Ethnomethodology*. Thousand Oaks, CA: Sage Publications.

Coupland, D. (1991) *Generation X: Tales for an Accelerated Culture*. New York : St. Martin's Press.

Densmore, L.F. (1995) Taking extreme mainstream, *InLine: The Skate Magazine*, 4 (8): 37.

Denzin, N.K. (1991) *Images of Postmodern Society: Social Theory and Contemporary Cinema*. London: Sage Publications.

Forkan, J. (1995) Crazy – like a fox, *Cablevision*, 3 July: 11.

Fowler, C. (1995) *The eXtreme Games*, ESPN, 25 June.

Gablik, S. (1984) *Has Modernism Failed?* New York: Thames and Hudson.

Gruneau, R. (1989) Making Spectacle: A Case Study in Television Sports Production, in L.A. Wenner (ed.) *Media, Sports, and Society*. Newbury Park, CA: Sage.

Hobsbawm, E. and Ranger, T. (eds) (1983) *The Invention of Tradition*. Cambridge: Cambridge University Press.

Kolber, S. (1995) *The eXtreme Games*, ESPN, 1 July.

Morgan, W.J. (1994) *Leftist Theories of Sport: A Critique and Reconstruction*. Urbana: University of Illinois Press.

Mountain Dew commercial (1995) ESPN, 24, 25, 26, 27, 28, 29, 30 June and 1, 2, 3 July.

NBC-TV (1993) Gatorade Ironman Triathlon Championship, 20 June.

Rojek, C. (1995) *Decentring Leisure: Rethinking Leisure Theory*. London: Sage.

*The eXtreme Games* Preview Show (1995) ESPN, 24 June.

Scott, S. (1995) *The eXtreme Games*, ESPN, 26 June.

Slowikowski, S.S. (1991) Burning desire: nostalgia, ritual, and the sport-festival flame ceremony, *Sociology of Sport Journal*, 8: 239–57.

Smith, S. (1995) *The eXtreme Games*, ESPN, 26 June.

Springwood, C.F. (1996) *Cooperstown to Dyersville: A Geography of Baseball Nostalgia*. Boulder, COL.: Westview.

*The eXtreme Games* (1995) ESPN, 25 June.

*Thrasher* (1995) For love or money? Extreme showcase predictably network, October: 50–53.

Tuchman, G. (1994) Historical social science: methodologies, methods, and meanings, in N.K. Denzin and Y.S. Lincoln (eds) *Handbook of Qualitative Research*. Thousand Oaks, CA: Sage.

# 18 | CONVERGENCE: SPORT ON THE INFORMATION SUPERHIGHWAY

## Brian Stoddart

Originally published in *Journal of Sport & Social Issues*, 21(1), 1997: 93–102.

In writing about Rupert Murdoch's incursion into the world of tele-vised sport, Charles P. Pierce (1995: 187) noted that 'there will be more of a market for ancillary sports industries as television brings more of these sports to more of the world'. For Pierce, as for other com-mentators (like Baldo 1994; Grover 1994), the Murdoch moves were simply further evidence supporting the view that, in sport, national geographical boundaries were becoming irrelevant. For sports sociolo-gists, of course, that is the starting point for a wide-ranging discussion about the globalization of sport, with all the attendant problems of cultural imperialism breaking down national traditions and practices – the 1994 battle between Rogers Communications, Inc. and Canada's ruling telecommunications body over the future of the Maclean group was an excellent case in point (Fulton 1994). After all, the critics argue, Murdoch was not interested in the long-term future or the intrinsic interests of the sport itself when his Fox network signed a 10-year deal to put badminton on the Star TV footprint.

There is much substance to this as basketball becomes a major global sport (much to the chagrin of culturally localised games such as cricket), *USA Today* reports routinely on the sumo wrestling championship results from Japan, Malaysian newspapers carry extensive reports on the NHL playoffs as well as most other major North American sports, and more and more sports are crowded onto television as the executives in charge of expansionist channels seek more and more product. Where some sociologists see problems, sports junkies find Nirvana, but either way the face of sports has changed.

Yet in Pierce's (1995) comment on the ancillary industries, there is the hint of an idea that the simple, quantitative globalization of sports forms may be just the beginning of change that could not only affect the ways in which people consume their sports, but also the current forms of revenue raising in which sports themselves are involved, ranging across merchandising, sponsorship, viewing, fan idolatry, and news dissemination. Indeed, at the very time that Pierce and others see an increasing monopoly created by the alliance of sport and television, that alliance may be challenged by the very consumers at whom it is aimed. Understanding this apparent paradox begins with the concept of *convergence*. In the telecommunications world, convergence represents the merger of television, computer, and telephone services to provide an expanded range of delivery and merchandising services to a broadening range of consumers. Sitting at home in the personal communications centre with access to these merged services, the consumer navigates the resultant information superhighway to select a chosen product. From the provider's viewpoint, this means a much more tailor-made service greeting a potential client. The client, however, takes increased control over the selection and, theoretically, can then pressure the provider for an expanded range of specific goods and services.

This goes far beyond the simple form of spread in which a global network gains access to a range of sports, say, to present that range to what is simply a bigger audience. If a true form of convergence comes to sport, not only will the current ancillary services profit, but an entirely new range of such services will arise over which the global convergence giants may or may not exercise control. In one view (Hearn and Mandeville 1995: 92) such a process involves 'the centrality of consumption in both the economic and the cultural infrastructure of late capitalism'. The captains of the sports industries might want to debate that, but the logical possibilities are clearly there. The foundations of such convergence development are undoubtedly present. The merger of sports and media systems is a necessary precondition, and this is happening apace. Cablevision Systems, for example, bought the Madison Square Gardens group in a deal that saw not only the famous stadium change hands, but also the MSG cable network along with the two major franchises of the Knicks and the Rangers ('Viacom Offloads', 1994). A partner in all this, significantly, was the ITT group that runs the Sheraton hotel chain. With ITT moving into the ownership of more Las Vegas casinos, strategists saw a great opportunity for controlling more in-house entertainment in a field much in demand by hotel patrons. Further evidence for this line of analysis came during 1995 when ITT joined with Dow Jones to take over the New York city public television channel, WNYC-TV, with the stated goal being to turn the channel into an America-wide provider of sports, financial news, and entertainment by way of satellite technology ('ITT-Dow Jones Corp's Offer' 1995).

A further example of convergence in practice concerns the group controlled by Miami-based Wayne Huizinga (Ozanian 1995). An owner with interests in the Marlins, Dolphins, and the Panthers, Huizinga began the empire with a national chain of video stores. His ambition now is to build a sports theme park where the franchises will play and have merchandising outlets and a cable channel to carry the product, thereby maximising the profit by realising as many marketing opportunities as possible. If the product is there, so are the means for conveying that product. The online revolution is here and exhibits a phenomenal growth rate. *Der Spiegel*, the prominent German weekly periodical, already has 120,000 subscribers online via CompuServe, the American agency (Resnick 1994). By mid-1994, there were more than 5 million paying subscribers to online services in the United States (Arlen 1994). Major test-bed sites for interactive services are springing up around the world. In Singapore, the local Telstra is in alliance with Hewlett Packard, Sybase International, and Mitsui to create a major network in the island state ('Media Partnership to Deliver' 1995). In Australia, the University of Canberra is in alliance with the local government, Telstra, and several service agencies to test a massive 3,000 homes involved in receiving interactive services. In the United States, Time-Warner has already tested its full-service network ('Video-on-Demand' 1995). Microsoft and TCI are merging telephony and software ('Media Partnership to Deliver' 1995), and TCI and Continental Cablevision are doing similar work with telephony and cable television ('Cable Going to Pots' 1994).

Almost without exception, sport is regarded as a staple product on these merged systems, and it is easy to see why. The creation of the Japanese J-League soccer competition, for example, was thought by many analysts to be economically adventurous. What proved to be its power to shift a product was completely unexpected. In its first year on television alone, it helped sell US$300 million (all following figures are in US dollars) worth of items for Sony Creative Products, won a million new subscribers to the Fuji Bank with a J-League passbook, and snack food manufacturers sold millions of units (Morris 1995). As further evidence for the importance of sport in the on-line marketing boom, we need turn only to the United States where, during 1993, the big four pro-leagues sold almost $9 billion worth of franchised goods. That same year, the American networks billed $2.2 billion in sports-related advertising, with the cable networks adding another $800 million. A less heralded set of shifts involves the online world itself and its connections with sport. There is an expanding range of sports services on the Internet as cyberspace surfing becomes more accessible to more people. According to David Noack (1994), for example, the Internet has been replacing more customary forms of information provision for many aficionados. One subscriber suggested that he was getting major results and information from the Net before he could get it on sports cable channels such as ESPN. By Noack's count, there were more than 70 user groups devoted to sport, but that is a major undercalculation or, at least, a too-narrow reading of the field.

For example, the recently published *NetSports* (1995), part of a book series devoted to finding aids for Internet users, provides sites for hundreds of sports-based interest groups. Almost all major world sports are covered, with an understandable emphasis on mainline or professionalised sports. There are some gaps: Australian Rules football does not have a reference although such groups exist, badminton boasts just one site, but other significant Asian sports such as *sepaktakraw* and *kabbadi* have none. Significantly enough, though, sumo does – there are at least five sites, with one of them an English language source based in Japan – and there is a vast picture archive as well as a multimedia collection. This phenomenon, in many ways, represents the general point being made here – that globalization is increasing side by side with commodification. That exception aside, the general absence of major non-Western sports as sites is notable at present. Although this might represent a lower use of the Internet in some areas (the government agency-controlled Jaring service in Malaysia, for example, is not long in service, has limited capacity, and is relatively expensive for a majority of potential users), it is interesting to note that at least some Western sports sites are located outside the metropolitan countries – one major cricket service is run from Sri Lanka. Again, this points toward the main argument.

What Noack (1994) is delineating, however, is a subculture of sports fans using the new communication forms to gain more information and foster interaction among themselves to raise their knowledge base about a sport or sports. This might be seen as a postmodern version of spectatorship and fan affiliation. In that sense, the Net offers a curious form of resistance to the mediated forms of information and attitudes fed to fans by mainline information sources. Given that fans themselves can feed the Net, they are taking control of the sports form and of the opportunity to bypass or supplant the major sources of supply to which they have been tied for generations. Although access currently is predominantly a function of economic or professional privilege (for example, for university academics), that is also rapidly breaking down as the technology becomes cheaper and more penetrable. The moment is not unchallenged, however, as the mainline suppliers themselves become aware of the opportunities and, perhaps, the threat that is already there. *Newsweek*, which now runs a regular column titled 'Cyberscope' (and which itself is connected to the Net) reported recently that the *Raleigh News and Observer* has set up home pages for each major league baseball team on the World Wide Web. Included in the data are progress scores for games being played. That is, along with radio and television sources, the Net actually provides progress result services. ESPN's response to the new conditions has been the establishment of *SportsZone* on the system to provide, among other services, interactive sessions with major league players ('Net Me Out to the Ball Game' 1995). *USA Today* has its *SportsCenter* online in full text and key-coded so that Net users can download any required material. Just to take the point a little further, the Home Shopping Network cable channel already has taken over the Internet Shopping Network, indicating how extensive the Net possibilities seem to be to more established entities ('Zirconia.com' 1994).

As an example of possibilities available to users in the converged sports condition, consider golf, which has long had a solid bloc of commercial interest at its heart (Hackney 1995). The new golf channel, which went to air in the United States in January 1995, has the Times-Mirror group as a major participant, adding to its outlets for the goods and services showcased in its golf magazine properties ('More TV Time' 1994). There are more than 20 Net services available to devotees of the sport, and one of the characteristics is that those services cater to the consumer rather than simply follow the elite player-oriented sources provided to date by major media blocs in alliance with leading manufacturers. Although the Net does provide golf shopping opportunities, most sites allow average golfers to talk to each other while planning vacations, address swing and equipment problems, and encourage just talking about the game of golf, which has the magical power to captivate its adherents to the point of enslavement. So logged-in golfers can pre-visit thousands of courses around the world, find a peer-assessed golf school and accommodation, discuss the iniquities of manufacturers' and providers' equipment, get up-to-date news on tournaments ignored by the major services, and contact fellow addicts around the world.

By now, the emerging picture indicates how the well-connected sports fan can vastly improve the amount of information to be taken in concerning chosen sports, and much of this information is coming from sources that supplant traditional lines of communication. The fan, in some cases, also can influence the material going out by inter-connecting with other fans in user groups. The consumers' point of view is now being fashioned in a way not previously possible. It is important to note, however, that the idea of consumer autonomy is being confronted by the major players. Symbolically and practically, perhaps the best example of this is Planet Reebok. By calling up http://planetreebok.com/ on the Web, the sports surfer gains information about how the sports shoe giant develops its product and deals with contemporary issues. Although the service does no merchandising as such, it is clearly a teaser in an age where the range of purchase options is expanding exponentially. The interesting question, of course, is how the average sports fan is to deal with these newly emerged options.

The pace of the change and its sheer dimensions constitute the key challenge for the consumer. Recently, for example, the biggest news has involved Rupert Murdoch again. In May 1995, he announced that News Limited, his company, was entering an alliance with MCI, the second-largest long-distance telephone carrier in the United States ('News, MCI Pact' 1995). MCI would take a 13 per cent stock position in News Limited, and jointly they would mount a $400 million venture to create and distribute globally a set of information, education, and entertainment services via the resultant network. By definition, this includes the sports options already contained within the News Limited conglomerate. The Murdoch product sprawl is well worth reviewing at this point, as are the networks over which those products are conveyed ('Media Partnership to Deliver' 1995).

At home base, with the Fox network, Murdoch already holds the NFC and the NHL and is likely to go all out to retain those when the rights are renegotiated. He bid considerably more than other contenders when the last decision was made, and with his subsequent moves is likely to do so again. In addition to those properties, he also has expressed a keen interest in golf, tennis, and baseball. One or all of them might well fall. Given the growing global consumer demand for all those sports, he is well placed to command the world market. Add to that his British holdings through BSkyB, the merged channel he controls following an expensive battle for market dominance. Premier league soccer was created by Murdoch, at further vast expense, and received massive consumer support in revolt over the previously poor services provided under cosy deals between traditional carriers and soccer authorities. Incidentally, the full complexity of the move and its clear financial rewards for Murdoch have escaped some analysts (such as Appleton 1995). In Australia, Murdoch challenged rugby league authorities in a bid to lure one of that country's major sporting attractions onto his nascent Foxtel network in which, significantly, he is partnered by Telstra. After that raid, he then moved into the other code popular across the southern hemisphere – rugby union (South African celebrations at winning the 1995 rugby union World Cup were cut short when the players rebelled over the authorities' deal with Murdoch, preferring one with his long-term Australian rival, Kerry Packer). Administrators in other codes such as Australian Rules football, which had come to rely on mainstream television for the bulk of its revenue (Linnell 1995), began to review their network contracts somewhat nervously (Westfield 1995). Then there is El Canal Fox, which goes throughout Latin America, and the Hong Kong-based Star TV, which has an enormous footprint throughout Asia, spreading from the Gulf states to New Zealand, even though local restrictions do not as yet allow it untrammelled entry to all countries under the satellite span.

This last point provides an important sidebar, a technological backdrop to all the activity mentioned so far. As Thomas (1995) points out, Malaysia, for example, has had a rigid policy of controlling access to its airwaves. In the face of technological expansion and sophistication, however, that policy is close to redundant. Cable and satellite broadcasting are being introduced cautiously as Panamsat's new PAS-4 satellite goes into action and Hong Kong's Asiasat-2 is readied for launch, dramatically increasing the possibilities for transnational intervention. In both those cases, sport is a big factor: ESPN on the former and Star-TV on the latter ('Panamsat Launch' 1995). Countries such as India and Malaysia now have to deal with the phenomenon rather than keep it at arm's length. By mid-1995, Turner Broadcasting officials were outlining a bid to tie up with a local Malaysian group financing a satellite ('Turner International' 1995). Again, one of the main points in the pitch was the possibility of a 24-hour all-sport channel. It was highly significant that Malaysia's Deputy Prime Minister Anwar Ibrahim was a guest speaker at Murdoch's annual meeting for senior executives in Australia in mid-1995. In what represented a significant policy shift, Anwar noted that countries such as Malaysia were now part of the global television system whether they liked it or not. There was now no option but to deal with the issues presented by Murdoch.

There is a simple economic equation that underlies the Murdoch expansion. Where some analysts see his high bidding for rights in specific markets as inflationary (such as the respective football deals in Great Britain and the United States), Murdoch and others think simply in a world market paying a vast sum for elite British football looks far more responsible when seen in a linked network, where Murdoch channels in soccer-mad cultures such as Asia and Latin America get an enormously enhanced product service at no additional fee. How might dominance such as this alter the practice of sports consumption around the world, and how will those ancillary services to which Pierce (1995) referred arise? In general, the process might be summarised in the following way. In the time BI (Before Internet), sports consumers were largely entrapped by producers, in the form of the sports themselves, and by mediators, in the form of the television operators. Even sponsors sometimes found themselves in a similar position. As some discovered with the Sydney Organising Committee of the Olympic Games (SOCOG) and its marketing agency, for example, there is pressure not only to sponsor the event but to build similar support into selling its own product (like 'for every loaf of bread we sell, "x" cents goes to the Olympic Games fund'). The most obvious point here, of course, is that as the consumer takes in the sport, he or she also has to take in the sponsorship messages. Channel shifting is no solution either because on-screen signage advertising has now been developed to highly sophisticated levels. The Masters golf tournament, one of the four 'major' events around the globe each year, is unique in not allowing any form of on-course advertising – the prestige of the tournament itself is enough to generate millions of dollars in advertising billings for the network, which pays hefty fees for the right to telecast.

The height of this bound-in process is best represented by Mark McCormack's omnipresent International Management Group (IMG), which has become so powerful in the sports world, notably tennis and golf. First, IMG 'owns' a vast number of the leading players. Second, IMG owns or runs a number of the leading tournaments. Third, IMG holds the television rights to such tournaments. What the consumers 'see' on their screens, then, is a product controlled tightly by IMG and returning profit to that company at every roll of the dice; the one event returns several profit lines to IMG. The sponsors pay a tournament fee (to IMG), pay appearance fees in one form or another to players (from which IMG takes a management fee), and is shown on a television channel (for which IMG takes another set of rights fees). Add incidental on-site fees levied for merchandising and concessions, and the tight control over the product or products is evident. Although this is the ultimate example, perhaps, it is also indicative of the closed nature of the product to which the sports consumer has become accustomed, unknowingly for the most part.

The new equation, though, looks something like this. First, vast numbers of sports consumers now have the potential to shift outside the sources on which they have relied for information and services for so long. Second, some of the major players are attempting to connect to the online revolution. Third, they are being joined by other players who have seized the opportunity to provide a service afforded them by the rise of the Net. Fourth, the sports scene is being joined by players who either were not there before or who, if they were, had only a minor role previously – the prime example here is that of the telephone carriers, most especially the long distance groups (Stoddart 1995). At this juncture, then, there is an intriguing challenge for control of the global sport empire. Put in its more spectacular form, it is whether a global mogul, Murdoch most likely, can through a series of strategic sports and communication alliances control the whole enterprise, or whether the fans can fight back through the Net to establish what would be a remarkable incidence of citizen power in which they controlled what they wanted to learn, buy, generate, and reject. It is a genuine struggle because the Net offers the potential for an alternative sports communication system, the first in a long time, if not for the very first time in the history of the modern communications industry. As a sidebar, it is inevitable that issues of the Net itself, involving players such as Bill Gates of Microsoft, who is even more powerful than Murdoch potentially, begin to intrude increasingly into the sports world. By way of example, consider the recent disquiet over Gates's very clear intention to have his new software constitute the major gate to the Net. If he had succeeded, one of the consequences would have been a narrowing of the range of sports materials to be put on and taken from the Net by those sports surfers now rolling in.

Ironically, Gates also represents the major salvation because it is his sort of human genius and creativity that led to the emergence of the Net in the first place and constitutes its principal hope for survival in any meaningful way. If it does survive, then the sports fan has access to what is effectively an unmediated form (in the traditional sense, at least) of goods and services and to a peer reference group. During the 1994 to 1995 baseball strike, for example, a Net site sprang up that offered enormous scope for those parties who knew how to gain access. Although it provided largely a forum for disgruntled fans to vent their spleens in a way not possible in other public media platforms, there was also the possibility for management and unions to contribute to the debate, perhaps even with each other. (Of course, all this raises another very real intellectual question about debate structured on knowledge versus opinion, but that is beyond the scope of this article). As the use of the Net grows, this type of interaction will increase, more so if the Net remains open rather than being closed by the activities of major global communications players such as Murdoch and Gates. If knowledge is power, then the Net is almost the only way forward. The current state of Malaysian soccer helps illustrate the point. Over the past few years the professionalised league, involving a large number of foreign as well as local players, has been shaken by allegations of match fixing engineered by bookmakers buying off players. By mid-1995, there had been a number of court cases, and more than 80 players and officials were under suspension pending further court cases or criminal investigation. In a situation where media commentary is monitored very carefully, rumour often has replaced fact as the basis for decision making, and official rhetoric has gone unchallenged. The Net provides an obvious alternative, in this case, for those interested in following the matter into its deeper realms, a far less consequential variation, perhaps, of the initiative shown by southern Mexico's rebels, who took a page on the World Wide Web to explain their cause.

That is an appropriate point at which to conclude, probably, because it suggests an even further convergence, that of sports into the general social fabric of cultures around the world. Historians of sport have noted for some time that over the past century and a half, sport has become increasingly marked features of modernising cultures. The major issue now is about whether indigenous cultural sports forms can survive the onslaught of globalized sports. Whatever the opinion and analysis about that, there can be no denying that politics, industry, economics, and media have now penetrated the world of sport in an unprecedented way. The rise of the Net may simply add to that penetration, or it may come to provide a redress in balance in favour of the fan.

## References

Appleton, G. (1995) The politics of sport and pay TV, *Australian Quarterly*, 67(1): 31–7.

Arlen, G.H. (1994) Tally finds five million users online, *Information & Interactive Services Report* [Online], 15 July.

Baldo, A. (1994) Thanks millions, *Financial World* [Online], 10 May.

Cable going to pots (1994) *Video Technology News*, 11 August.

Fulton, E.K. (1994) Showdown, *Maclean's* [Online], 3 October.

Grover, R. (1994) Murdoch's deals, *Business Week* [Online], 3 October.

Hackney, H. (1995) The new skins game, *Financial World Magazine* [Online], 14 February.

Hearn, G. and Mandeville, T. (1995) The electronic superhighway: increased commodification or the democratisation of leisure? *Media Information Australia*, 75: 92–101.

ITT-Dow Jones corp's offer for city TV station (1995) *New Straits Times*, 8 August.

Linnell, G. (1995) *Football Ltd: The Inside Story of the AFL*. Sydney: Ironbark.

Media partnership to deliver broadband, on-line services (1995) *Multimedia Week* [Online], 2 January.

More TV time for Times Mirror (1994), *Folio* [Online], 1 July.

Morris, Y. (1995) How Japan scored, *Financial World Magazine* [Online], 14 February.

Net me out to the ball game (1995), *Newsweek*, 21 May.

*NetSports* (1995) New York: Woolf.

News, MCI pact a global first (1995) *Australian*, 12 May.

Noack, D. (1994) Sports on the Net, *Internet World* [Online], September.

Ozanian, M. (1995) Following the money, *Financial World Magazine* [Online], 14 February.

Panamsat launch to fill programming gap in Asia (1995) *New Straits Times*, 8 August.

Pierce, C.P. (1995) Master of the universe, *GQ*, April.

Resnick, R. (1994) Going global, *Interactive Publishing Alert* [Online], June.

Stoddart, B. (1995) Sport and Australian pay-television: some global considerations. *Communications Research Forum, 1994: Papers, Vol. 1*, Canberra, Australia: Bureau of Transport and Communications Economics.

Thomas, A.O. (1995) ASEAN television & Pan-Asian broadcast satellites, *Media Information Australia*, 75: 123–29.

Turner International eyes Binariang tie-up (1995) *Sun*, 28 July.

Viacom offloads famous assets (1994) *Australian*, 30 August.

Video-on-demand trials move forward (1995) *Broadband Networking News* [Online], 10 January.

Westfield, M. (1995) AFL next battle in pay TV war, *Australian*, 17–18 June.

Zirconia.com (1994) *Multimedia Week* [Online], 12 September.

# 19 | INTERNET COVERAGE OF UNIVERSITY SOFTBALL AND BASEBALL WEB SITES: THE INEQUITY CONTINUES

## Michael Sagas, George B. Cunningham, Brian J. Wigley and Frank B. Ashley

First published in *Sociology of Sport Journal*, 17 (2): 2000: 198–205.

Despite the rise of female sport participation and the increase in intercollegiate teams for women since the inception of Title IX [the 1972 federal statute prohibiting sexual discrimination in educational institutions] (Acosta and Carpenter 1994, 1998), there has been little improvement in the media coverage of women's sport during this timeframe (Theberge and Cronk 1986; Lumpkin and Williams 1991; Coakley 1998). This phenomenon has stimulated many researchers to examine the coverage of men's and women's sport in the private sector, via magazines, newspapers, television, and journals, as well as media directly surrounding intercollegiate sport, such as the *National Collegiate Athletic Association (NCAA) News* and school newspapers. Much of the research in this area has taken place due to two fundamental principles. First, many maintain that 'the mass media have become one of the most powerful institutional forces for shaping values and attitudes in modern culture' (Kane 1988: 88–9). In doing so, it influences public perceptions as to what is appropriate, normal, and reasonable (McGregor 1989). Another motivation to studying media representation is the concept that the media provide female youth with possible role models (Rintala and Birrell 1984). If females are not represented in an equitable fashion by the media, then female youth are not provided the necessary icons to emulate. Additionally, equitable media coverage of women's sport can possibly instill a sense of female sport acceptability among males in society.

## Conceptual background

Most of the research concerning the coverage of men's and women's athletics has concentrated on the private media. Many of these endeavours have indicated that print and television media portray sport as a masculine venture (Theberge and Cronk 1986; Kane 1988; Lumpkin and Williams 1991; Cramer 1994; Duncan, Messner, Williams, and Jensen 1994; Tuggle 1996). These studies discovered that females have been predominantly featured in 'feminine' sports such as golf, tennis, and swimming (Kane 1988; Lumpkin and Williams 1991; Cramer 1994); that sport photographs reinforce sexist stereotypes (Rintala and Birrell 1984; Lumpkin and Williams 1991); that when women are shown in non 'feminine' sports, they are portrayed as supportive rather than participating (Tuggle 1996; Cuneen and Sidwell 1998); and that television media 'reflect the social conventions of gender-biased language' (Duncan et al. 1994: 267). Previous research has also indicated that the overall coverage of females is substantially less than that of men (Kane 1988; Lumpkin and Sidwell 1991; Coakley 1998; Cuneen and Sidwell 1998). Extensive studies of both *Sports Illustrated* (Lumpkin and Williams 1991) and *Sports Illustrated for Kids* (Cuneen and Sidwell 1998) demonstrated that male athletes were represented more often than were females. Coakley (1998) maintains that the coverage of women's athletics in big city newspapers has not increased over the past 25 years. Lastly, a study of ESPN's 'Sports-Center' and CNN's 'Sports Tonight' revealed that women's sport was covered only 5 per cent of the time (Tuggle 1996).

In addition to the examination of coverage and representation of women's athletics in the private sector, several studies have addressed the issue while exploring the media directly involved in intercollegiate athletics. These studies are unique due to the context in which they occur. Unlike the private media, which cater to the needs and wants of their consumers and advertisers (Steinem 1990), media surrounding intercollegiate athletics do not contend with external economic, cultural, or sociopolitical forces. In other words, due to the relative absence of external market forces affecting decisions and the presence of Title IX regulations, the representation and coverage of both men's and women's intercollegiate sport should theoretically be equitable, if not equal. Even school newspapers, which oftentimes partially rely on external advertising contributions, are under the scope of Title IX, thanks to the Civil Rights Restoration Act of 1987. Passed in response to the 1984 *Grove City* decision, this piece of legislation allowed Congress to restore 'the full reach of Title IX to any program of any institution that accepts federal funding' (Yasser, McCurdy and Goplerud 1997).

Two key studies have examined the inequitable coverage of women in media surrounding intercollegiate athletics (Shifflett and Revelle 1994; Wann, Schrader, Allison and McGeorge 1998). In examining the coverage of women's athletics in the *NCAA News*, Shifflett and Revelle (1994) found that females were under-represented in both articles and photographs. In a similar vein, Wann and co-workers (1998) noted that university newspapers from medium and large universities were apt to focus on men's rather than women's athletics, an occurrence that was not observed in small universities. This study looked to further the research of Wann and his associates (1998) by examining the coverage of men's and women's sports (like baseball and softball) through university World Wide Web sites. With the proliferation of users and potential usage options (Delpy and Bosetti 1998), the Internet has become a valuable medium through which universities can post timely information concerning men's and women's athletics. Based on the review of literature, several hypotheses were set forth:

(a) baseball sites would receive greater pre-season coverage than would softball;
(b) baseball sites would receive more timely information in the form of game results, team statistics, individual statistics, and longer game summaries than would softball sites; and
(c) regional differences would occur in the equitable coverage of softball and baseball.

## Methodology

### Description of target universities

Web sites from 52 different NCAA Division I universities representing 7 athletic conferences – the Big XII, the Southeastern Conference (SEC), the Big East, the Atlantic Coast Conference (ACC), the Big Ten, the Western Athletic Conference (WAC), and the Pacific-10 (Pac-10) – were analysed for the study. All institutions fielded both softball and baseball teams and maintained Web sites for both sports. The University of Florida (SEC) and Providence College (Big East) were not analysed due to testing error.

## Procedure

Each university Web site was initially analysed on February 7, 1999, since the majority of the baseball and softball seasons began after this date. To assess the pre-season coverage of the different sports, several variables were analysed. These included the availability of the head coach and assistant coach names, biographies and pictures, facility information, updated player rosters, player biographies and pictures, and the season outlook. While all of the aforementioned variables were analysed on a presence versus absence basis, the head and assistant coach biographies and season outlook were also analysed for length. The length of these variables was analysed in terms of number lines present in the text. Although different university Web sites utilize different sizes and fonts for their text, each university formatted their baseball and softball Web pages the same way, thus controlling for the variations between different school sites.

During the season, all sites for softball and baseball teams were analysed five different times for the presence of updated scores and the presence of and length of press releases. Thus, including the initial data collection, each Web site was examined six times, for a total of 624 total data sets. Press releases and scores were operationally defined as current if they contained information from the last game played. The site was analysed on Monday at 5:00 p.m. local time only if both softball and baseball teams had played the previous weekend. Of the total sample, 35 baseball sites and 31 softball sites offered statistical information, and consequently those sites were analysed for the presence of updated individual and team statistics. The same operational definition for current scores applied to the statistical data.

## Results

### Initial contact

Initial Web site examination revealed that universities consistently allotted better coverage to baseball than softball in several fundamental areas, including the presence of and length of specific variables. Specifically, z tests indicated that several variables, including the names of the head and assistant coaches, the biography and picture of the assistant coach, and player biographies and pictures appeared more often on baseball sites than on softball sites. Table 1 provides the statistical significance of these calculations. Univariate analysis of variance (ANOVA; $\alpha$ = .05) indicated that baseball assistant coaches were apportioned longer biographies ($M = 44.1$) than were softball assistant coaches ($M = 25.92$; $F_{1,55} = 13.8$, $p < .001$). Univariate ANOVA ($\alpha$ = .05) also revealed that the length of the season outlook for baseball ($M = 30.2$) was longer than that of softball ($M = 21.2$; $F_{1,55} = 4.70$, $p < .05$). Representations of these data are provided in Table 2. Data analysis revealed that softball also received inequitable coverage during the season as compared to baseball. Baseball sites were routinely updated in a more timely manner than were softball sites for scores, individual and team statistics, and press releases (Table 1). Univariate ANOVA

*Table 1*  Variables analysed for baseball and softball sites in pre-season and during the season

| Measure | Baseball % | Softball % | $z$ |
| --- | --- | --- | --- |
| Pre-season | | | |
|   Head coach name | 100 | 94.2 | −1.76* |
|   Head coach biography | 76.9 | 73.0 | −0.45 |
|   Head coach picture | 59.6 | 46.2 | −1.37 |
|   Assistant coach name | 96.1 | 82.7 | −2.27** |
|   Assistant coach biography | 65.4 | 46.2 | −1.99* |
|   Assistant coach picture | 42.3 | 26.9 | −1.65* |
|   Facility information | 34.6 | 21.2 | −1.53 |
|   Updated roster | 96.1 | 88.5 | −1.56 |
|   Player biographies | 65.3 | 46.1 | −1.99* |
|   Player picture | 51.9 | 30.7 | −2.22** |
|   Season outlook | 63.4 | 48.1 | −1.58 |
| During the season | | | |
|   Updated scores | 89.2 | 79.2 | −3.15** |
|   Any statistics | 90.3 | 71.2 | −2.54* |
|   Updated team statistics | 65.1 | 47.7 | 3.21** |
|   Updated individual statistics | 65.6 | 47.1 | −3.25** |
|   Updated press releases | 93.1 | 86.5 | −2.5* |

Note: *$p < .01$. **$p < .001$.

*Table 2* In-season and regional differences in the coverage of softball and baseball

| Measure | Softball | | Baseball | | F |
|---|---|---|---|---|---|
| | *m* | *(50)* | *m* | *(50)* | |
| In-season | | | | | |
| Assistant coach biography | 25.9 | (11.9) | 44.1 | (22.2) | 13.8 |
| Season outlook | 21.2 | (16.1) | 30.2 | (24.3) | 4.7 |
| Regional differences | | | | | |
| SEC | 34.4 | (21.6) | 75.4 | (67.8) | 16.5 |
| Big XII | 28.2 | (32.4) | 43.1 | (48.7) | 3.23 |
| WAC | 26.3 | (22.5) | 33.5 | (12.3) | 2.7 |
| PAC-10 | 27.5 | (20.3) | 35.8 | (23.0) | 2.58 |
| ACC | 23.5 | (7.07) | 35.5 | (29.7) | 2.0 |
| Big East | 25.2 | (21.1) | 32.7 | (30.6) | 1.16 |
| Big Ten | 24.6 | (15.4) | 25.2 | (21.0) | 0.02 |

Note: *$p < .05$. **$p < .001$.

($\alpha = .05$) indicated that the length of the baseball press releases ($M = 42.77$) was significantly greater than that of softball ($M = 28.45$; $F_{1,.518} = 20.28, p < .001$).

To examine regional differences in the coverage of women's athletics, conferences were divided into three regions: (a) the south (Big XII and SEC); (b) the west (Pac-10 and WAC); and (c) the north/east (Big East, Big Ten, ACC). To test the hypothesis, the length of the press release as measured by the number of lines was analysed for each university Web site in the region. Analysis showed that the south allocated the least coverage to their softball teams compared to their baseball teams, while the north and east provided the most equitable coverage of any of the regions. The SEC had the largest discrepancy between softball ($M = 34.4$) and baseball ($M = 75.4$; F1, 98 = 16.5, $p < .001$), and the Big XII rated next to last in providing equitable coverage for women (F $_{1,.98} = 3.23, p < .07$). University sites in the west region provided marginal coverage for women. A single factor ANOVA ($\alpha = .10$) showed that the WAC and the Pac-10 did not have a significant difference between the length of the press releases for baseball and softball. While the ACC and the Big East were among the most impartial in their coverage, the Big Ten provided the fairest coverage to softball (Table 2).

## Discussion

The primary purpose of the study was to extend previous literature by examining the coverage of men's and women's sport as reported in university baseball and softball Web sites. Malec (1994) has argued that researchers should compare the percentage of male and female coverage to an independent standard, such as the number of athletes for both genders. In comparing baseball and softball sites, this is a moot point due to the equal number of players participating and receiving scholarships for these sports (Bollig and Summers 1997). The findings in this study further the large body of research documenting the inequitable coverage of women's athletics (Rintala and Birrell 1984; Theberge and Cronk 1986; Kane 1988; Lumpkin and Williams 1991; Coakley 1998; Cuneen and Sidwell 1998) and specifically mirror the findings of others who have found the coverage of women's sport lacking in the media centred on intercollegiate athletics (Shiffiett and Revelle 1994; Wann et al. 1998). Results indicate that women received untimely and inequitable coverage in the pre-season as well as during the season. Further, regional differences were apparent as southern universities allocated inequitable softball coverage when compared to those universities from the west and north/east. Although further research is needed in this area, one possible explanation for this occurrence may be the political and cultural philosophies peculiar to each region.

The general findings of this study have particular significance in adding to the overall understanding of gender discrepancies in media coverage. First, this study extends previous literature that had concentrated on print media by expanding the scope to Internet resources. Also, the finding that universities provided inequitable coverage has both legal and social ramifications. In the 1992 case, Franklin v. Gwinnett County Public Schools, the Supreme Court ruled that if schools intentionally violated Title IX, the injured parties could sue for financial damages (Yasser, McCurdy and Goplerud 1997). According to Coakley (1998), this enabled coaches and other parties to hold institutions accountable for establishing gender equity. In fact, in 1997 the National Women's Law Centre filed sex-discrimination complaints against 25 colleges and universities due to unequal dispersal of scholarship monies (Huggins 1997). Accordingly, universities face possible litigation due to the Title IX infractions. In the social context, university athletic departments are not adequately providing for their stakeholders – the student athletes and their parents, the fans, potential recruits, and the coaches – when they fail to provide equitable coverage to both genders. Lastly, this is the first examination of media controlled directly by the intercollegiate athletic departments. While others have concentrated on media peripheral to and indirectly linked to intercollegiate athletics, this research provides the first comprehensive look at the dynamics of athletic department sport coverage. These findings suggest that discriminatory representation of women's athletics is not solely concentrated in external media sources but resides within the athletic programs as well.

In summary, the Internet coverage of softball was substantially less than that of baseball, thus furthering the findings of previous literature. Specifically, baseball received greater coverage in the pre-season and also during the season. Regional differences were observed as conferences in the south inadequately represented softball. Not only do the findings suggest that universities are in direct violation of Title IX, but major social ramifications could possibly result. Future researchers could benefit from extended research through all NCAA divisions in this area. Additional considerations might include an analysis of the coverage of 'gender-appropriate' sports such as tennis, golf, or swimming, or an investigation as to whether the success of the program contributes to coverage allotment. It is worth noting, however, that of the present sample, 18 softball teams finished in the final regular season Top 25 Poll while only 13 of the baseball teams accomplished the same distinction.

## References

Acosta, R.V. and Carpenter, L.J. (1994) The status of women in intercollegiate athletics, in S. Birrell and C.L. Cole (eds) *Women, Sport, and Culture*. Champaign, IL: Human Kinetics.

Acosta, R.V. and Carpenter, L.V. (1998) *Women in Intercollegiate Sport – A Longitudinal Study: Twenty-one Year Update, 1972–1998*. Unpublished manuscript, Brooklyn College, Brooklyn, NY.

Bollig, L. and Summers, J.G. (eds) (1997) *1997–1998 NCAA Division I Manual*. Overland Park, KS: National Collegiate Athletic Association.

Coakley, J.J. (1998) *Sport in Society: Issues and Controversies*, 6th edn. New York: Irwin McGraw-Hill.

Cramer, J.A. (1994) Conversations with women journalists, in P.J. Creedon (ed.) *Women, Media, and Sport: Challenging Gender Values*. Thousand Oaks, CA: Sage.

Cuneen, J. and Sidwell, M.J. (1998) Gender portrayals in *Sports Illustrated for Kids* advertisements: a content analysis of prominent and supporting models, *Journal of Sport Management*, 12: 39–50.

Delpy, L. and Bosetti, A. (1998) Sport management and marketing via the World Wide Web, *Sport Marketing Quarterly*, 7: 21–7.

Duncan, M.C., Messner, M.A., Williams, L. and Jensen, K. (1994) Gender stereotyping in television sports, in S. Birrell and C.L. Cole (eds) *Women, Culture, and Sport*. Champaign, IL: Human Kinetics.

Huggins, S. (1997) Scholarships are focus of new Title IX claims [On-line]. Available: http://www.ncaa.org/news/19970609/active/3423n02.html

Kane, M.J. (1988) Media coverage of the female athlete before, during, and after Title IX: *Sports Illustrated* revisited, *Journal of Sport Management*, 2: 87–99.

Lumpkin, A. and Williams, L.D. (1991) An analysis of *Sports Illustrated* feature articles, 1954–1987, *Sociology of Sport Journal*, 8: 16–32.

Malec, M.A. (1994) Gender inequities in the *NCAA News? Journal of Sport & Social Issues*, 18: 376–8.

McGregor, E. (1989) Mass media and sport: influences on the public, *Physical Educator*, 46: 52–5.

Rintala, J. and Birrell, S. (1984) Fair treatment for the active female: A content analysis of *Young Athlete magazine, Sociology of Sport Journal*, 1: 231–50.

Shifflett, B. and Revelle, R. (1994) Gender equity in sports and media coverage: a review of the NCAA *News, Journal of Sport & Social Issues*, 18: 144–50.

Steinem, G. (1990, July/August) Sex, lies, and advertising. Ms., 1: 18–8.

Theberge, N. and Cronk, A. (1986) Work routines in newspaper sports departments and the coverage of women's sports, *Sociology of Sport Journal*, 3: 195–203.

Tuggle, C.A. (1996) Television sports reporting of female athletics: quantitative and qualitative content analysis of ESPN SportsCenter and CNN Sports Tonight, *Dissertation Abstracts International*, 57: 2248. (University Microfilms No. AAC 9633959).

Wann, D.L., Schrader, M.P., Allison, J.A. and McGeorge, K.K. (1998) The inequitable newspaper coverage of men's and women's athletics at small, medium, and large universities, *Journal of Sport & Social Issues*, 22: 79–87.

Yasser, R., McCurdy, J.R. and Goplerud, C.P. (1997) *Sports Law: Cases and Materials*, 3rd edn. Cincinnati, OH: Anderson.

## Part II: Further reading

Andrews, D.L. and Jackson, S.J. (eds) (2001) *Sport Stars: The Cultural Politics of Sporting Celebrity*. London and New York: Routledge.

Baker, A. and Boyd, T. (eds) (1997) *Sports, Media, and the Politics of Identity*. Bloomington, IN: Indiana University Press.

Birrell, S. and McDonald, M.G. (eds) (2000) *Reading Sport: Critical Essays on Power and Representation*. Boston: Northeastern University Press.

Creedon, P.J. (ed.) (1994) *Women, Media and Sport: Challenging Gender Values*. Thousand Oaks, CA: Sage.

Denison, J. and Markula, P. (eds) (2003) *'Moving Writing': Crafting Movement in Sport Research*. New York: Peter Lang.

Hemphill, D. and Symons, C. (eds) (2002) *Gender, Sexuality and Sport: A Dangerous Mix*. Petersham, NSW: Walla Walla Press.

McKay, J., Messner, M.A. and Sabo, D. (eds) (2000) *Masculinities, Gender Relations, and Sport*. Thousand Oaks, CA: Sage.

Miller, T. (2001) *Sportsex*. Philadelphia: Temple University Press.

Rowe, D. (1995) *Popular Cultures: Rock Music, Sport and the Politics of Pleasure*. London: Sage.

Rowe, D. (2004) *Sport, Culture and the Media: The Unruly Trinity*, 2nd edn. Buckingham: Open University Press.

Schaffer, K. and Smith, S. (eds) (2000) *The Olympics at the Millennium: Power, Politics, and the Games*. New Brunswick, New Jersey, and London: Rutgers University Press.

Wenner, L.A. (ed.) (1998) *MediaSport*. London: Routledge.

Whannel, G. (2001) *Media Sport Stars: Masculinities and Moralities*. London: Routledge.

# INDEX

# SPORT, CULTURE AND THE MEDIA
## SECOND EDITION

**David Rowe**

This was the first book to comprehensively analyse two powerful cultural forces of our times; sport and the media. This new edition examines the latest developments in the sports media, including:

- Expanded material on new media sport and technology developments
- Updated coverage of political economy, including integration of large entertainment corporations and sporting organizations
- New scholarship and research in the field, recent sports events, new media texts and theory such as postmodernism, reception and spectatorship

This is a key text for undergraduate students in culture and media, sociology, sport and leisure studies, communication and gender.

### Contents

c288pp      0 335 21075 9 (Paperback)      0 335 21076 7 (Hardback)